"Without sentimentality, he writes about the ordinary and thrilling courtships as his family assembles itself over generations, as well as about the neurotic, semi-dysfunctional, often angry love of brothers and sisters, fathers and daughters, grandmothers and grandsons."
—*Raleigh News & Observer*

"*Family* is a book to savor."   —*Cleveland Plain Dealer*

"A beautifully understated, amazingly vivid, multigenerational family album. . . . This heartland saga has the artistry and emotional nuance of Frazier's bestselling *Great Plains*."—*Publishers Weekly*

"Frazier's *Family* is hard to put down. . . . A deeply moving book in a great American literary tradition."   —*Los Angeles Times Book Review*

FAMILY

IAN FRAZIER

HarperPerennial
A Division of HarperCollinsPublishers

Chapter 10 appeared in *The Atlantic Monthly* in somewhat different form.

This book was originally published in 1994 by Farrar, Straus & Giroux. It is here reprinted by arrangement with Farrar, Straus & Giroux.

HarperCollins books may be purchased for educational, business, or sales promotional use. For information please write: Special Markets Department, HarperCollins Publishers, Inc., 10 East 53rd Street, New York, NY 10022.

First HarperPerennial edition published 1995.

ISBN 0-06-097677-2

---

95 96 97 98 99 RRD 10 9 8 7 6 5 4 3 2 1

TO DAVE, SUZAN,

AND MAGGIE

FAMILY TREES

Thomas Benedict — Mary Bridgum
1617-1690
Daniel
Daniel
Jonas

Thomas Wickham
1624-1688
Samuel

Abraham Wildman
1670-1750
Abraham

Joseph Wanton
1705-1780

Thomas Wickham
1700-1777

Samuel   Comfort Hoyt — Eunice
                              b. 1751

Platt Benedict — Sally DeForest
1775-1866   1777-1852

Thomas Wickham — Elizabeth Wanton
1736-1817   1742-1814
Frederick y
Eliz. Christian

Timothy Taylor
1751-1851

Charles Patch   James Deaver
1787-1835 &
Catherine Husted

Jonas Benedict
1809-1851
Fanny
Fanny Buckingham

David D. Benedict — Harriott M. Deaver
1833-1901; great-   1835-1909
grand-father.
Brother of Fanny,
who married Louis Severance

John Frazier (?)

William Wickham — Catherine Christian Samuel Preston
1778-1815   and Esther Taylor

Ezra Wildman — Anne
1715-1858

Frederick A. Wildman — Mariette
1813-1891   1814-1891

Absalom Frazier — Clarissa Bundy
1797-1865
3-greats-grandfather

Frederick Wickham — Lucy Preston (Wickham)
1812-1901   1814-1897

Emily Jane Wildman
(Wickham) 1838-1919;
great-great-grandmother
(also called Emma)

siblings: Mary
Harriott
Agnes
Fanny
Frederick
Susan Rose

Thomas Vaughn
3-greats-
grandfather

Charles P. Wickham
1836-1925; great-great-
grandfather

Louis W. Wickham — Ellen Eliza Benedict (Wickham)
1866-1951;   1868-1942; great-grandmother
great-   (also called Bss)
grandfather
(also called Boa)

siblings: Susan
Fred
Anne Belle

William Brenneman — Sara Newman

Simeon Frazier — Lucy Vaughn (Frazier)
1832-1907
great-great-grandfather

Maude Brenneman (Frazier)
1866-1957; great-grandmother

Cora Wickham (Frazier)
1895-1985;
grandmother (also called
G-Grandmother)

David Frazier
1919-1967

siblings: Louis
Edwin Ray, Jr.
(Teddy)

Harry Edwin Frazier
1868-1938; great-grandfather

Edwin Ray Frazier
1891-1951; grandfather
(also called Ray)

siblings of:
Ruth
Dorothy
Donald
Charles Richard
Sarah Margaret (Peg)

Margaret Kathryn Hursh
1921-1986

Me, and siblings, David, Susan, Fritz, and
Maggie

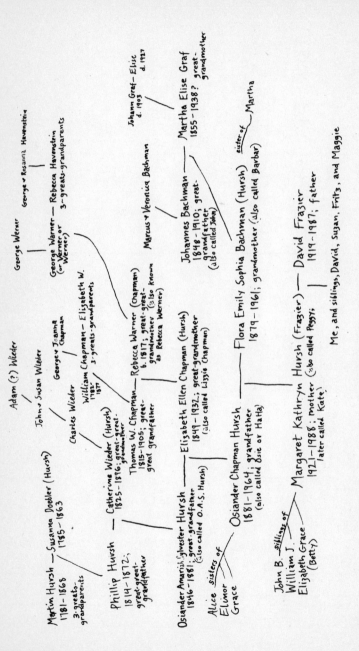

MOTHER'S SIDE

We can believe in the nothingness of life,

we can believe in the nothingness of death

and of life after death—but who can believe

in the nothingness of Ben?

—THOMAS WOLFE
Look Homeward, Angel

C H A P T E R   1

THE TWENTIETH CENTURY began on a Tuesday. On that day, all
my great-grandparents but one were living in Ohio or Indiana. Mr.
and Mrs. Harry E. Frazier and their four children lived in Indianapolis, in a neighborhood of many vacant lots and telephone poles.
Mr. and Mrs. Louis W. Wickham and their three children and hired
girl lived at 237 Benedict Avenue, Norwalk, Ohio. The Reverend John
Bachman and his wife and two daughters lived in New Knoxville,
Ohio, where he was pastor of the First German Reformed Church.
Mrs. Elizabeth C. Hursh and her three grown daughters and one son
lived at 86 Greenfield Street, Tiffin, Ohio; her husband, Professor
O.A.S. Hursh, lay in a nearby cemetery, beneath a $200 monument
inscribed with a Latin quotation and the years, months, and days of
his life.

*Reverend John Bachman (seated) and his family in 1909. His wife, younger daughter, and
sons-in-law stand behind him. The young man on the left is my grandfather Osie Hursh.
The seated woman is my grandmother Flora Bachman Hursh. Uncle Bill, the baby in the
dress, has just been christened*

O.A.S. Hursh's initials stood for Osiander Amariah Sylvester. At his birth in 1846, his parents decided to leave the choice of a name to their minister; when the minister announced it at the baby's baptism, they were surprised. Osiander was a figure of the Protestant Reformation in Germany whose stridency in debate won him many enemies and created disputes which sometimes required the intervention of Martin Luther himself. The name was self-invented; it means "holy man" in Greek. Amariah came from the Old Testament, where it is the name of a number of walk-on characters. It is Hebrew for "God has spoken." Sylvester was apparently added just for meter and flourish. Taken together, the three names are a small sermon in themselves, and suggest that naming babies was a job which the Hurshes' minister would have liked to do more often. In later years, however, his efforts turned out to be wasted; the child he baptized almost never wrote his names out full, and people generally referred to him by his initials. If he ever had a nickname less formal than O.A.S., nobody today remembers it.

O.A.S. Hursh had a dark beard, dark eyes set well apart, a broad forehead, and dark, fly-away hair which he sometimes controlled with a tonic of one part Jamaican rum mixed with two parts cod-liver oil. He grew up on his father's farm near Ithaca, a town in southwestern Ohio which has a hitching rail on its main street to this day. When he was fourteen, he taught in a country school to earn money for college, and he continued to teach full- or part-time for the rest of his life. In his twenties, he kept a pocket diary, which I have. It begins with the eclipse of the sun on August 7, 1869, and ends with his first day as professor of Latin and Greek at Heidelberg College.

O.A.S. Hursh was a fan of sermons. Sometimes he attended several in one weekend. Afterward he kept notes on them, and went over them in his mind the way a person today might do with movies. His family was Lutheran, but he went to other churches as well. When he had a free afternoon, he would harness a colt to a light hickory buggy and go sailing along the Miamisburg and Eastern turnpike, just for something to do. He began to give orations himself in the Heidelberg chapel. At his commencement he delivered the Heidelberg Address, titled "The Study of Mind." In the audience was a young woman named Elizabeth Chapman, whose brother and sister went to Heidelberg. She was from Stark County, in the eastern part of the

state. Her father farmed, raised cattle and merino sheep, and served
a term in the state legislature. The family had the first square grand
piano in the county, a Boardman & Gray. O.A.S. Hursh and Elizabeth
Chapman met at the commencement, and married at her father's
house on Christmas Day, 1873. They returned to Tiffin, and with a
loan from her father built a brick Victorian house across the street
from the campus. In 1874 they had a daughter, Alice, and in 1876,
Elinor, and in 1879, Grace. During the summer, O.A.S. studied at
the Heidelberg Theological Seminary, and soon was ordained a minister in the German Reformed Church. He never had a parish of his
own but filled in for other ministers when they went on vacation.
On Sundays in July and August he gave a sermon called "Christianity
the True Manhood" in churches in Navarre, Richville, and Mohican,
Ohio. In August 1881, maybe after a hard schedule of traveling and
preaching, he came down with typhoid fever. He died two weeks
later. The monument his wife bought for him, a six-foot stone obelisk
and pedestal, now leans slightly to one side. The years have weathered
the Latin inscription until it is no longer readable; some of the pencil
notes in his pocket diary look as if they might have been made last
month.

Sunday, Aug. 29 1869. At home greater part of the day . . . Sister Amanda
and I took a buggy ride to Uncle Simon's to bid the folks farewell. They
emigrate to Ill. next Tuesday. We called at Mr. Robeson's this evening—
Traded breastpins.

Monday Aug 30 1869. Started for Tiffin this afternoon by the way of Dayton.
Traveled nearly all night. Met Zerbe at Urbana. Reached Tiffin at 7 a.m.

Wednesday Sept 1st. School opened today . . . a number of new students in
attendance. Prospect encouraging.

"The private acts, the secret walks of men, if noble, are the noblest of their
lives."

New Year—1870. In Tiffin. Weather unpleasant. Snowed all day. Spent the
day in meditation, prayer, and reading. Attended Firemen's Fair this evening.
Oysters.

Tuesday Jan 4th 1870. The twenty-fourth anniversary of my birthday. Arose early this morning. Consecrated myself anew to the Service of Almighty God.

Importance and necessity of Union. An alliance against Satan. When I hear persons talking in a selfish manner about the excellence and superiority of their own denomination I am reminded of Christ's rebuke to his disciples &c.

4th of July 1870. Cramer and I went to Put-In-Bay Island to-day. Set up a tent on the beach . . . spent one week on the Island. Were employed in fishing, rowing, bathing, reading, walking about the Island &c. Had a huge time of it.

Mr. and Mrs. Harry E. Frazier were good at math. Harry met Maude Breneman when both were working in the bookkeeping department of a lumber company in Canton, and they married in 1890. Maude had a cute face, with a mouth that turned down at the corners, and hair in tight curls around her forehead. Harry was a short, natty man whose mustache, nose, and round spectacle lenses seemed to be jostling for control of the center of his face. In company, Harry would sit quietly and then all of a sudden come out with something that showed he'd been listening all along and had had enough tomfoolery. He was an active member of the Christian Church (Disciples of Christ), and taught and superintended Sunday schools. At meals, he said long graces—sometimes, on special occasions like anniversaries, very long. In the evening he and Maude would get out a card table and play double solitaire.

In 1891, Maude and Harry had their first child, Edwin Ray. They would have five more. They moved from Canton to Indianapolis, where Harry's family lived, and he got a job as cashier with the Indiana Car and Foundry Company. Harry was promoted from cashier to treasurer. In 1899 he left the company and started an accounting firm with three partners. Then he became secretary and treasurer of the Taisey Pneumatic Service Company. Maude's mother and sister moved in with them. Harry got a job with Rogers Brown & Company, pig-iron commission merchants of Cincinnati, and the family moved there. In 1908 Harry was sent as vice president and general manager of the Huron Steel and Iron Company of Norwalk, Ohio, to try to get that company back in the black. The family rented a big house with

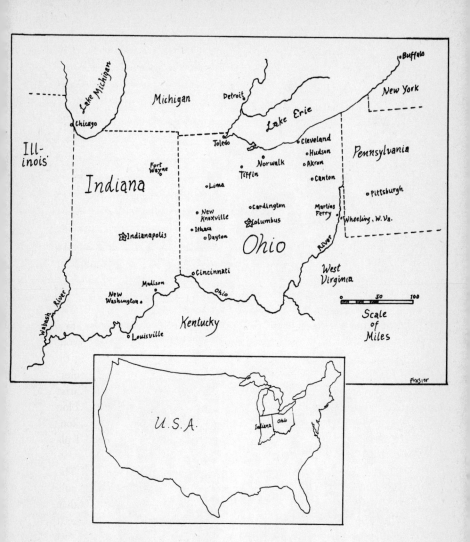

Indiana and Ohio, with principal cities, and small towns where my relatives settled

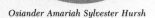

Osiander Amariah Sylvester Hursh

The first page of one of his sermons. This sermon was a standby, and he gave it a number of times

O.A.S. Hursh's father, Phillip Hursh, a farmer in southwestern Ohio

Osiander C. Hursh, son of O.A.S. Hursh, about 1900

a veranda running along two sides and a round cupola with leaded-glass windows at 107 West Main Street, Norwalk. Edwin Ray, now called just Ray, enrolled in his second high school. He was seventeen.

Norwalk, Ohio, is an inland town in an inland state. It is about 107 miles from the Pennsylvania border on the east and 112 miles from the Indiana border on the west. Its founders, for fear of fevers, did not want to live near swamps or river bottoms, so the site they chose was a long sand ridge above the forks of the Huron River, twelve miles in from Lake Erie. The town's population was about 7,000 in 1900, and it is about 15,000 now. A hundred years ago, most Americans lived in towns Norwalk's size and smaller. I have visited many towns where ancestors of mine once lived, but I like Norwalk best. Although highway sprawl has grown along its larger roads, it still looks like a small town. In some directions, farmland is still close. As I drive on Highway 20 in late fall, the first snowfall of the year whitens the gravel alongside the road and dusts the furrowed fields like fingerprints. In the summer, when I come out of the library in the evening, cicadas sing in the maples along West Main Street with a sound like a lawn sprinkler coming closer and then fading away. All my Norwalk relatives have died or moved away long ago. I can find more relatives in Norwalk's Woodlawn Cemetery than in any other one place.

In 1900, Norwalk was a farm town. It also had a brewery, two small steel companies, a carriage-body shop, and a company that made umbrellas. It was (and is) the county seat of Huron County; on busy days when court was in session, West Main Street was a thicket of wagon and buggy wheels. Several passenger trains a day stopped in Norwalk bound for New York or Chicago, and freights went through all the time. The freights brought tramps, whose numbers increased in the spring. They left scrawls on back gates to indicate to other tramps which houses were most generous with handouts. The town had electricity, but since most of the houses had been built without wiring, extension cords hung here and there in the rooms. A local telephone company, Harrison Telephone, provided phone service. A typical phone number was 81.

Nights then were dark and quiet. If you were lying awake, you might hear the tread of a driverless horse hauling home his drunken owner, passed out in the wagon box. People rarely locked their doors, and when they did, they had to hunt all over for the key. Everyone

knew everyone. Most would also talk without hesitation to any stranger
who resembled themselves. Con artists went through the region like
viruses. One borrowed $3,000 from a notoriously stingy Norwalk man
using a phony deed to a farm as collateral and then disappeared,
causing the lender to fret until he lost his mind; another sold door-
to-door as a sure moth repellent special beans imported from Manila,
which turned out to be lima beans soaked in cinnamon oil; others
brought counterfeit pennies from the East and used them in slot
machines and for groceries. People died as a result of falls more often,
apparently, than they do now. Either they fell off wagonloads of ice
or stacks of straw fell on them. They also died in accidents caused by
runaway horse teams and were run over and ground to pieces by
trains. In the St. Charles Hotel in Norwalk, a thirty-eight-year-old
stenographer and typist named Hattie Norman died of an overdose of
headache powder. In Hug and Cook's Saloon, Cook shot himself behind the right ear with a pistol; observers said he had been suffering
from "dementia" for days.

Thoroughfares like Main Street had a gravel surface, but roads
in general were dirt. Between spring and summer, they sometimes
went from liquid to gas with barely a pause at solid. In August the
dust on some roads might be so deep you couldn't ride a bicycle. Dust
rode up wagonwheel spokes and then fell in showers like water off a
paddlewheel. In town, roads were oiled or were sprinkled regularly
by a water wagon. Because all laundry dried outside, housewives hated
dust. They got up extra early on Monday to see who would be the
first to get her washing on the line. It was considered improper to
hang dark clothes and light clothes together. In winter, ice and wind
were another problem; clothes wore faster when they froze and flapped
on the line.

When people got together, they often played whist or cribbage.
Some had their own personal cribbage boards. On Sundays they went
to church and then came home and had a big dinner and sat quietly
the rest of the day, and they made the children sit, too. Some didn't
even allow reading, except of the Bible, on the Sabbath. In that part
of Ohio, natives pronounced creek "crick" and buried "burried," and
"root" to rhyme with "foot." Most would use the word "jew" as a verb
without a second thought. Instead of "almost," they usually said
"pretty near," pronounced "pret-near": "I believe that harness cost

pret-near twenty dollars." Their trouser flies buttoned. They had fewer clothes than people do today, and wore them more. Proper dress for men included high starched cotton or linen shirt collars; the highest ones were called "four-story" collars. Cheaper shirt collars made of celluloid were considered bad style, like clip-on neckties today. Striped celluloid collars were worst of all. A local school administrator said he would have some qualms about trusting a boy or girl of his to a teacher who wore a celluloid collar.

Kids who grew up in Norwalk around that time said later that they'd had a ball. Three-ring circuses came to the playing fields on Milan Avenue north of town once or twice a year. There were picnics, and excursions up to the lake on the electric railway, and parades on Decoration Day and the Fourth of July. Boys and girls picked black raspberries along the roadside and climbed apple trees for eating apples. In the fall they went into the woods and brought back gun-nysacks full of butternuts, hickory nuts, and black walnuts. During husking, the walnuts stained their hands a golden brown that wouldn't fade until late winter. Boys took their dogs into the fields at harvest time, when the hired men were taking apart the shocks of corn, to watch the dogs kill the mice that had been nesting there and ran in every direction. Some kids had ponies, and pony carts with rubber tires. In winter kids loved to go to sleep with the ground bare and wake up with it white with snow; then they'd go for sleigh rides, sometimes taking down fence rails so they could cross from one field to the next. Boys hunted squirrels and partridge in the woods and shot at old outbuildings for target practice. Their parents told them they must never, ever throw stones at a train. In the early spring they had a contest to see who could be first to go into the muddy snowmelt of Norwalk Creek up to his neck, a difficult feat before mid-March. Girls picked wildflowers, and knew poems about them, and made May baskets of them the first of May. Young people smoked dried mullein leaves, courted in orchards, and went to corn-husking bees; if you got a red ear, you could kiss the boy or girl of your choice. Pranks included removing a nut from someone's rear buggy wheel, and putting a brick in a paper sack on a downtown sidewalk and waiting for someone to kick it. Little kids often went barefoot outdoors in warm weather. They stubbed their toes and chipped their toenails and got stone bruises. They were supposed to wash their feet at a basin on the back porch every evening when they came in. So many people were related to one another that households were partly interchangeable. Mothers set extra places at table and fed whichever kids happened to be around.

Mr. and Mrs. Louis W. Wickham lived next door to his parents on a street named for her great-grandfather. Louis Wickham's father, Charles P. Wickham, was the first citizen of the town. He was a brevetted lieutenant colonel in the Civil War, a two-term congressman, and a judge of the Huron County Court of Common Pleas. Mrs. Louis Wickham, born Ellen Eliza Benedict, was the great-granddaughter of Platt Benedict, who had come out from Connecticut in 1817 to found the town. Louis Wickham stood six feet two, with dark eyes and round cheeks and straight dark hair parted in the middle, and he liked to dress. He believed that when a man got down to his last hundred dollars, he should buy a good suit. Ellen Wickham, called Lil or Lillie, was long-legged and high-hipped and long-necked, with blue eyes and a strong jaw. Louis Wickham worked as junior partner in his father's law firm, handling divorce and alimony suits, delinquent-payment and petty-larceny cases, and fenceline disputes. A lot of the firm's money came from defending the railroads that passed through Huron County against damage suits by people who had lost relatives, limbs, or property. No railroad ever paid such a claim until it had taken the plaintiff to every court it could. Lillie Wickham socialized in town on the committees of various women's groups and in the women's guild of St. Paul's Episcopal Church. She also gardened and looked after some rental properties she owned, going in a carriage the first of the month to collect. Louis and Ellen had four children: Suzan, born in 1893; Cora, in 1895; Fred, in 1900; and Anne Belle, in 1907. In the 1911 Norwalk City Directory, Louis Wickham noted that as of October 1 the family would be living at 153 West Main Street. This move, to an Italianate brick house in the more fashionable part of town, put them about ten doors up the street from the Harry Frazier family. Ray Frazier was now nearly twenty, a student at Princeton who came home for visits. Cora Wickham was sixteen.

In the homes of New Knoxville, Ohio, a town much smaller than Norwalk about 100 miles to the southwest, people spoke a dialect of German called *Plattdeutsch*. New Knoxville was like a German village transplanted to America. Local families included the Fledderjohanns, the Meckstroths, the Schroluckes, the Katterheinrichs. The first set-

bucktoothed
Rabbit in garden, sign: "Hi There!"

Cemetery right in town — next to
New Knoxville tel. co.   no fence around it

"First United Church of Christ

Rev. Jon R. Coddington, Pastor
(on sign)"

"Erite Deutsch
Evangelisch —
Reformirte Kirche"

on church above door

quite a church   ~~drinking~~ fountain
out back by pkg lot

smelling all kinds of small town smells:
leaves along sidewalk   moldy wood smell in
church

[what I'm trying to show by above
sketch is that church v. Bavarian ~~looks~~]

built 1922 — no; 1894

little brick house next to church ~
this where Barbar was a girl — no
parsonage on up street. at corner of Werheim & W. Bremen

photo in church of Sunday morning;
a throng outside church; buggies

A page from my notebook with a sketch of the church where Reverend Bachman preached

tlers of New Knoxville came in the 1830s from Ladbergen, in what
was then Prussia, to dig the Miami-Erie Canal, and after Ohio's short
canal era stayed to farm. They convinced many relatives and friends
from Ladbergen to join them. The center of town was the steeple of
the First German Reformed Church, with its turrets, its four-sided
clock face, and its high spire topped by a multipronged ornament
symbolizing the Apostles and the first four books of the Gospels. Fewer
than a thousand people lived in New Knoxville, but on some Sundays
nearly two thousand came to the church. Farm families traveled for
hours down roads that in summer were aisles through rows of corn.
Photos show the church on Sunday morning rising above a sea of
fringed buggy roofs. Services were in German. Church members used
Martin Luther's Bible and hymnal, but considered themselves more
liberal than Lutherans on matters of doctrine and personal expression.
In 1898 the pastor of the First Reformed Church, Reverend Moritz
Noll, died suddenly. His friend the Reverend John Bachman came
up from the Reformed church in Cincinnati to preach the funeral
sermon. The people in New Knoxville liked Rev. Bachman and asked
him to stay.

Rev. Bachman was born in Switzerland in 1848. His family had
a small farm with vineyards and pasture outside the town of Binningen,
near Basel. His parents called him Johannes; he was the second youngest of eight children. As a boy, Johannes wanted to be a surveyor,
and when he was sixteen he began to work for one. He tramped all
over his canton surveying property lines, and he helped mark the
grade for a new railroad leading into Germany. The surveyor liked his
work and hoped that someday they could be partners. Johannes's
father had a bad temper and whipped Johannes often, so hard he bore
the stripes on his back for the rest of his life. Once when Johannes
was eighteen his father tried to beat him and Johannes grabbed his
hand and told him firmly that he could no longer whip him like a dog.
He left home the same day and got a job on a nearby farm. About
that time he experienced a strong spiritual calling to enter the ministry.
He enrolled in the St. Chrischona Mission Institute in Basel and
graduated in 1872. The surveyor regretted his loss to the profession
and said he feared Johannes would always be just a poor preacher.
Johannes said, "I would not change with a king. I am an ambassador
of the Most High, and have the greatest privilege on earth, to point
immortal souls to God."

After graduation, Johannes heard that Reformed churches in America were in need of German-speaking preachers, and he left Switzerland for good. He was ordained in Philadelphia and became pastor of a Reformed church in Egg Harbor City, New Jersey. The next year his friend Moritz Noll came over, too, accompanied by Rev. Bachman's fiancée, Martha Elise Graf. Martha was a graduate of the New Girls School in Berne, where she had studied to be an elementary-school teacher. On the boat, a woman saw Martha's long golden curls and told her that no women in America wore their hair like that, so Martha let her cut her hair short. She later decided the woman had wanted the hair to sell. When Martha arrived and Johannes saw her, he threw a fit and made her wear a cap. They were married in Egg Harbor City. In 1875 Rev. Bachman was called to be pastor of the First Reformed Church of Cincinnati. In 1879, they had a daughter, Flora Emily Sophia. Two years later they had another, Martha.

Mrs. Bachman suffered from a respiratory condition which sometimes caused her to cough uncontrollably for hours at a time. Some years she spent the summer months away from her family in northern Michigan, where the air was better for her. She did not do much housework or cooking. She had maids, and when Flora and Martha got old enough, they helped. They cooked the big Sunday dinners the family had after morning services, and they packed their father's suitcases when he traveled on church business. Flora was such a good ironer that everyone left the more delicate ironing to her. A spring morning might find Martha in the potato bins, sprouting potatoes. The move from Cincinnati to New Knoxville was a shock to Flora. She had never been anyplace where people watched her so closely or made so much of every little thing she did. Some of the kids called her and Martha "P.K.s," for "preacher's kids." She became best friends with a young woman named Lizzie Mahn. She and Lizzie used to sit on the stairs leading down to her father's study when he was performing a marriage there and spy on the ceremony through the transom. Flora's nickname was Floss. She directed children's pageants at the church and embroidered little pillows to give as gifts. She had a sweet voice, and sang hymns and played the piano. Her father thought he might let her take some classes at Heidelberg College.

•

Three months after O.A.S. Hursh died, his wife, Elizabeth, had a son. She named him Osiander after her husband and Chapman after her family. Through life he was called O.C., or Osie. Mrs. Hursh now had an infant and three little girls and no means of support. Her parents tried to get her to move back to the farm with them, but she was determined to stay in the house her husband had built. She had money from life insurance; the trustees of the college and her father gave her a few hundred more. She took in boarders, usually students or teachers at the college. She made small loans and collected the interest. She sold rags, papers, and iron to the junk man. She kept chickens and a milk cow. She grew a big vegetable garden out back with fruit trees and elderberry and raspberry bushes, and fertilized with horse manure her children collected in a wagon on Greenfield Street. Supplies like coffee and raisins she ordered in bulk from Sears, Roebuck & Co.

She had three "definite opportunities" to remarry, according to her daughters, but turned them all down. "She said that she had had her husband and was true to her children," her daughter Alice later wrote. It was a loyalty she expected to be returned. Alice, Elinor, and Grace grew into young women who could sing, play the piano, draw, and look handsome in white dresses sitting on a porch swing. Their mother wore her hair up off her neck and parted in the middle, with the sides of her head bare. Her level gaze came through oval pince-nez glasses on a fine chain which looped over one ear and pinned to the yoke of her blouse. When any of her daughters paid too much attention to a young man, she put a stop to it. Alice was going with the son of the president of Heidelberg College when her mother observed him walking her back from church on a cold morning with his hand in her coat pocket; she said no gentleman would do such a thing. Elinor's young man friend had an excellent singing voice, but was found to owe forty dollars to a tailor. Grace's beau was a candidate for the ministry, but wanted to take her off to Japan where he planned to go as a missionary. In the end, none of the girls—as they would be called for most of their lives—ever married. Alice gave piano lessons and played the organ in Tiffin churches. Grace taught in the elementary school. Elinor lived during the school year in the Ohio towns where she taught high-school music and art. They loved their mother and said her faith was an inspiration. In photos, they stand behind her or off to one side, a little out of focus, like backup singers.

When Osie came of age, his mother watched him as jealously as she had his sisters. He graduated from high school in 1899, taught in a country school for a year, and entered Heidelberg. There he met Flora Bachman, whose father had told her if she continued to do good work he did not mind paying the necessary expenses. Osie had a strong baritone singing voice, Flora a light soprano; he played the flute, she the piano; he knew Latin and Greek but wished to learn German, she said she would teach him. There were walks in the country, conversations at crossroad benches, summer-evening musical sessions when even the mosquitoes seemed to be in an exalted mood. Mrs. Hursh discouraged the romance from the beginning. When Flora came to call, she was suddenly not at home. She told Osie to wait, that he had plenty of time, that she and the girls needed a man to help them. One day Osie, inspired by meeting Rev. Bachman, announced that he was thinking of becoming a minister and going to Japan himself, and his mother really got alarmed.

Osie's solution to the problem of his mother had always been to work. Work provided her with money, which she always needed, yet at the same time let him be away from her and on his own and free. Osie was a big-boned, dark-eyed young man with black hair that stood up and a chin that stuck out. As a student he had jobs in a tile yard, in a shoe store, on a farm. He could work a twenty-hour day on the farm and like it. After graduation he got a job offer from a high school in Cardington, Ohio, and for some reason could not take the train there, so rode the fifty-plus miles down and back over country roads on his bicycle. The school board hired him as principal, teacher of several subjects, band director, and basketball coach in a high school of sixty-nine students. He wrote Flora from Cardington every few days. She was back in New Knoxville—her father had begun to show signs of nervous disorder and needed his daughters to look after him. Osie wrote that he had lost every bit of his heart to her and didn't see how he was getting along without it. Often he apologized for something he had to do that prevented him from going to see her; that pattern would continue for as long as they knew each other.

Another pattern their lives would follow was the school year, with its exam periods, holidays, and vacations. In March of 1905, Osie wrote Flora that he would visit her in New Knoxville over his Easter vacation. When his mother heard of this, she asked him to come to Tiffin instead, to fix some things around the house. Osie wrote again to Flora and said that he couldn't come, that he'd see her in the

summer. Then he suddenly changed his mind and went to New Knoxville anyway. On Easter Sunday he asked Flora to marry him. She
accepted. He asked her father for his permission and got it. He was
so happy he didn't know that he was walking on the earth. He said
he would appoint that day a day of thanksgiving always. He rode the
train back to Cardington still in a glorious dream and finished grading
all the papers he had brought with him before he reached Galion. In
deference to Mrs. Hursh, Osie and Flora asked her to set the date—
but she wouldn't, so they set it themselves. They were married by
Rev. Bachman in late May of 1906, after school had let out for the
summer.

•

Louis and Lillie Wickham's daughter Cora was a tall, slim girl
with blue eyes and a prominent nose. Growing up, it seemed to her
that just about everybody in Norwalk was in some way her relative.
Her grandfather Wickham, who people around town called Judge or
Colonel, awed her so that she could barely speak in his presence, but
among her many cousins she was lively, even bossy. Throughout her
life she had a quick tongue which could sometimes make people cry.
She loved to go to her parents' summer cottage on a bluff above Lake
Erie, where the big mayflies called Canadian soldiers hung from the
rafters and caught in her hair and popped underfoot, and where in
the evenings all the relatives from the cottages nearby would gather
on a porch in the light from kerosene lamps and listen to the old men
talk about the Civil War. With cousins, she explored along the lakeshore and up the creeks that ran into it. She tanned beautifully. When
her father went fishing, he took her along until her brother Fred got
big enough to go; then he stopped taking her.

Cora got high marks in algebra, had heard of Freud, and could
recite the poetry of Alfred Noyes. She had many ideas and opinions,
but if somebody told her something funny, she did not hesitate to
laugh and lose her train of thought. She thought a man should be
smart, and Ray Frazier was. When he graduated first in his class at
Norwalk High, some people in town said it wasn't fair, because he'd
only been going to the school for a year. Ray played blocking back in
football, in the old single-wing offense, even though he was just five-
four. He had finely drawn features and sandy hair. He was quiet,
dour, and unsociable. He knew how all sorts of machines worked and

when he got going on that subject could explain anything to anybody. He wrote light verse, and rolled his own cigarettes of Bull Durham tobacco with one hand as he drove, scattering flakes all over. Later he switched to Lucky Strikes; as an adult, he'd reach for a cigarette every morning the moment his feet hit the floor. To judge from photos, he rarely smiled. Cora said he was the funniest man she ever met. He had a strong attraction for her—she was a tall woman who preferred short men. Her family, especially her mother and her sister Anne Belle, did not like Ray. But for Cora, who had spent her life surrounded by her family and its history, that may have been another plus.

Ray graduated from Princeton, and worked for steel companies in Norwalk and in Cleveland, Ohio. During the First World War he joined the army. Cora graduated from high school, went to Wooster College in Wooster, Ohio, had to leave after being caught organizing a sorority in defiance of school rules, went to Smith College in Massachusetts, graduated, and taught high-school math in Tennessee and Norwalk. In 1918 Ray was a regimental sergeant major stationed at Valparaiso, Indiana, and Cora was living at home. They planned to be married August 8. Cora's older sister, Suzan, an instructor in English at Smith, came back to visit her family and attend her sister's wedding. While in Norwalk, she got appendicitis. She had her appendix out, but afterward developed an infection, and she died at her parents' house on the morning of July 27. The whole town felt the blow. People remembered Suzan as a sunny child and an excellent student in the Norwalk schools. Hundreds came to the Wickham house on West Main Street to pay their last tribute. The flowers they brought filled the downstairs.

Cora's parents suggested that it might be a good idea under the circumstances if she and Ray postponed the wedding. Maybe Cora felt that she had already waited long enough; maybe she was angry at Suzan for dying and leaving her and getting all the attention, too; maybe she was just trying to be brave and carry on. In any case, eleven days after Suzan's funeral, as scheduled, Ray and Cora were married in her parents' living room. Ray's youngest sister, Peg, who was there, says it was a quiet ceremony. "I was worried—Ray was so sort of depressed," she says. "I thought people were supposed to be happy before they got married." Cora's family was angry at her. The Norwalk newspaper called the ceremony "a nuptial event of unusual interest," and noted the improvised altar of potted plants and white phlox and the presence of only immediate family. The couple spent their honeymoon at the Wickhams' cottage on Lake Erie, and when Ray got out of the army moved to Bay Village, a suburban town west of Cleveland.

In 1919 they had a son, David. In 1925 they had Louis, and in 1931, Edwin Ray, Jr., called Teddy. Ray worked six and a half days a week running the blast furnaces at the Otis steel mill in the industrial flats of Cleveland. Cora worked for the Bay Village school board. The sense of tragedy that shadowed their wedding never completely went away. One of Ray's younger brothers fell into the hold of the lake freighter he was working on and died in the summer of 1919. Ray continued to suffer from depression and in his thirties apparently had a nervous breakdown. David and Louis were healthy, but Teddy was born with congenital heart disease. He remained a near-invalid, frail and thin, with bluish lips and fingernails. He liked to read, write stories about boys sailing away on adventures, watch the barometer for approaching storms, and listen to the shortwave radio his father and brothers helped him make. Cora spent much of her time taking care of him and seeing to his diet. He could not drink cow's milk, so Cora kept a goat, which David, my father, milked.

If I had to piece together a picture of my father's childhood from the little he told me of it, I would include the goat, which he disliked, and his paper route, and the golf ball he was bouncing along railroad tracks one day that came up off a tie and hit him in the mouth, and his brother Louis pushing him into the goldfish pond, and his bad skin in high school that made him want to go around with a paper bag over his head, and his father's absence, and his parents' arguments, and his lifeguard job at a public beach near his house, and his mother not wanting him to play high-school football, and always the family's hope that Teddy would someday be well. People have emerged from worse childhoods with hopeful dispositions; David learned from his a scientific pessimism which could darken in a moment to black dread.

•

Osie Hursh got a job as high-school principal in Martins Ferry, a town on the Ohio River, and after he and Flora were married they moved there. In 1907 they had a son, John Bachman. They moved to Lakewood, a larger suburb on Cleveland's west side, where Osie

Harry Edwin Frazier and his wife, Maude Breneman Frazier

Their oldest son, Edwin Ray Frazier,
at his graduation from Norwalk High School in 1909

taught math and German at Lakewood High. In 1909 they had William Joseph, and in 1911 they had Elizabeth Grace (Betty). Flora made dresses for all her babies, and playsuits with short pants for John and Bill, and frocks and pinafores for Betty. Her stitching was fine and regular, her smocking came out even, and the plaids of her jackets met invisibly at the seams. She disdained store-bought clothes for children. All day she did housekeeping tasks of the sort which people today would have trouble even to identify—like mixing laundry starch and water in a big kettle, heating it on the stove, applying it to freshly laundered bedskirts, and ironing the dust ruffles on the skirts with a special curved iron. Everything in her house, it seemed, had a skirt or scarf or antimacassar or quilted cover; the whole interior appeared embroidered by hand. To make soup she first made noodles, to make sandwiches she made white bread and brown bread. She had her everyday baking and then her extra, holiday baking. Fruitcake season began in mid-November: chopping, hand-mixing, baking, steaming, cooling, wrapping the cakes in cheesecloth, storing them in cake tins in a closet to ripen for Christmas. Nothing about the world of today would puzzle her more than the contempt it has worked up for fruit-cake. For family birthdays she might make three or four birthday cakes, beating air into the thirteen egg whites for the angel food with a wire whisk on a flat pan until her arm nearly dropped off.

John, Bill, and Betty were near enough in age that they played together. John got mostly A's in school; he wanted to be a doctor. He was discouraged by how much harder it was to learn to ride a bike for him than for Bill. Neighbors told Flora how handsome little Bill was, and what a cute couple he and Betty made. Betty had black wavy hair to below her waist. She didn't like John to boss her; she told him he was an old lady sometimes. All the children adored their mother and worried about how hard she worked. Osie was often gone from five-thirty in the morning to after dark in the evening, working extra jobs—doing the books for a bank, running a vegetable stand, teaching night school—to add to his salary. In the evenings Flora's eyes and head sometimes hurt her so she could not read or hold a pen. Her family kept trying to get her to take a rest. The summer Betty was nine and the boys were eleven and thirteen, Flora went by herself to stay with her old childhood nurse in Cincinnati. The visit so restored her that when she returned she got pregnant. At first, Flora felt very bad—the pregnancy was entirely accidental, and she and Osie already had so many burdens. But then they accepted it as God's blessing. After her hardest term ever and a long labor, she gave birth on June 15, 1921, to Margaret Katherine, my mother. The family called her Peggy. Osie took Bill with him to the furniture store and bought the best wicker baby carriage they had.

Peggy had curly black hair which her mother stroked to make curlier while nursing her, and eyes that seized on things. Her mother told herself she would never forget those eyes. She called Peggy her "*nesthäkchen*," German for nestling. As a toddler, Peggy was little and round. Her brothers used to stand a few feet apart and throw her back and forth like a ball. ("Questionable judgment in a couple of teenage kids, but what the heck, they loved her," says Bill's wife, Ginny.) She sat in a high chair and smiled and cooed and played with an empty talcum box. At Christmas when she was a year and a half, her sister and brothers couldn't look at their own gifts, they were so absorbed in watching her delight. When she was three, she said she wanted to be an actress when she grew up. When she was nine, she changed her wish to movie actress; her grandmother Bachman wrote from California advising her to give up that ambition, in the interest of her spiritual welfare.

Rev. Bachman was long dead by then. His nervous condition had progressed from minor upsets over lost railroad tickets and baggage checks, to near-panics over misplaced funds collected for the church missions, to prolonged states of general agitation that convinced his wife he was no longer himself. He had a condition of the esophagus that made eating difficult, and after an operation improved it he felt so good he went back to work sooner than the doctors advised. In a few months he suffered a complete nervous breakdown, and he died in the summer of 1910. His wife and daughter Martha and her husband moved to the West Coast. For the Hursh children, this meant that their closest relatives during childhood were their grandmother Hursh and aunts Alice, Elinor, and Grace. Mrs. Hursh never did get over her dislike of Flora, but she loved her grandchildren. They stayed with her in the summers and played all over her big house and yard. Their aunts made up games for them, and on their birthdays sent them U.S. savings bonds, and wrote them poems and made watercolors of animals. They were the only children the aunts had to fuss over.

Grandmother Hursh remained in the house O.A.S. Hursh had

built until she died in 1932. The aunts continued to live there as before. Grace and Elinor contributed most of the income; Alice sometimes drew an allowance. Grace recorded in a ledger book every penny the household spent, including the quarter paid to a plumber to thaw out their drain and the nickel paid on November 13, 1939, to a Donald Smith "for helping with leaves." They kept a list of all their callers—once in the space of a couple of months they had 118. Alice showed the callers Christmas cards she had for sale. They took vacation trips to Lincoln's farm in Illinois and to Washington's house at Mount Vernon in a gray sedan they called Lady Jane Grey. On winter evenings they sat in the parlor around the fire in the coal grate and talked. They wrote out stories they recalled about their mother and grandparents in scripts that might have come from the handwriting workbook, attended meetings of the Daughters of the American Revolution and the Women's Christian Temperance Union, and met missionaries of the Reformed Church who were visiting Tiffin; one missionary told them that in Central Africa people ate sliced elephant trunk, which resembled doughnuts because of the hole in the middle. On Sundays they went to the Trinity Reformed Church, to which they and their mother had given a set of organ chimes in memory of their father.

John, Bill, and Betty grew up and went off to college. By the time Peggy was eight, she was the only child living at home. She helped her mother with the little nursery school she ran in her house, especially when the school put on shows for the parents. She studied acting and dance at the Cleveland Play House and knew the name of every grown-up actor in the company. After high school she went to Stephens, a women's junior college in Missouri, mainly because the famous actress Maude Adams was a teacher there. When Peggy first saw Maude Adams she was surprised at how ordinary she looked, but felt so unworthy she could hardly meet her eyes. She got parts in many school plays. She was Straforel in *The Romancers*, by Rostand; Maude Adams noticed her, and told her she was almost breathing right. Peggy also continued to dance. After one recital she wrote in a journal: "Tonight my soul was filled with music. My whole body swayed to the rhythm of the dance. I danced tonight, and my heart danced with me."

Maude Adams told Peggy that she had talent and should continue in the theater. Back in Ohio, Peggy's family—her parents, brother

Bill, his wife, Ginny—were doubtful. Her mother was thrilled that Maude Adams, an idol from her girlhood, should say such a thing, but feared that if Peggy pursued acting she would be hurt. She always hated to see Peggy hurt. Bill and Ginny were of the opinion that a college education should prepare a person for something definite and that Peggy needed a profession. Peggy's father said that if she enrolled in the special third-year apprentice program in acting she'd been offered at Stephens, that year would be the last of her education he would pay for. Peggy decided to take two years of college at Cornell instead and get a degree in English so she could teach. She graduated from Cornell in 1944 and that fall began to teach high-school English in Sidney, New York.

Peggy told her mother that she enjoyed teaching, that her father did not force her into it, and that in fact she had wanted to teach for a year as sort of a tribute to him. But she added that she still had a bug about the stage. At Sidney she directed a production of *Our Town* which the principal said was the best high-school play he'd ever seen. After school was out she left Sidney, intending to get a job working on shows for the USO, but by August the war was over. She looked for teaching jobs in the Cleveland area, and at the last minute was hired to teach drama at John Adams, a high school on the east side. She had many talented students there and enjoyed directing them in plays like *Papa Is All*.

In the summer of 1947 she went to New York City and stayed with a friend of her mother's who had an apartment on Riverside Drive. She rode on the top of double-decker buses down to midtown and the Village looking for acting jobs. She wrote her father that New York made her feel free, and he wrote back that freedom was a feeling you made for yourself wherever you were—it wasn't just in the air. She met a sculptor and may have fallen in love with him. The sculptor told her that their spirits touched, and always would. He did nude drawings of her in pastels and wrote her letters on the back of student report sheets from the Newark Public School of Fine and Industrial Art, where he taught. He was twenty-four years older than she was, however, and had a wife and children. She went back to Cleveland when school started in the fall.

A year or two later, she applied for graduate study at the Yale School of Drama and was accepted. She took a leave of absence from teaching at John Adams to go to Yale, but in the end never went. First she had to direct a benefit performance for the Cleveland Community Chest, which conflicted with the start of fall semester; then she got a part-time job writing and producing scripts for WBOE, the radio station of the Cleveland Board of Education. She continued to appear in local little theater productions. Lakewood audiences remembered her as Vinnie in *Life with Father* and *Life with Mother*, Mavis Wilson in *Love from a Stranger*, and Jessie in *I Remember Mama*. When she was twenty-eight she was teaching remedial English in a junior high school and living in her parents' house, which was so snug the staircase was nearly vertical. As much as she wanted anything of her life, she did not want to end up an old maid schoolteacher like her aunts.

C H A P T E R 2

AFTER MY PARENTS had been married for thirty-two years, my father began to show signs of Alzheimer's disease. His family—my mother, my brother Dave, my sisters Suzan and Maggie, and I—did not believe at first the symptoms were real. But he was sure he was getting sick. "Don't forget, I'm *inside* this thing," he said, and it turned out he was right. His slow decline seemed as if it might go on indefinitely, but in 1987 he got pneumonia, went into the hospital, and died. My mother was proud that she had never put him in a nursing home. In pictures taken then she looks haggard. People said his death would be a blessing for her, but she did not see it that way. I thought she was like a flower someone had cut at the stem by accident and set back among the uncut flowers. She died of liver cancer in November 1988, a little more than a year after my father.

Recently I went back to Hudson, Ohio, the town between Cleveland and Akron where we used to live. My parents moved to a house

My mother in the kitchen of their apartment in Lakewood, Ohio

in a development in Hudson in 1957 and left for an apartment in
Cleveland in 1977. Hudson is the one place we lived as a family—
after Maggie, the youngest, was born, and before I, the oldest, went
away to college. As I often do, I stopped first at Merino's Beer &
Wine, off Main Street. Rich Merino has been running that store since
1946. There was no one in town my father saw more regularly. Rich
is trim, tan, big-eared, nearly bald; he has big arms and forearms. He
grew up in Hudson and once played on the same football team as
Hall-of-Famer Dante Lavelli. He was asleep in a lawn chair in front
of the counter when I came in. "Yeah, your dad—" he said. "He'd
come in here. He had that stride. He'd buy six-packs. I don't remember him buying much wine. I could tell when your mom was pregnant
'cause he'd buy that Guinness Stout for her."

I bought a quart of beer from Rich and got in my rented car. I
drove out of town, past houses where people we used to know used
to live. The Coluccis, the Beemans, the Edelmans, the Deans. The
place where Grissom's farm used to be; a woman moved the house
into town a while ago and fixed it up and lives in it; there's a high
school there today. A lot more people live in Hudson now than did
when we moved there. The Hendersons: he used to play the bagpipes
in the early evening on his side porch. The bridge where the veter-
inarian's son died one night in a car crash; my friend Kent and I went
down the next morning to look at the wreck, and all we found were
tire ruts in the muck, splinters of rearview mirror, and lots of 45 rpm
records with bright labels scattered along the creek bottom in the clear
water. The Adolphs, the Rickeys, the Douds. In Hudson everyone
was plural. Our Christmas card from the Douds was signed, "The
Douds." I passed the development where we used to live but did not
go look at our old house. I drove beyond the township line and down
a dirt road to Tinker's Creek State Park. I pulled into the four-car
parking lot and got out.

It was December. The sun had just set. A red dusk came through
the bare trees, and I could see the evening star. I walked along the
railroad tracks that run next to the park drinking from my quart in a
paper sack. A lot of this park is swamp—the sort of place developers
are leaving for later. Friends and I used to come out here in the spring
and cantilever ourselves out on the scrub willows and shoot dozens
of little frogs we called spring peepers with slingshots and BB guns.

I stopped at a culvert where one of the swamp ponds flows under the tracks. There was a layer of ice on the pond. I picked up a rock from the track bed and threw it at the ice, expecting to punch a hole; instead, the rock bounced across the ice with a noise like an electric synthesizer makes, a sort of metallic *wahng wahng wahng*. At each shorter bounce the noise got higher, until it was like chirping. This tickled me and I threw several more rocks. I picked up my beer from the tie where I had set it and took some swallows. I put my hands in my jacket pocket and hopped from foot to foot. Even here I could hear traffic—the faraway noise of trucks on the turnpike or the interstate—and see headlights of cars on a bridge or bouncing across the grade crossing to the south. Then I heard a non-unison cackling, a windy, fast-moving sound that became a honking right above me as a flock of Canada geese appeared over the treeline. They were in a V, with one goose and then another dropping down out of the formation. The geese banked away to my right, around a point of trees, evidently heading for open water beyond. In the next few minutes more Vs flew in from the same direction. Just at last light, a small flock came. They were dark against the sky, then dim against the trees. When they were over the pond, all the geese stopped beating their wings at exactly the same moment and began to glide. My heart jumped; everyday thoughts fell away and I felt the full weight of how much I loved my mother.

For some reason I did not think of my father, although I loved him, too.

•

Because of the difficulties of my father's illness and the swiftness of my mother's, their departure from life was not so much a retreat as a rout. My mother had not had time to do a lot besides work and take care of my father. Their apartment was full of miscellany they had accumulated or never got around to throwing away, and unsorted personal papers. As we cleaned out the apartment so the urologist and his wife who had bought it could move in, we found dozens of fingernail clippers, bud vases, and seashells; lots of handbags, woven baskets that floral arrangements come in, electric razors, clothes irons, and books on how to teach yourself to speak Chinese. Many items had nothing in common except that they commemorated trips my parents had taken or plays my mother had directed or been in. Suzan found several suit boxes of scraps from clothes my mother sewed—

bright, mint-condition leftovers from shirts, costumes, and dresses that had worn out and vanished twenty or thirty years ago. Maggie looked in the phone book and found a store in a far suburb that sells supplies to Amish women who quilt. When I dropped the scraps off at the store one afternoon, the lady told me I should look for them turning up in a year or two in quilts at the Geauga County Fair.

As a kid, I had always wanted to go through my parents' papers—now I could. I tried to tell which ones were less important. The apartment building has a trash chute running next to the freight elevator with a door at every floor. I took some papers and opened the chute door and tossed them in; a few hung in front of me in a warm updraft from the basement filled with dumpster smell. Usually, any paper I looked at closely I couldn't throw away. In falling-apart manila envelopes, file folders, gift boxes with the names of defunct Cleveland department stores, accordion files, my mother's desk, my father's bureau drawers, I found:

A pack of 260 gummed foil stars in assorted colors and sizes.

A pad of detention notices, with blanks for student's name, room number, and offense.

An article from *National Geographic* magazine on potatoes, with notes in Cora's handwriting; it was a contention of hers that my father's illness had something to do with his eating habits, particularly his habit of setting the potatoes to one side of his plate and leaving them.

An abstract of a paper given in 1951 at an American Chemical Society symposium saying that Negroes almost never get kidney stones, and women only seldom, as a result of protective colloids in their urine.

An envelope of photographs my father took from the balcony of the apartment through a high-powered Quasar telescope: many of the full moon, Saturn with its rings, other planets, and a few of women in bikinis sunbathing by neighboring buildings.

A notebook of daily and other reminders my mother kept at around the time of my birth:

> Write Thank-you letters
> Akron
> Lydia
> Betty

"Main Street"
"Babbitt"   Sinclair Lewis

Cleaners for green dress
         blue suit

Toothpowder
Slippers
"Kim"—Kipling;

A recipe for applesauce cake in an aunt's handwriting with the note "Keeps good, if you hide it."

A photocopy of an article dated November 1956, about the effect of a nuclear attack on Washington, D.C. Our father often told us what to do in the event of nuclear war, and kept jugs of water and cans of food on the basement rafters against the possibility. He usually ended his lesson to us something like "Then you'll come out of your hole and look around and get on with the job of rebuilding the world."

A road map of Alaska and western Canada.

A bicycle license from the village of Oberlin, Ohio, valid from December 12, 1939, to October 31, 1940, in my father's name.

A .44 caliber slug in a glass pill bottle, with a prescription from an Ocean Beach, California, drugstore; the slip reads, "Use as directed for pain. 1—Colt Slug / Chawed Flat." The name of the prescribing doctor is Kirkby. Harold Kirkby was my father's roommate at Stanford graduate school. Like my father, his doctorate was in chemistry.

A three-subject school notebook, blank except for what my mother had written on the first page in inks of different color:

The end was part of the adventure—the dark part.

Trying to find a way back into life.

He was so gallant—he would go anywhere, do anything he thought I wanted him to. "Do you think we dare risk it?" he'd say, sometimes.

Silver dollars in my bracelet box.

A list of people I never heard of who were sent announcements of my birth, including Florence McGlenn, Paul Yaple, Mr. Butterfield,

Mrs. Hexamer, Girls in 1-2-3, the L. Bramer Carlsons, Gen Marko, Eliz. Tilley, and Mary Linda Do.

An article clipped from *Scientific American* of September 1977 on the subject of why hot water freezes faster than cold.

A military photograph taken from the air of a submarine with German markings bleeding oil, survivors around it in the water.

A card admitting my father to the Pacific Fleet Commissioned Officers' Mess on Guam, good through 1946.

A booklet, *How to Refinish Furniture at Home*.

A typescript, "Summary of uses of the comma."

An English test on Ibsen's *Hedda Gabler*: "People who are bored often are suffering from some inner conflicts. What are Hedda's conflicts? Discuss."

Pencil silhouettes of all us children which my father later had made into sterling-silver silhouettes to hang on the wall.

A small shopping bag decorated with John Singer Sargent's portrait of Mrs. Fiske Warren and her daughter.

A sheaf of textbook condition reports filed by students at the beginning of the school year so that they would not be charged for pre-existing damage: "Michelle Anderson: Corners damaged (outside) Spine damaged (dirty)"; "Larissa Hritsko: First couple of pages are stained"; "Ed Stein: Beat up cover"; "Monica Lanigan: cover chewed <u>all</u> pages have bent corners and/or are ripped pen writing on pg 41."

A carbon of a report from my kindergarten teacher: "Ian follows directions in a haphazard manner. He often does not think things through and becomes excited or in a hurry. He often answers in a hurry without thinking. He is cheerful and popular in the group and anxious to please. He knows many songs and verses."

A review from the Akron *Beacon Journal* of a production of *Macbeth* at the Kent State University Theater in which my mother played Lady Macbeth: "Kate Frazier . . . gave the outstanding performance of the evening. She has obviously thought through the part carefully so every word and gesture had purpose. Her sleepwalking scene was gripping."

A jar of matchbooks my father collected on business trips, from the Arizona Hotel in Phoenix ("air conditioned"), the Van Curler Hotel in Schenectady ("200 Rooms"), the KoKo Motel in Joplin, Missouri ("Enjoy Our Television"), the Cornell Heights Residential Club in

Ithaca, New York ("Your Headquarters"), the Town Park Motor Hotel in Memphis ("America's Most Beautiful Motor Hotel"), the Hotel Kirwan in Lima, Ohio ("Known for Clean Rooms and Good Food"), the Granot Lodge in Clinton, Oklahoma ("T-V In Lobby").

A brochure advertising luxury service flats in London's Knightsbridge district for rent by the day or week.

A copy of the deed to our house in Hudson. A clause states that the owners agree not to raise hogs or have an outhouse.

A five-year diary kept by my father, which begins on January 1, 1938, with the death of his grandfather Harry E. Frazier.

A poem written by Ray Frazier after the death of his son Teddy:

> We pray, dear God, that somewhere,
> In the land beyond the blue,
> The dream for which he dreamed so long
> Has now come true.

An article Ray wrote for his company newsletter about scrap iron, describing its different grades, from machined particles the fineness of talcum powder, to used razor blades, to car fenders cut into eight-inch squares, to old railroad locomotives.

An obituary for Ray clipped from *The New York Times* of October 11, 1951: "Edwin R. Frazier, 59, Veteran Steel Man."

Several portfolios of drawings in pencil and pastels done by my sister Suzan. She made enough money for a trip to Europe by sketching portraits on the midway across from the break-a-plate booth at a local amusement park.

A set of three-by-five cards with notes in my father's handwriting on the subject of a rare chemical compound called oxazole (C_3H_3NO), mostly incomprehensible to me.

A folder of clippings and reviews having to do with the later career of the sculptor my mother once knew in New York.

A folded piece of paper inscribed *Keys to Cottage*, containing two brass house keys. The cottage on Lake Erie we went to on weekends in the summer—the same place Cora had played as a little girl—was sold in 1967.

A price tag from my mother's mink coat. It cost $1,495, on sale.

An obituary notice clipped from a newspaper for Flora Bachman

Hursh, dated 1961. Also, notices for Osie Hursh (1964) and Cora Frazier (1985).

A file folder of letters my father wrote to universities, mostly in California, looking for a job teaching chemistry or statistics in 1964. Also, a number of rejection letters he got in return.

An envelope of papers having to do with my father's contest of a traffic ticket in which the judge gave him the decision but scolded him for remarks he made about the arresting officer, "most unbecoming for a man of the defendant's educational and professional background."

Several copies of my father's patents. He had ten of his own and shared four others with colleagues.

An optometrist's card with the prescription for my father's lenses.

Several faded construction-paper penguins which Maggie made and hung in her bedroom when she was in elementary school and liked penguins.

Hundreds of issues of *Theatre Arts* magazine.

An assessment of modern teaching, written by my mother: "The classroom has changed; students are much less controlled; they speak when they want to regardless of what is being taught. They whistle; they fix their hair; they chew gum; they pass notes; they sleep; they work on other homework; they look at magazines. They come to class tired after working at their jobs until ten or eleven o'clock; they come after a night of partying or attending a rock concert. They don't have much to give to their English . . . nor do they want to. Their interest lies particularly in receiving a good grade." One of the students at the high school where she taught was Jeffrey Dahmer, later a mass murderer.

A piece of yellow notepaper with my father's shaky latter-day printing:

DEPRESSION

ANXIETIE

ANXIITY

ANXIIETY   DEPRESSION

ANXITY

A folder of magazine articles written by Jamaica Kincaid.

A card that says, "Season's Greetings from Antarctica"—two figures in a white landscape walking toward a Quonset hut with a steeple and a cross—sent by a cousin who was stationed there in the navy.

A photograph, taken after my father had gotten sick, of my brother Dave standing next to him by the dining-room table with his arm around him.

Thousands of other photographs.

A draft of a speech by my mother in praise of the high-school custodians.

My brother Fritz's library card. It expired in 1976, four years after he did, at the age of fifteen, of leukemia.

•

A while ago, Maggie and Suzan were talking about Fritz in Maggie's living room.

Suzan: Fritz used to get really mad . . .

Maggie: It was like having a homicidal maniac in the house.

Suzan: . . . and one time I made him mad when I cut a decorative border into a permission slip he needed for school—I mean, the slip was still perfectly serviceable, but he blew up and tore in half some notes I'd taken for English, which happened to be one of the few times I'd taken notes . . .

Me: How old were you? How old was he?

Suzan: Oh, fourteen.

Maggie: He was big. I think he was sick by then—it was after he didn't have hair.

Suzan: No, it was before that. He had hair. Anyway, I took a bowl of chili and dumped it on his head while he was sitting on the couch. He was really surprised.

Maggie: The bowl just sat there on his head. He had to take it off like a hat. The chili was still there.

Suzan: We ran away really fast. He was so furious. I locked myself in the bathroom. He pounded and pounded on the door.

Maggie: I knew he'd get me if he couldn't get her, so I locked myself in my room.

Suzan: I thought I'd have to stay in the bathroom forever, and I realized there really wasn't a lot to *do* in the bathroom.

Maggie: He kept pounding on the bathroom door and on my door, and then I heard him start laughing.

Suzan: Yes, I remember he said it was pretty funny. I got to come out of the bathroom a lot sooner than I expected.

•

Fritz was in a difficult position in the family—the fourth of five brothers and sisters. He probably felt overlooked. When he was little, his sayings, which we would tease him for, were "You make me mad, mad, mad!" and "Big deal!" The second he used whenever someone would point out something of interest when we were on vacation. Dinnertimes often pivoted on the moment when he would suddenly pound his fist on the table, rattling the dishes, and storm off. For a while I would be sent to look for him, but he could be hard to find and I stopped making much effort. Years later my mother said that if Fritz hadn't been sick, she didn't think she would have ever gotten to know him. He was the only person in the family besides me who liked to fish. Once, on the banks of the Chena River in Alaska, he accidentally let go of his little Zebco spinning rod as he was casting and without a pause sprinted at top speed after it into the water. Just before he got sick, when I came home from college on Christmas vacation, he wrestled me to a draw although I had twenty pounds and six years on him.

His death was the worst thing that ever happened to me; I hesitate to think what it was like for him. Once, being a wise guy, I said something making fun of my father which Fritz took as making fun of his illness. Probably it wasn't such a good idea to be a wise guy at all right then. Fritz told me I had no compassion. I remember the accuracy of his eyes as he said it, the rage-filled, glittering, comprehending blue of them. The look plugged into me. I saw myself for a child and knew a breathtaking instant of what he knew.

•

Then there were the letters—in bundles and bales, some taped together by adhesive tape that had turned amber, some formerly held by rubber bands that had melted to the envelopes in spots. My father's parents wrote him regularly when he was in graduate school and in the navy, and he wrote to them and to his brothers. My mother and her mother wrote each other every two or three days for years. My mother and father wrote each other before they were married. Letters and telegrams survived from close relatives, friends, distant relatives, unidentifiable people. Some of the letters had come down through the family for generations. The earliest one was dated 1855; a great-great-grandfather, a student at Kenyon College, telling a cousin that the young woman in love with the cousin appears to be of respectable family from all reports. The latest were sent to my mother in 1988 just a few days before she died.

Nowadays, evening is the usual time for family and friends to make long-distance telephone calls. Evening used to be when people wrote letters. I found the letters a cache of nighttime hours: in Atlanta, during the Civil War, in camp, the writer lit by a candle held by a bayonet stuck in the ground; in a farmhouse in 1868, "evening and children all in bed, and for two or three hours I can think and know what I am about"; in a small-town boardinghouse in midwinter, the pages of the stationery curling from the heat of the coal stove; in a dormitory room at a boys' school in 1896, before glee-club practice; in a front parlor, the writer feeling wasteful for keeping the electric light on so late; by a coal grate, the writer warming his feet after playing the piccolo that day in the mud and slush at a GAR funeral; in a college dormitory in 1940 while rain came down and a radio played and a girl talked on the phone and someone shouted and a roommate sucked on a sucker and coughed and sat on the bed tracing a map of France for French class; in Bay Village, the writer babysitting for a little girl named Louisy, who would not stop bouncing on the gorgeous satin damask davenport; in a kitchen, midnight, 1944, while the writer cooked sweet potatoes to can from her victory garden; in an armchair under a lamp, a book serving as a desk "with bad effect on the chirography"; on a couch in 1964, the writer half asleep from watching the Republican convention on TV.

In the end, I did not throw many papers away. I collected all the letters to or from my father and put them with a bunch of his other things in a box I labeled THE DAD MUSEUM. I did the same for my mother in a box labeled THE MOM MUSEUM. The papers that remained filled other boxes. I took all the boxes back to New York and went through them during the next several years. I held each item under the light and looked at it. In notebooks I wrote down what all the items were and what almost every letter said. If the writers were still living I went to see them; usually this meant traveling not to the Midwest but to one coast or another, where most of my relatives now are. I read books my ancestors had referred to—The Bible, Fleetwood's *Life of Christ*, Swan's *Treatise for Justices of the Peace*—and books that referred in passing to them, such as *A Captive of War*, by Solon Hyde, in which the author and Great-great-grandfather Benedict are taken prisoner by the Confederates at the Battle of Chicamauga. These books caused me to read lots of others.

One summer I read for a few weeks in the main reading room of Butler Library at Columbia University—first-person travel accounts, mostly, by people who had gone to the Ohio and Indiana frontier in the early 1800s. The reading room is long and lofty, with many study tables, and bookshelves along the walls. From the first day I always sat at the same seat, at the end of a table not far from the door. One afternoon a young Asian woman sat just behind me at the next table. She had a lot of plastic shopping bags. She worked quietly for a while and then all of a sudden began to rustle the plastic bags like mad. She would rustle and rustle and rustle, and when I thought she was done she would rustle a little bit more. Then she would go back to work and after a while start up again. The next morning when I arrived I saw by the plastic bags that the woman had chosen the same seat. I scanned the vast, nearly empty room—no shortage of places to sit. I thought for a bit and decided I couldn't change a seat I was so used to just because of a little noise. I took my usual chair and read, through outbreaks of rustling, for five or six hours. I became bored and leaned back in my chair and stretched. I noticed that the bookshelves just to my left held bound volumes of Ph.D. thesis abstracts—from the University of Iowa, Michigan State, Ohio State. On a lower shelf I spotted a volume, *Stanford University Abstract of Dissertations 1943/44–1946/47*. I did not have to get up. I leaned over in my chair, took the book, flipped it open to my father's thesis: "A Further Study of the Relationship between Echinocystic Acid and Oleanolic Acid." There must be twenty-five thousand books in that room.

I untangled genealogies that I found in my parents' papers or that relatives lent me. I drew family trees in which, no doubt, errors of fact imitated the errors of chromosome replication in DNA. I studied census data at a branch of the National Archives at a military base in Bayonne, New Jersey, where I had to get a pass at the gate from a woman sergeant in camouflage and the road went through acres of hardware bound for Saudi Arabia, and I read documents of the Connecticut Legislature from the Revolutionary War at the Mormon li-

brary on Sixty-fifth Street in Manhattan, where the director was Elder
Henry Rock. I looked at family photographs with a small magnifying
glass. In a picture taken at the beach in the 1950s I saw the sand on
the back of my brother's legs, a paper carton of bait, the burned place
on the half-buried log where we used to build fires. In a picture of
the dining room at a Thanksgiving dinner I saw the table settings and
the turkey and the sweat on the black windowpanes. I scanned, shingle
by Necco-wafer shingle, the candy house my mother made and somebody photographed one Christmas. I rented cars from a garage in the
basement of the World Trade Center and drove to many places within
eight hundred miles that had been of importance in an ancestor's life.
I read gravestone inscriptions disappearing like movie credits into the
advancing sod.

I wanted my parents' lives to have meant something. I hunted
all over for meanings of any kind—not, I think, simply out of grief or
anger at their deaths, but also because the stuff they saved implied
that there must have been a reason for saving it. The smell of an old
hymnal, the weave of a black mesh hat veil, the tone of a thank-you
note, each struck me with the silent force of a clue. Something was
going on here. I believed bigger meanings hid behind little ones, that
maybe I could follow them to a source back tens or hundreds of years
ago. I didn't care if the meanings were far-flung or vague or even
trivial. I wanted to pursue them. I hoped maybe I could find a meaning
that would defeat death.

C H A P T E R   3

ANCESTORS:

One was named Godwyn of Cornwall, maybe. One might possibly have been mentioned in the Domesday Book of 1085–86. Some came from the north of England, some from near the town of Rowley in Yorkshire, some from Scotland, some perhaps from the Palatinate districts in Germany. Several seem to have been named Melchior; one, Melchior Breneman, a Swiss Mennonite, was born in Berne in 1631. One lived for a hundred years in the seventeenth and eighteenth centuries. One sailed to America in 1635 on the ship *Defense*; one landed at Ipswich, Massachusetts, on the *Elizabeth*. One was a tanner in Scituate, Massachusetts. One was said to have been an ensign in the army of Oliver Cromwell. One was a dealer of wool in New Haven in 1664. One died of a cold he caught fighting the Great Fire of London

Platt Benedict (1775–1866) and his wife, Sally DeForest Benedict (1777–1852). Platt founded the town of Norwalk, Ohio. In his garden, Platt was said to have grown a parsnip five feet three inches long

in 1666, reportedly. Several served in King Philip's War, the series of bloody Indian battles that spread from Massachusetts throughout New England in 1675; one survived the Great Narragansett Swamp Fight, another received twelve acres for his participation in the Direful Swamp Fight of December 19. Several were colonial governors; one died in Boston in 1676 while attending a meeting of the commissioners of the United Colonies. One took the oath of allegiance to Charles II in Massachusetts in 1678, and later accused a woman named Mary Currier of bewitching a cow that had wandered away. One served as deputy to the general court of Norwalk, Connecticut. One was a carpenter in Andover, Massachusetts, in the 1690s. Of one, little is known besides her maiden name: Smith.

Following the trail of remote ancestors reminds me of when the army used to chase an Indian tribe on the prairie and the Indians would all split up and the trail would grow faint and then disappear completely. Much of what I learned of ancestors before 1700 comes from a careful genealogy done by a distant cousin whose mother was a Wickham. That family, and the Benedicts—who combined in my grandmother Cora—were impressed with the people they were descended from and kept records. Parts of their handed-down histories have glazed over into myth. The other branches of the family cared who they came from, but not as much, and in some cases hardly at all. Together these various impulses created the vagueness in which genealogies usually begin. A family tree that goes back to 1600—to the twelfth generation, say, the generation of Pocahontas—can contain direct ancestors to the number $2 + 2^2 + 2^3 \ldots + 2^{12}$, or a possible 8,190 names.

One ancestor, Thomas Benedict, a sometime weaver's apprentice, left England for the Massachusetts Bay Colony in 1638 with his stepsister, Mary Bridgum. They married in 1640, moved to Long Island, then to Norwalk, Connecticut. They had five sons and four daughters. Thomas's will parceled out among them his calf pastures, boggy meadow, salt meadows, upland acres, commonage, "sticky plaine lot," "fruiteful spring lot," sheep, barns, plows, chains, and the mare "yt is now running in ye wood." Seven of his nine children had children. In a genealogy of the Benedicts published over a hundred years ago, the index of Thomas and Mary's descendants runs to twenty-two pages of small type.

One ancestor was a brother of the Indian fighter John Lovewell, who killed Indians the way you'd kill rats in your basement and who was himself killed by a Pequawket Indian with a shotgun near the present town of Fryeburg, Maine. One served for thirty-two weeks as surgeon's mate during the French and Indian War; later he practiced medicine in New Ipswich, New Hampshire. One was married to another on December 28, 1762, by the Reverend Marmaduke Brown. One's tombstone describes her as the "meek benevolent and virtuous Consort" of another, buried beside her; most of the conversations you hear today near their gravesite in a small New England city are in Spanish. Three or more were hatters: "He was very much bent when first I knew him, brought on as some of his family think by his position over the kettle in planking hats," a relative recalled of one. One would use no expression stronger than "Swizzle." One had many great-grandchildren, who referred to him as "Grand-sir," pronounced "Granser." One was so fat she went to church on Sunday mornings and stayed there all day, rather than go home and then return for evening services. One was a heavy drinker who died from a fractured skull suffered in a fall down the stairs of the newspaper he founded. One continued to wear knee breeches into the 1820s, long after they had gone out of style. One resisted buying a mechanical clock, saying that his sundial was good enough for him. One's favorite expression was "Maybe it is all for the best."

One or more may have been related to the man who preached the funeral sermon for Mary, Queen of Scots. One might possibly have given a birthday party for James I in 1617. One had a brother-in-law who knew the Marquis de Lafayette and entertained him in his home. One had a first cousin who was an army engineer on the staff of General William Sherman. One's granddaughter married the uncle of newsman Lowell Thomas.

Many had wives who died young; for years, the two leading causes of death in women were childbirth and household accidents with fire. A few of the men lie in cemeteries next to a row of wives. None that I know of got divorced. Some had marriages that lasted for more than fifty years, a few for more than sixty. Families with five or more children were common. Old census records list only the names of heads of households, almost always males; everyone else was just a vertical stroke of the pen.

One or more were slave-ship captains. Joseph Wanton (1705–80) made many voyages to the western coast of Africa to trade for slaves. In 1758, during the war between England and France, he was captured by a French privateer at the Dutch trading post of Annamaboa, on the coast of what is now Ghana. He lost his vessel, the *King of Prussia*, and his cargo—sixty-six hogsheads of rum, twenty ounces of gold dust, and fifty-four slaves. The privateer set him ashore, and eventually he made his way home with the remnants of other stranded slave-ship crews on a ship given to them by a local Dutch slave trader. Joseph Wanton lived in Newport, Rhode Island, then the main port for slave ships in North America. An abolitionist minister described Newport as "built up by the blood of poor Africans." Wanton's son-in-law Thomas Wickham, also of Newport, was very likely the same Thomas Wickham described in Newport Custom House records as master of the sloop *Diamond*, which arrived in port from Africa in May 1762. A Notice of Sale in a Boston newspaper of that month advertises, "Just Imported, From the Coast of Africa, a Parcel of likely Negroes; To be Sold on board the sloop *Diamond*, Capt. Wickham, now lying at Mr. Avery's Wharf, near the South Market." In 1763 the same paper reported that Thomas Wickham and other captains had written from the coast of Africa that the trade there was discouraging, and that the price of slaves had gone up to two hundred gallons of rum a head.

A number of my ancestors owned slaves. Wills and other documents preserve the names of men and women known simply as Bell, Nancy, Bet. One will bequeathed to a daughter a runaway mulatto boy named Daniel "if he be found." One ancestor (Abraham Wildman, 1670–1750) freed in his will "for faithful service my black man Mingo." Woodcut illustrations in history books and TV specials make slavery seem of the distant past, but really slavery was just the day before yesterday. My grandfather Osie Hursh, who I knew well, knew well his grandfather Thomas Chapman (1815–1905); as a young man in Western Virginia, Grandfather Chapman owned a man named Black Bill and a woman named Aunt Rindy, who had been wedding presents from his parents.

•

Mostly, my ancestors were Protestants. In fact, of all the ancestors I can name over the last three hundred years, only one or two were possibly not. I imagine myself in a grange hall full of ancestors—their dark clothes, perhaps a woolly, smoky smell, their inward demeanors—and I think conversation between me and them would be even more strained than usual at family get-togethers. My ancestors talked and wrote a lot more about God and Jesus Christ than I do. They prayed out loud, cited Scripture in conversation, and generally gave a strong appearance of belief. They approved of mirth, but not "dissolute mirth." They could be a tough audience. In church, they often hummed when they liked what the preacher was saying and sometimes hissed softly when they didn't. Many of my references come from popular culture; theirs usually came from the Bible. A person who moved fast they might say was "going like Jehu," from Jehu, a King of Israel, the fastest driver in the Bible (II Kings, 9:20), whose chariot a watchman could identify in the far distance from the tower of Jerusalem: "The driving is like the driving of Jehu . . . for he driveth furiously."

Compared to them, I suppose I am an infidel. They might call me a Nothingarian—the name regular churchgoers in the nineteenth century sometimes applied to those who weren't. I attend services at an Episcopal church in Brooklyn four or five times a year. Except in church, if a person uses the name of Jesus Christ, I prefer that it be as an exclamation; anyone who comes up to me talking in a serious way about Jesus Christ makes me uncomfortable. If a friend were to mention Jesus Christ in a serious way, I would probably assume that he or she was about to have a breakdown. Months and years sometimes pass without my giving any thought to religion. The only religious observance I perform every year without fail is on Good Friday, when I call my friend Mark Singer and discuss the charges and counter-charges of this whole Crucifixion snafu. In the past, when I have felt I needed a minister—usually at times of birth, marriage, or death— I have gone to an Episcopal church and one has helped me.

A note in a genealogy compiled by Aunt Grace says that Thomas Chapman's parents were Old School Presbyterians. So remote is my experience of religion from theirs I had no idea what that meant. I thought a Presbyterian was a Presbyterian. It turns out that in the mid-nineteenth century there were at least eight kinds of Presbyterians: Associate, Associate Reformed, Reformed, Reformed Dutch, German Reformed, Constitutional, Cumberland, and Old School. The differences among them were many and complicated. For example, most disagreed on predestination, the Calvinist refinement of Luther's idea that man was saved by divine grace through faith alone. Believers in predestination said that not only was man saved through grace, he could do nothing about it; some souls were predestined for salvation from birth, and others for hell. This idea, also called infant damnation, got people almost as upset as the abortion debate does today. Some Presbyterians, like the Associate and Associate Reformed sects, were strict predestinarians; others, like the Cumberland sect, rejected the doctrine as "fantastic" and called its believers "baby burners."

Old School Presbyterians inclined to strictness on predestination, but the real difference between them and other sects had more to do with politics. Old School Presbyterians were anti–New England. Some of them lived in more recently settled parts of the country, and the event that caused them to divide the church and form their own sect in 1837 was a planned merger of Presbyterian churches with Congregationalists, since Pilgrim days the church of New England. Old School Presbyterians didn't like the Congregationalists' supposed disregard of Scripture, their liberality in letting each congregation govern itself, and especially their views on slavery. Many Congregational churches preached abolition. The Old School sect came to represent the strongest pro-slavery position within Presbyterianism. Thomas Chapman's move from Virginia to a free state in the 1840s and his membership in a Reformed Presbyterian church suggest that his opinion on slavery changed.

Back then, it almost went without saying that a person here, if religious, was a Protestant; people of other Old World faiths did not exist in America in large numbers until the late 1840s. Churchgoers identified themselves not as Protestants but by denomination. Some of my ancestors were Mennonites, some were Lutherans, some Congregationalists. Those who went to the Episcopal church were low-church Episcopals—as opposed to middle-, high-, or Puseyite (ultra-high). One relative was a Swedenborgian, or follower of Emanuel Swedenborg, an eighteenth-century polymath and mystic who wrote a lot about self-realization and believed the Second Coming had already occurred. Nowadays we may think of Protestantism as a single faith, one among many. In fact, there has never been just one Protestant Church; from the beginning, the Protestant movement has been made up of sects. In the early United States, after the Revolutionary War,

Protestant sects proliferated like diet colas. Besides the Presbyterians and Episcopalians and Congregationalists, all split internally by various schisms, there were newer churches like the Methodists and Baptists, who won so many souls on the frontier with their circuit riders and tent-meeting revivals that they became the two largest denominations in the country. Methodists soon subdivided into three or four different sects, and among the Baptists, the Hard Shell, Free Will, Particular, Seceder, Seventh-day, Six-Principle and Two-Seeds-in-the-Spirit Predestinarian congregations all formed sects of their own. Then there were Shakers, Quakers (four different kinds), Mormons, Sandemanians, Finneyites, Rappites, Zoarites, Millerites, Universalists, Pietists, Transcendentalists, Osbornites, Moravians, Swiss Brethren, Plymouth Brethren, United Brethren in Christ, Dunkards (also called the Brethren), Unitarians, German Lutherans, Dutch Lutherans—"an almost endless variety of religious factions," as the English visitor Mrs. Trollope observed in 1831. Many of the churches further divided into separate black and white congregations; many were split by the Civil War. The number of sects puzzled Indians visited by different missionaries, amused Catholics and Jews, and embarrassed Protestant religious historians. No one has yet written a detailed history of the Protestant sects in America.

When my great-great-grandfather Simeon Frazier was fourteen, he joined a church known at different times as the New Lights, Christians, or Disciples of Christ. This church was the result of a spontaneous uprising of many frontier churches against their parent bodies, usually Presbyterian or Baptist. Its two founders were renegade Presbyterian ministers named Barton Stone and Thomas Campbell. Stone preached mostly in Indiana and Kentucky, Campbell in western Pennsylvania. In the 1820s, followers of Stone and followers of Campbell found that they were opposed to the same things: church hierarchies, forms of worship not mentioned in the New Testament, and all statements of creed. They wanted to forget systems and dogmas and return to the basics—"the Bible, the whole Bible, and nothing but the Bible." They hoped also to do away with sects, which they deplored, by absorbing them all into a simple faith based on the practices of the early Christians. The Stoneites and the Campbellites united in 1832. Their ideas made sense to lots of people; hundreds of thousands joined them, creating one of the largest indigenous religious movements in American history. After Simeon Frazier became a member, so did his

father, Absalom. Simeon preached in Disciples churches, served as a
trustee of a Disciples college, and helped found a church in Green-
wood, Indiana. His son, Harry E., taught Sunday school in Disciples
churches for much of his life. The beliefs that meant a lot to those
Fraziers meant nothing to my father or his father, Ray. Ray worked
Sundays. His son Louis says he never saw Ray go into a church vol-
untarily in his life. Before I started looking through the papers in my
parents' apartment, I had never heard of the Disciples of Christ.

The church where Simeon Frazier became a Disciple in 1846 still
stands. It is in New Washington, a town of about five hundred, several
miles in from the Ohio River in southern Indiana. One Sunday in
June, I went there. This part of Indiana, away from interstate highways, beyond the reach of Cincinnati and Louisville, is rural. Sometimes you pass through miles of hardwood forest without any farms.
Electric current from a nuclear generating plant on the river sputters
on powerlines overhead. On a country road lined with wild roses and
black-eyed Susans I saw an animal—an otter?—staring into a pool in
a nearly dry creekbed, the angle of its diamond-shaped head limning
concentration. I stopped the car and walked back; the animal was
gone, but the trapped shiners were still swimming around in panic.
In New Washington, vacant lots where buildings once stood had been
recently mowed. A house or two on the main street was boarded shut.
Sheets of plywood sealed the windows of the Presbyterian church, a
three-story brick building covered with vines on a lawn of tall maples.
Above the maples rose the aqua-blue legs of the town water tower.
A few lots had one-story pre-fab buildings, wild strawberries growing
beneath the air-conditioner drips.

I found the Disciples church at the corner of two gravel streets.
Its white board front, in keeping with the founder's doctrines of simplicity, is plain as a packing crate. The lines where the boards meet
are perfectly straight; the carpentry seems not so much joined as fused.
A few shingles are missing on the small roof above the entryway.
Above the double doors, a narrow window in modest stained-glass
reads CHRISTIAN CHURCH. The original church building is wood; a
more recent addition, at the far end, is brick. I stood on the street in
front of the church and looked at it from steeple to ground. Then I
sat in the car and waited until enough people had arrived for morning
service that I wouldn't be too conspicuous and went in.

The plain wooden pews had been refinished and fitted with cushions. Glass-globe light fixtures replaced the candle holders with tin reflectors on the walls. Blue carpet covered the floor, electronic speakers faced the congregation from either side of the pulpit, and the new addition had blocked some of the stained-glass windows. The high vaulted ceiling of tongue-and-groove boards was the same as in 1846. I sat in the back, and several people greeted me. A woman named Velma said, "We're not many, but we're mighty!" Among the two dozen in attendance were one young woman and no young men besides the minister; nearly everyone was over sixty. Some of the women had neat white hairdos that looked fresh from the hairdresser. The service proceeded without a prayerbook—simplicity. The minister gave a sermon taken from the Second Book of Chronicles, on the subject of man's unwillingness to admit he has sinned. The minister said that the author of Second Chronicles refuses to blame circumstances for the Jews' captivity in Babylon, blaming it instead on their sins. Something in the sermon led me into a train of thought that brought tears to my eyes, as happens a lot to me in church. Then we said some prayers, including one for the recovery of a man who had been run over by a bulldozer. The Communion wafer was a compressed pellet of bread, and the wine came in small plastic cups like the kind used in hospitals for liquid medication; it turned out to be grape juice. I tried to concentrate on the blood of Christ, but my tastebuds said, "Welch's." Seated, we sang the hymn "Amazing Grace." I was expecting the versions I remembered from the radio, the ones by Judy Collins or Willie Nelson. This version was different—the congregation sang it slowly, pausing a beat after each phrase, the voices high and wavery. As I read this vision of forgiveness and salvation written by a former slave trader, a lens of new tears blocked the words. I had not known there were so many verses.

'Twas grace that taught my heart to fear,
And grace my fears relieved . . .

I thought of all the country churches where this hymn has lived, lives still. I thought of my great-great-grandfather as a teenager under this ceiling almost a century and a half ago. I thought of the frankness of the building's front, of the intention that had nailed together its boards.

I thought of amazing grace that could cleanse a person of terrible sin
for no reason at all.

•

In a bigger town near New Washington I found a local history
which said that in the early days there were people in the county who
knew the Bible so well that together they could have reproduced the
whole book from memory if they had to. Probably a lot of them were
Disciples. Disciples took seriously the Protestant ideas that no inter-
cessor was required between an individual and God, that divine truth
could be found by searching the Scriptures. Many families owned
almost no books besides the Bible; reading it and thinking about it
were their pastimes. Among other denominations, Disciples got the
reputation as tough opponents in arguments about religion. They loved
a debate. Thomas Campbell's son, Alexander, who became the movement's main leader in the 1830s and after, debated Catholic Bishop
John B. Purcell in Cincinnati on the subject of Catholicism; the debate
drew a crowd of thousands and lasted a week. Some denominations
defended themselves with ministers—"Campbellite killers"—who
specialized in debating Disciples. The Disciples argued among themselves as well. They argued about the spelling of their name—should
it be with a capital or small "d"? (Those who still resisted the whole
idea of sects and denominations said small "d.") They believed in
baptism by immersion, but argued about whether or not the minister
should wear baptismal robes of India rubber. Some said that if John
the Baptist had had India rubber robes, he would have worn them.
They argued about whether the Communion drink should be wine or
grape juice; some said that Jesus Christ never intended his followers
to use as a symbol of his precious blood a substance 17 percent of
which is poison. (Eventually, the anti-wine faction prevailed.) A bitter
and long-lasting argument involved the playing of musical instruments,
usually foot-pump organs, in the service. Some said never, some said
only occasionally, some said every Sunday. All these arguments caused
schisms of various sizes; the instrumental-music deadlock led eventually to the formation of a whole new sect, later to be a large church
of its own.

In fact, to judge by contemporary accounts, the United States in
the early nineteenth century was one big religious argument. No single
denomination had had a majority in the colonies; none was able to

become established as a state church after the Revolution. This left plenty of room for competition. In a growing country full of souls to win, the sects went after each other. Methodists hit Presbyterians at the weak points of infant damnation and the innate corruption of man, saying that Christ had died for everyone, not just the elect. Presbyterians replied that Methodism attracted such numbers because it appealed to all those who were "strangers to the plagues of their own hearts." East Coast ministers made fun of the ignorance and lack of couth of frontier ministers. Frontier ministers made fun of the fancy pipe organs and stained glass of East Coast churches. Lots of people called each other heathens and infidels and apostates and heretics and errorists. Mormons called (and call) non-Mormons gentiles, and a chorus replied that Mormons weren't even Christians, called them "filthy dreamers," sometimes tarred and feathered them, burned their churches, killed them, and eventually drove them across the Mississippi and out of the United States. As for Catholics and Jews, forget it. Protestants argued about everything from was Isaac Watts a blasphemer for adapting Psalm verses into hymns, to whether celebrations at Christmas and Easter contributed to Sabbath-breaking, to why the New Testament didn't contain more details about Christ's childhood (would make the book too bulky and hard to carry, some said), to whether the Bible forbade dancing and, if so, did it forbid walking in time to music without crossing one's legs, to whether suppers served buffet-style furthered the purposes of the devil by providing no opportunity to say grace.

One idea on which all the disputants would have agreed was that God intended this new land specially for them. The Mormon leader Joseph Smith said that all of America was Zion, from north to south. The Presbyterian Jonathan Edwards said that the millennium of Christ's rule on earth would begin in Northampton, Massachusetts. Protestantism, the noisy brawl that began with Luther's theses in 1517, that recast Christian theology and energized capitalism and changed Europe, traveled well with the pioneers. A man with a Bible, whatever his sect, made a little unit of Protestant civilization all by himself. And a religion split into many sects fit well with a big and varied landscape waiting to be settled: if this spot right here turned out not to be the Promised Land, due to the doctrinal errors of its inhabitants, then maybe that spot over there would be. Dividing and subdividing, the

Protestant sects spread out across America and filled its valleys, hollows, notches, and glades like grouting.

•

In 1800, all the ancestors I know of lived east of the Allegheny Mountains. Absalom Frazier was three. He lived in North Carolina, probably, the son of a recent immigrant from Scotland whose name may have been John. Martin Hursh, nineteen, and Susannah Doebler, fifteen, lived in Pennsylvania; after they married they would have a farm in Rush township, almost in the mountains, where the horizon was always just above eye level and plowing left the fields scalloped against the sky. George Werner and Rebecca Havenstein also lived in Pennsylvania. Later they gave birth to a daughter, Rebecca, my great-great-grandmother, in Fort Loudon, a town on the Pittsburg Pike just below where it climbed to the first difficult pass in the Alleghenies. William Chapman, eighteen, lived near Martinsburg, Virginia (now West Virginia), and Elizabeth Wilcoxon, fifteen, across the Potomac Valley and downstream, in Maryland. William Wickham, twenty-two, may have lived in a brick house on Washington Square in New York City, where his father had moved the family's shipping business after being imprisoned as a loyalist in Newport, Rhode Island, during the Revolution. William's future wife, Catherine Christian, twenty-three, lived in Philadelphia.

Samuel Preston was in southern New Hampshire, probably running *The Village Messenger*, a weekly newspaper he founded in the town of Amherst. Esther Taylor lived in a town seven miles away. He was twenty-two and she was nineteen. Their marriage in 1804 combined two families that had been in New England for 150 years or more, moving slowly from eastern Massachusetts to new settlements farther north and west. Esther's father, Timothy, had served in the Continental Army during the Revolution. One of Samuel's grandfathers went on the Crown Point expedition in the French and Indian War; the other fought at Concord in the first battle of the Revolution at the age of sixty-six. Samuel grew up in the valley of New Hampshire's Souhegan River, and Esther at the place where that river and the Merrimack join.

Platt Benedict, his wife Sally DeForest Benedict, Ezra Wildman, his wife Ann Hoyt Wildman, Charles Patch, and Catherine Husted all lived in Danbury, Connecticut. Charles Patch and Catherine

Husted, who would marry, were still school age; the others were in their early or mid-twenties. Sally Benedict was from Wilton and Platt from Norwalk, where his great-great-great-grandfather (the original Benedict, the one with many descendants) had come in the 1660s. The others had grown up in Danbury. That town, because of its location on a road convenient to the fur trade of the Hudson River, its nearness to the fashion industry in New York City, and its population that included many English-born hatters, became the hat-making capital of America. Except for the Benedicts, my Danbury ancestors either worked in the town's hat factories or had relatives who did.

All of these young people—Revolutionary War babies, for the most part—would die on the other side of the Alleghenies from which they were born. The work of their lives would be to leave places their families had settled, some for generations, and move to what was called the Black Forest of the West. Later, when they recalled their lives, only a few details from the years east of the mountains would survive. All the emigrants who started in Connecticut, and some of the others, ended up in a section of northern Ohio called the Connecticut Western Reserve. It happened like this:

During the Revolution, Connecticut towns made good targets for the British, whose main base was in New York City. The British fleet controlled the sea and often raided up the coast. Connecticut provided a lot of the rebels' supplies, and supplies from all over New England passed through Danbury. Early in 1777, General Washington established a forage depot and hospital at Danbury. The British, who knew that Washington had to keep most of his troops in New Jersey to counter a move against Philadelphia, and who needed stores themselves, decided to attack it. They loaded six regiments, about 1,500 men, into transport ships off Manhattan, sailed up the East River and into Long Island Sound, stopped at Oyster Bay to board about 300 loyalist American soldiers, sailed to Compo Beach on the Connecticut shore, and landed on the evening of April 25. They marched that night and the next day, went through Weston, Redding, Bethel, met small resistance, and entered Danbury about three o'clock on the afternoon of Saturday, April 26.

Most of the inhabitants had fled. Comfort Hoyt, my five-greats-grandfather on my father's side, had a house and store in the middle of town. He was slender, bald, and already prosperous at twenty-five.

He began loading goods into wagons and carts, but rebel officers came and requisitioned them to move supplies from the hospital. His goods were thrown down. His wife, Eunice, who was very pregnant, hid her coin-silver spoons and other silver in the ashpit of the chimney. In the Episcopal church across the street, supplies for the Continental Army—barrels of pork, beef, nails, saltpeter, and tar, hogsheads of biscuits, rum, and brandy—were piled up to the gallery. Out of respect for the Church of England, the British took the supplies out before burning them. Hot pork fat ran ankle-deep in the street. The British could find no wagons to carry the spoils, so they spent that afternoon and night burning—five thousand pairs of shoes and stockings, a thousand tents and several marquees imported from France, medicine, Indian corn, hospital bedding, coffee, oats. Maybe they marked crosses with a chunk of lime on houses belonging to Tories to spare them from burning; in any event, they did burn at least nineteen houses, including Comfort Hoyt's house and store. At eight o'clock the next morning, they marched out of town headed back to the seacoast.

Comfort Hoyt's younger brother Isaac, perhaps influenced to Tory sympathies by his Anglican minister grandfather, went with them. This grieved Comfort's mother; Comfort's father was away fighting in the 16th Connecticut Militia. Eunice had her baby the day the British left. The child, Anne, lived for only a year and a half. Eunice's next child, a daughter also named Anne, would be my four-greats-grandmother. Eunice herself would die after the birth of her seventh child at the age of thirty-five. When the Hoyts returned to their house, they found nothing standing but the chimney, the silver still safe in the ashpit. Near the ruin was their other remaining possession, a round low table the British officers had set "in the meadow" to mix their drinks on. The family later said that when they found it its top was crusted inch-deep in brandy and sugar.

People who lost property petitioned the Connecticut legislature for reparation, and in June the legislature sent agents to meet with the sufferers and take statements. One claim was from a Samuel Smith, who had owned a slave named Ned. Ned, an enthusiast of the rebel cause, had been one of the few to fire at the British when they entered the town. They had attacked the house he and some allies were in and killed them; Samuel Smith wanted repayment for the loss of his slave. The legislature eventually accepted 186 claims from Danbury. Comfort Hoyt's losses came to 657 pounds, 15 shillings, and one penny.

The raid was so successful for the British they later hit New Haven, Fairfield, Norwalk, New London, Groton, and Ridgefield—the destruction escalated as the war went on. The Continental Army could not spare troops to guard all landing points on the coast, and the British wanted to punish Connecticut for supporting the rebellion. As in Danbury, the sufferers afterward submitted claims to the legislature; by the end of the war, the claims numbered more than 1,800. The legislature proposed to pay not in money but in western land. As a colony and then as a state, Connecticut had never accepted the finality of her western boundary. She preferred to think that her territory extended in a strip between the 41st parallel and two minutes above the 42nd parallel—her northern and southern boundaries—clear across the continent, as per her original charter from Charles II. Connecticut Yankees had even vaulted intervening parts of New York and New Jersey to start colonies in what they considered their territory in Pennsylvania, causing all kinds of trouble between that state and theirs. During the Revolution, nearly 300 of those colonists in the Susquehanna Valley were killed by a force of British, Tories, and Indians in one of the worst massacres of the war.

After the war, when other states were giving up their western lands, Connecticut said she would yield all but a strip of the Ohio country 120 miles long and about 50 miles wide. She said she reserved this section for herself, which is how it got the name Western Reserve. Congress finally accepted this reserve, maybe because of the losses Connecticut had suffered, maybe because of the massacre, maybe because Connecticut was so persistent it was just easier to let her have her way. In 1792, Connecticut used half a million acres of this western land to pay the sufferers' claims.

Many of the sufferers sold their grants immediately for cash. Comfort Hoyt held on to his, and bought more. In 1795, Connecticut sold the remaining 3 million acres of the Reserve—an estimate, as none of it had been surveyed—to a syndicate of investors which later became the Connecticut Land Company. The purchasers paid $1.2 million in bonds to the state treasurer secured by mortgage. No cash changed hands, although of course it would later, as the lands were resold throughout New England. Purchasers were told they assumed the risk of the conflicting Indian title, described as "unextinguished and unquieted"—which was to say that a lot of Indians still lived there. Many of these Shawnees, Senecas, Onondagas, Wyandots, Miamis, Ottawas, Massasagoes, Pottawattomies, Chippewas, and Delawares had helped the French fight the British in the French and Indian War, and the British fight the Americans in the Revolution. After that war was over, they fought on; the Miamis and Shawnees with British aid killed almost 700 militiamen led by General Arthur St. Clair in western Ohio in 1791, and an army led by General Anthony Wayne killed a lot of Miamis and others in 1794 at the Battle of Fallen Timbers, which resulted in a treaty and a brief peace.

The Connecticut Land Company sent Moses Cleaveland west to buy some of the Reserve from the Indians and make a survey. His party met with representatives of the Six Nations of the Iroquois, whose own claim to the land was debatable, at Buffalo, New York, in the spring of 1796. The Connecticut men feasted the Indians from Tuesday to Friday and provided whiskey. Among the Indians was Joseph Brant, who had helped plan the attack on the Connecticut colonists in Pennsylvania and had translated the Bible into Mohawk. At the signing, a Seneca, Red Jacket, said that white people made a great parade about religion, but all they wanted was money. The Indians received $500 "New York currency," two beef cattle, and a hundred gallons of whiskey; some also got provisions for the trip home. The Connecticut Land Company got all of the Western Reserve from the Pennsylvania border to the Cuyahoga River, about 400,000 acres.

Seven years later, representatives of that company, the war-claim holders (incorporated in a separate company called the Sufferers), and the U.S. government met with the other Indians to buy the rest of the Reserve. They tried to persuade the Indians to come to a council site on Lake Erie, but the the Indians wouldn't, so the agents had to go to them, at Fort Industry on the Maumee River. This time the price for 2.75 million acres west of the Cuyahoga was about $19,000 ($4,000 down, the rest in installments), payable by the land companies, and an annuity of some thousands payable by the government from then on. Witnesses said the Indians signed the treaty with reluctance and afterward many of them wept. No one pointed out to the Indians that the lands they were giving up had already been sold, and perhaps resold many times, for a lot more. A photostat of the treaty of July 4, 1803, hangs in the Firelands Museum in Norwalk. Among the white signatories are Charles Janett, Esq., the U.S. commissioner; Henry Champion and Isaac Wells, of the Connecticut companies; and below, in full flourish, the President, "Th Jefferson." Among the Indian or part-Indian signatories are Wyandots named The Crane, Leather Lips, Adam Brown, Chuskee Boy; Shawnees named Black Hoof, Isaac Peters, Blue Jacket; the Pottawattomies Magawh and Tahee; the Chippewas Cat Fish, Young Boy, Tonquish, and Little Bear; and an Ottawa named Eddy.

•

People talked about the Western Reserve and traded its lands, but for years not many moved there. The new state of Ohio assumed legal jurisdiction in 1803. Then the British lost the War of 1812, which removed any last danger of Indian attack, and real settlement began. Platt Benedict was the first of my ancestors to go to Ohio. At forty he had all his hair, deep-set eyes unclouded by doubt, and a thin mouth that drooped like a mustache. He left Connecticut on horseback in August 1815, and by September had examined a townsite in Huron County, satisfied himself that it had good water, and decided to buy it. He liked this sand ridge a mile or more in length because it was airy and well drained; emigrants' guidebooks warned that the good soil in bottomlands was not worth the risk of fevers from the bilious, swampy vapors. One of Platt's partners, Elisha Whittlesey, of a Connecticut family which had been involved in the Western Reserve since its beginning, was behind the deal and probably financed it. Platt rode back from Ohio to Connecticut in eleven days, found out who owned the land, paid a man from New Milford $1,260 for 560 acres, paid a Polly Bull $1,624 for about 800 acres, received the deeds the next spring, and sent them to Whittlesey. In January of 1817 Platt returned to the townsite, traveling most of the way by sleigh. He named the new town Norwalk, after the Connecticut town he had watched the British burn when he was four. He built a cabin in a day with the help of people already living in the area; some would later complain that Platt was not, in fact, the town's first settler, as histories claimed. He stayed a few weeks, left a man to clear and fence four acres for ten dollars an acre, and rode back to Danbury suffering from dysentery so severe the journey took him a month.

In July of 1817, Platt and Sally loaded a horse wagon and a bigger wagon drawn by two yoke of oxen and said goodbye to their relatives and friends. Sally and the children—Clarissa, twenty; David, fifteen; Daniel, fourteen; Jonas, eight; and Eliza Ann, four—climbed on. Platt rode his saddle horse. Perhaps his sister Elizabeth and her husband, Samuel Darling, came, too. Supposedly the group had gone just a little way when Sally stopped her wagon and ran back to cut a slip from the English ivy on the wall of their old house; ivy from that slip later grew on buildings all over Norwalk and at Kenyon College. The Benedict party crossed a corner of New York State and into New Jersey, went through Morristown, into Pennsylvania, through Harrisburg, and at Carlisle joined the pike heading west to Pittsburg (spelled then without the h). They took the Pittsburg Pike all the way across the state, through Shippensburg, Chambersburg, Fort Loudon (where others of my ancestors, the Werners, were living), and Ligonier. At Pittsburg they took a flatboat a short way down the Ohio River to Beaver, Pennsylvania. They crossed into Ohio and traded their sore-footed oxen for fresh ones. They went through Warren, the oldest settlement in that part of the state, and Cleveland, which had only five or six houses. They continued west through wilderness with fewer and fewer clearings. They reached Norwalk September 9.

The cabin Platt had built had burned down. The man he had hired was gone, as were, Platt noted, the barrel of flour and barrel of pork provided to feed him. The Benedicts found a place to stay with Mr. and Mrs. David Gibbs ("who were also entertaining Capt. John Boalt's family, nine of whom were sick with ague," says a family history). In four days, with the help of all the men around, Platt built a square cabin twenty feet on a side. The cabin had no windows or chimney, just a hole in the roof at one end to let the smoke out. Sally and the children moved their bedding onto the damp dirt floor.

Soon the Benedicts made bunk beds with mattress supports of woven linden bark, and other improvements. Years later, Sally wrote:

Two miles from any neighbor, our little cabin stood; the floor of logs split in the middle, not smoothed by plane or chisel; our chairs made in the same rude manner; our table was of pieces of boxes in which our goods had been packed . . . On one side of our cabin was a large fire place, on the east and

west sides were our doors, on the north our only windows, in which, to supply
the place of glass we had pasted pieces of greased paper.

And many pleasant evenings we spent beside that fire place, cracking
nuts, and eating—not apples,—but turnips. You need not laugh, these raw
turnips tasted good, when there was nothing else to eat, and as the flames
grew brighter, our merry party would forget they were not in their eastern
homes, but, far away in the wilds of Ohio.

We heard the howl of the wolves, and the whoop of the Indians resounding through the forest; for a favorite hunting ground of these wild men
was situated near our cabin, and often would the Indians assemble and renew
their noisy sports, little dreaming of the tide of emigration which should
finally sweep them away.

One night the loud barking of our dog attracted our attention, followed
by a knock at the door; on opening which, in stalked a large Indian, dressed
in furs and blanket, and fully armed. The children huddled close to me, as
he came near and asked for "Daddy." He was evidently intoxicated, and I
did not dare let him know that "Daddy" was not at home. I asked him to sit
down, but he preferred to stretch himself before the fire, where he soon fell
asleep. When he awoke he was nearly sober, and quite inclined to be talkative.
He told me of the many wrongs the Indians had suffered; that the white man
had planted corn over his father's bones, and the poor old Indian wept. Finally
he started up, exclaiming, "Daddy no come. You go sleep. I go to my
brother's," and he went away.

Sleep was a stranger to our eyes that night. We kept ourselves in read-
iness for flight, for we expected the "red-face" would return with his brothers,
and murder us all. The riches of a Kingdom would not repay me for another
such night of anxiety. But as time passed on, we gained the friendship of the
denizens of the forest, and they brot us many many presents in their own
crude way.

The year after the Benedicts arrived, Platt assisted at the hanging
of two Ottawa Indians, One Who Walks Far and another, for the
murder of muskrat trappers John Wood and George Bishop. The Indians were accused of killing the men in the forest and taking their
traps and furs. Other Indians turned the accused over to white au-
thorities. The hanging took place on a knoll behind where the Episcopal church now stands. Thanks to Elisha Whittlesey, Norwalk had
been made county seat by then; Whittlesey, on his way to becoming

a congressman and one of the most powerful men in the state, had convinced the Ohio legislature, thus guaranteeing the town's survival as well as the partners' investment. Platt replaced his log house with one of brick on the same site, and built the first frame barn in town. He got caught up in the mania for merino sheep that swept England and America. The herd he imported was the town's first improved stock. He planted apple orchards and the maple trees that lined the town's main street for a century or more. Vegetables grew so well in the virgin soil that people all over northern Ohio started vegetable wars, to see who could produce the biggest. In his garden, according to one history, Platt grew a parsnip five feet three inches long.

He served the town as postmaster for ten years, losing the job in 1828, when Jackson and the Democrats won the election and threw out the Whigs. He sustained a dislike for Jackson from then on. He oversaw the building of the first academy in Norwalk and knew to the brick how many bricks it took. When Episcopal churches in the East raised about $1,600 to build a church in Norwalk, Platt received $550 on contract to begin construction. He spent $850 getting the church partly built and put in a bid to finish it for $1,000. His bid was rejected, and the church was finished for $1,200. He figured he lost about $200 on the deal, not including the land he had donated for the site; he spent much of a reminiscence published years later on the details.

Norwalk elected him justice of the peace, and then mayor four times. He began his final term at the age of eighty-one. His hair had turned a patriarchal white. When he was eighty-two, he and others formed a local historical society, with him as president and chief resource. He rode horseback at ninety, outlived Sally by fourteen years and all his children but Clarissa, remarried in 1866 at the age of ninety-one, and died that fall of a cold he caught after attending the Grand Encampment of Masons in Toledo. Special trains from there and from Cleveland brought mourners to Norwalk for his funeral.

C H A P T E R 4

DURING THE YEARS when my ancestors went West, so did millions of other people. The parents of many Americans who would become famous in the second half of the century were on the road in the first half—the Lincolns, the Grants, the Shermans, the parents of Jefferson Davis and James A. Garfield and Carry Nation and William McKinley. Many families moved again and again; only a few headed back East across the mountains. Jesse Grant, born in the West, moved from Maysville, Kentucky, to Ravenna, Ohio, to Point Pleasant, Ohio, where he had a son, Ulysses S. Charles Sherman moved from Norwalk, Connecticut, to land in the Western Reserve acquired from his father, and had a son, William, whom he gave the middle name Tecumseh after the recently defeated Shawnee chief. In the Western Reserve alone, other arrivals included Daniel Decatur Emmett, who wrote the words and music to "Dixie"; the abolitionist John Brown,

An engraving from a book of American frontier scenes published in 1841 by the English painter George Harvey (Courtesy New York Public Library)

whose family moved to Hudson when he was five; and the parents of William Dean Howells, Jay Cooke, Thomas A. Edison, and John D. Rockefeller.

In 1790, almost all Americans lived along the coast in the original thirteen colonies; by 1850, only half did. A French observer said that a true American's life was like a soldier's, here today and tomorrow fifty miles off. An Englishman who walked the Pittsburg Pike from McConnellstown to Pittsburg in 1817 just weeks in advance of the Benedicts wrote: "Old America seems to be breaking up, and moving westward. We are seldom out of sight, as we travel on this grand track, towards the Ohio, of family groups" whose dream was owning "as many acres as they possess half-dollars." He said that, in general, Americans were better acquainted with the vast expanse of their country and its eighteen states than the English with their little island.

Travelers to the West took the Genesee Road from Albany past the Finger Lakes to Buffalo and then skirted Lake Erie, on a trail that went along the beach, then inland, then turned north for Detroit; or they took the Cumberland Road through Maryland and across south-western Pennsylvania to Wheeling on the Ohio River. Later, many went via New York City, Albany, and the Erie Canal. But for years the heaviest traffic was on the Pittsburgh Pike. It was also called the Glade Road, the Pennsylvania Road, or Forbes's Road, after Brigadier General John Forbes, who led the British forces building it during the French and Indian War. He and his men spent months scaling passes and hacking through laurel thickets to threaten the French at Fort Duquesne, at the future site of Pittsburg; when they got within thirty miles, the French abandoned the fort and burned it down. Forbes was carried all the way back to Philadelphia on a litter, and he died soon after. Indian war parties found the road convenient for raiding settlements in the East, and soldiers used it to pursue them. The British and then the Americans maintained forts along it. Traders carried whiskey and guns west on it, and brought back furs and ginseng. Pennsylvania spent two years improving it beginning in 1785; it has not been out of use since. Today, much of it is U.S. Highway 30.

The pike was broad and flat in the lowlands, steep and narrow in the defiles. Sometimes a slope was strewn with wrecked wagons and the bodies of oxen and horses. At the summit of Mt. Cove, above McConnellstown (now McConnellsburg), wagons stopped so that passengers could look at what was advertised as the first view of the West. Travelers in the summer of 1817 and the ones that followed said that the road was like the cavalcade of a continuous fair, that single wagons carried as many as twenty people, that some families were barefoot carrying packs on their backs, that some pushed handcarts and begged their way. Some rode in fancy carriages, which enraged teamsters who tried to run them off the road. Some emigrants sang hymns or phrases of campaign songs. Some shouted, "Hurrah for Ohio!" The more religious would not travel on the Sabbath, but started again early Monday morning to make up the time. A few women traveled alone with young children. Some travelers spoke German, many were Scots-Irish. People said you could tell the emigrants from New Jersey by the women riding in the wagon, the ones from Pennsylvania by the women lingering behind, and the ones from New England by the women walking cheerfully before.

At night the travelers generally stayed at inns, then called taverns. By 1810, there were plenty of taverns along the pike. A tavern might be just a one-room cabin where supper and breakfast were served cold, the coffee was "a libel on diluted soot," and you slept beneath the bed of your wagon in the yard. Or the tavern might be like one on the Cumberland Road, where the horse trough was filled with clear water and the ground around the trough sprinkled with peppermint, where you could get two drinks of whiskey for a fip (half a bit, or six and a quarter cents), where $1.75 bought meals, feed for the stock, and all you could drink, and where you spread your bedroll on the puncheon floor next to a barroom fireplace that held six bushels of coal. In any tavern with sleeping quarters people usually shared one large room and slept two or more to a bed. When it was time for the ladies to retire, the men would all go outside to see what weather they were likely to have. People who hung blankets around their beds for privacy were mocked—"powerful proud doings of stuck-up folks," such modesty was called. A good breakfast in the morning might be coffee, rolls, toast, biscuits, waffles, salted Lake Huron pickerel, veal cutlets, ham, gooseberry pie, currants, cranberry preserves, butter, and cheese.

The pike ended at Pittsburg, a place almost everyone had something bad to say about. The town's location at the forks of the Ohio and its many coal deposits made it a manufacturing center from the beginning. In 1820 it had glass works, steam-driven sawmills, carding mills, gristmills, flax-crushing mills, fulling mills, iron foundries, and the largest nail factory west of the Alleghenies. Coal smoke was everywhere: "The citizens move enveloped in a cloud—like Aeneas entering Carthage—and hence are known rather by their voice than by their face." "In approaching this dirty hole I felt the height of disappointment . . . I might say with truth I did not see a white man or woman in the place. The more you wash, the blacker you get. I am confident that I carried some of this coal dust 1,000 miles in spite of my efforts to get rid of it." At Pittsburg, travelers might board a flatboat and float three miles an hour with the current down the Ohio to a landing somewhere along its cross-country course to the Mississippi. Or they might head due west, cutting off the river's long northern bend, and ferry across it into Ohio at Steubenville. People going to the Western Reserve took the river just thirty miles or so to Beaver, another smoky mill town. A main road led northwest into Ohio from there. It was an excellent road of stiff clay for part of its length, but muddy in the spring and fall.

Those bound for western Ohio, Indiana, and Illinois took a continuation of the Cumberland Road which cut almost straight across the middle of Ohio and then angled down through the other two states. Later, when the road was improved, it would run all the way to St. Louis. It was also called the National Road. It passed through Columbus, Ohio; Richmond, Indiana; Indianapolis; Terre Haute; and Vandalia, Illinois. In 1820, the farther west you went, the worse it got. Contract specifications for builders who worked on it in Indiana required that only trees twelve inches and smaller be cut level with the road; eighteen-inch trees could have stumps nine inches high, and those over eighteen inches could have fifteen-inch stumps. The stumps were supposed to be trimmed and rounded, but travelers naturally avoided them, and wheels dug holes next to them. A wagon box needed to ride well off the ground to clear them all. Some places had ruts deep enough to bury a horse. By the time you reached Illinois, taverns were scarce, and you might have to spend a night or two in the woods.

Once you left the main roads, it was easy to get lost, sometimes even to lose your rig entirely. In Indiana, roads went through "buttermilk land," "spouty land," "rooty and snaggy land"; in Ohio, the roads inland from the lake in the northwest had to cross the Black Swamp, where there were said to be entrepreneurs who staked out certain mudholes as their own for the income they made pulling out wagons. At rivers, you generally had to ford across or be ferried; it took Easterners a while to learn to holler properly at ferry crossings. Roads meandered around from farm to farm as new settlers came in and the land filled up, with a lack of system which drove some travelers crazy. In Indiana, roads were marked by blazes on tree trunks: three perpendicular blazes indicated a legislative road, or "blaze road"; a single blaze meant a neighborhood road, called an open road. Despite the signs, a careful traveler might continue for hours on a road only to reach its end in someone's partly cleared yard.

•

When Absalom Frazier came to Indiana he was no more than twenty-two. One county history says he was a wheelwright and edge-tool maker. Another describes him as a mechanic and inventor of a widely used spinning wheel. As far as I know, he left no memoirs and founded no historical societies; I imagine him as a silent man living in a world of mechanisms. He was one of many Southerners who chose to settle in Indiana. Almost all of Indiana's first settlers came from the South, almost none from New England. People from New England —"narrow-nosed Yankees," they were called—usually knew they weren't as welcome past the Indiana state line. Absalom's appearance in Wayne County in the 1820 U.S. Census suggests that he came west via the National Road, which ran through the county. He had a wife, Barbara, a one-year-old, Simpson, and a baby on the way. Wayne County was really the frontier; until recently, the land adjoining it to the west had been Indian territory. In 1812, a Shawnee war party had killed three settlers and their dog at a sugar camp in the county. Indians hanging around the taverns still bragged that they had killed enough white people for themselves and their ponies to swim in the blood. At Fort Wayne, about ninety miles to the north, Indians were said to be killing each other in drunken quarrels at the rate of about fifteen a month.

By 1830, Absalom had moved from Wayne County to New Washington, in Clark County, where he was one of the first settlers. Barbara had died, and Absalom had married Clarissa Bundy. When she died after twenty-two years of marriage, Absalom married a third time. He would have a total of eleven children. Clarissa bore my great-great-grandfather Simeon in New Washington on May 20, 1832. A problem for all frontier farmers was getting their grain to a gristmill, and any town that hoped to flourish needed one; in 1824 Absalom built a steam-driven gristmill in New Washington. Probably he ordered the parts and had them delivered by boat on the nearby Ohio River. Later he added a sawmill, which almost certainly milled the lumber used to build the New Washington Disciples of Christ Church.

Samuel and Esther Preston, of New Hampshire, went West via the Genesee Road. In 1819 they left Nashua with Mrs. Preston's mother; their two children, Charles and Lucy; and a small black dog named Nero. They stayed for several months with friends in Pepperell, Massachusetts, and set out in October; emigrants' guides advised that travel was healthiest in the months before or after the summer fever season. They went by wagon and stopped at taverns at night. Charles was three and Lucy, my great-great-great-grandmother, was five. She was afraid she would be killed by Indians—she thought they were four-footed animals like bears or wolves. The family crossed through snow in the Green Mountains in Vermont and went down to Bennington, where the weather was warm and pleasant. They met up with the Genesee Road in Albany and followed it without incident across the state. In Black Rock, a town on Lake Erie near Buffalo, they stayed in a tavern where a young chambermaid had committed suicide a few nights before. People told them that the girl had sewn some black strings on her nightcap, said she was mourning for her sins, and died of an overdose of laudanum.

At Black Rock they took a schooner bound for western Ohio, but got only as far as Erie, Pennsylvania, before adverse winds made the captain refuse to go on. By now it was November. The Prestons continued overland on muddy roads and falling-apart corduroy bridges. A big dog followed them and they named him Mose. When they reached the ferry crossing of the Cuyahoga River at the foot of Superior Street (now Superior Avenue) in Cleveland, the crew of the ferry refused to let Mose and Nero aboard. Lucy and Charles cried. After the family had crossed, Mr. Preston went back, hired someone with a canoe, and ferried the dogs. Mr. Preston was an alcoholic, and Lucy would have sad memories of him, but she held on to this memory all her life.

The Prestons' last stop before they reached Norwalk was a tavern in the town of Eldridge (now Berlin Heights). Mr. and Mrs. Walker, who ran the tavern, had an infant son with crooked feet, and Mrs. Preston said, "Why, you ought to have them straightened!" But years later, when the boy came to school in Norwalk, he was still reel-footed. The Prestons arrived in Norwalk the next morning, a Sunday. A woman whose husband had the first tavern in town gave the children a biscuit spread with butter and honey. South of town the family ran into Mrs. Preston's father, Timothy Taylor, on his way to services at the Baptist church. Mr. Taylor had moved near Norwalk and started a farm earlier that year at the age of sixty-five.

The next spring Mr. Preston got homesick and decided to move back East. The family went up to the lake and boarded the *Walk-In-The-Water*, the first steamboat on Lake Erie, named after a Wyandot chief who switched sides between the British and Americans at least three times in the War of 1812. The boat's engine burned hardwood and pine, and blue-white woodsmoke came from her stack. The Prestons went to Buffalo and then to a town called Waterloo, in Canada. Bad feeling remained from the war—children teased Lucy and called her Yankee, and she refused to go to school. In the fall the Prestons returned to Norwalk. Soon they were living in a house at 50 West Main Street. Mr. Preston worked as a carpenter. Later, with a partner, he founded a newspaper, the Huron County *Reflector*.

My Wickham ancestors went West earlier than the others, but they didn't go as far. The family had lived in Rhode Island for almost a hundred years, much of the time at the same address on Fair Street in Newport; a remote cousin who grew up there later wrote a long poem in rhymed couplets of iambic pentameter describing their house, from the rainbow light that came at certain hours through the green-tinted windows of convex glass around the front entry, to the dishes and china in the kitchen closet, to the low doorway of the storage room where the author often bumped her head. Sometime after Thomas Wickham got in trouble for his politics during the Revolution, he moved to New York City, a place more congenial to loyalists, and there ran a shipping business with his son, William. (The business may or may not have involved carrying slaves.) They made a lot of money trading with the West Indies until President Thomas Jefferson got Congress to pass the Embargo Act of 1807. This act was a reprisal against England and France, who in the ongoing Napoleonic War had each embargoed trade to the other. Jefferson's embargo forbade all American ocean shipping; it had no effect on England or France, but it did wreck the American shipping business and help to bring on a national depression. William Wickham, who was young enough to start over, moved to Sodus Point, a town in western New York on Lake Ontario. He and his wife, Catherine, built a house and store and established a post office. Then, in the War of 1812, British forces came ashore at Sodus Point, saw an American flag flying at the Wickhams', and burned house, store, and outbuildings.

This probably struck William as a hell of a note, considering that his family had suffered for being loyal to the British in the past. He and Catherine rebuilt, and spent the rest of their lives at Sodus Point. One of their sons, Frederick, became a sailor on the Great Lakes in his teens and master of a ship in his twenties. Sometimes he docked at Milan, Ohio, a port at the head of navigation on the Huron River, which handled most of the wheat shipped from the Western Reserve. Milan (pronounced *My*-lan) is about eight miles from Norwalk.

In 1825, the first boat bound for New York City left Lake Erie and entered the newly completed Erie Canal. Observers at the point where the canal met the lake saw the boat and fired a cannon. Some miles to the east, people heard the shot and fired a cannon there; when sound of that shot reached a cannon farther east, someone fired that one; and so on, in a sequence of hundreds of cannon placed at intervals along the canal route, down the Mohawk River, and down the Hudson River all the way to New York City. At the final shot, an hour and twenty minutes after the first, the sequence was reversed, from the city all the way back to the lake. The Echo Cannonade (as people called it) announced the opening of the canal and began a big celebration in the city. The canal, which the state of New York built with its own money, drained traffic from other routes to the West and made New York City. When Ezra and Anne Hoyt Wildman and a party of fourteen children, in-laws, grandchildren, and friends left Danbury for the West on the second Tuesday of October 1828, they came first to New York City. They spent a few days seeing the sights and staying at a hotel on the Bowery run by a man they knew from Danbury. Then they went up the Hudson on a steamboat and boarded a line boat on the canal.

Some travelers wrote that the canal boat was the most monotonous means of travel ever invented, but the Wildmans enjoyed it. They cooked their meals on the crew's cookstove and, as they had all their stuff with them, slept in beds on their own sheets. The children often jumped off the boat and strolled along the shore; when they wanted to get back on, they would run ahead to a bridge and drop from it as the boat passed under. Anne and Ezra's fifteen-year-old son, Frederick Augustus (they would not let their children give each other nicknames, so first he used Augustus, then he decided he preferred Frederick), my great-great-great-grandfather, was almost left behind when he lost track of time gathering chestnuts on a shortcut across a bend. He had to run for miles along the towpath to catch up.

At Buffalo, the party and maybe three hundred other emigrants got the westbound steamboat *William Penn*. It was supposed to stop at Huron, Ohio, but went to Sandusky. The Wildmans landed there in a thick fog and hired a two-horse wagon and driver to take them to their destination about twenty-five miles to the southeast. They spent their first night in the state of Ohio on the floor of the Eagle Tavern in Milan. At three o'clock the next afternoon in a drenching rainstorm they arrived at Clarksfield township, where they had land —160 acres given originally to Comfort Hoyt in repayment for his losses in the British raid on Danbury. Comfort's nephew had lived on the land for a while and cleared a few acres; Comfort sold half the land to Ezra Wildman and gave half to his daughter Ann. In 1830, Comfort, an old man, came to Ohio on horseback to see for himself the final result of having his house and store burned by the British fifty-three years before.

Charles and Catherine Patch, the last of my Danbury ancestors to go West, also took the Erie Canal part of the way. They and their eight children arrived in October of 1831 at Milan and rented a house. Charles and two of his sons got jobs in a hat factory. (Charles was the one whose shoulders may have become stooped planking hats.) A number of people in that family made hats at one time or another. Charles and Catherine's daughter Mariette had a job in a factory trimming them. At sixteen, she was slim, dark-eyed, and vivid. A mutual cousin introduced Frederick Wildman to Mariette not long after her family arrived. He was very attracted to her. The two took it for granted that they were designed for each other. Charles Patch soon gave up hatting and bought a farm next to Frederick's parents' farm in Clarksfield. Frederick had worked in other towns as a carpenter and a schoolteacher; he began to teach in a school near enough that he could see Mariette every day.

Other ancestors who went West left sketchier records, or none. William and Elizabeth Chapman, both born in the Potomac Valley, were in the valley of the Ohio by 1815. Their son Thomas was born in northern Brooke County, Virginia—now Hancock County, West Virginia—that little finger of the state extending between Pennsylvania and Ohio. Their descendants recalled that they had a big stone house by the river. Eventually they ended up in Stark County, Ohio. George and Rebecca Werner's (or Warner's) daughter Rebecca married Thomas Chapman when she was nineteen and settled with him in western Virginia. Probably her parents had also moved West from Fort Loudon, Pennsylvania, by then. The only evidence of Martin and Susannah Hursh's move West is in the census records: in 1820, he appears in the federal census in Rush Township, Pennsylvania; by 1830, he is gone; in 1840 he reappears in Wayne Township, Butler County, Ohio. By 1850 he has a household of nine and a farm worth $7,200. His son Phillip is living in a nearby county with his wife, Catherine, and their four-year-old son, Osiander.

•

People went West to have better farms, to make money, to get out from under parents and grandparents and neighbors who had known them since they were born. Of the people from Connecticut who went to the Western Reserve, a history written about a hundred years ago explains, "Connecticut federalism was the most ironclad variety anywhere to be found . . . 'old families' were the pride and weakness of their respective localities." The history says that Connecticut had "shelled over" with tradition and family. To many emigrants, the West was not just new and wide-open and free of past associations, it was holy—the place where God wanted people like them to go. Often they left districts where the only land yet to be farmed was up on the sides of hills, where everything was cleared except the tops of rocky knolls, where getting firewood involved a journey.

When they went West, what they found on the other side of the mountains, mainly, was trees. Much of Ohio was covered by a hardwood forest that dated from the last ice age, interrupted here and there by small prairies, swamps, or stretches of wind-downed timber. An English traveler described Indiana as a forest larger than England. Emigrants rode through unbroken forests for days on end. Some said you had to have the experience to understand how solitary and unrelieved it was. They called the tree-covered expanses wastes and the occasional sunlit openings oases. Tree trunks often grew sixty and seventy feet straight up before the first branch, in an unending series of columns receding into green gloom all around. Squirrels ran on limbs in the leafy umbrella almost out of shotgun range. A view extending two hundred yards was rare enough to draw comment. When travelers came out into an opening where they could see sky and clouds and distance, they rejoiced.

Settlers talked about the hurricanes of pigeons that passed overhead in flights several layers deep, about shoals of white bass and pickerel in the rivers so dense you could catch dozens by hand, about squirrels so numerous the state of Ohio passed a law in 1817 requiring a quota of squirrel skins from every taxpayer on penalty of fine. But for most settlers, the trees made the personality of the country. There were white, black, red, and yellow oaks, shagbark hickory, beeches, butternuts, chestnuts, and elms—red, white, and slippery. There were three kinds of maple, four kinds of ash, linden, dogwood, locust, poplar, black birch, white birch, ironwood, sassafras, wild cherry, crab apple, black walnut. Pecans, cottonwoods, and sycamores grew in the river bottoms, giant grapevines hanging among them. Sycamores sometimes grew to great size and then in time became hollow; a hollow sycamore could hold a dozen horses, thirty standing men. Trimmed, roofed, fitted with a door, a sycamore trunk might serve as an outbuilding or a smokehouse. People knew that chestnuts made the most durable fence rails and second-growth hickory the strongest ax handles and beech the best fuel, that linden blossoms made the best honey, that ironwood was almost impossible to burn or break, that butternut hulls made a yellow dye and oak leaves purple. Cabins of unfinished logs sometimes sprouted new shoots in the spring until they were all over foliage on the outside. Settlers asked new arrivals, "How do you think you will like our wooden country?"

The settlers did not just attack the forest, they smote it. When they founded towns, they generally cut down all the trees on the site first thing: later, sometimes much later, they removed them. Clearing land of trees, stumps, and roots took a long time. Often farmers began by girdling the trees on their property—cutting a section of bark all the way around the trunk so the tree would die. When they planted corn among the dead trees it came up fine and lush. They applied to the timber verbs almost extinct today: they frowed, they scotched, they hewed, they mauled, they rived. (A frow is a tool like an ax but with the blade at right angles to the handle, used for splitting; to scotch meant to trim the bark from a log on one side only; to hew meant to trim a log all around; a maul is a heavy wooden hammer used to drive wedges; riving is wrenching apart by main strength.) Always, they used fire. Setting a fire to burn the dead timber off a field was called niggering off a field. They made big piles of brush and timber and burned them; for years, the smell of the settlements was the smell of burning woodpiles. They got together for stump pullings and log rollings. They had noticed how a strong wind sometimes knocked down acres of trees at a time; near Medina, Ohio, axmen cut halfway through the trunks of trees on several acres, and then, when a good blow came, toppled the trees on the windward side against others in a chain reaction that knocked down trees by the hundreds.

Some settlers began with no implements but an ax. In conversation, the subject of axes—their ideal weight, their proper helves—was more popular than politics or religion. A man who made good axes, who knew the secrets of tempering the steel and getting the center of gravity right, received the celebrity of an artist and might act accordingly. The best ax maker in southern Indiana was "a dissolute, drunken genius, named Richardson." Men who really knew how to chop became famous, too. An ax blow requires the same timing of weight shift and wrist action as a golf swing, and as in golf, those who were good at it taught others; sometimes all the men in one district learned their stroke from the same axman extraordinaire. A good stroke had a "sweetness" similar to the sound of a well-struck golf or tennis ball, and gave a satisfaction which moved the work along.

A generation of men chopped and burned and rooted until they made a landscape which, to judge from photographs, was less wooded than today's. Stands of original-growth forest became so hard to find that historians made note of them. None of the people who cleared the trees and none of the travelers who observed them doing it had a second thought about it, apparently, except for Charles Dickens. The author, his wife, and his private secretary made a tour of America in 1842, with stops in New York and Washington and a western journey through Virginia, Kentucky, and Ohio. In Ohio, they went north from Cincinnati to Tiffin by stagecoach via Columbus; from Tiffin they took a train to Sandusky, where they got a steamboat for points east. He described the experience in his *American Notes*, published the same year. Tree stumps they passed on the western leg reminded him of a Grecian urn, a woman weeping at a tomb, a student poring over a book, a crouching Negro, a horse, a cannon, an armed man, a hunchback throwing off a cloak and stepping into the light. Traveling through new settlements, Dickens wrote:

The eye was pained to see the stumps of great trees thickly strewn in every field of wheat . . . It was quite sad and oppressive to come upon great tracts where settlers had been burning down the trees, and where their wounded bodies lay about like those of murdered creatures, while here and there some charred and blackened giant reared aloft two withered arms, and seemed to call down curses on his foes.

•

Many of the settlers were pale yellow. Fevers sometimes turned whole families the same malarial hue. Every summer brought fevers of several varieties—dumb agues, which made the jaw muscles clench, and cold chills, which produced shivers, and shaking agues, where the sufferer shook until the walls rattled, and intermittent fevers, which came and went so predictably sufferers could plan around them. Many settlers loved to borrow things from their neighbors and to know their neighbors' business. Visitors from the East and Europe found frontier people almost too nosy to endure; the frontier provided solitude but not much privacy. Men on the frontier often had to be reminded to remove their hats indoors. Children stared at strangers and giggled, and laughed at the expressions on the faces of worshippers during church. Most frontier people said they believed that all men were created equal, although one visitor noted that he never heard that sentiment from the lips of a lady. Another observed that Americans loved to lean their chairbacks against a wall. He said that if you put a hundred Americans in chairs, ninety-nine would immediately shuffle backward and lean themselves against the nearest prop.

The settlers also liked to shoot their guns. Many owned accurate, long-barreled, small-caliber flintlocks—"Kentucky rifles"—made originally by German gunsmiths who emigrated to central Pennsylvania in the mid-1700s. Almost every cabin had a shooting tree nearby on which the men sighted in their rifles and tried out different bullets and charges of powder. Social gatherings often involved shooting contests. Men shot at charcoal circles marked on shingles of white pine for prizes, or they shot at the prize itself, a live turkey confined behind a log so that only its head was visible. Hits on the bird's bill did not count. Everybody ate a lot of wild game, which made a tedious diet unseasoned, as it often was, by salt or spices. Once farmers had cleared the neighborhood of wolves and other predators, they raised skinny, agile hogs. Hogs ran free—Dickens said they swarmed in the settlements like grains of sand on the seashore—but they came when you fed them. The best way to slaughter them was to stick them while they were alive, so they would run and bleed themselves out. They provided meat for salting, bristles, lard, tallow; some people made door hinges out of bacon rind. Also, hogs kept down the rattlesnakes, which they liked to gang up on and eat. Hogs were said to be immune to snake venom.

In a cabin without cupboards or much furniture, a visitor could see the household's possessions at a glance. Some families kept a trumpet to blow for people who were lost in the woods. On the frontier, it was hard to replace items that broke, so the condition of shoes and utensils showed how long ago their owners had arrived. A table setting might be augmented by a half pair of scissors or a bone-handled straight razor. If a mirror broke, the owner took the bigger fragments and reframed them. Because the bed was the most prominent piece of furniture in the cabin's one room, women made pretty quilts for it, and because the part of the quilt that rested on top of the bed faded more quickly than the parts that hung at the sides, they sometimes made the middle part with darker colors.

When settlers went to see a neighbor, they went to the front of the cabin and yelled at the door, "Who keeps this house?" A person inside would reply, "Housekeepers! Come in." Indians, when they came to a cabin, generally approached from the back, then looked in a window, then knocked on the door. Settlers recalled hearing the whoops of Indians resounding in the forest; Indians traveled single file down trails in groups that might stretch for miles, and they whooped to communicate along the line. Many Indian villages were uninhabited by the time the first wave of settlers came. Boys explored the villages and found them overgrown, except for the hard-packed circles of earth where the Indians used to dance. Settlers dug up Indian burial mounds and admired the thickness of the skulls and the soundness and regularity of the teeth. Some of the bones were burned or had stone arrow points stuck in them.

An upper-class Englishman who traveled the frontier in 1817 and 1818 and lived for a while in Illinois said that the people he saw looked old at an earlier age than people in England. He thought this was because frontier people had few comforts and bad clothes and poor hygiene, because they married very young, and because they drank whiskey. He called the last "the greatest pest, the most fertile source of disorders, amongst them." Most frontier farms could be made to produce a crop of corn or wheat within the first or second year; selling the crop and shipping it were more difficult. As whiskey, it traveled better, kept longer, and could be sold or traded. Many of the Scots-Irish settlers not only knew how to distill whiskey, they were good at it. People said that some of the whiskey you got on the frontier— "squirrel whiskey," one of its names—tasted fine. For years it was much easier to find good whiskey there than good coffee. A traveler to Ohio and Indiana in 1827 reported that whiskey was drunk like water. An Indiana county history says that in those days people thought it was impossible for any man to work in the harvest field without the use of whiskey. People drank it out of bowls, teacups, gourds. Most preferred to take it straight, or "barefoot." It was watered down and given to children. Schoolteachers were paid in it. Lake schooners were christened with jugs of it. Before elections, candidates for public office often left barrels of it in their names for customers at groceries to help themselves. It entered even the most casual social encounters. Etiquette required that a person drink, wipe the mouth of the jug him- or herself, then pass. This may all sound raffish and fun, but for many of the children who watched the effect of whiskey on their parents, it wasn't. The first generation to grow up on the frontier produced tens of thousands of anti-liquor reformers, members of the Women's

Christian Temperance Union and Sons of Temperance, whose cause became a nationwide movement which would eventually result in the prohibition of alcoholic beverages with the Volstead Act of 1919.

Another reason the Englishman suggested for people on the frontier looking so old was excitement of the passions, in the form of religious enthusiasm. The years when emigrants first went West were the age of the great tent-meeting revivals all over the country, and especially on the frontier. The new interest Americans had in religion, plus the loneliness of living in what had recently been a wilderness, made the revival meeting the big social event of the summer for many. Methodists understood better than others how lonely frontier people could get, and Methodist circuit riders traveled all over visiting isolated cabins, where the family was usually so glad for the company they killed a chicken for dinner; it was said that chickens soon learned to recognize the circuit rider, and hid when they saw him coming. Methodists held revival meetings on the middle frontier, and Baptists concentrated on the southern, and other denominations began to sponsor revivals of their own. The biggest gatherings might have a half-dozen preachers of various denominations exhorting the crowds at one time.

People got ready for the tent meetings days in advance. Men did extra chores and women baked, prepared hams, and mended. Tent meetings generally took place at a clearing in the woods convenient to a number of settlements. People arrived throughout the day and filled the clearing with wagons and tents improvised of wagon tarps. In the evening they gathered at one or more open-sided tents at the clearing's center. It took a while for everyone to get warmed up, usually. Dusk came on, and preaching continued by torch and lantern light. Here and there people began to faint and fall down as the minister called them to the Lord. At a revival meeting at Cane Ridge, Kentucky, an eyewitness said that five hundred worshippers fell to the ground in a moment, as if a battery of guns had fired on them. When the spirit grew upon the congregations, people screamed and flopped and jerked. Women's bonnets came off, then their combs, then their long hair flew loose, then it began to crack "almost as loud as a wagoner's whip" as they flung themselves back and forth. Men and women struggled in wrestling matches with the devil while others cheered them on. Preachers prayed for those yet to be saved, using the subject's full name and occupation; one skeptic said they failed to convert him because they left out his middle name. Camp-meeting oratory involved exhalation at the end of phrases—"We shall beseech the Lord-ah"—which TV evangelists still use today. When the camp-meeting preachers got even more inspired, they might begin to chant in a high nasal psalmody called "the holy whine," or to laugh a special deep hearty laugh known as "the holy laugh." Sometimes they also made a noise known as "the holy bark." Their preaching echoed from the dark woods all around, where hidden smart alecks sometimes mimicked them. An observer not involved in the proceedings was surprised that after a night of hysteria people could get up so cheerfully in the morning and tuck into the provisions the women had prepared. Participants said that after searching their souls and weeping and suffering and finally coming to Jesus, they slept better than ever before in their lives.

Revival meetings probably needed to be out in the woods for best effect. By 1850, they had lost popularity. Cultural attractions like lectures, debates, recitations, and moving panoramas of the Holy Land painted on canvas began to replace them. Old settlers said the country had gotten all peopled up. Little towns were everywhere. Railroads built from the cities and connected with the East. The endless tree-covered wastes had disappeared. Geologists who study sediments taken from the bottom of Lake Erie can identify the year 1850, approximately, by a change in the sediments' pollen content: those from before 1850 contain pine pollen, but those from after contain less pine pollen and a lot more pollen of the ragweed plant, which spread where trees used to be. Sediments from a hundred years later contain the radioactive isotope ^{137}cesium, which settled to earth after atmospheric testing of nuclear weapons; they mark the horizon of 1952 $\pm$ 2, about when I was born.

CHAPTER 5

FREDERICK WICKHAM came to Norwalk one day in the early 1830s and saw Lucy Preston in her yard picking lilies of the valley. She was about eighteen, small, blond, with sharp blue eyes. Lucy's mother had died when she was twelve. She ran her father's household by herself. Frederick was about twenty. He sailed the Great Lakes and was getting accustomed to telling people what to do. Very likely, he had just left his ship in Milan. Maybe he came to Norwalk on business for his brothers, ship chandlers at the nearby port of Huron, who owned a house in Norwalk. The moment he saw Lucy he decided to marry her. Their many descendants would tell different versions of this first encounter. My grandmother, Cora, told me that when she was six years old she saw Frederick lying in his coffin looking fine in his black suit, and holding lilies of the valley in his hand.

Lucy and Frederick were married on January 13, 1835. As a wedding present, her father gave them a house he built mostly by

Frederick and Lucy Preston Wickham, in their later years

himself at 38 West Main Street. Lucy and Frederick's marriage lasted sixty-two years and produced thirteen children; twelve lived to adulthood and eleven had children. She also helped raise her brother Charles's six after he lost his second wife. Nephews and nieces who went to school in Norwalk but whose families lived elsewhere sometimes boarded at her house, as did boys who worked as apprentices at her father's newspaper. The last survivor of her children, Emma, stayed in the house until she died in 1953, and after that the house became the museum of the Firelands Historical Society, which it is today. The first time I visited the museum I signed the full guest book and then told the museum guide that I was a descendant of the woman whose house this used to be. The guide laughed and said that nearly everybody who comes there is, seems like.

Lucy Preston Wickham was more famous—among her descendants, at least—than any of my other ancestors. She usually gets the longest write-ups in any genealogies that include her. My grandmother called her a "Pauline Bunyan" figure. Lucy grew up with a father who drank and who died of a fall in 1852, and perhaps because of this Lucy developed strong temperance views which she passed on to her children. People said that she was once walking down Main Street when a drunk came out a saloon door and fell down on the sidewalk. Lucy called through the door to the proprietor, "Come out here, please. Your sign has fallen down." People said that she baked thirteen pies every week; that she fed so many people at a meal she served two of every dish and cooked a peck of potatoes; that seventy-five relatives came to her Christmas dinner; that for breakfast on winter mornings she made wheat cakes, corn cakes, buckwheat cakes, and hot bread, with white sugar syrup, brown sugar syrup, honey, and New Orleans molasses; that she cared for her grandfather Taylor until he died at age ninety-six; that she proofread the paper and sometimes wrote editorials; that she learned sign language to talk to a woman who sewed for her and who could not hear or speak; that she had studied music and painting; that she spoke and read French; that she regularly attended the Presbyterian Church. She made sure that all the children did their homework, which back then meant a preparation of a Bible lesson every Saturday night for Sabbath school the next day. "Of a cheerful and amiable disposition," a family history describes her, "with a fund of wit and humor inexhaustible, her chief delight was in ministering to others: when remonstrated with for such unceasing and unwearied efforts she made reply: 'The Lord came not to be ministered unto, but to minister.' "

(My cousin Ellen Harding Anderson, a great-great-granddaughter of Lucy's, says, "That's a textbook definition of an adult child of an alcoholic!")

Lucy and Frederick's new house was not ready for them to move into for more than a year and a half after their wedding. They finally did in September of 1836; the next week, Lucy had her first child, Charles Preston, in the master bedroom. The rule that a person should not have favorites among his or her children does not apply in reverse, especially to ancestors from far in the past. Great-great-grandfather Charles Preston Wickham is my favorite ancestor. I have a photograph of him sitting in a rocking chair on a front porch at the turn of the century. I will probably never be able to sit like that: justified, in place, coinciding completely with myself. He looks as if he had once been at war but was now at peace. Charles Preston Wickham was a devout Christian, a war hero, and a lifelong teetotaler, all things I am not. He was also a lawyer, a judge, a congressman. He was chairman of the Congressional Committee on Coinage, Weights, and Measures. He never wrote or said anything funny that I know of. A portrait of him, larger than life size, still hangs above the judge's bench in the Huron County Court of Common Pleas; aside from the face and hands, the canvas is dark tones, now aged mostly to black. I imagine that, at his most charitable, he might find me a mystery. If he'd run into me on my way home at about two o'clock last Tuesday morning, his charity would have really been put to the test. His obituarist for the Norwalk newspaper called him "as brave as a lion and as tender as a woman." Overlooking the obituarist's ideas about lions and women, I choose my great-great-grandfather because that's what I think a person should be.

Charles was the oldest of the tribe of Lucy's descendants. Everybody called him Charlie. Next came Catherine—"Aunt Kate"—Lucy's second self and chief assistant. Then William, called Will, antic as Charlie was serious, who would spend some of his later life editing the family newspaper. Then Frederick, who weighed 150 pounds when he went off to the Civil War and 75 when he got out of Andersonville Prison. Then John, who died at age two. Then Mary, who married a general, and Sara, who lived at home and never married. Then Lucy, Albert, Caroline, Emma, Jessie, and Frank. Lucy had Frank in 1860; Charlie was a young man starting a family of his own by then.

Mariette Patch and Frederick Wildman, the young hat trimmer and schoolteacher who had known for years they belonged together, married at his father's house in Clarksfield on February 3, 1835—three weeks after Lucy married Frederick Wickham. (Clarksfield is ten miles from Norwalk, but it does not appear the two couples had met each other then.) Mariette's father was very ill with tuberculosis, and before the Patch family left for the wedding ceremony Mariette's sisters could not decide who should stay behind with him, since they both wanted to go. Mariette finally said, "Very well, you may all go and I will stay." This made everyone laugh, and Mr. Patch said he would be fine by himself for a while. The Reverend Xenophon Betts married Frederick to Mariette, and Alfred R. Seger to Frederick's sister, Cornelia, and Warren Cooley to Alfred's sister, Amaryllis, all in the same ceremony. Local people called it the Triple Wedding. Frederick's landlady said that such an arrangement was bad luck and that all the newlyweds would not live out the year. In fact, all of the six lived to their fortieth anniversary, and Frederick and Mariette to their fifty-sixth. For a honeymoon, the couples drove to Norwalk in a hired stagecoach, had dinner, drove to Strong Ridge, had supper in a tavern, spent the night, drove back to Norwalk, stayed another night, and went home. On a steep hill, one of the wheelhorses slipped and fell on the ice, and the stage came within inches of going over a precipice and possibly killing everybody. The newlyweds were saved by the presence of mind of the driver, who kept the horse calm and straightened out the traces. Frederick and Mariette's first child, Charles Ezra, was born about ten months later. In 1838 they had their second, Emily Jane.

Like many settlers, Frederick Wildman had many jobs. Besides teaching, he clerked in a dry-goods store, made cabinets, was a justice of the peace, did surveys for the Vermilion & Ashland Railroad, practiced law, assisted the county tax assessor, farmed. His parents gave him thirty acres of their land in Clarksfield and he began to clear it. In the evenings, he and Mariette enjoyed setting fire to the brush piles and watching them burn. One day after he had cleared a few acres he was using a pair of steers to drag some rails to make a fence when suddenly the rails hit a stump and swung around and knocked down his little boy, Charles, who was running along behind. No bones were broken, but Charles limped from that day on. About then, Charles became sick with what his father called a brain fever. It was probably the reason the boy never developed normally and lived in his parents' care all his life. He became a figure around Norwalk; younger relatives remembered him wandering in the woods and coming home with sacks of nuts on his shoulders. He liked to read and "could write a fair letter," a niece said. Frederick and Mariette had four more children. One, Samuel, died when he was almost three of scarlet fever. In about 1850 the family moved to Norwalk, where Frederick became clerk of the Court of Common Pleas.

Emily Jane was twelve or thirteen. Probably, she enrolled at the Norwalk Academy, where, probably, she met Charlie Wickham. After the academy, Charlie learned to be a printer during several years at the newspaper. Then he studied law in the offices of Worcester and Pennewell, attorneys, and attended Cincinnati Law School. He graduated in 1858 and began to practice law in Norwalk. He was also the local agent for the Liverpool and London Fire and Life Insurance Company. Emily Jane Wildman married him in August of 1860. In a photograph taken about then she wears her dark hair parted in the middle and tight to her head, her eyes dark in her intent little face. Everybody called her Emma. To her many nieces and nephews, she would be Auntie Em. She and Charlie's sister Kate, also in the photograph, wear dresses of identical pattern and style, each with a white collar and a brooch at the neck. Charlie, standing behind Emma, is tall, sharp-nosed, long-necked, with straight hair combed to one side off his high forehead and cut at the middle of his neck in back. Charlie loved Emma's family, especially her father; Frederick Wildman would be one of the close companions of Charlie's life.

Platt Benedict, Norwalk's patriarch, did not have the luck with his children that he had with towns and vegetables. Only one of his five lived half as many years as he did. Most of them were teenagers or younger when the family went West—maybe they did not like pioneering. The next-to-youngest, Jonas, was my three-greats-grandfather. A Benedict genealogy which goes on at length about Platt and others tells nothing about Jonas but the dates of his birth, marriage, and death. So far, that is the only record of him I have found. Oral history sort of explains why—it says Jonas was another drunk. Was he the one who fell in the fire and burned to death, or died from eating too much green corn? The stories shift and change. In any case, Jonas's wife, Fanny Buckingham, died in 1840, and Jonas died in 1851 at the age of forty-two. They left two children—David DeForest, seventeen, and Fanny, twelve. Probably Platt and Sally took them in.

David D. Benedict, my great-great-grandfather, was the sort of person whose life reaches its peak in college. He entered Kenyon, in Gambier, Ohio, in 1852; maybe he was just happy to get away from the memories in Norwalk. People at Kenyon still remembered him fifty years later. He was slender, light-boned, clean-shaven except for a fashionable fringe of chin whiskers. He became a member of Delta Kappa Epsilon fraternity, along with his friend Fred Tennard, of Baton Rouge, Louisiana. For under fifty dollars David and other DKEs built a log cabin fraternity house which a Kenyon history says was the first fraternity house in the United States. He founded *The Collegian*, Kenyon's first monthly magazine, and was its first editor. He founded *The Reveille*, the college annual, the third college annual in the country. He wrote letters on stationery embossed with a woodcut of the dormitory building where he lived. "It can be truly said that no undergraduate ever did the work that Dr. Benedict did for Kenyon," says a college history of years ago. He graduated in 1856, married Harriott Deaver, went to Cleveland Medical College, and received a degree there in 1861.

•

Thomas and Rebecca Chapman left their farm in western Virginia for one in Ohio in 1839. After 1840 they farmed 160 acres in Bethlehem township, near the town of Navarre. The Ohio and Erie Canal, which joined Lake Erie to the Ohio River, ran through Navarre, and big four-square houses of brick and stone with roofs that didn't come to a peak—a style known as Ohio Canal—stood on the main street. Apparently the Chapmans brought their wedding presents, Black Bill and Aunt Rindy, with them; a granddaughter said that Black Bill and Aunt Rindy begged to stay with the family after emancipation. Thomas Chapman raised improved stock and became one of the richest farmers in the county. He was a leading Democrat who served in the state senate in 1858 and 1859. His family liked to think of him as the Honorable Thomas Chapman. I have a photograph of him, long-faced,

Charles Preston Wickham is in the center of this group portrait taken about 1860. His wife, Emily Jane, sits in front of him to the right. She and Charles's sister Catherine—"Aunt Kate"—wear identical dresses

in a black wide-brim hat and black string tie. He kept a team of carriage horses, and Aunt Alice, his granddaughter, said the mountings of their harnesses were of gold (silver, said Aunt Grace). He and Rebecca had six children, and Elizabeth Ellen, called Lizzie, was the fifth.

Lizzie was born in 1849. Aunt Rindy took care of her. She went to singing lessons in nearby Massillon and sang a solo in a concert program when she was eight. She painted watercolors of ruins with trees growing out of them. One time on her way to school she lost a leather purse her father had given her, and she couldn't go back to look for it right away, and snow fell and covered everything, and then the next spring her father's sheepdog, Shep, found the purse and brought it to her in his mouth, and it was almost as good as new. Another time, her mother bought her a silk dress and she wore it on a visit to her grandparents across the Ohio River, and she fell in the river while getting off the ferry and spoiled her dress and had to go to a nearby house and change into one of her older dresses.

Meanwhile, O.A.S. Hursh was living on his parents' farm. Phillip and Catherine Hursh had two other children, Mary and Amanda. The family's land lay between the towns of Ithaca and Arcanum in the flat expanse of southwestern Ohio. Probably they grew corn; today their farm is part of a corn sea stretching for miles in every direction. Phillip Hursh died when he was fifty-eight as a result of a tree falling on him. "Sanctified by affliction, firm in true faith—securing the crown," his minister described him, improving on II Timothy, 4:6 ff. Phillip was buried on a low ridge, and has the best view of any ancestor: woodlot groves one behind the next receding to the horizon like an archipelago, the yellow veins of wheat fields in the green, silos at various distances, the dull metal shine of sun on a barn roof, a near cornfield waving in the wind like a classroom full of kids who know the answer. As a widow, Catherine Hursh lived in neighboring Baker's Store, a crossroads town almost no one remembers today. She also would die because of a fall. In her seventies, she went through the wrong door of two doors side by side and fell to the cement cellar floor of the house of her granddaughter, Mrs. Eva Fellers Wagner.

•

Simeon Frazier grew up in New Washington, Indiana. He went to a school there and worked in his father's grist and lumber mills. People called him Sim. His mother died when he was sixteen. When he was twenty, worse misfortune hit the Fraziers: his older brothers,

Jesse and Nathaniel, and his younger brother, Ransom, all died in
one year. Probably they died of polio—"child paralysis"—an epidemic
in the region in 1852. Simeon quit working for his father and got a
job clerking in a general store. Then he went to Louisville, Kentucky,
to study bookkeeping. His older half brothers, Simpson and Jacob,
moved to Centralia, Illinois, and his father and his new wife soon
followed them. Simeon did not go along. He came back to Indiana
and became a freight agent for the Jamestown, Madison & Indianapolis
Railroad, a position he would hold with a few interruptions for the
next thirty-one years. He continued active in the Disciples of Christ
Church, and in 1856 married Lucy Vaughn, daughter of Thomas
Vaughn, one of the early Disciples preachers in Indiana. Simeon
helped the church in his capacity as freight agent by arranging transportation to Disciples gatherings. He also joined the International
Order of Odd Fellows. He was elected junior warden of their Grand
Encampment in Indiana in 1862, and senior warden in 1863.

•

I have to look hard in the lives of some of my ancestors up to
1860 to see the approach of the Civil War. Some apparently did not
feel strongly enough one way or the other about slavery or secession
to fight about it. Thomas Chapman was a Democrat, and Democrats
generally favored compromise over war. O.A.S. Hursh was fifteen in
1861, and did not interrupt his schooling to enlist. Simeon Frazier
waited until 1864 to join the 132nd Illinois Infantry Regiment for a
hundred days' service guarding lines of transportation. The ancestors
I know the most about are the ones who did the most in the war. The
two facts are related. Without the war, many people would have
continued marrying and bearing children and making a living unsure
that anything that happened to them was remarkable enough to record.
When they went to war, every event became important. The war filled
the journals and letters of all sorts of people with good handwriting
who until then had not had much to write about. Men who could not
tell you ten occurrences from the first ten years of their lives could
give you a detail from every day of the hundreds they served. War
slowed down time and reduced space to small units. Ancestors who
fought in the war could say where they were on almost every day from
1861 to 1865; for certain days, they could tell the spot where they
were standing almost minute by minute.

The Western Reserve was the most solidly antislavery region of its size in the country. Its settlers, many of them sons and daughters of clergymen, tended to take a new look at their Christian ideals when they came to Ohio, and acted on what they believed. The Reserve was the trunk line for the Underground Railroad, which smuggled runaway slaves to Canada. Thousands of blacks came through, hid in the trim New England–style houses, and fled across Lake Erie. Some stayed at Lucy Preston Wickham's house, according to her grandson. Whole towns ignored the Fugitive Slave Law and resisted federal marshals who tried to enforce it. People in and near the Reserve gave slave catchers from the South an especially hard time. In Iberia, Ohio, when slave catchers accompanied by a marshal seized two young black men, a mob of citizens surrounded the group, freed the captives, gave them beech switches, and let them whip the slave catchers and the marshal and cut their hair. The Reserve produced some of the country's leading abolitionists, including Joshua R. Giddings and Benjamin F. Wade. John Brown raised money to pay for his raids from contributors in the Reserve.

My ancestors in Norwalk all served in the war or otherwise supported it. They may have been as antislavery as anybody else, but to judge only from what they wrote, they did not give slavery or its victims much thought before the war began. Frederick Wickham, who quit sailing to work on the *Reflector* at Lucy's urging and became its editor in 1852, wrote lots of editorials, often composing them as he set them in type on the press. I cannot find one on the evils of slavery. Perhaps in the back of his mind he recalled Joseph Wanton and his slave-trading Newport ancestors of the not-too-distant past. What seemed to make Frederick really mad was not slavery but secession, which he considered treason. Nor did he and the others seem to hate slaveholders or Southerners in general. Instead, they hated local Southern sympathizers, treasonous copperheads, Democrat supporters of rebellion, and especially the opposition newspaper, the Norwalk *Experiment*. It and its editors came in for plenty of invective at the typesetting hand of Frederick Wickham. When it published what he said were lies about the *Reflector*, he compared it to a llama, "defending itself from those who are disposed to annoy it, by blowing its filth upon them." His newspaper was for the Union and Abraham Lincoln all the way. After the war began, the *Reflector* noted with approval the arrest and jailing of local individuals suspected of treasonous beliefs or of discouraging young men from enlisting in the army.

My grandmother had a favorite story she used to tell about each of her grandfathers. Of her mother's father, David Benedict, she said that during the war he was an army doctor. He and his best friend, Fred Tennard, of Louisiana, had written to each other often before the war, but during it and after they lost touch. David wrote to Fred many times, but never heard back. After the war, David went on a train trip that took him through Baton Rouge, Fred's hometown, and he wrote Fred and told him he was coming. Again he received no answer, but when he reached Baton Rouge he and his wife stopped anyway. As a veteran of the Union Army, David wore a button called a Loyal Legion button. At some point, he took it off. Fred Tennard was there to meet the train. The two men hugged each other and jumped up and down and yelled. Then David and his wife went to Fred's house. Fred asked David, "Where's your Loyal Legion button?" David said he had taken it off. Fred said, "The war is over, boy! Put it on!" (Here, tears always filled my grandmother's eyes from the bottom up, like a glass.)

David Benedict was commissioned assistant surgeon with the 17th Ohio Volunteer Infantry Regiment in January 1863. The 17th served with the Army of the Cumberland in western Tennessee. David was assigned to a field unit that treated the wounded near the front lines and then sent them to hospitals in the rear. At the Battle of Chickamauga, in September, he worked all the first day among piles of amputated arms, legs, and feet. As the battle went back and forth, the Confederates captured the hospital, then the Yankees drove the Confederates back, then the Confederates recaptured it. As the enemy approached the first time, David's orderly, Solon Hyde, watched the doctors work under fire as long as they could bear, then run for the woods. Solon Hyde thought it was funny the way the surgeons carried their instrument bags and scuttled across the open field through sharpshooter fire, then stretched out to their full lengths and ran like deer when they reached the trees. He and David Benedict delayed longer than the others. When they finally decided to run, he noticed there was nothing funny about it. They heard troops moving in the night but did not realize they were prisoners until the next morning, when the Confederate generals Nathan Bedford Forrest and Benjamin Cheatham rode up in a leisurely way to join them for breakfast at the doctors' mess. The Yankees offered the Confederates coffee, a luxury in the blockaded South, but General Forrest refused it. He said he scorned to drink coffee until he could flaunt his flag in the face of his oppressors in a free and independent South. General Cheatham, however, had several cups. David Benedict and Solon Hyde and other prisoners were shipped in freight cars to Libby Prison, in Richmond. Because David was a doctor, he was held in better quarters and exchanged North after six or eight weeks. Solon Hyde, an enlisted man, stayed in prison for almost a year and a half.

David went back to the 17th Infantry and accompanied it as it marched with Sherman's force through Georgia. For a while he was detailed to run a smallpox hospital in the town of Ringgold. He stayed up all night with a one-year-old boy who opened his mouth for medicine just like a young bird and who died soon after. When the Yankees reached Atlanta, David got his mail, including the last two issues of *Harper's Magazine*, which his wife had sent. He liked reading its installments of Dickens's *Our Mutual Friend*. He watched a Southern lady in a fine green dress cross a muddy street; when she lifted her skirts, he saw her petticoats were very dirty. The army continued its March to the Sea. David spent Christmas in Savannah. The next spring General Sherman led his men into South Carolina, reminding them that this was the state that had started the war. They burned so many barns and rail yards and sawmills and cottonseed piles and turpentine factories it was impossible for them to keep clean of soot. They were supposed to go easier on North Carolina, but there the burning continued. "Our boys were over in Rockingham [N.C.] and say it was a very pretty little place," David wrote. Turpentine factories went up like fireworks and spread flames all around, the burning resin floating down streams and setting bridges afire. David saw children whose houses had been destroyed, and an old man who had been tortured by near-hanging to say where his valuables were, and women who had had keepsakes snatched from their bosoms, and drunken Yankees dressed in looted finery from the previous century riding in looted fancy carriages one day and burning them for cooking fires the next. He did some minor looting himself in abandoned doctors' offices; the prescription books in which he kept a lot of the diary I read were among his plunder. "In some respects this Army has got to be a perfect mob, a band of thieves and robbers. The old Army of the Cumberland is not now the noble band of patriots that it once was," he wrote. Perhaps this was what crossed his mind years later, in Louisiana, when he took off his Loyal Legion button.

The story my grandmother told of her other grandfather was about his funeral. Charles Preston Wickham lived to be an old man. He continued to practice law and to attend the Presbyterian Church. One day he came out of the church, began to cross Main Street to his house, and stepped out between two parked cars. He was hit by a car driven by a salesman for his grand-nephew's Ford distributorship. He survived three weeks and died in his sleep on March 18, 1925, in the same room in which he had been born almost eighty-nine years before. My grandmother said that she wanted to take my father, who was five, to the funeral, but people told her not to. She finally agreed that he was too young to understand about death. "I didn't take him," she said, "and I always wished I had. Hundreds of people came to the church and then to the cemetery, and there was an American flag draped on the coffin, and a trumpeter played 'Taps,' and then these old veterans from the Civil War, these old, feeble men, stood by the coffin and slowly raised their rifles and fired a salute."

My grandmother lived most of the last two decades of her life in Florida. She became the tannest of all my relatives. She wore her silver hair up in a chignon, with little curls at the temples. Her faded blue eyes looked at you over a sill of wrinkles. Like most people who loved my grandmother, I had trouble with her sometimes. She could be a pain. But tears always filled my eyes, as well as hers, when she said how old the veterans were. The last time she told me that story, she was approaching ninety herself.

CHAPTER 6

PROBABLY THE VETERANS were the last survivors of the 55th Ohio Volunteer Infantry. Charles Preston Wickham and at least 1,383 other men served in the regiment. At least 247 were killed in battle or died of accidents or disease during the war. Hundreds more were discharged for illness or wounds or on expiration of term of service, or they left for other reasons. Only about 300 remained in the ranks when their colonel made a farewell speech and then declared the regiment officially disbanded at the fairgrounds in Cleveland in July of 1865. Veterans of the 55th held a reunion in 1866 and every year after that for half a century and more. In 1887, many attended the dedication of a monument honoring the regiment on the Gettysburg battlefield; because the regiment was stationed on the Union right, at the junction of the Emmitsburg and Taneytown roads, today its

Veterans of the 55th Ohio Volunteer Infantry, with wives. Lt.-Col. Stevens (seated, left) has only one arm and uses a cane as a result of wounds suffered at the Battle of Chancellorsville

monument is one of the first you see when you visit the site. In 1904, a veteran named Hartwell Osborn with help from other veterans wrote a book, *Trials and Triumphs: The Record of the Fifty-Fifth Ohio Volunteer Infantry*. Charles Wickham gave a copy to his son that year for Christmas. I found it among my parents' books when I helped them move to their new apartment in 1977. I took it, and have read it over the years until I know parts of it almost by heart.

Much of it is not exciting: marches described in terms of mileage and destination, discussions of which officer replaced which, small events in succession without narrative. Much of it is lists. Reading the roster of the command—

ADAMS, ALBERT. Age 18. E.S. [Entered Service] 17 Sept. '61. 3 years; Private Co. C; discharged 5 Nov. '62, on surgeon's certificate of disability.

ADAMS, ALONZO. Age 21. E.S. 2 Jan. '62. 3 years; Private Co. C; no further record.

ADAMS, CHAUNCY. Age 29. E.S. Jan '62. 3 Years; Private Co. D; discharged 12 Jan. '62, on surgeon's certificate of disability.

ADAMS, EBENEZER. Age 40. E.S. 20 Sept. '61. 3 years; appointed Sergeant Co. B; discharged 14 Oct. '62 at Alexandria, Va., on surgeon's certificate of disability—

I imagine that I know some of them. Benjamin Taber, the first man to enlist in the regiment, served as regimental quartermaster for most of the war and later owned the biggest mercantile store in Norwalk. Abner Twaddle, slow but sure, took army life without complaint and died shot through the left breast at the Battle of Resaca, Georgia. Edward Sharp was captured near Atlanta, sent to a prison camp, released at the end of the war, and died in the disastrous explosion of the steamboat *Sultana* on the way home. Twenty-two-year-old Jonathan Shell was wounded at the Battle of Kennesaw Mountain. Probably Raymond Burr's comrades did not give him the same nickname they would today. The Quackenbush boys, Alvarado and John, stayed privates throughout the war. Randolph Beard was wounded at Second Bull Run in '62, wounded at Chancellorsville in '63, and killed at Resaca in '64. Arthur Cranston left the regiment, went to West Point, and later died in battle with Modoc Indians in California. Benjamin Pease charged a brick barn at Gettysburg unaware that no one was charging with him and captured the five Confederate sharpshooters inside all by himself. Moses Pugh picked up a shiny new musket from the body of a Confederate at Gettysburg, ignoring his friends who told him the gun would turn traitor; two days later the gun went off by accident and killed the colonel's horse. Cheerful, jug-eared Frederick Boalt, said to be the laziest man in the regiment but the bravest in battle, amused himself while under fire by catching hot bullets after they bounced from the pile of fence rails in front of him. He was murdered years later by claim jumpers in Kansas who shot him through the window of his sod house after they realized they couldn't scare him off.

And then there was gentle Sumner Wing, the regimental nurse, who cared for the men when they were sick, who held many when they died. I say his name to myself over and over: Sumner Wing, Sumner Wing. He wrote in his pages in the regimental history: "I am proud of my hospital work," and signed himself, "Your Loving Comrade." Charlie Wickham said that for care of him when he had the fever he owed Sumner Wing a debt he feared he could never repay.

•

Lincoln was elected President in November 1860. Seven Southern states had seceded and formed a confederacy by the time he was inaugurated in March 1861. The Confederacy demanded the surrender of all U.S. forts within its territory. On April 12, 1861, Confederate forces fired on Fort Sumter, in the harbor of Charleston, South Carolina, and the United States declared war. Four other Southern states, including Virginia, seceded. In July, the Confederate Army beat the Union Army at the Battle of Bull Run. Lincoln then called for 500,000 to volunteer for the army for three years. At Norwalk, leading citizens sent a petition to the governor of Ohio suggesting that a regiment of infantry be raised from Huron and Erie Counties. In early September the War Department commissioned Norwalk lawyer George H. Safford a lieutenant colonel and ordered him to begin recruitment of the 55th Ohio Volunteer Infantry. Charlie Wickham enlisted on September 13, as did his brother, Will, and his father-in-law, Frederick Wildman. All were assigned to Company D.

Lieutenant Colonel Safford held recruiting meetings in Norwalk and neighboring towns; the ladies were respectfully invited to be present. The *Reflector* ran ads, "To Arms, Ye Brave!" In mid-October,

(left) Charles P. Wickham later in life; (right) Charles's brother Will Wickham

(left) Hartwell Osborn, who wrote the chronicle of the regiment; (right) Frederick Boalt, said to be the bravest man in the regiment

(left) Henry Husted at about age 21. Died at the Battle of Chancellorsville; (right) Moses Pugh. A gun he took from a dead Confederate later went off by accident and killed the colonel's horse

MEN OF THE 55TH OHIO VOLUNTEER INFANTRY

thirty tons of uniforms, tents, and other camp equipment arrived by train. The regiment, now numbering three or four hundred, was mustered into service. The men marched from Norwalk in a drizzling rain and set up a camp they called Camp McClellan on a farm field outside of town. Each company elected officers; Company D chose Frederick Wildman captain, Charlie Wickham first lieutenant, and Will Wickham sergeant. Charlie told his son years later that the men had wanted to elect him captain, but that he thought it wasn't right for him to hold a higher rank than his father-in-law. He also said that if he had started out as captain he would probably have risen through the ranks more quickly and gotten himself killed in battle.

In November, John C. Lee, a lawyer from Tiffin, was appointed the regiment's colonel. All the officers who organized and trained the regiment were local men without military experience. A group of citizens headed by Mrs. Samuel Worcester, the congressman's wife, formed a Soldiers' Aid Society and began to collect supplies like blankets and heavy socks. In December the society announced that the Norwalk high and grammar schools had collected about 800 towels and a quantity of washcloths for the regiment. The grammar-school students also made enough pincushions to give one to every officer and man, and filled the pincushions with 43,360 pins donated mostly by private individuals.

People took picnics to Camp McClellan to visit the recruits and watch them drill. The regimental band gave concerts and held a ball at Whittlesey Hall in Norwalk at which a fight broke out, no one injured. The week before Christmas, the regiment and a cavalry regiment held a grand review at Camp McClellan. Most of the people in Erie and Huron Counties, a crowd of about 10,000, came. As the troops paraded by, spectators laughed at a little dog that rode behind the saddle of one of the cavalrymen. Citizens made speeches and presented the 55th with a stand of colors. Colonel Lee promised that these colors would never fall into rebel hands.

Early in January 1862, the men were issued their new guns, French-made rifled muskets with a range of a thousand yards. On January 11 they received an order to report immediately to Romney, Virginia; then the order was countermanded. On January 24, they were again ordered to move, and to bring rations for five days. The town ladies roasted dozens of chickens and packed other food. The

regiment marched to Norwalk and spent the night in church basements
and elsewhere in town. The next morning, a Saturday, 967 officers
and men marched to the depot, where cars of the Cleveland & Toledo
Railroad were waiting for them. Thousands of friends and relatives
came to see them off. Wagons of camp equipment were hurrying to
and fro. At a quarter of twelve the soldiers heard the order to get
aboard. Those with wives or sweethearts kissed them goodbye; many
would never see their loved ones again. Frederick Wildman still remembered the thrill of that kiss when he was an old man.

The regiment went to Cleveland and changed trains for Wheeling,
Virginia. As it crossed the Ohio River, Frederick Wildman noted the
exact moment he entered onto slave soil. At Wheeling the regiment
changed to the Baltimore & Ohio Railroad. Officers rode in stove-
heated B&O passenger cars and men in freight cars provided only
with straw, where they nearly froze. The train climbed into the Alleghenies on a track so full of twists and turns that for hours at a time
the twenty cars were never in a straight line. The darkness in the
longer tunnels was so complete the men said it hurt their eyes. Fifty
miles from Wheeling, they began to see Union soldiers guarding the
road. They arrived in Grafton, Virginia, at ten o'clock on a Sunday
night. The men slept in the freight cars and officers at the hotel. The
next morning the regiment pitched camp on a hill above the town and
sent out pickets; the rebels were said to be within fourteen miles. The
Reflector printed the first of many letters from the 55th which it would
run throughout the war. Will Wickham wrote that he thought they
would smell gunpowder within the week, and also that he was taking
Ayer's Cherry Pectoral for his cold. Ayer's Cherry Pectoral happened
to be one of the patent medicines—gargling oils, pulmonic wafers,
ague remedies, corn cures, bonesets, "female pills," vermifuges, febri-
fuges, blood purifiers—which provided most of the *Reflector*'s advertising.

Because the route of the B&O went through both slave and free
states, the railroad strongly opposed secession. Its influence had a lot
to do with keeping Maryland in the Union, luckily for Lincoln, as the
secession of Maryland would have made Washington, D.C., almost
impossible to defend. The B&O also linked the capital with the Midwest, and Confederate forces attacked points along the route in Virginia early and often during the war. The 55th belonged to the 30,000-

man Army of West Virginia, commanded by General William S. Ro-secrans, whose job was to keep the B&O open. After a few days in Grafton, the regiment broke camp and moved east on the railroad to New Creek, Virginia (now Keyser, West Virginia). It pitched camp and then marched sixteen miles over the mountains to the town of Romney, found the Confederates had just left, and marched back in a sleet storm.

On February 9, men from the 55th and other regiments—a force of about 1,600 in all, with cavalry and two brass cannon—headed forty miles south into enemy territory to the crossroads town of Moore-field. Colonel Lee told the men to watch and pray and keep their powder dry. They marched, slept, and marched another day and night, through mountain scenery grander than any Charlie Wickham had ever seen; he wished his wife could see it. They reached the ferry at the South Fork of the Potomac about three miles from Moorefield early in the morning and made fires of fence rails while they waited for dawn in the bitter cold. Suddenly they heard pops from the op-posite shore, and rebel bullets flew overhead. A soldier from another regiment described the phonics of a passing minié ball: "It was a swell from E flat to F, and as it passed into the distance and lost its velocity, receded to D—a very pretty change." The men quickly doused the fires and got back into ranks, breathless and silent, shot at for the first time.

The column moved out on a rough road so slippery with sleet the men could hardly stand. The road sort of paralleled the river and took them past the town. When sunlight came streaming through the moun-tains they were near the river on the west side of Moorefield. They marched down a narrow lane to a ford and saw the enemy, about 1,500 strong, on a level expanse above the town. The Confederates began firing at them. A man of the 55th just in front of Charlie Wickham fell to the ground, struck in the cheek; the enemy was too far away to do much damage, however, and the spent ball only cut him. The Yankees forded on top of empty baggage wagons run into the river at a spot about three feet deep where the channel divided around several islands. Musket fire rattled sharply for a while, but the Confederates had no cannon, and the Yankees' brass field pieces soon dispersed them. No Yankees and perhaps fifteen Confederates died. The 55th and the other regiments marched into town and down the main street like a Fourth of July parade. They went down each side street and searched every house for prisoners. They took thirty-two men who had been captured before and released on parole. The men had not violated parole and so were released again. Most of the people in town were children and chagrined-looking women. Most of the valuable property had been removed, but the Yankees did round up 240 head of cattle and confiscate a load of bacon. They detailed a force to hold the town, and then the rest, including the 55th, marched back to New Creek. Before they left they had second thoughts, apparently, and returned the bacon.

No history of the Civil War that I know of describes the skirmish at Moorefield. *The War of the Rebellion*, a many-volume compilation of Union and Confederate records published by the Secretary of War after 1880, gives it little more than a mention. It was one of those small actions of no real consequence which history leaves out. However, it infuriated the soon-to-be-legendary Confederate general, Stonewall Jackson. From his headquarters at Winchester, across the mountains to the east, he wrote to his friend A. R. Boteler, a representative in the Confederate Congress:

Winchester, Febry 12th 1862

Hon. A. R. Boteler,
Dear Sir:
An official dispatch received this morning informs me that the enemy are in possession of Moorefield. Such is the fruit of evacuating Romney. Genl. Loring should be cashiered for his course.

Very Truely Yrs
T. J. Jackson

Thomas Jonathan Jackson was himself from northwestern Virginia. He was born in 1824 in Clarksburg and raised there by a half uncle and other relatives after his parents died. He had a high forehead and a deep brow and very large feet. He attended West Point, where he made up for his poor early education with dogged study and graduated in the first third of his class. A classmate said if the course had lasted another four years, he'd have been at the top. He served in the Mexican War and won distinction at the Battle of Chapultepec. While in Mexico he studied Catholicism. He grew a beard which came in a lighter shade of brown than the hair on his head; he never was without a beard from then on. Assigned to Fort Hamilton, on Long Island, he had himself baptized an Episcopalian. At his next post he got into an involved dispute with his commanding officer and resigned from the army to teach at the Virginia Military Institute, in Lexington, Virginia. There he joined the Lexington Presbyterian Church, became a deacon, and began to tithe his income. He said he believed the Bible sanctioned slavery, that it was decreed by Divine Providence. He owned six or seven slaves himself. He began a Negro Sunday school for children in Lexington and opened most of its meetings by singing "Amazing Grace" off-key.

At V.M.I. he taught Artillery Tactics and Natural Philosophy. The second today might be called physics, and included optics, astronomy, mechanics, and higher mathematics. Jackson always memorized his lectures word for word; if interrupted by a question, he had to go back a ways and begin again. He disapproved of the phrase "you know" sprinkled in conversation and might remind anyone who used it that he did *not* know. One time he misunderstood the superintendant to say that he should remain in a building on campus and sat there all night waiting to be dismissed. Some students, among themselves, called him Fool Tom. Some walked behind him in imitation of his long stride. Some complained to the trustees about his teaching. A group of alumni tried to have him fired.

His first wife died giving birth to their first child, a daughter who also died. His second wife, Mary Anna Morrison, said Jackson was a kind and gentle husband who loved to play with children. He rolled on the floor with them and teased them in Spanish baby talk. He did not hunt, ride to hounds, or fish. He enjoyed gardening, and worked alongside his slaves in his garden behind his house on Lexington's main street and on his eighteen-acre farm plot outside town. He would attend musical parties, so long as they did not involve dancing. In the privacy of his home he sometimes danced a polka for exercise. He never read or mailed a letter on Sunday, and believed the government sinned by delivering mail on a Sunday. He never used his eyes by artificial light and instead spent evenings after supper thinking and staring for two hours at a time at a wall. He experimented with his diet and set himself a daily regimen which began with a 6 a.m. cold bath winter and summer. He never ate between meals. At social gatherings he ate little or brought his own food. He worked out with Indian clubs—dumbbells—and read about hydropathy, visiting spas from Virginia to Vermont. He believed that the Alum Spring of Rockbridge, Virginia, was the "water of waters." On a five-month tour of Europe he saw the sculpture in Florence and understood then how a person could love art above all things. When John Brown was hanged at Charles Town, Virginia, Jackson commanded a guard detachment from V.M.I. He wrote his wife a detailed description of the hanging seen close up, from Brown's composed ride seated on the box containing his coffin to the last clench of his hands.

Jackson got his nickname at Bull Run, which the Confederates won mostly because of him and his brigade of five Virginia regiments. As they repulsed a Yankee advance, the Confederate General Barnard E. Bee supposedly said, "There stands Jackson like a stone wall!" Jackson was afterward put in charge of the Valley District—the Shenandoah Valley in Virginia, from Harpers Ferry to Staunton—and in the winter of '61–'62 set about to attack the Yankees near it. With his brigade and three others commanded by General W. W. Loring he marched northwest from his headquarters at Winchester toward the town of Romney. He wanted to drive a wedge between the Union forces to the east and west of him; he hoped this could be the first step on an invasion of the North via the valley of the Monongahela River that would cut the Union in half.

Back then almost no one fought winter campaigns. Jackson's force of about 9,000 suffered in the cold and struggled on the icy roads. Men and horses fell and broke bones. Some of Loring's troops almost mutinied, and Loring did not discourage them. At Romney Jackson found the Yankee garrison gone. He left Loring and his troops at Romney and returned to Winchester. Loring complained, and Jackson's subordinates sent a petition to the Confederate War Department asking that his brigades be withdrawn. The War Department ordered Jackson to withdraw them. Jackson complied, and submitted his resignation. He said he could not be of service when what he did in the field was undone at the War Department. With no threat of attack from Romney, the Yankees easily took Moorefield. Jackson's friends, including Congressman Boteler and the governor of Virginia, talked him out of resigning. The War Department never undercut him again.

For me, Stonewall Jackson is the essence of the frontier Calvinist.

He sometimes said he preferred God's will to his own. He believed in sweeping the enemy from the earth, and that he was an instrument of God in a holy war. No general on either side had his God-haunted fervor. He knew his own spiritual nature perhaps as well as a person can, and he saw spirit moving in the world, in the real American places where he fought. He was one of those few people whose eyes create what they see.

•

Back in Norwalk, the *Reflector* printed rumors of Southern atrocities—that an unnamed Confederate brigadier general had sent a professor at New York University a piece of tanned skin from the thigh of a son of John Brown, who had been skinned after he died at Harpers Ferry; that a woman in northwestern Missouri had offered a premium for enough Yankee scalps to make a bed quilt; that an un-identified man had beheaded a fifteen-year-old boy for being a Union sympathizer and disemboweled him and put his head in the cavity. The ladies of the Soldiers' Aid Society held a Masquerade Exhibition in town which raised nearly seventy dollars. They had sent Canton flannel shirts, flannel drawers, forty-four cushions for wounded limbs, towels, handkerchiefs, etc., to the Soldiers' Aid Society of Cleveland. For the 55th they asked local citizens to donate mutton in tin cans, applesauce, apple and peach butter, pickles, dried beef, maple sugar, and eggs packed safely in oats.

Dr. Jay Kling, the regiment's surgeon, returned to Norwalk in poor health early in March and said that the boys were well, except for a few who had the measles. The next week, more than forty were down with the disease. They had caught it from bedding left at their campsite in New Creek by an infected regiment that had camped there before. The 55th returned to Grafton on the railroad, pitched hospital tents, and began to fill them. One night, nineteen-year-old Horace Smith got out of his sickbed when the nurse's back was turned and went down the steps to the railroad tracks and fell face-first in a puddle. He was found half an hour later, dead—the first of the regiment to lose his life in the war. Soon, seven more had died. A hundred were down sick, and 350 were reported unfit for guard duty.

The Norwalk ladies of the Soldiers' Aid Society got busy and packed trunks with hospital stores, delicacies, and clothing. Then a doctor from Norwalk; Charlie Wickham's wife, Emma; her mother,

Mariette Wildman; and a man from Milan whose son was sick went to Grafton with the trunks to nurse the men themselves. They found them lying on cots using knapsacks for pillows. Emma and Mariette made pillows of calico mattress ticking and stuffed them with hay. Most of the sufferers were boys of eighteen and twenty who had never been sick away from home before. The women made tin pails of lemonade to cool their fevers. Bondy B. Gaines and Hiram Ganty and Roland Jacoy and James Doughty and John Patterson and David White and Rush Sloan died. The measles took nearly twenty young men of the 55th before it was through. After two weeks the sick who were going to survive had begun to convalesce. The regiment had just received six months' pay, and many of the men asked Emma and Mariette to take the cash to their families. The women hid about $5,000 in their dresses and left on the train. A suspicious-looking stranger who rode much of the way in the same compartment with them made them nervous, but they and the money reached Norwalk all right.

Spring came, and the armies took the field. The 55th left Grafton on March 31 and went about a hundred miles east on the B&O to Green Springs, Virginia. There the regiment was issued wagons, and green mules the men had to break to harness. With its new supply train the 55th marched to Romney, waited out some bad weather that made the roads impassable, and then headed south. The men knew that now the real soldiering had begun. From then on, most days called for a march—of eight miles, fifteen miles, eleven miles, thirty-four miles. As part of an army now commanded by the celebrity John C. Frémont, the men of the 55th marched over cloud-filled passes in the Shenandoah Mountains, down valley trails where they crossed and recrossed the same stream a dozen times, through rainstorms that left them covered with mud, along dusty country roads where the heat nearly melted the gutta-percha in their suspenders and stragglers fell by the way in squads. They went from one little Virginia town to another, and sometimes back again. In Norwalk, Lucy and Frederick Wickham followed the regiment's progress on the map on the dining-room wall.

•

I rented a car—a red one. I double-parked in front of my apartment in Brooklyn and loaded my golf clubs in the trunk. I laid my garment bag flat across the back so as not to wrinkle my shirts, and put my road atlas, briefcase, and copy of *Trials and Triumphs* on the passenger seat. I had a big argument with my wife and left. Then I came back, made up, and left again. I drove out Ft. Hamilton Parkway, stoplight by stoplight. Then the Verrazano Narrows Bridge jacked me into the air, and I was in America—or Staten Island, anyway. I crossed New Jersey and into Pennsylvania. After about three hours, the songs on the radio began to repeat, and I turned it off. Then I turned it back on. Hank Williams, Jr., the country and Western star, had a song addressed to Saddam Hussein: "Don't Give Us a Reason." It was about the troops we had just sent to the Persian Gulf, and it said we weren't afraid of his starving army and rusty tanks. I saw my first yellow ribbons. I stopped for gas, stayed in a motel, ate. The next morning I was in West Virginia, along the Ohio River some miles north of where the 55th crossed it on their way to the war. I pulled over and got out and went down a trail through some alders to the bank.

Powerlines marked with orange balls to warn low-flying airplanes crossed the river in a long swoop. The morning was windless and already hot. The river lay smooth and wide as a shopping mall parking lot. A flood had left driftwood and part of a Styrofoam cooler in the first branches of a poplar tree and buried a piece of raft up against it in river gravel. Empty sixteen-ounce cans of Keystone beer lay around, near stump logs someone had dragged to the water. Forked sticks that had held still-fishing poles stuck out of the sand. The green tail of a carp broke the surface, and the ripples it made widened as they went downstream. Near the bank the current moved at the speed of a wedding procession. Dragonflies policed the surface for littler insects. Out in the channel a coal barge stubbed its way upstream.

I drove south to Wheeling and got lost. In the convenience store where I asked for directions, a distant look came over the face of the straw-haired teenager behind the counter as he tried to picture to himself how I should go. I finally found U.S. 250, the road that follows the old B&O tracks heading southeast. Soon it left the flat land along the Ohio for the West Virginia hills. The men of the 55th had not exaggerated how winding the route was. It climbed, it turned, it snaked, it teetered around bends shadowed by the forest. It seemed to take advantage of every little valley it found. Then suddenly it would be in a town of brick buildings next to the road, NO TRESPASS-

ING signs all around, and on the boarded-up windows signs advertising POLICE DOGS ON PATROL—a sketch of a snarling Doberman, open-mouthed, a strand of saliva connecting a top fang to one on the bottom. Most of the time I had to keep a foot ready to brake, and both hands on the wheel.

Grafton, West Virginia, is a town of five or six thousand stacked like cartons on the hills above the Buckhannon River. The first sign I noticed in town was one saying TAYLOR COUNTY JAIL in blue neon. Church steeples overhung the street. I parked, and then walked out on a long metal footbridge over the rail yards and the river. The metal vibrated under my shoes with the idling of the diesel engines below. The old B&O passenger station of red brick and marble, with its concrete columns, its carved sandstone capitals, its ornate brass light fixtures, was closed and boarded shut except for a door marked EMPLOYEES ONLY. I went through the door and stood for a while reading safety memos on the bulletin board. Then I got back in the car and drove up and down the hilly streets until I came to National Cemetery, the first U.S. military cemetery in West Virginia. Among the thousands of identical white stone markers in three levels terraced above the train tracks I found those of Roland Jacoy and David White, teenage measles victims from the 55th.

Rain fell as I drove for some more hours on winding roads to Keyser (formerly New Creek), West Virginia. This town changed hands fourteen times during the war. The railroad right-of-way here is as wide as an eight-lane highway. I climbed the long flight of metal stairs to the bridge over the rail yards in the drizzle. On one of the landings someone had written "KKK Revenge" in orange spray paint. The tracks disappeared in the distance around a bend. Trains have been running on them since 1851. In another direction stretched a part of town with single-family homes, garden plots, stand-up swimming pools. Two wet dogs were running and humping down the street.

I climbed back down to the rail yards and walked around. An older man in a black windbreaker, his hands in his pockets, his eyes pouchy, stood by a blue pickup truck with a camper top. He wore a blue hat with an old Chessie System insignia on the front. I asked him if passenger trains stopped there anymore. He said, "Noooooooohhhhh!" as if I'd just asked whether people ate gravel. "Hasn't been a passenger train here in six years," he said. "I was a conductor on the last passenger train through here. I worked this division for every passenger line came through. I was twenty years old when I hired on in '44 and was promoted to conductor in '51. We used to carry Presidents of the *Yew*-nited States on their trips. Sometimes we'd have a train fo'teen cars and 600 people. Hard to believe. Now I'm retired."

As I drove out of town, I passed a person in a penguin costume waving to traffic from a sidewalk at an intersection. From a row of houses close to the road, a man wearing nothing but a blue bath towel opened a front door, leaned out on the stoop, spit, looked up and down the street.

Getting to Romney took about half an hour. I fooled with the radio; out here in the smaller markets it plays better country music. Some men of the 55th feared they would die of exposure as they marched this road. I kept one eye on the taillights of the car in front of me. Romney is shady and genteel, in the valley of the South Branch of the Potomac. Lots of old brick buildings survive on its main street. The second time Charlie Wickham was here with the regiment, he wrote that he had gone through the books and papers of a Reverend William Foote, whose departure in advance of the Union troops led them to assume he was a rebel. Charlie wrote that he "confiscated" Rev. Foote's copy of Pascal's *Provincial Letters*.

I parked by the library and went in and asked the librarian if she had ever heard of Rev. Foote. She said she hadn't but she'd call someone who might have. She talked on the phone for a while and said, "Okay, Miz Pew, thanks," and hung up. Miz Pew had heard of Rev. Foote and said he was a Presbyterian minister. She said he didn't have any kin still in the area as far as she knew. The librarian gave me two county histories; one noted that Rev. Foote died in 1869 and the other that he had dreamed of making Romney an educational center. In Romney's Indian Mound Cemetery I found Rev. Foote's ten-foot-high stone marker with an inscription: "On the fiftieth anniversary of his first sermon he preached his last, both from the text 'For by the grace of God are ye saved through faith; and that not of yourselves; it is the gift of God.'"

Charlie Wickham also poked around the county courthouse in Romney. War had left its offices in chaos. I went into the courthouse (built 1922) that stands on the site today and walked down echoing halls that smelled of floor polish. A woman in the office of the clerk of the county court told me that they were having a party, and then she disappeared somewhere. I heard faint voices singing "Happy Birthday." When Charlie Wickham had looked in the clerk's office he found "an undistinguishable mass of papers covering the floor to a depth of at least a foot"—processes dated in the second year of the reign of George II, leases on parchment signed by Thomas, Lord Fairfax, Baron of Cameron, Proprietor of the Northern Neck of Virginia. He contemplated the ruin and wondered what the rebels had gained.

From Romney I went to Junction, where the 55th camped on the expedition to Moorefield. Charlie wrote that they slept in a field; I saw a likely-looking one with new-cut hay lying on it in S-curves. U.S. 220 from there to Moorefield is the same route the 55th took. Long hills parallel the road on either side, their wooded profiles notched here and there where powerlines go over. Sometimes the hilltops were airbrushed out by low clouds. Rows of corn climbed rises and disappeared over the other side. A bronze-colored Chevy, its hood up, sat aslant on a bare ridge. The road went through a pass and into the valley of the South Branch of the Potomac. All those little roads you see on the map, even in rural West Virginia, are actually stiff and throbbing with traffic. Charlie wrote that as they came down this valley "we passed in the stilly night vast farms and fine farm houses." The fine farmhouses are still there, red-brick mansions with multiple chimneys, balconies over the front door, white pillars, and crescent-shaped third-floor windows. But whenever I slowed down to look at them, someone decelerated to within inches of my rear bumper and traffic piled up in my mirror.

I spent the night at the Evans Motel in Moorefield. The next morning I went back to the bridge over the river three miles north of town. This is the old ferry crossing—the spot where the 55th was fired on for the first time. I pulled into a rutted place just down from the bridge. A man and a boy were launching a canoe on the foggy water; they put two fishing rods, strung and slightly bowed, and a blue picnic cooler in the canoe, and the man pushed off. There was the hollow sound of paddles on aluminum and the splashing of gravel that fell through the grates of the bridge as cars went by. Beneath the mark of the canoe's spine in the mud I found concrete with worn-down rusted metal in it—an old ferry mooring possibly. At a house by the bridge I met Wayne Sherman, who had come out to get the paper. He said this definitely was the site of the ferry and that the river hadn't moved much at all. Years ago, his grandfather had a blacksmith shop there. Wayne Sherman was wearing a polo shirt, khaki shorts, white kneesocks, and Nike running shoes. He had a fringe of white hair and a blacksmith's bulging forearms. He said he had found several minié balls in his vegetable garden on the other side of the road, and I said how they might have got there. His nephew Roger, a younger version of Wayne, came up. Roger said that when his grandparents were digging the basement for a house nearby, where he now lives, they found a human skeleton. He said that as a child he used to play with the skeleton, until his father decided that wasn't right and buried it in the yard.

Later, I learned who the skeleton might have been. The 55th camped here on an occasion after their first expedition to Moorefield, and the locals, to harass them, cut the ferry from its moorings and let it drift downstream. The 55th sent men after it, and as they were towing it back, Charlie wrote, "a member of Company E . . . was drowned . . . He was trying to swim the stream with his shirt, drawers, and boots on; and although remonstrated with, persisted in doing so, the result being that the current was too rapid for him to withstand, and he was carried down crying for help which could not be rendered." Charlie does not say what happened next. Maybe they recovered the body and, unable to ship it home, buried it here. The regimental roster gives the drowned man's name as George Minus.

I couldn't find a road that matched the description of the one the Yankees took when they assaulted the town, except for a private lane with a locked gate. So I drove to a bridge on the other side of Moorefield, parked, walked on slippery stones next to a levee, plunged through brush filled with spiderwebs that hung from my hat brim, woke up a whippoorwill that flew away with batlike wingbeats, passed some towering sycamores, climbed a ridge, saw a partly eaten ear of dried corn on a log, descended a ridge, and came to a place where the river divided around islands. Maybe this was where the Yankees crossed. I waded in; the water was waist-deep, cool, clear enough that I could see a pair of sunglasses drifting on the gravel bottom. On the other side I strolled through a field next to a single-strand electric

fence. Bluish-gray waterbirds with orange feet trailing behind flew
low along the bank at my approach. Swallows dove down and unzipped
the river's surface with their beaks as they plucked floating insects.
Goldfinches scattered, flying with quick wingbeats, then holding their
wings to their sides. There were lots of wildflowers—yellow daisies,
thistles, honeysuckle, touch-me-nots. Bees fumbled in the wildflowers
like thumbs.

Sometimes it was easier to walk in the water than on the bank.
Crossing an outcropping of shale slick with brown silt I almost fell.
Then the river bottom got siltier and siltier, with gray, eutrophic-
looking algae everywhere. I got out of the water and read a sign:
TOWN OF MOOREFIELD WASTEWATER DISPOSAL OUTLET. I
went back upstream, where the river was less dirty, and rinsed my
pants and shoes. Then I crashed through some more brush and invaded
the town through the elementary-school playground. I walked down
the sidewalk, leaving wet footprints. In Fox's Pizza Den I had an
Italian hero with sweet peppers, onions, lettuce, and oil, and a soda.
Someone had tied a big yellow ribbon around the pillar supporting
the town clock. I overheard a woman talk quietly with another about
a son who had just been sent to the Persian Gulf. I heard a young
woman say, "Man, I'll fight for my car!"

I walked along the highway back to where I'd parked. My shoes
were still wet, but my pants were almost dry. I drove another mile
or two until I came to the Valley View Golf Course. I felt like hitting
a few balls, so I pulled into the gravel parking lot next to a farmhouse
with a pro shop on the first floor. I took my clubs out of the trunk. A
woman in her sixties with a broad face and genial crow's feet around
her eyes watched me from a lawn chair on the side porch. She was
wearing a white blouse, light-blue culottes, and white sneakers. I asked
her if I could play some golf, and she said, "Sure enough." We went
into the pro shop and she said she would charge me only five dollars,
because it was off-peak or something. She asked me where I was from
and I told her. She said they'd been getting a lot of rain and I said I
knew, I'd been out in some of it. She asked if I was on vacation and
I said I was interested in the Civil War and had been visiting Civil
War sites in West Virginia. She said that sounded interesting. I remarked that, as a matter of fact, my great-great-grandfather was in a
Union Army regiment that went through Moorefield during the war.

The woman did not stop smiling, but her face became cement. The geniality vanished from her wrinkles; suddenly she was looking at me over an imaginary gunsight. As I put my scorecard in my back pocket and opened the screen door, she sang, "Now you have a good time!"

I played pretty well, as I recall. Maybe I was tired enough to be relaxed, maybe it was my new metal drivers—I don't know. Usually I spray the ball all over the place and even miss it entirely once in a while. I'm always half afraid I'll injure someone or lose my ball, so I'm always coming up out of my swing to watch where the ball goes, which means I don't keep my head down. This time, I was staying down over the ball. You have to stay down, bring your shoulders all the way through, get a good turn with your wrists, and—*whack!* Into the wild blue it goes, disappearing like a dot in the middle of an old TV screen. The front nine was hilly, the back nine flat. I like hitting on hills, especially down hills. It gives me a psychological boost, which is important. Stay down, stay relaxed, get a mental picture of your ball way out there on the fairway just where you want it. A misty rain fell off and on. There was no one in front of or behind me. Hitting from a rough next to some trees I smelled witch hazel, a smell I associate with courting (if that's the word) my first girlfriend the summer when I was sixteen. I remembered the summer breaths the fields exhaled, the declining evening light, my anticipation. Then I felt kind of sad when I realized that witch hazel still smells exactly the same, but I will never again be as I was twenty-five years ago. *Whack!* I cleared a water hazard neatly; my ball lay on the apron of the green just as if I'd gone up there and placed it by hand (which I sometimes do). It looked so great there I decided I didn't really mind that I'd never be sixteen again. The rain started to come down hard as I played the eighteenth. I ran back to the car, drove to town, and reregistered at the Evans Motel. I ate dinner someplace and then bought a six-pack of beer and talked on the telephone to my wife and friends for a few hours, and went to sleep.

I woke up early and drove to Petersburg. The road from Moorefield led through rocky hills with fog ebbing around them like tide. "Of all the rocky scenery, this march capped the climax," wrote a chronicler of the 55th. Uplifted plates of granite next to the river slump against each other like books on a shelf, uplifted cliffs in the distance continue their lines. Sometimes the road squeezes between a cliff and a guardrail above the river. The 55th found this trail difficult and spent a day covering its ten-plus miles. Twenty minutes of car radio put it behind me.

The 55th camped at Petersburg for two nights. Here the regiment was part of a brigade—including two other regiments, an artillery battery, and a cavalry battalion—under the command of General Robert C. Schenck. On May 3, the brigade was ordered to move south. First it had to cross the South Branch of the Potomac at the Petersburg ford. The ford was about half a mile wide, with a fast current. Two regiments crossed safely, but then some artillery got into deeper water, and two men and eight horses drowned. When an ambulance of the 55th lost a wheel in the ford and was almost swept away, Colonel Lee went to General Schenck and said, "Not another man of my command shall cross there." General Schenck asked him if he intended to disobey orders. Colonel Lee said not when they were according to the regulations of war. Then, ever the lawyer, he produced a copy of the regulations from his portmanteau and turned to the page that said no man or beast shall be forced through water more than three feet ten inches deep. General Schenck halted the crossing and set about building rafts.

At or near the spot where the ford used to be I found a municipal park. The river is now no more than eighty yards wide at this point, confined on one bank by a fifteen-foot-high levee of stone and concrete that people jog along, and on the other by a high, brushy bank. The water was running shin-deep through bleached gray rocks. Wild grapevines grew from the side of the levee and almost down to the waterline. The rocks by the river were dotted with periwinkle-like shells. I put sunblock on my forehead, bridge of nose, and bald spot, and sat among them. By my feet bobbed a soggy green tennis ball that had escaped from the public courts nearby. I picked a grape and polished the wax from it and put it in my mouth. It was so sour all my salivary glands went into action at once. A red-winged blackbird flew by, the red and yellow of his wing patches making an orange streak. The rocks in the streambed looked like the kind that roll under your feet and get you running in slow motion when you try to wade on them. I imagined them drowning eight horses and two men.

Once across, the 55th marched with the brigade down what is now Highway 220 to Franklin. The route is wooded, hilly, with here

and there an expanse of fields green as a green fire. I passed dusty
sheep sleeping on a bare patch beneath an oak. Clouds drifted against
far hills like snow against a snow fence. A drive-in theater of unpainted
cinder blocks featured a twin bill: *Ford Fairlane*, starring Andrew
Dice Clay, and *Nuns on the Run*. When the 55th reached Franklin,
rations were so short and the men so hungry some ate feed intended
for the mules. Here General Schenck was surprised to learn that a
Union force under the command of General Milroy had encountered
more than 8,000 Confederates near the town of McDowell, thirty-four
miles to the south. Schenck immediately ordered a forced march to
support Milroy. The brigade left its supply trains behind and covered
the distance, including a climb over Jack Mountain, in twenty-four
hours.

I figured that my suitcase, briefcase, and golf clubs probably
weighed about the same as the full kit and rifle carried by a private
in the 55th. I considered parking the car and trying some of this march
myself, fully loaded, just to get an idea what it was like. Then I decided
not to. I stopped for lunch in Monterey, Virginia, a town that has
several mountain-crafts stores and no fast-food restaurants. At a table
by the window I read a copy of the *Valley Banner*, from Elkton,
Virginia, that someone had left there. The question in the person-in-
the-street interview column, "Street Talk," was "Would you support
the use of nuclear weapons against Iraq?" Four of the six interviewed
said yes, if necessary. One woman said only if it would not hurt
innocent people.

Schenck's brigade passed through Monterey and turned onto what
is now Highway 250 to McDowell. Tired and hungry, it arrived at
McDowell about noon. The Confederates were threatening Milroy's
men in the valley of Bull Pasture River by taking position on a hill
above. Leaving the 55th in reserve by the artillery, Schenck ordered
the 82nd Ohio and the 5th West Virginia to join Milroy's men in
attacking the hill. A hard fight followed; Schenck's brigade lost over
250 killed and wounded. When darkness came, all the Yankees retreated up the road to Monterey. The Confederates followed them
and took some prisoners, including Private Henry Hess of the 55th,
who later died in prison.

The soldiers referred to McDowell as a hamlet, and it still is that
today: a convenience store, a gas station–grocery–post office, a funeral
home. White frame houses with green shutters stand a good distance

apart from each other. People in McDowell bus their children to school in Monterey; the one-story school building has been converted to a Ruritan Hall. I parked in front of it next to a van with the name of a pest-control company. In the field near where the battle took place three men were going over the ground with metal detectors. Each was working a section far from the others. I walked to the nearest one. He was wearing a blue short-sleeved uniform shirt with the same name on the pocket as on the side of the van. His face was broad and tan and his eyes squinty beneath hair streaked beach-boy blond. The metal detector hummed. He didn't see me until I spoke.

"Well, *first* we're money-huntin'," he said, "and second we're looking for Civil War stuff."

"Do you know anything about the battle that was here?"

"No. We're not even from around here. We're from over in Harrisonburg."

"Have you found anything?"

"So far all I've found is four pennies."

"You haven't found any bullets or anything?"

"No, you never find any old stuff around schools . . . We just do this when we don't have nothin' else to do."

"This is your lunch hour?"

"This is my whole afternoon."

Next to the volunteer fire station across the street a big oak tree grew through an O-shaped picnic table. I sat at the table in the shade and reviewed my notes. Two kids were riding their bicycles around town, doing wheelies and spraying gravel. They spotted me, a new face, and came swooping over. One boy was little, blue-eyed, snub-nosed, with an apostrophe of blond hair sticking from the back of his "Goodwrench Racing Team" baseball cap. The other boy was stocky, round, with dark eyes and straight dark hair. They skidded to a stop, and the blond boy asked, "Do you know where you are?"

"McDowell, Virginia."

"Do you know what county you're in?"

I looked at the map. "Highland."

"Oh." He was disappointed.

"Do you ever find any Civil War relics around here?" I asked.

"Timmy Kirkpatrick found a cannonball but he's gone to Monterey today," the blond boy said.

"Where'd he find it?"

"Up that dirt road. They're building a house and putting in a fence out front and he found it right there."

"Did you see it?"

"Yeah."

"How big was it?"

"About so big [indicating a size between a golf ball and a baseball—a grapeshot]. It was one of the little ones."

"It was pretty," the dark-haired boy said.

•

At McDowell, the 55th began what it and many thousands more Yankees would spend the spring doing—trying to catch and whip Stonewall Jackson. In March of '62 Jackson was still an unproven commander whose recent winter campaign had revived his reputation as a nut. By June he was the hero of the Confederacy, a tactician of swift marches and surprise, winner of battles in the Shenandoah Valley and beyond against four different armies. His small, lightly equipped army ricocheted around northern Virginia and lit it up like a pinball machine. Mainly, he and General Robert E. Lee, then military advisor to President Jefferson Davis, wanted to keep Federal troops in northern Virginia from leaving to reinforce those advancing on Richmond, who were already so close they could see the city's church steeples. Jackson's Valley Campaign (as it came to be called) began as a diversion. By the time it was over, Lincoln had set aside plans to take the Confederate capital and had diverted troops to protect his own.

First, Jackson hit a force under General Nathaniel Banks near the town of Winchester. Jackson had withdrawn from there at the approach of Banks's superior numbers, but when he learned that some of them were about to leave for the east, he attacked with 4,000 men at Kernstown, just south of Winchester. The part of Banks's army he met outnumbered him more than two to one, and beat him. But everyone from Banks on up assumed that Jackson must have more men than he did to have attacked in the first place. Lincoln ordered the brigades who had been about to leave to stay. He took others from before Richmond to strengthen the defenses of Washington. Jackson retreated up the Shenandoah Valley, and Banks was ordered to pursue.

The Shenandoah River enters the Potomac at Harpers Ferry. Forty or fifty river miles upstream, near the town of Front Royal, the Shenandoah divides into the North Fork and the South Fork. Each of these continues to the southwest in parallel valleys separated by a spine of mountains. More mountains enclose each valley on its other side. Jackson went up the valley of the North Fork, then crossed to the valley of the South Fork, called the Luray Valley. He stopped at Swift Run Gap, a strong defensive position near passes that led east and west. Banks followed slowly. He did not see Jackson and assumed that he had chased him out of the valley. In fact, Jackson had taken a position not only easy to defend but also easy to move from should he decide to drop down on Banks. Jackson asked Lee for reinforcements, and Lee sent General Richard Ewell, who had some 7,000 men near Culpeper to the east, to join him. As Ewell approached, Jackson moved to the southeast, hardening Banks's conviction that he was in retreat. When he reached the railroad at Mechum's River Station, suddenly he turned west, met up with a Confederate force led by General Edward Johnson, crossed another mountain range, and descended with 8,000 men on Milroy and his 3,000.

He whipped Milroy and chased him and Schenck all the way back to Franklin. The men of the 55th kept expecting another attack, but all Jackson wanted to do was stop the advance. Frémont, the Union commander following some distance to the north, had hoped to continue with his army through Virginia to Tennessee, and take Knoxville. Jackson's victory at McDowell ended that idea.

Jackson marched back east over the mountains to the valley of the South Fork, where he met up with Ewell. Now he had about 17,000 men. Banks, who had about 9,000, was marching back down the valley of the North Fork unaware of the size and position of the enemy approaching on his flank. Jackson came down the Luray Valley, hit a garrison of a thousand men at Front Royal, captured or killed more than half of them, and swung west to attack Banks. Banks retreated, but not in time to save his supply train. Jackson's men hit the moving column, sent Yankees running in both directions, and captured medical supplies and commissary stores worth hundreds of thousands of dollars. Banks outraced the rebels to his defenses at Winchester. Jackson pursued all night. The next morning—a Sunday, to Jackson's regret, but it couldn't be helped—Jackson ordered an assault on Federal emplacements on the hills above the town. By now many of his men hero-worshipped him so that they broke into cheers when they saw him. A Louisiana brigade, ordered to keep silent so as not to draw fire, removed their hats and gave a silent cheer as he rode by. Shortly after, seeing the battle was won, Jackson ordered his whole line to advance into the town. "Now let's holler!" he said. Screaming the rebel yell, his men turned the Yankee retreat into a rout. By the next day, what remained of Banks's army had withdrawn across the Potomac into Maryland.

Jackson knew that bigger armies would be coming after him soon; caution would dictate a withdrawal south. Instead, Jackson marched north, to the Potomac at Harpers Ferry, purposely increasing fears in Washington that he planned to keep on going and attack the capital. Lincoln and his Secretary of War, Edwin Stanton, had ordered Frémont's 15,000, as well as an army of 20,000 in eastern Virginia, to move against Jackson. Frémont left his supply train and started east. He had to go the long way around because the nearer mountain passes had all been prudently filled with obstructions at Jackson's orders when he was in the neighborhood fighting Milroy.

The men of the 55th did not think much of Frémont. They said he was haughty and surrounded himself with a retinue of aides in gold lace. His personal staff of more than fifty included many foreign-born soldiers of fortune who sat their horses in the English way, rising in the stirrups with the motion of the gait. The American soldiers thought this looked funny, and they annoyed the aides by saying, "Don't rise for me, sir," whenever they saluted. It took Frémont's army about a week to get over the mountains and to the North Fork of the Shenandoah. Frémont caught up with Jackson near the town of Strasburg just as some of the 20,000 Yankees under General Shields arrived from the east, but Jackson slipped between and retreated south. Frémont, misguessing that Jackson had a much larger force, kept his distance as he pursued up the valley of the North Fork, while Shields took the valley of the South Fork. The men of the 55th slept in fields of rye churned to mortar by men and horses, and on piles of fence rails to stay out of the wet. Will Wickham slept on a pile of fence rails and woke after an hour aching in every bone, cold as a wedge. He said that he went days without food as they marched after Jackson and that he had worn the same pair of drawers for a month. Charlie said he had had his clothes and boots off only once in two weeks and didn't wash his hands and face in five days. He said he wasn't tired of the business, that he was "in for the war."

Frémont and Shields finally caught up with Jackson at the south
end of the valley. Frémont advanced tentatively against Jackson at
the Battle of Cross Keys, got into a sharp fight, and withdrew. The
55th, briefly under artillery fire, was ordered to lie on the ground; in
the evening it marched back in the direction it had come. Jackson
then turned around and threw back Shields. Then he and his army
got away over the mountains and went to join Lee and the troops
defending Richmond. The exhausted Yankees marched north, made
camp, and rested.

The Richmond *Whig* called Jackson the Hero of the War, the
Game Cock of the Valley, the Confederate Boomerang, the Great
Gyrator. After June 1862, Stonewall Jackson was one of the most
famous generals ever in America. When he rode through towns, admirers came alongside and hugged the neck of his horse, Little Sorrel.
The Confederate Congress passed a resolution of praise and gratitude for Jackson's victories. Northern newspapers referred to him as
"the wily foe" and "the canny Rebel." People in the South talked
about the battered V.M.I. cadet cap he wore pulled down to his eyes,
about his ability to sleep standing against a fence for minutes at a
time, about his love of secrecy which excluded newspaper correspondents from his campaigns, about his habit of always turning to face
enemy fire to keep any wounds in front, about his way of standing or
riding with one arm upraised for the imagined benefit to his health,
about the lemons he sucked on regularly to relieve his dyspepsia.
Some joked that the reason he always fought so hard to avoid the
capture of even a single supply wagon was that he feared to lose the
one carrying his lemons. Some said that his blue eyes shone with a
strange light when he went into battle, and called him "Blue Light."
Some laughed at his style of giving orders for a morning march—he
never said "at dawn," he always said "at early dawn."

In prison hospitals, wounded Federal soldiers climbed over each
other to get a glimpse of him. Confederate soldiers embarrassed him
with their constant cheering. Other officers knew, if they heard a
cheer in camp, Jackson must be passing by. He always waved his cap
and rode away at a gallop. People wrote songs about him and sent
him presents. He told his wife he had enough gift handkerchiefs, socks,
and gloves to last until peace. English admirers sent him fancy riding
gear. Souvenir seekers cut locks from Little Sorrel's mane and tail.

Virginia ladies wore bracelets made of the tail hairs. In Martinsburg (now West) Virginia, a group of ladies surrounded Jackson and cut buttons from his coat. Crowds called at the windows and rattled the shutters of the place he was staying, then opened a window and threw red and white roses around him. When he was riding through Leesburg, Virginia, a woman laid her scarf in the road in front of him. Jackson reined up, surprised. The woman asked if he would ride his horse over her scarf, and he did.

C H A P T E R   7

I FEEL AS IF I more or less understand what the men of the 55th went through up to August 30, 1862. They had suffered hardship and disease, they had seen battles and been in them, but not a man had yet died in action. On that day, in the Second Battle of Bull Run, they faced a Confederate assault for the first time. They were posted on Bald Hill near one end of the Union line when a Texas brigade commanded by John Bell Hood, a general who would lose a leg and part of an arm in the war, attacked from their left flank. The 55th quickly changed fronts and threw the Texans back, then advanced with cheers. Suddenly from the woods on both sides the enemy appeared "in overwhelming numbers," as Colonel Lee said in his report. The troops were some of 30,000 in five divisions under General James Longstreet, whose counterattack on this second day of the battle won

The Union Army crosses the Rappahannock River at Kelly's Ford. The men of the 55th Ohio marched with this wing, part of General Joseph Hooker's grand flanking movement around the Confederates and General Lee (Courtesy New York Public Library)

it for the Confederates. Regiments on either side began to fall back, enemy fire cut the 55th's flagstaff to pieces, and a solid shot killed the color bearer, Corporal William Bellamy. The 55th retreated with the colors, leaving dead on the field. It lost ninety-five killed, wounded, or missing.

At Second Bull Run and after, the men of the 55th saw and did things that I, who have never been in a war, can only imagine. Some weeks after the battle, the regiment camped on the very ground where it had fought. Will Wickham wrote that he saw a hole in the ground which turned out to be the mouth of a partially buried rebel with teeth protruding above. He recalled the way another corpse looked with its brass buttons torn off and its pockets turned inside out by scavengers. He saw body parts sticking from the dirt and joked that the dead must have thought the regiment's bugler was Gabriel blowing his horn for them to rise. "May God deliver me from a rebel ever using my skull as a spit box!" he wrote. Confederate success in this battle and others toward the end of '62 caused some in the North to talk of settling for peace. "I suppose the Democrats in the next Congress will be for offering some compromise to the infernal rebels," Charlie Wickham wrote; ". . . if such a thing is done, in my opinion, where blood has heretofore trickled, it will run rivers. The Government must be sustained in its dignity and integrity, and without any *compromise whatever* with rebels! *Let the traitors of the North understand this!!*"

The list of the regiment's casualties came to Norwalk by telegraph. A telegraph operator, George Kennan—brother of the great-grandfather of George Kennan, the Russian scholar and diplomat—took the list over to Frederick Wickham at the office of the *Reflector*. As the war went on, the sight of a telegrapher walking to the newspaper office must have filled people in Norwalk with dread. The large number of wounded at Second Bull Run caused the U.S. Surgeon General to ask that women and children scrape lint for bandages. The Norwalk Soldiers' Aid Society said it would forward immediately any lint left at the store of D. H. Pease in town. The society asked that all lint be packed smoothly and close in paper boxes. Soon after, scurvy hit the hospitals, and a call went out for onions to combat it. Norwalk women collected onions from local farmers and made onion pickle. When the onions ran out, the women pickled artichokes and, when those ran

Ladies of the Norwalk Soldiers' Aid Society. (top) Mrs. Samuel T. Worcester; (bottom) Mrs. Lizzie H. Farr and Mrs. Henry M. Wooster

out, potatoes. The society later estimated it sent over a thousand gallons of pickles to the war that fall.

So many in Norwalk wanted to participate in the society that it formed an auxiliary organization, the Alert Club, mostly of younger women and girls. Very young girls joined a group called the Beehive Society. Frederick Law Olmsted, the general secretary of the U.S. Sanitary Commission, announced that dried apples could not be sent to him in too great numbers; the women got together for apple-paring bees. To the 55th the society sent bed ticks, feather pillows, shirts, a dressing gown, forty cans of prepared chicken (most of which spoiled; some women said they never did get the smell out of their noses), sixty-five pounds of dried beef, nine packages of dried herbs, three gallons of wine . . . One woman sent the finest linen from her trousseau. The little girls of the Beehive Society raised almost twenty-two dollars at their booth at a Fourth of July festival and spent it all on tobacco for the soldiers, their mothers having decided to suspend their prejudice against tobacco for the war.

Every few weeks the society held an ice-cream-and-cake party and sold tickets for a dime. The boys who churned ice cream for hours in Lucy Wickham's kitchen received honorable mention in the newspaper. Often, the society sponsored stage performances to raise funds. At Whittlesey Hall, the young ladies of the Alert Club put on a program of tableaux ("Washington's Dream of Liberty," "Eugenie and the Ladies of the Court," "The Witch of Endor," "Il Penseroso"), calisthenics, and music. The calisthenics alone were said to be worth the price of admission. Artemus Ward, the humorist, gave a benefit lecture titled "Sixty Minutes in Africa"—"rich and side-splitting," declared the *Reflector*.

Women worked on tasks for the society seven days a week. Thoughts of where they would get supplies and how they would send them filled their minds as they sat in church. They spent so many hours bent over in empty flour barrels packing them for shipment that one woman believed they may have permanently affected their posture. All that the women had done would never be known until the final reckoning on Judgment Day, a memoirist of the society wrote. She believed the war changed some things in women's lives for good: "Women found out then what they could do, especially if organized . . . the knowledge of the usefulness of allied womanhood dates from 1861."

The 55th was in no battles for some months after Second Bull Run. It spent the rest of the fall in the defenses of Washington, missing the Battle of Antietam, in which 13,000 Yankees died turning back an invasion of Maryland. The Confederates lost almost as many and retreated across the Potomac into Maryland. In November the 55th was posted at Centerville, Virginia, where a detective officer of the Union Army told the officers to be on the watch for a man and two women smuggling quinine into the South. Charlie Wickham, as provost marshal, detailed men to watch the roads, and Corporal Frank Hunt of Company I caught the smugglers. They had fifty-eight one-ounce bottles of quinine under their wagon and more in a can labeled PULVERIZED CINAMMON. The younger of the women, "a comely woman, aged 25 years," had eight pounds of quinine and a quantity of morphine concealed in her bustle. Quinine, a malaria remedy badly needed in the South, was said to sell for $80 an ounce in Richmond. Charlie forwarded the smugglers to Washington and prison.

After Antietam, Lincoln wanted the Union Army to pursue the Confederates and get between them and Richmond and force a battle. When his commander, General George B. McClellan, didn't, Lincoln replaced him with General Ambrose Burnside. Burnside moved the army south, intending to cross the Rappahannock River at the town of Fredericksburg. The Rappahannock was the biggest obstacle to be crossed on the way to Richmond. General Robert E. Lee, since June the commander of the Army of Northern Virginia, met Burnside at Fredericksburg on December 13 and repulsed him, with 13,000 casualties to 5,000 for the Confederates. On the day of the battle the corps to which the 55th was assigned marched toward Fredericksburg to support Burnside, but arrived after the fighting was over. Then Burnside decided to take advantage of dry weather to make a flanking march around Lee. Soon after the army set out, rains came, and the whole column became a bogged-down mess of pontoons, artillery, wagons, and hundreds of buried horses and mules—a march that came to be known as the "Mud March." After that, the armies went into winter quarters.

The 55th's camp was near Stafford Court House, Virginia. The men made shelters of tents nailed to cribs of split pine, or dug holes into hillsides and floored the dugouts with puncheon logs and roofed them with kitchen tents. Some men slept on mattresses of cedar and pine boughs. The regiment kept the camp neat, swept the streets every morning, and set little cedars and holly bushes in the ground like the maples along the streets of Norwalk. They called their camp "Little Norwalk." On December 22 Charlie Wickham wrote a letter to his brothers and sisters in Norwalk. Four years before, they had all agreed to meet this Christmas or to write letters explaining their absence. Back then they had no cares, Charlie said. Now they had felt pain, sorrow, loss, defeat, and the blight of life's animosities and hates. But, he added, four years ago the chains of slaves clanked in more than half the country; now the slaves were about to be set free. He was referring to the Emancipation Proclamation, which Lincoln had issued in September after the Battle of Antietam. The Proclamation declared that all persons held in bondage in those states in rebellion against the federal government would be free as of January 1, 1863. Charlie had never written so openly about slavery before: "I see in the future a glorious consummation of our strife in behalf of the freedom of man, in which we are so awfully, so grandly engaged." Neither had the *Reflector*, which published the letter. Now ending slavery was an official cause and not just a controversial idea about which people had opinions. Now it was patriotic. Charlie finished writing and then sat down to his Christmas dinner "(!)" at a table made of an empty cracker box set on four stakes driven into the ground.

The 55th had served under Generals Rosecrans, Frémont, and John Pope, whose appointment to a superior post caused Frémont to resign. Pope made a speech about how in the West, where he had fought, he and his men were used to seeing the backs of their enemies; he promised he would "bag" Stonewall Jackson. The 55th hoped he would lead it to glorious victories, but he moved too slowly against Jackson at Second Bull Run. Lincoln removed him and sent him to a command on the Minnesota frontier. Then the 55th became part of the Army of the Potomac under General Burnside. After the disaster at Fredericksburg and the Mud March, Lincoln replaced Burnside with General Joseph Hooker.

Hooker was a handsome, ginger-haired West Point graduate, loud, affable, and confident. The men of the 55th pronounced him "a picture of manly beauty" when they saw him on horseback. He had served with distinction in earlier battles and was wounded in the foot at Antietam. The newspapers called him Fighting Joe, a nickname that Robert E. Lee, his opposite number, sometimes shortened to

"F.J." What made Hooker especially qualified, from the point of view of Lincoln and the Republican cabinet, was his lack of political aspirations; the Republicans did not want to create a rival for the Presidency should he succeed. He was forty-eight years old, with a reputation for liking whiskey and the company of prostitutes, although a friend said he stopped drinking when he assumed the command. He had contempt for Burnside and often talked against him when he served under him. He told a newspaper reporter that the army and the government needed a dictator. When Lincoln appointed him in late January '63, he asked him for military success and said he would risk the dictatorship.

Hooker's army consisted of seven corps. To improve discipline and morale, he ordered that each corps identify itself by a badge sewn on the cap. Each corps contained three divisions, each division contained two or more brigades, and each brigade contained three or more regiments. The 55th belonged to the 2nd Brigade, 1st Division, 11th Corps, whose emblem was a crescent. Their brigade included four regiments from Ohio and was known as the Ohio Brigade. The 55th had served with the other Ohio regiments since early 1862 and the men had many friends in them, especially in the 75th and the 25th. Hooker got his army new coats and uniforms and tents, added vegetables to the rations, increased enlistments, and reduced desertions by allowing more furloughs. Charlie Wickham, now a captain, was able to go home for the first time in many months. Without mercy, the brigades drilled in the mornings and in the afternoons. The army's strength and confidence began to return.

In February, a bill authorizing the raising of 300,000 Negro soldiers passed the House of Representatives. When it became law, it would provide Colonel Lee of the 55th with a reply to opponents back home who chided him for "fighting for the nigger." "It may have been so," Lee told an audience at a ceremony when he was in Norwalk, "but now the nigger is going to fight for us!"

Also in February, Frederick Wildman resigned from the regiment. He was nearly fifty, and the marching and exposure had worn him down. His wife told him he had done enough for his country and should come home.

In March, Hooker appointed General Oliver O. Howard to command the 11th Corps. Howard was just thirty-two, a man of strong religious beliefs. He graduated from West Point in the same class as the now-famed Confederate cavalryman J.E.B. Stuart. When other cadets had ostracized Howard for being so religious and an abolitionist, Stuart was one of the few men to be friendly to him, along with Colonel Robert E. Lee, the school's superintendent. Lee invited Howard and Stuart to visit him in Virginia. Howard had lost most of his right arm at the Battle of Fair Oaks. All the men of the 55th who saw Howard liked him. They reported that he had banished liquor from 11th Corps headquarters.

In April, Lincoln came from Washington to review Hooker's refurbished army. Many from the 55th tried to get a glimpse of him when they heard he was in camp. Everywhere Lincoln went he was surrounded by a throng. On April 8 he reviewed the 6th, 5th, 2nd, and 3rd Corps: "Immense bodies of troops arranged in solid masses, as far as the eye could reach . . . It seemed to me as if there were men enough to walk all over the Southern Confederacy," wrote a member of the 55th. The soldiers marched by the President from ten o'clock in the morning until four in the afternoon. Also in attendance were Lincoln's son Tad and Mrs. Lincoln, "a remarkably good-looking woman, for her age." On April 10 Lincoln reviewed the 11th and 12th Corps. The same correspondent reported that for marching and military appearance, the palm went to the 11th Corps. There were whispers afoot that the 55th was the best regiment in the whole corps, he added. Morale was splendid; Hooker had rescued the army from despondency and gloom. The writer concluded, "I believe that when this Army shall get into a collision with the enemy, there will be a battle fought, that, in the language of the gallant Hooker, will 'shake the Universe,' of which the issue cannot, must not be doubtful."

•

After the Shenandoah Valley campaign, Stonewall Jackson did some all-night traveling without his army to confer with General Lee in Richmond. The young officers of his staff—Sandy Pendleton, Wells J. Hawks, Kidder Meade, Dr. Hunter McGuire, Ned Willis, Stapleton Crutchfield, Henry Kyd Douglas—for the moment on their own, had a good time as they passed through the rich Virginia counties of Albemarle and Louisa, "seeking new Desdemonas at the close of each day," Douglas recalled. When Jackson's staff and troops rejoined him he was in command of a wing of Lee's army fighting General McClellan

(left) General Joseph Hooker, who commanded the Union forces during the Chancellorsville campaign; (right) General Oliver O. Howard, commander of the 11th Corps

(left) Mary Anna Jackson (Eleanor S. Brockenbrough Library, The Museum of the Confederacy; Richmond, Virginia); (right) her husband, Thomas Jonathan "Stonewall" Jackson (Library of Congress)

and a force of 110,000 advancing up the peninsula toward Richmond. Historians debate why Jackson was so ineffective in this series of battles, the Seven Days battles, at the end of June '62: he didn't know the country, he had no maps, Lee's organization was poor, Jackson was not yet comfortable working with Lee. Most likely he moved so slowly and contributed little to the fighting because he was as exhausted as the Yankees he had left behind in the valley.

Even without Jackson at full strength, Lee forced McClellan from the peninsula. Jackson and 14,000 troops marched north and camped near Richmond. Jackson could have entered the city a hero if he had wanted to, but chose instead to make just two brief visits, one without display on a Sunday to hear the famous Presbyterian orator Reverend Moses Drury Hoge. Jackson sat in a side pew and slipped out after the service. Lee learned that General Pope was advancing on the important rail junction of Gordonsville, so sent Jackson's force to defend it. In Gordonsville, Jackson stayed at the house of the Presbyterian minister, the Reverend D. B. Ewing. Then came the Battle of Cedar Mountain, which Jackson almost lost by committing his troops too early. Then Lee got the idea of sending Jackson on a long flanking march around to Pope's rear. Jackson's men—people called them his "foot cavalry"—marched fifty-four miles in under two days, captured Federal stores at Manassas junction, started the fight at Second Bull Run, and held on until Longstreet arrived.

As Pope retreated, Lee sent Jackson on another flanking march, which resulted in a brief, fierce fight at Chantilly, Virginia. Then Jackson's force joined the rest of the Army of Northern Virginia on its invasion of Maryland. In Frederick, Maryland, Jackson never saw Barbara Frietchie or did any of the things John Greenleaf Whittier described in the poem of that name. He did, however, attend services at the Reformed church, as the Presbyterian church was not meeting that evening, and he slept through the sermon and the prayers. He also left a note at the residence of the Presbyterian minister, the Reverend Dr. Ross. From Maryland Lee sent him back across the Potomac to take the Federal post at Harpers Ferry; Lee felt insecure with such a large enemy force in his rear. Jackson set guns on the heights around the town, outmaneuvered the defenders, and captured 12,000 Union prisoners with the loss of only 300 men. Then he rejoined Lee. At the Battle of Antietam his forces on the far left of the line saw some of the bloodiest fighting around the Dunker church.

When the army retreated to Virginia, Jackson camped in the Shenandoah Valley not far from his old headquarters at Winchester. Lincoln had been right to want McClellan to pursue the retreating Confederates; the month of inaction that followed restored their army. Jackson's men were visited in camp by the Reverend Joseph C. Stiles, an evangelical Presbyterian who held outdoor prayer meetings every night. Everyone stood silent when Jackson knelt on the ground and prayed aloud.

As the Yankees and Burnside advanced on Fredericksburg, Jackson left the valley and marched quickly to help Lee. En route, he received a letter from his wife announcing the birth of their daughter. He named her Julia, after his mother. He had asked his wife not to send him a telegram, because he didn't want anybody else to know. He told his wife they must not get too attached to the child or God would punish them by taking it from them. He also told her not to spoil it or let anybody tease it. Jeb Stuart, who loved Jackson, had given him a uniform with gold braid which some of his soldiers thought out of character. On the eve of the Battle of Fredericksburg a chaplain found him behind a gun battery wrapped in an overcoat to conceal the uniform, reading the Bible.

After the battle was won, Jackson wanted to follow it up with a night attack. So his men would be able to identify each other, Jackson considered giving them armbands of white bandage, or having them attack naked. Lee vetoed the whole idea. Jackson spent the winter at Moss Neck, a plantation about twelve miles downriver from Fredericksburg. He established his headquarters in an outbuilding which had been the office of the owner; its walls were hung with fishing tackle, animal skins, and pictures of horses, bloody game cocks, and a famous rat terrier. He spent much time thinking about the spiritual welfare of his men and chose the Presbyterian minister Dr. Beverly Tucker Lacy for the task of improving it. Dr. Lacy tried to provide more chaplains according to Jackson's instructions that denominational differences be set aside and even Roman Catholics welcomed. He succeeded so well he began a religious revival among the troops. Jackson attended prayer meetings at Moss Neck every day. He did not insist that his aides attend, but always welcomed those who showed up, with a big smile. At Moss Neck he spent some of the most contemplative Sabbaths of his life, meditating and discussing theology with James P. Smith, a Presbyterian divinity student on his staff. He

caught up on his letter writing, corresponding with Congressman Boteler and others about a legislative bill to prohibit Sunday mails.

At about the time that Charlie Wickham was writing his Christmas
letter home, Jackson received a letter with a lock of Julia's hair. His
wife referred to her as a cherub, and Jackson said not to—"No earthly
being is such." Jackson had a Christmas dinner of oysters, turkey, and
ham for Generals Lee and Stuart and some staff officers in his headquarters. Stuart kidded him about the pictures on the walls and said
they were a sign of Jackson's moral decline. As the days passed, Jackson
prayed, began to write up reports on the battles he'd been in, and
recommended against pardon for three deserters sentenced to be shot.
He told his officers how important it was that they stay with their
commands and discouraged them from taking leaves. Again and again
his wife—he called her Anna—wrote and asked why he couldn't come
to see her and the baby. He explained that he had to set an example.

Finally, late in April, Anna and the baby came up by train to see
him. He had moved his headquarters by then, to Hamilton Crossing.
Anna brought along Hetty, a maid she had owned since Anna was a
girl, to help with the baby. Hetty was a good maid (according to Anna)
but had been opinionated and difficult before Jackson took her in hand.
Julia, nearly five months old, woke up from her nap just as the train
pulled into the station. Jackson walked into the car wearing an India-
rubber overcoat wet with rain, and the baby looked up at him and
smiled. He did not want to pick her up for fear of getting her wet.
When they got to the house where he was staying, he removed his
overcoat and held her, and he rarely put her down for the rest of the
visit.

Sometimes he knelt over her cradle and watched her as she slept.
When she cried to be picked up, he ignored her, then picked her up
when she stopped, so that he soon had her perfectly trained, Anna said.
Dr. Lacy baptized the baby. Everyone wanted to see her. Anna held
the baby up for the soldiers to see when they passed in review. Officers
and ladies came to call. Henry Kyd Douglas felt so awkward holding
the baby that everyone laughed and Jackson told Hetty to take her.

On the morning of April 29, a messenger knocked on the Jacksons'
bedroom door. Jackson guessed what the news was. He dressed and
told Anna she must get ready to leave immediately. They said goodbye
and he sent her and Hetty and Julia by escort to the train. He was in

fine spirits and ready for a fight. The dispatch from General Early had
informed him that Hooker was crossing the river above Fredericksburg.

•

In conversation, Hooker often said, "When I get to Richmond . . ." or, "After we have taken Richmond . . ." In anticipation
of a siege there, the army quartermaster had been told to be ready
with 10,000 shovels, 5,000 picks, thousands of axes, shingling hatchets,
and sandbags. Preparations were made to lay railroad tracks in the
wake of the soon-to-be-victorious advance. "That is the most depress-
ing thing about Hooker," Lincoln confided to a friend with a sigh. "It
seems to me that he is overconfident." Hooker said that his was "the
finest army on the planet," and knew that it greatly outnumbered
Lee's. He issued an order which warned against overestimating the
strength of the enemy. Officers who did that out of fear, he said, were
cowards who deserved death just as much as deserters in battle.

Hooker's plan of attack took the idea behind Burnside's flanking
march in December—the unlucky Mud March—and elaborated on
it. Hooker would send a large force to fords of the Rappahannock
upstream from Fredericksburg and outflank Lee's position there. A
smaller force would cross just below Fredericksburg to confuse Lee
and hold him. The combination was supposed to give Lee no choice
but to retreat or attack Hooker on his own ground. Meanwhile, the
Union cavalry under General George Stoneman would get between
the Confederate Army and Richmond, and cut lines of supply. As it
turned out, sending the cavalry so far from the rest of the army was
Hooker's biggest mistake.

On April 26 the men of the 55th received an order to be ready
to march the next morning. They were issued bread rations for eight
days and beef, in the form of a cattle herd, for three. Each man carried
a hundred rounds of ammunition and an overcoat and a blanket. The
55th and the rest of the 11th Corps were on the march by 9 a.m.
More than half of the 12,000 men in the corps had been born in
Germany. Many others were German-speaking. The German regiments carried lots of baggage and took a while getting in line to march.
The large number of their wagons caused Hooker to reprimand General Howard. Everyone was glad to get out of winter quarters, and
the men shouted and sang. Many soon discarded their blankets and

overcoats along the road. The 11th Corps reached Kelly's Ford on the Rappahannock twenty-five miles upstream from Fredericksburg on the next afternoon. They crossed the river at night on a pontoon bridge the engineers had built, and marched another day. At three o'clock the next morning they crossed the Rapidan, a tributary of the Rappahannock, at Germanna Ford. Again they used a bridge which soldiers in the advance had built. On the far side they could already see Union campfires. Moonlight shone on the bayonets; the jubilant men laughed and joked in the quiet night.

Three other corps—under Generals Slocum, Meade, and Couch—combined with the 11th Corps in the flanking movement. Slocum's corps took the same route, Meade's crossed the Rapidan at a ford farther downstream, and Couch's crossed the Rappahannock closer to Fredericksburg. All made their marches and crossings without serious difficulty. By April 30, Hooker had put more than 60,000 men in the rear of Lee's position at Fredericksburg, while another three corps were safely across the river downstream from the town. The 10,000 men of Stoneman's cavalry had gotten a late start, but now they, too, were across the river and far in Lee's rear to impede the expected retreat. To fight this force totaling perhaps 132,000 Lee had no more than 62,000.

The flanking corps converged on a crossroads called Chancellorsville on roads that led through a tangle of second-growth forest called the Wilderness. The original timber of this region had been cut down to make charcoal to smelt the local bog ores. When the foundries went out of business in 1846, new forests took over; only a few mostly poverty-stricken farms in clearings remained. Meade and Slocum met at Chancellorsville on the afternoon of April 30, and Meade said, "This is splendid, Slocum; hurrah for old Joe; we are on Lee's flank, and he does not know it. You take the Plank Road toward Fredericksburg, and I'll take the Pike, or *vice versa*, as you prefer, and we will get out of this Wilderness." He was disappointed to hear that Hooker had ordered them to stop there and wait.

General Lee did know about the enemy on his flank, and had guessed correctly that the force he could see downstream was intended as a feint. Leaving just 10,000 men to hold the position at Fredericksburg, he ordered the rest of his army, about 45,000, to march in the direction of Chancellorsville. On the morning of May 1 they were within four miles. Hooker, meanwhile, ordered the corps at Chancellorsville to advance. They had not gone far before they met the Confederates and the battle was begun. Then suddenly Hooker ordered all his corps to withdraw to their former position. The Union generals, with superior numbers and anticipation of success, were surprised and chagrined. Meade was furious. Howard's men, marching in the rear of Slocum's, had come two miles at the most after standing in ranks since morning. They could not believe they were just supposed to go back. "It gave to our whole army the impression of a check, a failure, a defeat," Howard recalled.

Hooker himself was at Chancellorsville by then. He seemed to be in a state of nervous exhaustion, but explained to his returning generals that now he had Lee just where he wanted him, that now Lee must attack him on his own ground. General Couch later said that "to hear from his own lips that the advantages gained by the successful marches of his lieutenants were to culminate in fighting a defensive battle in that nest of thickets was too much, and I retired from his presence with the belief that my commanding general was a whipped man."

The Army of the Potomac sat and waited. Its lines extended for perhaps six miles, from the Rappahannock to Chancellorsville, and from there out the Orange Turnpike. The position resembled, very roughly, a flattened V, with Chancellorsville at the point. Military tactics say that a flank should rest against a natural barrier so that the enemy cannot get around it. The left flank of Hooker's army rested against the river, but the right flank had no barrier other than the tangled woods to protect it. In military terms, it was "up in the air." On the end of this right flank was the 11th Corps; the regiments of the 1st Division occupied the very end. The 55th was posted along the turnpike next to a rail fence, only a few hundred yards from the farthest right of the army. On a small rise nearby stood a farmhouse owned by a family named Talley, the headquarters for the brigade and the division.

•

Chancellorsville is about a seven-hour drive from my apartment. Once you leave the city you can take multilane roads the entire way. Like many Civil War battlefields, Chancellorsville lies within the commuting radius of Washington, D.C.; if it were not so historical, sub-

urban growth would have covered it by now. I got to the visitor center
at the battlefield early in the afternoon. A guide there let me look at
a gazetteer of historic sites which said that the Talley farmhouse was
torn down in 1926. The gazetteer described where the house used to
stand and had a picture of a brown utility building near the site now.
I left the visitor center and got in the westbound lane of Highway 3
and sped up to 60. The Orange Turnpike may have been a country
road in 1863, but the highway that runs on top of it is more of an
autobahn. Spotting historic sites at a mile a minute can be tricky, and
twice I missed the brown utility building and had to make vexing
crossovers in the traffic stream. Finally, I pulled off the eastbound
lane and got out the passenger side.

I didn't see any NO TRESPASSING signs. I walked down a gravel
drive that led to a two-story metal building with broken windows and
yellow insulation hanging from holes in the walls. In the weeds closer
to the road I found the foundations of a house. A shade tree that had
once been in the front yard now stood hard by the humming pavement.
Pink bloomed on a rambling rose along a stretch of old plank fence.
Underfoot I smelled mint. Here would have been where the generals
and staff tied their horses. A battery of six-pound cannon had defended
the position from the yard. I walked to the highway and looked west
to where the 55th was posted. Bulldozer work and the eastbound lane
have erased the exact location. If I didn't know that where I was
standing had been all-important high ground, I would not have
guessed. It looked like just an old forgotten place by the road. Next
to the utility building I found a stack as tall as I am of old fiberglass
golf-cart bodies, and a heap of golf-cart seats.

The visitor center suggests that people see the battlefield by self-
guided auto tour. The tour begins just off Highway 3 at the site of
the Chancellorsville Inn, about three miles east of where the Talley
house used to be. The inn Hooker made his headquarters is gone;
there is a small parking lot, a few foundations, historical markers, and
an expanse of open ground. Here on May 1 Hooker announced that
the rebel army was now the legitimate property of the Army of the
Potomac, that God Almighty could not deprive him of them—a blas-
phemy that shocked many of his men. As I stood reading the markers,
another Civil War buff pulled into the parking lot, got out, and approached each marker when I moved on. He was wearing a camouflage

parka, a U.S.S. *Something* baseball cap, and shorts. He had strong-looking skinny legs and carried a tape recorder which was playing a cassette of a narrator talking about the battle. The buff got back in his car when I got in mine, and through his open window I heard the tape recorder say, "It must have been from such a scene that men in ancient times rose to the dignity of gods." Then our automatic seat belts moved up around the window frames and clasped us across the chest.

The next stop on the tour is at an intersection of smaller roads in the pine woods about a mile south. Here Lee and Jackson met at night on May 1 to discuss the next day's strategy. A granite monument on the springy pine straw beneath the dark trees marks where they sat. Unlike Hooker, Lee and Jackson still had their cavalry handy; as they conferred, Jeb Stuart rode up in the moonlight with the interesting news of Hooker's unprotected right flank. Then an aide of Lee's and Jackson's chief engineer returned from a scout to inform them that an attack on Hooker's entrenched front appeared unpromising. Lee and Jackson decided to attack on the flank, and made a plan as bold as any in military history. Lee had already divided his force once, when he left a part of his army at Fredericksburg and marched with 45,000 toward Chancellorsville. Now he would divide that 45,000, leaving about 12,000 to face Hooker and sending the rest, under Jackson's command, on a long march to envelop the Union right. Making the flanking force so large was Jackson's idea.

The night was clear and cold. Jackson slept for a while on the ground without a blanket. An aide lent him his cape, but Jackson returned it, and caught a cold. As it happened, Dr. Lacy, the Presbyterian divine never far from Jackson's side, had once had a church in the neighborhood and knew the roads. He and Jackson's cartographer, Jedediah Hotchkiss, talked to a local man and came up with a route that led a roundabout twelve miles or more to the turnpike west of the Union Army. Seeing to the details took a while, and Jackson's troops didn't start moving until after dawn. First came twenty-two regiments in a division under the command of General Rodes, then twenty regiments under General Colston, then twenty-eight under General A. P. Hill. Jackson ordered that stragglers were to be bayoneted, and placed a guard of strong men behind each regiment. More than a hundred pieces of artillery accompanied the infantry. A Federal cavalry demonstration delayed the march. Then Federal artillery on high ground spotted the movement across their front and shelled the column, and infantry attacked it. But a counterattack stopped pursuit, and by midday Jackson's flanking column had disappeared down a back road into the woods.

The back road is not part of the main tour. When Jackson took it, it was called the Furnace Road; today it is called Jackson Trail East. It and its continuation, Jackson Trail West, are among my favorites of all the back roads I have ever driven. The way is just wide enough for two cars to pass if both edge off onto the brief shoulder. Jackson's columns filled the road from one side to the other, causing slow going for aides who had to make their way through on horseback: "Say, here's one of Old Jack's little boys; let him by, boys! . . . Tell Old Jack we're all a-comin'. Don't let him begin the fuss till we get there!" Today this road still feels sneaky. Even with my foot off the gas, the car went about five miles an hour; I wished I could go slower. The traffic was all on the four-lane; none, for the moment, was here. Tree trunks filed by, some lit by sunlight, some darker. Now and then the sun made a bunch of leaves stand out from the shaded places. I moved through the flickering shade as if through a sleeve. Staff physician Dr. McGuire said he could never forget how Jackson's eyes flashed in his pale face as he said, "Press forward, press forward!," leaning over on his horse's neck in his eagerness. The road had been wet enough to be easy on the marchers' feet, and dust-free. My tires turned slowly, sometimes pressing down on a piece of gravel and popping it out to the side. Most roads are about destination; this road was about destiny.

I stopped at a historic marker by a little creek that ran across the road. The soldiers churned this creek to a mudhole as they passed, the marker said: "Many would never cross another earthly stream." I put my hand in the cool current in its channel paved with flagstones. On the edges, water striders pinched the surface film with their long legs as they balanced above their shadows.

The marchers continued down this road until it ended at the larger Brock Road. This road, now Virginia Route 613, is paved. I stopped and waited as cars sped by. Here Jackson could have taken a right and headed up toward the turnpike. Instead, he turned left, or south. He hoped that any Federal observers who saw the column going south here would assume he was retreating. But after a quarter

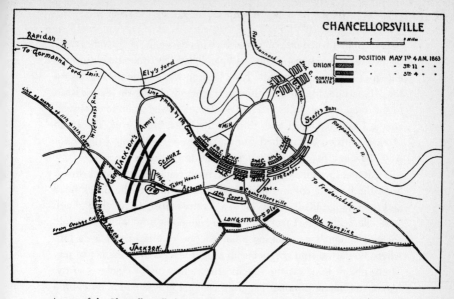

*A map of the Chancellorsville battlefield taken from the 55th Ohio's regimental history.
The dotted line shows, somewhat inaccurately, the line of march Jackson's force took
through the Wilderness to a position on the Union flank*

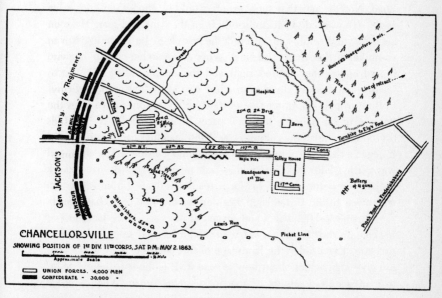

*Deployment of troops at about five o'clock in the afternoon of May 2, just before the attack
began. The 55th Ohio is at the center. In the lower left are the skirmishers of its picket
line, which slowed the right wing of Jackson's advance*

mile or so he turned onto a track which appears only as "Private Road" on a contemporary map. This road paralleled the Brock Road through a deeper screening of woods. Now Jackson was aiming north, toward the Union line, for the first time in the march. I took the Brock Road to this road (today, Jackson Trail West) and slowed again to minimum speed. I saw mailboxes and, through the trees, big houses. The snout of an expensive car pushed from a driveway, but turned the other way. To some people, this is just a road they drive every day.

After a few miles Jackson Trail West rejoined the Brock Road. Soon the flanking column came to the intersection of the Brock Road and the Orange Plank Road. Here a cavalry officer, General Fitzhugh Lee, offered to escort Jackson to a vantage point from which he could see the Union lines. Jackson followed Lee to a farm and up a hill, where he parted some branches to a sight few people ever get to see. There before him was the enemy, the right wing of Hooker's army, his for the taking. Smoke rose from cooking fires, soldiers butchered cattle, men lounged in groups. Muskets were stacked in long rows. Jackson's lips moved as he watched; Fitzhugh Lee thought he was praying.

Jackson had planned to make his attack up the Orange Plank Road. Now he saw that such a route would hit the Union lines at an angle. He wanted to hit it entirely from the flank and rear. He rode back down the hill and ordered the march to be extended to the turnpike, farther north and west. When the marchers finally reached the turnpike, they turned right and then deployed in the woods. Jackson put Rodes's division in a line two miles long, perpendicular to the turnpike on either side of it. He put Colston's division, when it came up, in a line a hundred paces behind Rodes's. A. P. Hill's division, the tail of the column, was still some miles back. As it arrived it began a third line a hundred paces behind Colston's. The afternoon was getting late; Jackson couldn't wait much longer. By five o'clock he had the better part of his force ready to advance from a position which was to the Union right as an eraser to a line on a chalkboard.

I came to Highway 3 and turned at the same place Jackson and his column did. I was not yet ready to go fast and so pulled over to the side. Even today the landscape of this onetime Wilderness does not give many clues about how to read it. It is the sort the eye skips over in search of someplace that makes more sense. When it was a nest of thickets it must have been even worse. I sat with the engine idling not far from where Jackson gave his division commanders the order of battle. Once the attack began, he said, it was not to stop under any circumstances until it carried the Union position at the Talley farmhouse.

•

Hooker learned of the Confederates moving across his front at about nine that morning. He could see the column himself from his tent. Examining a map, he said, "Lee is trying to flank me." At nine-thirty he sent General Howard a message ordering him to prepare the 11th Corps for an attack from the west. Howard later said he never received the message. Howard believed the thickets on his right were impenetrable. But he, too, had seen signs of enemy movement in that direction and informed Hooker that he was taking defensive measures. He did little besides facing his reserve artillery west. Soon Hooker came riding down the lines on his white horse to inspect the defenses in person. The men of the 55th were relieved to see him and felt reassured that their position was safe. Hooker told Howard he would send a cavalry division to occupy the gap between the 11th Corps and the river (according to the chronicler of the 55th). Where he thought he would get a cavalry division is hard to see; in any case, no such force arrived.

Cavalry could have given Hooker a bigger picture of the enemy's position and movements. Instead, he had to rely on reports from artillery observers and infantry pickets. Early in the day, these all seemed to confirm an idea which had been in the front of his mind ever since he came up with his grand strategy: Lee's inevitable retreat toward Richmond. General Daniel Sickles, who had recently arrived with his 3rd Corps, observed the rebels heading south near his position and asked Hooker if he could attack them. It was Sickles's men who caused the delay in Jackson's march on the Furnace Road. Hooker ordered Sickles to pursue slowly and with caution. Soon the sounds of battle to the south and certain defensive movements of Lee's removed the last of Hooker's doubts. He sent all his corps commanders an order to prepare ammunition and supplies for an early start, presumably after the retreating rebels, the next morning.

Men from the 55th on picket duty in the woods south of Union lines saw Jackson's columns moving and began exchanging shots with the enemy. Between one and two in the afternoon, Captain James Sauter of Company B on the picket line sent his first sergeant back to report to Colonel Lee that enemy infantry and artillery were massing on the right. Colonel Lee told the brigade commander, General John McLean, and he sent scouts to confirm the report. General McLean then referred Colonel Lee to General Charles Devens, commander of the 1st Division, who had immediate responsibility for the defense of the flank.

Charles Devens was forty-three years old, from Massachusetts, a graduate of Harvard College and Harvard Law School. He had won commendations for bravery at Fredericksburg and Fair Oaks, where he was severely wounded. He was handsome and single and wore a flowing mustache. He apparently did not think much of the troops in his command, and they found his manners austere. He had been appointed to the division, his largest command so far, just nine days before. If most generals in the Union Army had small understanding of the Wilderness, General Devens had less. When one of his regimental commanders asked him, "Do you know where you are?" Devens replied, "No, don't know as I do!" Someone found an old Yankee clock peddler and he made a map for Devens, but with little effect. Devens received Colonel Lee's report coldly. As the afternoon wore on and more news came in from the pickets, Lee made several more trips to Devens. Devens said that the rebels were retreating, and if that was not true he would have heard from corps headquarters. Finally he lost patience and told Lee, "You are frightened, sir," adding a remark about these Western colonels being more scared than hurt.

Reports of danger came from other line officers of the corps, but no one higher up took them seriously. One reason may have been that the rest of the army had a certain hostility toward the 11th Corps. Probably it was regarded as unproven, foreign, and strange. Eleven of the corps's twenty-seven regiments had never been in a battle, fifteen were German-speaking. The corps was perhaps the most mixed body in either army. It included a Scandinavian and Swiss regiment from Wisconsin and an all-Irish regiment from Ohio and a company of Jews from Chicago. Some of its officers had fled failed European revolutions of the 1840s: Frederick Hecker, veteran of the revolution in Baden in 1848; Carl Schurz, who fought in another Baden uprising the following year; and Wladimir Kryzanowski, exiled from Poland by the

Revolution of 1846. The engineer of the corps, Major Ernest F. Hoff-
man, had served on the staff of Garibaldi. Other officers were from
German military families or had taught in European cadet schools.
Some were freethinkers and sophisticates of a type not yet common
in backcountry America. Prince Salm-Salm, who commanded a New
York regiment, had a beautiful young wife who at the review of the
troops in April kissed Lincoln on a bet.

Colonel Leopold von Gilsa, formerly of the Prussian Army, commanded a brigade in the 1st Division. Two of his regiments, the 54th
New York and the 153rd Pennsylvania, were posted in the woods on
the farthest right. Unlike the rest of the division, their lines faced
roughly west. In mid-afternoon, Major Owen Rice of the 153rd, on
picket duty, sent von Gilsa a message:

"A large body of the enemy is massing in my front. For God's
sake, make dispositions to receive him!"

Von Gilsa took the message to General Howard at corps headquarters, but Howard dismissed him "with taunts" (said Major Rice)
and informed him nothing could get through those woods. Other
officers who came to Howard with similar reports were told not to be
afraid of a few bushwhackers or were accused of cowardice. Perhaps
Howard remembered Hooker's order characterizing officers who over-
estimated the strength of the enemy as cowards who deserved death.

Captain Hubert Dilger, an officer of the Baden Mounted Artillery
serving with an Ohio artillery battery, decided to make a reconnaissance on his own. He was known as a daredevil who often wore leather
breeches. He rode through the woods beyond the Union right until
he emerged in a clearing and saw thousands of rebel soldiers waiting
in line of battle. Enemy cavalry chased him, he became lost in the
woods, and finally he made it all the way to Hooker's headquarters.
An aide there laughed at him and told him to go tell his yarn to General
Howard. By the time Dilger got to Howard's headquarters, however,
the general was no longer there. He had gone with one of his divisions,
his 3,000-man reserve, to accompany General Sickles in southward
pursuit of the presumed retreat. The lines of Sickles's corps had ad-
joined Howard's; now there was a wide gap next to Howard's remaining
divisions, and no reserve to support them. Dilger went back to his
artillery unit and turned his guns to face west.

By late afternoon, the men on the Union right were playing poker

in the woods or resting. Some were cooking supper and had their
arms stacked. Here and there groups of officers could be seen talking
quietly on the road, looking now and then to the west. Some officers
and their aides kept close to their horses and did not even take the
bits out for the horses to graze. The 55th's regimental band, in some
pines across the road, was playing jaunty airs like "The Girl I Left
Behind Me." Between five o'clock and six, foxes, rabbits, and quail
began to break from the woods to the right. Then some deer emerged,
and a cheer went down the line as they ran by.

In the next instant, History, that force which always seems to
choose people who are richer or poorer or in a different place, caught
my relatives and the rest of the 55th square on the point of the chin.
There was a crash of cannon down the road and the loud boom of a
shell exploding directly overhead. Fragments of hot iron rained all
around. Noncombatants—commissary officers, clerks with armloads
of papers, teamsters, officers' black servants on spare horses—scattered. Bullets began to fly out of the woods, clipping the new leaves.
Musket fire in the near-distance sputtered, then grew to a roar as
Jackson's men hit von Gilsa's regiments on the right. Some of those
troops got off a few volleys, most did not. Soon hundreds were running
from the woods into the Talleys' pastures. Colonel Lee went to General
Devens and said that his flank was turned; could he change front?
Devens said "Not yet."

Bullets were zipping through the regiment from the side and
rear. Lee again went to Devens and said his men were being shot in
the back. Devens dismissed him with a wave of his hand. Now the
men could hear the rebel yell from thousands of throats. On his own,
Lee ordered the regiment to move across the road and change front.
The line pivoted from right to left under unbroken grapeshot and
canister fire from up the road. Captain Sauter, the officer who had
known the rebels were coming since early afternoon, was hit in the
head crossing the road and died instantly. Lee's horse was shot from
under him, Lee was injured. The 55th re-formed in the rear of the
25th Ohio, posted nearby.

Just to the west, the 75th Ohio could not fire for fear of hitting
von Gilsa's men as they came pouring through their ranks. Von Gilsa
shouted, "Colonel Riley, don't shoot my men!" When the 75th's front
was finally clear, the rebel line was thirty yards away. The 75th fired,

but in a minute or two it was overlapped on both sides and had lost 150 officers and men. The rebels came on, dusty, powder-blackened, their clothes in rags from the whipping branches. Many had not eaten in two days, and they grabbed the Yankees' abandoned suppers, and advanced eating and yelling and firing.

The 25th fired a number of volleys; more than half the regiment fell killed or wounded before it broke. The 55th stood to perhaps three volleys. Owen Lynch and Thomas Wilson and the Rumbaughs, James and William, were killed. Henry Husted fell dead, shot in the forehead; his family had the shoe store in Norwalk. Major James Stevens was hit in the rib, leg, and arm, Captain Horace Robinson in the leg, Corporal T. M. Wood in the elbow, Captain Hartwell Osborn in the foot, Hiram McGlone in the knee, Eri Mesnard in the shoulder, Peter Pixley in the left thigh. Benjamin Nye and David Reynolds and Edward Hinchy and Philip Livensparger were killed. Jacob Brown, called "Little Jake" because he was the smaller of two Jacob Browns in the regiment, came to Will Wickham and said, "Lieutenant, something is wrong with my gun—I can't fire it." Just then Charlie Streeter spun around and dropped to the ground. Will Wickham said, "There, Charlie Streeter is killed—take his gun." Little Jake did, and went on firing. Charlie Streeter, shot through the arm and lung, survived.

"There was, there could be, no effective attempt at resistance," said Captain Henry Kyd Douglas, who observed the attack with other Confederate officers advancing up the road.

"The best and bravest troops that ever existed would, under the same circumstances, have been terrorized," said a member of the 25th Ohio.

"It was a terrible gale! The rush, the rattle, the quick lightning from a hundred points at once; the roar, redoubled by echoes through the forest; the panic, the dead and dying in sight and the wounded straggling along; the frantic efforts of the brave and patriotic to stay the angry storm!" remembered General Howard, who had returned (without his reserve division) just as the attack began.

Will Wickham later wrote: "I am not now, I never have been, and I never shall be, in a frame of mind to blush for the part which fell to my individual lot that day, nor to apologize in the faintest terms for the conduct of my comrades in that awful time." Which is to say, they ran. Of 442 officers and men on line that afternoon, the 55th lost

175 killed, wounded, and captured, most in the space of ten or fifteen minutes. People would later debate which regiments ran the soonest, fastest, and farthest; a consensus of observers said the German regiments seemed to outdo the rest. Certainly, the panic was general. Men slashed at their knapsack straps with knives in order to unburden themselves more quickly, they overflowed the road, they dropped their muskets and ran full speed, they trampled through hospital tents and over gun carriages, they pleaded with those who tried to stop them to let them through. Driverless wagons careened here and there, cattle and mules joined the stampede. It was hard to locate an officer, because after the first few minutes nearly every officer had been shot or unhorsed or both. Every colonel but one in the 1st Division, 2nd Brigade, was killed or disabled. General Devens was shot in the foot but remained on the field to the last. General Howard sat on his horse in the middle of the road and exhorted his men to stand and fight. Observers said he wept as he held a regimental flag under the stump of his arm and pleaded bareheaded with the fugitives streaming by. Some men ran so far they went clear through the Union defenses ahead of them and were captured by Confederates on the other side.

The picket line of the 55th, now commanded by Captain Rudolphus Robbins and Lieutenant John Lowe, was at its post in the woods south of the turnpike when the attack began. It kept up such a steady fire at the rebels advancing there that it convinced their commander, General Colquitt, that he had somehow run into a large force, possibly part of Sickles's corps. He halted his troops, reconnoitered, and fell far behind the line of Jackson's advance. The picket line withdrew slowly, firing all the while, until many of its men had been captured. By delaying Colquitt it kept almost 5,000 men from the fight and saved the 11th Corps from worse disaster.

Charlie Wickham came across his friend Lieutenant Edward Culp of the 25th after their regiments had broken. They agreed to stay together and do what they could for the cause. Will Wickham "drifted" across a half mile of open field and was about to enter some woods when he stopped to watch a group of artillerymen trying to free a brass howitzer from a ditch. Suddenly he heard a sound like a smart slap on the face and turned to see a soldier standing erect as if at attention with a hole through his forehead the size of a half-dollar. The soldier did not fall until after Will had looked away.

Captain Hartwell Osborn, later the chronicler of the 55th, had trouble keeping up with the retreat. He took off his shoe, found it full of blood, and sat down by the side of the road to rest. He watched the rebel troops come on, "clad in as motley an array of uniforms as could be imagined," but well-disciplined and eager. He heard a rebel officer cry, "Oh, for only one more hour of daylight!" At about seven o'clock, General Jackson and his staff rode by.

Sunset that evening was at 6:48. The troops of Colston and Rodes had become disorganized in the headlong assault, and many of them were exhausted. In just half an hour they had killed, wounded, or captured thousands of Yankees, and had pushed ahead nearly two miles. Rodes told Jackson he had to stop and re-form his line. Evidently the idea of stopping the attack never crossed Jackson's mind. An officer said he had never seen Jackson so pleased with the progress of a fight. When another officer had said that the enemy were running away too fast, Jackson replied, "They never run too fast for me, sir! Press them, press them!" Now he ordered his third line of assault, the still-fresh troops of A. P. Hill, to move forward. He wanted Hill to get between the Yankee army and its escape route at a ford across the Rappahannock a mile or more away. A full moon rose, encouraging him further.

Whole regiments of Union troops were wandering around lost in the woods. A single entrenchment might be occupied at different points by both Union and Confederate men. The 8th Pennsylvania Cavalry, ordered to go to Howard's aid but unaware of the attack, stumbled onto a North Carolina infantry regiment and a fierce exchange of fire. General Sickles tried to return from his southward probe and got into a three-way shoot-out with both Union and Confederate forces in the dark. In some places the underbrush caught fire, and wounded men screamed as they burned.

Jackson decided to make a forward reconnaissance in person before continuing the advance. With a group of officers he rode unannounced through Confederate lines, perhaps on a smaller road that ran next to the turnpike. One officer suggested that this might be the wrong place for him, but Jackson replied that the danger was over, the enemy was routed. He told the officer to go back and tell General Hill to "press right on." Then he turned back himself and soon met Hill, with staff. As the party, now perhaps twenty riders, approached Confederate lines, picket firing broke out. Little Sorrel bolted in the opposite direction, but Jackson managed to turn him. Hill shouted to the Confederate pickets ahead, "Cease firing! Cease firing!" Another officer yelled that the pickets were firing into their own men. The troops here happened to be from the same North Carolina regiment which had earlier encountered the 8th Pennsylvania Cavalry; their colonel yelled, "It's a lie, boys! Pour it into them!"

The North Carolinians fired a volley at twenty paces. Four of the officers and perhaps fourteen horses were killed outright. Jackson, riding with one arm upraised to ward off low branches, was hit in the palm of that hand, and twice in the left arm. A bullet about three inches below the left shoulder shattered the bone and severed an artery, another entered his wrist. Little Sorrel again bolted toward Union lines, and Jackson again turned him, using the wounded hand. A branch hit Jackson across the face and scratched him. Someone grabbed his bridle, helped him from his horse; he was already weak with loss of blood. An officer ripped through his India-rubber overcoat with a penknife to get at the arm to stop the bleeding. Others brought litters to carry him and the rest of the wounded, including Major Crutchfield, his chief of artillery, shot in the leg. Crutchfield always used to say there ought to be an international law against fighting or marching in the winter, before eight in the morning, or after sundown. When the litter bearers reached the turnpike, the Yankee artillery half a mile away spotted the activity in the moonlight and began lobbing shells. General Hill, who had escaped the volley, was wounded in the legs. One of Jackson's bearers was hit and he dropped Jackson on his wounded arm. Jackson groaned aloud.

An ambulance carried Jackson back along the turnpike to a field hospital. His lips were compressed so tightly the impression of the teeth showed through. His surgeon, Dr. McGuire, dressed his smaller wounds, waited for the left arm to stiffen, gave Jackson chloroform ("What an infinite blessing," Jackson said), and amputated. When Jackson came to, he said he had imagined he heard beautiful music, but it must have been the sound of the saw. Rev. Lacy took the arm, bundled it up, and buried it in the small cemetery on his brother's farm nearby.

•

Hooker first learned of the flank attack when he was sitting in the evening on the veranda of the Chancellorsville Inn. An aide, looking west with binoculars, happened to see the 11th Corps fugitives coming up the road. Hooker ordered a division to advance and meet the enemy. Soon darkness fell and the rout slowed. By midnight much of the 11th Corps had been reassembled and posted behind strong fortifications on the left of the line. By morning Hooker was in a retracted defensive position, a smaller V which ran from the Rapidan to the Rappahannock. May 3 was the bloodiest morning of the war, as each side lost over 8,000 casualties in a back-and-forth fight. Rebel artillery took over positions Hooker had abandoned in his retrenchment, and Union lines came under heavy fire. A solid shot struck a pillar on the Chancellorsville Inn next to Hooker, and the pillar split and knocked Hooker down. He was more or less dazed for the rest of the battle.

After Lee had hit Hooker at Chancellorsville, he left a token force to watch him while he dealt with the three corps below Fredericksburg. Eventually he pushed that part of the army, commanded by General John Sedgwick, into a defensive position by the river. Hooker met with a group of his generals on the evening of May 4 to discuss whether or not to withdraw. After the meeting, some of the generals were annoyed when he announced that he had already made his decision. He withdrew the next evening, and he was one of the first across the Rappahannock. The 55th's survivors never forgot that gloomy march in the mud and rain. By then the force under Sedgwick had also withdrawn. Lee's army of about 60,000 had defeated an army more than twice its size and sent it back over the river.

News of the outcome did not reach the North right away. In Norwalk, a dispatch received on May 9 said that Richmond had been taken and Hooker was in pursuit of Lee. On May 12, readers of the *Reflector* learned that the 11th Corps had "disgracefully abandoned" their position and that Hooker had recrossed the river. Not until May 19 did the paper run a full report of the battle. Lincoln learned of Hooker's defeat in a telegram of May 6. A friend said that Lincoln's face turned the same shade as the French gray wallpaper behind him when he heard the news. He clasped his hands behind his back and paced up and down. He said, "My God, my God, what will the country say! What will the country say!"

The Union Army lost about 17,000 killed, wounded, and captured at Chancellorsville, the Confederates about 13,000. The 11th Corps lost about 2,500 of the 9,000 engaged. It also left about 6,000 knapsacks on the battlefield; the total left by the army was about 31,000 knapsacks. General Rodes said that, as a result, his men were comfortable in their newly acquired oilcloths and shelter tents despite the rainy weather. The victory convinced Lee that his army could do almost anything, and may have disposed him to ruin a big part of it on the famous, near-suicidal charge at Gettysburg two months later.

Lincoln replaced Hooker with General George Meade. Partial paralysis caused by the injury in the battle troubled Hooker for the rest of his life. General Howard served out the war with distinction and afterward became head of the Freedmen's Bureau, and the founder of Howard University. He and Hooker always blamed Chancellorsville on the 11th Corps. Some of the officers of the German regiments never retrieved their reputations. Colonel von Gilsa suffered from the shame and died shortly afterward. Colonel Lee of the 55th resigned from the regiment in disgust at the criticism and at his treatment on the field by General Devens. Lee later commanded another regiment, and after the war became lieutenant governor of Ohio. General Devens never had much to say about his errors at Chancellorsville. He survived the war, returned to Massachusetts, served three years as U.S. Attorney General, and became president of the Harvard Alumni Association.

Newspapers in the North dwelt on the supposed cowardice of the 11th Corps and called its Germans "Flying Dutchmen." Some soldiers tore the corps's crescent insignia from their uniforms, most just endured the scorn. Today it is hard to believe people could be so willing to accept blame. If anything, the rout at Chancellorsville made the 55th more eager to take risks and prove its courage. At Gettysburg, the regiment was among the troops organized for resistance by General W. S. Hancock on Cemetery Ridge. It spent most of the battle behind a low stone wall by the cemetery and lost many men killed and wounded by sharpshooter fire. Charlie Wickham served as a courier on a general's staff there and kept track of how many times he was shot at. He would escape the war without serious injury; his brother Will would lose most of his hearing from the cannon fire.

After Gettysburg the 55th marched south into Virginia, boarded a train, and joined thousands of men sent to western Tennessee to reinforce the Army of the Cumberland. The regiment spent the next two years of the war in the West and marching with Sherman through Georgia and the Carolinas. At the Battle of Resaca, Georgia, it lost the most men in a single engagement since Chancellorsville. When its colonel, Charles Gambee, received the order to advance, he turned pale and trembled in his saddle; the defenses at Resaca were designed to repulse just such an attack. He fell soon after, shot through the heart.

The 55th was about twenty miles from Raleigh, North Carolina, when the army learned of Lee's surrender at Appomattox. Charlie Wickham had risen to second in command of the regiment by then, brevetted lieutenant colonel for bravery and merit. The army marched all the way from Raleigh to Washington, D.C., via Richmond. There it paraded in triumph past the capitol building of the former Confederacy and Jefferson Davis's deserted White House. The 55th camped at Chancellorsville near ground familiar to many veterans; they showed their comrades over the battlefield without shame. In Washington the army held a Grand Review from the Capitol up Pennsylvania Avenue, attended by densely packed, cheering crowds. The 55th camped outside Washington, and then it and other regiments were sent west to Louisville by train and steamboat. When the Ohio men first saw the shore of their home state as they passed by, they rushed to the rail in numbers that almost caused the boat to swamp. In Louisville the regiment took part in its final review and heard General Sherman praise his soldiers and tell them to make as good a record in civilian life as they had in the army. From there the 55th went by boat to Cincinnati and train to Cleveland, where it was paid and mustered out.

By the time I was born, the deeds of the 55th had been forgotten, and its members were scattered in cemeteries in Huron County and beyond. People I knew who must have heard the veterans' war stories as children did not tell them to me; perhaps the stories weren't the same secondhand. I see now that evidence of the regiment's service was everywhere in Norwalk. The ranks of maples along Main Street, the monument in front of the library, the polish on the courthouse floors—the town's general air of certitude—all spoke of a time when Norwalk had raised a regiment and won a war. The pain the veterans had suffered made the places they chose to live afterward more real;

the regard they never lost for each other fastened those places to the earth. They and their families came out of the war remade, into a remade country. They built summer cottages on the Lake Erie shore and sat on the porches in the evenings and talked about the war.

•

Mary Anna Jackson was staying in Richmond at the house of the Reverend Dr. Moses Drury Hoge when word came that her husband had been wounded. Rev. Hoge was the Presbyterian orator Jackson had once made a special trip to Richmond to hear; his wife and other Richmond ladies had since befriended Anna. Due to the danger of capture she did not go to Jackson for five days, until after the railroad had been repaired. He had been moved in the meantime to a house on the Chandler farm at Guiney Station, a stop on the railroad south of Fredericksburg. Again Anna brought Hetty and the baby. After the surgery Jackson at first had recovered well, resting comfortably and discussing theology and military strategy with his aides. But by the time Anna arrived, his condition had worsened. She had last seen her husband just over a week before; now she saw him semiconscious, one arm gone, his remaining hand bandaged, his cheeks flushed with fever, his breathing labored, his face scratched and the scratches dressed with isinglass plaster. He revived, recognized her, and said, "You must not wear a long face. I love cheerfulness and brightness in a sickroom." The doctors—several had been sent to assist Dr. McGuire—told Anna that Jackson had developed pneumonia of the right lung. They blistered him with vacuum cups and gave him morphine and opium. He was in and out of consciousness from the time she arrived. He said things like "Tell Major Hawks to send forward provisions to the men! Order A. P. Hill to prepare for action! Pass the infantry to the front!" Anna spent so much time with him that her baby got hungry. One evening, Anna read him psalms and sang hymns.

On Sunday, May 10, the doctors told Anna that Jackson would die in a few hours. She sat by his bedside and held his hand and told him that he would that day be with his Maker in heaven. He regained consciousness and asked her what she was saying, and when she told him he replied, "Oh no; you are frightened, my child. Death is not so near. I may yet get well." Anna flung herself across the bed weeping. Then he asked Dr. McGuire if what his wife had said was true, and the doctor affirmed it. Jackson said that was all right, later adding, "I have always desired to die on a Sunday." Anna set Julia on the bed next to him. He saw his daughter and said, "Little darling! Sweet one!" The baby smiled at him as long as he continued to notice her. At about three in the afternoon he became restless. He called out orders and murmured disconnected words. Just before he died, he seemed to relax. He smiled as if in relief. He said, "Let us cross over the river, and rest under the shade of the trees."

A short talk given by historians at the Chancellorsville battlefield usually concludes near the visitor center at the spot where Jackson was shot. I stood with a small group of visitors and listened to historian James McKee describe Jackson's wounding and death. Next to me, a boy in a black T-shirt and drawstring camouflage pants sighted the pistol of his forefinger at joggers and bicyclists on a nearby road as James McKee repeated Jackson's last words, and I began to cry silently and blink the tears so they wouldn't overflow, as I almost always do when I think of those words, as I have done sometimes late in the evening when repeating them to dinner-party companions. "Let us cross over the river, and rest under the shade of the trees." In this sentence, perhaps the most famous dying utterance in American history, Jackson concentrated a lifetime of prayer and struggle and aspiration—his, and that of the young country he had fought to divide. So many crossed water to get here, so many wanted to rest under the shade. The trees of Jackson's vision are the ones we could have cut down but decided not to. His river pertains to the Shenandoah of his early triumphs, and the dangerous Potomac, and the moatlike Rappahannock, and the strategic Chickahominy. But it is the same spiritual water as the river Jordan and the River of Life and the river we shall gather at in the hymn. It is what the historical marker on Jackson Trail East has in mind when it mentions the soldiers never crossing another earthly stream. In his last words, Jackson created America's best-known imaginary landscape.

"Let us cross over the river, and rest under the shade of the trees." In the staccato rhythm of the words I can see each step of the action. The sentence ascends in terraces to rest and peace, it undoes knots inside me, it exhales like a sigh. I can see the shining, whorled river sliding by and the gently rising bank and the shaded grass trodden down after a day-camp picnic, across the river and under the trees. I see the columnar trunks almost in a row and the high ceiling where the leaves begin and the sketchier clouds and sky somewhere above. And then I get kind of carried away and I extend this landscape indefinitely in every direction and I imagine it as the new good place America in its best moments has hoped to be and I populate it from the whole globe and I fill it with faces like those in a poster from an old epic Western movie and with cooking smells and music and maybe even a few car-burglar alarms for verisimilitude—I will spare you all the details. Suffice it to say that all the drinking fountains work, across the river and under the trees.

Before the Civil War, America didn't know if it was a country or lots of different Promised Lands. People invented the America they wanted to live in and then struggled to live there. Across the river and under the trees combined all these invented countries into one. Across the river and under the trees descended like a beneficence in the last moments of a fierce man's life and crystallized his fierceness to purity. Across the river and under the trees carried no demurring subclauses or riders. It included us all—people Jackson considered infidels, men he would have shot unblinking in life. Across the river and under the trees was poetry to equal the nation-making poetry of Lincoln, and the only line of public poetry to come from the South in the war. Even though Stonewall Jackson fought for the Slave Power and though his faith is beyond me and though he did not like newspaper correspondents and though he killed the boy whose family had the shoe store and though the flag of his cause still scares me when I see it on the radiator grille of a truck in my rearview mirror and though I am more than glad his side lost, I dream of across the river and under the trees.

C H A P T E R 8

AFTER THE CIVIL WAR, Americans in general got bigger. The crews of Irishmen building the Union Pacific Railroad west met the crews of Chinese building the Central Pacific east in Utah in 1869, linking the coasts, and soon California fruits began to appear in stores in New York City. As rail lines spread, they brought to market canned salmon from Oregon, canned New Jersey tomatoes, salt beef and pork from Chicago, canned corn, oysters, sardines, milk, peaches, peas, and beans. People stopped regarding beer as a foreign beverage, and drank hundreds of thousands of gallons from breweries in Milwaukee and Cincinnati. Many people saw oranges, lemons, and red bananas for the first time. Cooks used more spices. Improved milling made better flour, and Americans ate the best bread they ever had. A road-house near Saratoga, New York, invented the potato chip, and eventually barrels of "Saratoga chips" could be found in grocery stores everywhere. Americans ate quickly, and a lot. A French visitor said

Oil and sulphur magnate Louis H. Severance. My richest relative

that in restaurants Americans ordered three times as much as they could eat. He was shocked by the amount wasted at a meal. Dealers in ready-made clothes had to go to larger sizes. A clothier in Baltimore reported in 1887 that an average-sized suit had increased a full inch around the chest and waist, with no increase in the legs. A Texas clothier said he thought people were becoming stouter built.

The lean, angular American was seen less often after the war. Men began to shave their beards; by the 1890s very few had them. Women wore the same clothes Madonna wears today, only with dresses over them. In public, middle-class men wore black suits and black silk hats, and if yours was a hat of brown felt, they asked you about it. People had more teeth, and more dentists to fix them. The postwar years saw a tremendous increase in the number of dental schools. Coincidentally or not, chewing became a recreation. Women and girls used store-bought chewing gum, a new product, which came in fruit, peppermint, and medicinal flavors. Men chewed tobacco, and spat. One historian described tobacco chewing as "well-nigh universal" in the South. Public places everywhere had spittoons, also called cuspidors. It was the Spittoon Age. Spittoons dotted the floors of hotel lobbies, saloons, railway stations. A conference room with twenty-six chairs might have twenty-six handy spittoons. Fashionable churches had spittoons in the pews. At a convention of Civil War veterans in Indianapolis, the spittoons were replaced by tubs. Army officers, dry-goods drummers, college professors, and little boys chewed. President Grover Cleveland (elected 1884 and again in 1892) chewed.

When Cleveland developed a sarcoma on his upper left jaw, Dr. J. D. Bryant saved his life with an operation performed in secret on a yacht in New York Harbor. These years produced more advances in medicine than the previous two thousand. Antiseptic surgery, improved microscopy, better medical instruments and anesthesia and suturing helped doctors perform operations which had not been possible before. People began to accept the idea that some diseases were caused by germs, a word which had at first seemed comical and which newspaper editors liked to set in quotation marks. Dr. Wilhelm Röntgen invented the X-ray machine. Alexander Graham Bell, whose wife had lost her hearing to scarlet fever as a child, set out to invent a talking machine as an aid to the deaf and came up with the telephone. After he patented it in 1877, hundreds of other inventors claimed they had done it first and filed lawsuits, none of which succeeded. America teemed with inventors. Thomas Edison invented the incandescent light bulb and the phonograph and the mimeograph machine. Other people invented the dynamo, the air brake, vulcanized rubber, internal-combustion engines, the air hammer, the structural I-beam, the arc light, the zipper, and the screw-back earring. A Midwestern man said he had invented a flying machine which suffered from only one defect—"the inability to rise."

In Milwaukee, a former newspaper publisher and postmaster named C. L. Sholes had an idea for a typewriting machine which he thought might help the blind. He built a model which could type only one letter, W. Later versions could produce the whole alphabet, but broke down a lot. Sholes and his partners reasoned that a gunsmith might be able to solve their problems making small metal parts that were strong enough, so they took their typewriter to the Remington Arms Company in New York. Remington improved the machine and put it on the market in 1874. Mark Twain bought one. His *Adventures of Tom Sawyer*, which he copied on a typewriter, was perhaps the first typed book manuscript. It was all in capital letters—the refinement of the shift key, which added small letters, came a few years after. Twain asked the Remington Company not to mention that he owned a typewriter; he said he was tired of people always asking him how he was making out with it.

There were lots of new companies starting up, and they looked for new ways to advertise. They bought space in newspapers, persuaded editors of magazines which had never taken outside ads before to take theirs, hired literary men to handle their publicity, offered lecturers big fees to mention products from the podium. The famous Congregational minister Henry Ward Beecher appeared in testimonial ads for Pears Soap. At the time, many people liked to look at picturesque scenery, and advertisers put ads on it. Picnickers in New England were used to seeing signboards inscribed VISIT OAK HALL (a Boston clothing store) all over the countryside. The cliffs above the Pacific near San Francisco where tourists went to see the sea lions were blistered with signs for things like Little Bile Beans. Placards for Schlitz beer and Sapolio soap and Bull Durham tobacco and Dr. J. H. Shenck's Mandrake Pills and P. H. Drake's Plantation Bitters and Kodak cameras and Dr. Munyon ("I Am for Men") covered rocks and fences and barns. Ads for aperients and perfumes and malaria remedies followed beside the railroad tracks out from the cities and deep into the woods. No traveler who saw America in the later nineteenth century fails to mention the ads.

National transportation and national markets made for national crazes. The first of these after the Civil War was the baseball craze. Soldiers had played baseball in the camps during the war, and when they got home they organized clubs and held practices and set up matches with other clubs. The craze took off so fast that people were referring to baseball as the national game as early as 1867. Clubs traveled to other towns to play, debated club rules, made up funny rules ("No man is allowed to break any more than two bats at one strike"). Then there was the bicycle craze, which attracted millions after the introduction of the "safety bicycle"—a machine with two wheels the same size, less likely to pitch a rider on his head than the earlier model with the high front wheel. Crazes also developed for roller skating, croquet, football, and spelling bees. Some wondered if the spelling-bee mania might be a scheme by Webster's to sell more dictionaries. In 1880 it seemed as if everybody was reading *Ben-Hur*, the romance of Christian-era Rome by Lew Wallace. John D. Rockefeller, usually not much of a reader, couldn't put it down as he walked the streets of Paris on his first trip abroad. Soon after the book came out, people were building Roman chariots, dressing in Roman costumes, and holding chariot races.

Our time resembles the period 1865–1900 in that both were oppressed by the sounds of the sixties. We can probably expect to be hearing classic 1960s rock-and-roll on the air waves into the next century; people back then heard over and over songs from the Civil War, and oratory and reminiscences about it. Veterans were always getting together for one kind of reunion or another. Nearly every town and city erected statuary memorials to the war ("horrible," a French critic pronounced most of them; "disastrous . . . for American art"). Orators revived the sacred dead at every dedication ceremony. As the important survivors of the war began to die off, eulogies filled the newspapers. The commemorative mood was continued in celebrations of the country's centennial, with the Centennial Exposition in Philadelphia in 1876 the largest of many centennial events spread out over fifteen years. The veterans of the victorious Grand Army of the Republic remained the strongest political force in the country. Republican politicians played to their antagonism for the Democratic South, telling them to vote as they had shot.

The Southern night riders who called themselves the Ku Klux Klan informed the freedmen in shantytowns they hoped to terrorize that they were ghosts of the Confederate dead come straight from hell. The Klan was founded in eastern Tennessee in 1867, and elected the former Confederate cavalry general Nathan Bedford Forrest its first Grand Wizard; he resigned and attempted to dissolve the organization two years later after its violence got bad. KKK riders did not wear only white hoods and robes; they wore rubber "doughface" masks bought in stores, false noses, long tongues of red flannel, animal horns, and cloth horns stiffened with whalebone from corsets. Sometimes they just turned their jackets backward or inside out and blacked their faces with lampblack. Klansmen's wives sewed skull-and-crossbone symbols or daggers on robes with their new sewing machines, and starched robes for horses and men so they would rustle and glisten in the moonlight. Klan-led and other white violence killed thousands of blacks and injured or terrorized many more. Klan terror—"kukluxing"—generally let up around planting and harvest time, so as not to distract black workers from jobs in the field.

The federal government passed laws against the Klan and sent troops to enforce them. White people North and South did not like the Klan's violence, but this did not mean they had friendly feelings for "the Negro." Most white Northerners and Southerners shared a contempt for blacks and recoiled at the idea of social equality; however they may have felt about slavery, most were agreed on that. In writings of the time you can hardly find a good word about the freedmen. Even former abolitionists thought they were human, but just barely. When the radical Republican Secretary of War Edwin Stanton said he favored black enfranchisement, his wife expressed a horror of Negroes sitting at her table. The humorist Artemus Ward, who had lectured to raise money for the Union cause, heckled a black American tragedian playing Othello in London. Oberlin College, which had accepted black students before the war, had fewer and fewer after it; an observer said the college unofficially discouraged them from attending. Robert Todd Lincoln, son of the Great Emancipator, regretted that colored porters employed by his multimillion-dollar Pullman Car Company had to subsist mainly on tips, but added that the arrangement was "old" and the colored race accustomed to it. White churches excluded black members and supported racism generally; "The color line is distinctly drawn by Jehova himself," said *Presbyterian Quarterly*. Many intellectuals had recently absorbed Darwin's theory of natural selection and applied it to the races. This logic argued that the stronger, more vital Anglo-Saxon was destined by nature to survive, while certain weaker races—the Negro, the American Indian—were not. The Harvard scientist Louis Agassiz (though not a Darwinian) conjectured that Negroes in the United States, removed from the care of slavery, would eventually die out. Softhearted people who agreed with him regretted the process and averted their eyes.

The second U.S. census, in 1800, counted a population of about 5 million; by 1860 it had grown to about 35 million. By 1900 it was about 76 million, a fourteen-fold increase for the century. No country had ever grown so fast. The population of Europe, reduced by the millions who emigrated to America, slightly more than doubled over the same span. America was the fifth leading manufacturing nation in the world in 1860, the first by 1900. Despite depressions in 1873 and 1893, despite poverty in the South and among city immigrants and Midwestern farmers and many wage earners, America became rich. The middle class multiplied, mostly in the larger towns and the cities, where it bought houses and tended the soft green lawns foreign travelers admired. People had more money in savings than before. The income tax imposed on the North during the war was repealed in 1872, and another income tax law that passed in the 1890s soon was declared unconstitutional by the Supreme Court. Dozens of Americans made fortunes that put them among the richest individuals in the world. After 1876, America exported more than it imported nearly every year. Perhaps the newly rich in New York and Chicago and elsewhere thought that adding a foreign title to the family would be a good way to balance the trade; many looked for lords and marquises to marry their daughters. American women were said to have an undemocratic longing for European aristocracy, and newspaper columnists and preachers chided them for it. Plenty of European nobles were ready to oblige. One history says that by 1900 an estimated $200 million or more had left America for Europe through marriage.

European culture intimidated many Americans less than it used to. The laying of the first successful transatlantic telegraph cable in

1866 gave Americans news from Europe and elsewhere, and they began to pay more attention to international events. People crossed the Atlantic in ever-faster steamers and kept track of the number of their crossings. They traveled all over Europe, bringing back the eclectic tastes in art and architecture they reproduced in the large brick Victorian mansions which later generations would find so ugly. Some Americans talked of annexing Canada or invading Mexico. At the end of the century America fought a war with Spain more or less for the thrill of it and won far-flung possessions, including Puerto Rico and the Philippines; the country began to think in terms of empire. Rudyard Kipling, who traveled across America in 1889, found the people money-mad, embarrassingly patriotic, and spiritually barren. But he concluded they were too friendly and naïve to fight with. A man he met on a train told him, "We kin feed all the earth, just as easily as we kin whip all the earth."

•

Dr. David Benedict returned to Norwalk after the Civil War and never practiced medicine again. He had a sentimental love for childhood and for children; perhaps he could not stand to watch any more of them die. The other side of the optimism that followed the war appeared in veterans like David, who lived out their days disengaged, often damaged. He and his wife, Harriott, already had four daughters: Mary, Harriott, Agnes, and Fannie. In 1866 they had a son, Fred; in 1868, another daughter, Ellen Eliza; and in 1873, their last child, Suzan.

David had studied pharmacy, and with a partner he opened a drugstore in Norwalk at the corner of Whittlesey and West Main. Besides drugs, Benedict & Burton's sold wine and liquor ("for Medicinal purposes only"), splints, cologne, dolls of all sizes, machinery oil, wallpaper, English repp stationery and envelopes, toilet seats, writing desks. With his wife and a daughter, David took trips to New York City to buy merchandise. In the spring he sold "New Regulation Base Balls," in December toys and "holiday goods." The store installed a soda fountain and sold cold phosphates and sodas, except sometimes toward the end of the summer, when the ice ran out. Back then America had very few bookstores, so Benedict & Burton's also offered the latest popular novels—*Doctor Ox*, by Jules Verne, and *Tempest Tossed*, by Theodore Tilton.

David had inherited a lot of land in and near Norwalk from Platt

Benedict, his grandfather. From time to time he sold some of his acres to businesses or farms. Like his grandfather, he grew big parsnips, and in 1870 he brought to the newspaper office five of them, with a total length of twenty-seven feet, two and a half inches. The longest fell just inches short of Platt's five-foot, three-inch record. David served as senior warden of St. Paul's Episcopal Church. When the church moved part of its adjoining cemetery in an expansion, one of the graves moved was Platt's. David's eight-year-old daughter, Ellen Eliza, called Lillie, was present at the disinterment, and she got a chance to examine Platt's skull. She would later tell her grandchildren that it still had all its teeth, despite Platt's reputation for never brushing.

David wanted a house big enough for all his family and plenty of guests. On his land at 80 East Seminary Street he built a nine-bedroom brick Victorian—an immense pile, with high windows, multiple chimneys, rococo trim, and additional brick structures like subclauses extending from the back. When young men began coming around to court his six daughters, they called it the Fortress. Relatives who later played there said its attic was filled with more junk than they had ever seen, hats and clothes and swords and whatnots going back to the beginning of Norwalk. The house still stands. Out back, there used to be a shed where David did his woodworking, and a barn with a horse stall and a place to park the family's surrey and two-seater sleigh. In the middle of the floor of the hay mow David spread walnuts, butternuts, and hickory nuts to dry before cracking them for the children.

Dr. Benedict, as people around town called him, wore black and always rode a black horse. One day in February a horse he was riding ran away with him and threw him, injuring him some. He tried a number of enterprises other than his drugstore. He opened a brickyard on the outskirts of town, with a brick- and tile-making machine and hundreds of cords of wood for the kilns, and ran it for a while. He became treasurer of Norwalk's Home Savings & Loan. He experimented with his own patent-medicine formulas, manufacturing a headache remedy called Rego's and a tonic called Maple City Cough Syrup. His relatives gave these products enthusiastic testimonials in the newspaper. He was often whistling; people around town could recognize him by his favorite tunes without looking up. He wrote reminiscences of his childhood—like about the time he and some friends scrounged up all the scrap iron in town and took it to the blacksmith and the blacksmith made them a cannon. He attended class reunions at Kenyon, teased his sedate second-oldest daughter, Harriott, planned family parties, and worked in the greenhouse he added off the east wall.

With his sister Fannie's husband, a man named Louis Severance, he developed a cow pasture across Norwalk Creek into residential property. The partners built a long bridge across the creek bottom to reach it. His children and Fannie's children saw a lot of each other; the Severances often came to the Benedicts' for visits. In 1874, at the age of thirty-five, Fannie died. Apparently this only made the families closer. The Severance cousins continued to visit, and regarded the Benedict place in Norwalk as their second home. Louis Severance did not remarry for twenty-two years. He and David were lifelong friends.

Louis Severance is my richest relative. The family has always been quick to claim him, considering he married into it back in 1862; being a multimillionaire makes a distant relative closer. We used to recall the connection when we went to a concert in Cleveland at Severance Hall or shopped at Severance Center, a shopping mall on land where his son used to have an estate. Louis Severance was born in Cleveland in 1838, went to public schools, and at eighteen began working for the Commercial National Bank. He was one of a group of young businessmen starting out in Cleveland at the time, men like John D. Rockefeller and Marcus Hanna and Henry Flagler. The Commercial National Bank lent Rockefeller millions for the petroleum refineries his oil company was building on flat land above a creek a mile or so from the center of Cleveland. In 1864, Louis Severance moved to Titusville, Pennsylvania, and got into the oil business himself.

Titusville and neighboring parts of western Pennsylvania were in the middle of the world's first oil boom, begun in 1858 when "Colonel" E. L. Drake found oil by the unlikely method of drilling a hole in the ground. Oil was selling for as much as twenty dollars a barrel at the time, and when Drake hooked a cistern pump to his well it pumped twenty or thirty barrels a day. Suddenly thousands of people descended on western Pennsylvania and started drilling. Many of the wells struck oil, some were gushers, some flowed thousands of barrels a day. Men who couldn't afford steam-powered drills "kicked down" drill shafts into the earth by jumping on a stirrup attachment to drive them. Towns like Pithole and Oil City grew instantly into oily expanses of derricks and shacks further grimed by the smoke from hundreds of steam engines. The Allegheny River sometimes ran black with oil for miles, and caught on fire. Oil stored in wooden barrels leaked and burned or made a black gumbo with the mud that was everywhere. Pennsylvania Dutch farmers became the oil sheiks of their era. Lacking tanks, the drillers dug reservoirs in the ground and stored oil behind mud banks. Wells caught on fire and sometimes burned for days in the winter, causing trees near them to bud and leaf.

Biographical notes about Louis Severance don't say exactly what he did in Titusville. Probably he was a refiner. Refiners had a more stable business and could make more money in the long run than drillers. (The price of crude oil fluctuated a lot, falling sometimes as low as ten cents a barrel.) At the beginning of the oil boom, petroleum was used mostly as a salve or liniment, or it was taken internally as medicine. Then people discovered that it could be boiled and distilled to produce an illuminating oil better than any on the market. Refiners called the illuminant kerosene. Whale oil was getting expensive as whales became scarce; kerosene provided a fuel that was cheaper and burned brighter than whale oil, lard oil, candles, or camphine. Kerosene from Pennsylvania crude oil illuminated with little smoke or odor at a cost of about thirty-five cents a gallon. Within a few years you could find a kerosene lamp in every home in America. Trimming a lamp became a task every girl was supposed to know how to do, just as every boy was supposed to know how to harness a horse. America used only about a third of the kerosene it produced, so the rest went for export. Kerosene lamps lit Europe, they replaced tallow lamps in Japan and China and olive-oil-burning lamps in the Middle East. All over the world people stopped going to bed at dark just for lack of anything better to do. They read more and socialized more and stayed up later. The world has been brighter at night from about 1870.

The businessman who had the most to do with this change was John D. Rockefeller. He became a partner in a Cleveland refinery at first as a sideline to his grain and commodities business. Then he figured that Cleveland would lose out geographically to Chicago in the grain business in the long run, but had advantages in location and transportation over any city for refining oil. He formed another company called Rockefeller & Andrews, and went into refining full-time. Samuel Andrews, the partner, was an English-born refiner whose methods were said to yield the most kerosene. Other partners got impatient with Rockefeller's practice of paying low dividends and putting money into expansion, so Rockefeller bought them out. In 1870 he changed the name of the firm to the Standard Oil Company of Ohio. "The Standard," as it came to be known, would soon be the largest oil company in the world, then the largest company of any kind. Rockefeller believed that ordinary free competition was not possible in the oil business; he constantly expanded his volume and his capital as a defense against price wars and crashes. He said, "The day of combination is here to stay. Individualism has gone, never to return." He consolidated the business by persuading smaller refiners to sell out to him and by using railroad freight discounts, paid by rebate, to bankrupt others. The Standard bought tank cars, built its own pipelines, built a big cooperage to make barrels. The blue oil barrels of Standard Oil were recognized all over America and in Europe. Standard Oil would eventually control 90 percent of the American oil industry; abroad, its chief competition would be kerosene from Russia. Rockefeller moved to New York and built a big house on Fifty-fourth Street off Fifth Avenue, near where Rockefeller Center is now. Oil made him one of the richest men in the world years before most people had heard of the automobile.

In the 1870s, Rockefeller began to buy the refineries in the Pennsylvania oil fields. He bought the company of a major Titusville refiner, John D. Archbold, a man who would one day succeed him as head of Standard Oil. After Archbold sold out, other Titusville refiners—including, probably, Louis Severance—did, too. Some refiners said that Standard Oil had threatened and crushed them, others became executives with the company. Rockefeller managed to include many good businessmen in his enterprise, men like Flagler, Archbold, Charles Pratt, Oliver Payne, Henry H. Rogers, and Stephen Harkness, whose faces are now forgotten or replaced in people's minds by the buildings named after them. Rockefeller not only made nearly a billion dollars for himself, he helped many associates become millionaires. Standard Oil's holdings had long eclipsed the boundaries of Ohio, multiplying into Standard Oil of New Jersey, of New York, of Indiana, and other divisions. A corporation lawyer named Samuel C.T. Dodd devised a new business organization to hold these companies together. Because there were laws against a company owning shares of a competitor's stock, Dodd put shares of all the companies into a single trust; this giant interstate combine, called the Standard Oil Trust, was run from headquarters in New York by its "trustees," who happened to be Rockefeller and his top executives.

Louis Severance joined the Standard Oil Company of Ohio in 1876, probably after the purchase of his refinery, and became that company's treasurer. He held the position for almost twenty years. Standard Oil of Ohio had grown from Rockefeller's first refinery to a sixty-acre plant southeast of Cleveland, with refinery buildings numbered 1 through 6. Its fumes filled the valley of the Cuyahoga River; people said you could taste them in the butter and the beer. In refinery number 5, a German-born chemist named Herman Frasch worked on problems which today would be called research and development. Frasch found out how to retrieve sulphuric acid, used to purify kerosene, from the sludge left over after refining. Reusing sulphuric acid saved money; at the time most sulphur had to be imported from Sicily. Frasch also worked on how to sweeten the high-sulphur crude oil pumped from new fields in western Ohio and Canada. Rockefeller acquired millions of barrels of this oil when the Pennsylvania fields began to dry up. A single drop of it on the clothes made a person smell like a rotten egg, and kerosene refined from it burned poorly, smoked, and stank. Frasch discovered that adding copper oxides to that oil would precipitate stable copper sulphides from it, effectively removing the sulphur. Oil from the new fields went from fourteen cents a barrel to a dollar a barrel.

Frasch often came around the treasurer's office, and he and Louis Severance got to know each other. Apparently Frasch had an affinity for sulphur. From the fact of sulphur's low melting point, he deduced that the mineral could be mined more easily in a liquid state. He envisioned sinking a tube into a sulphur deposit, pumping superheated water down to melt the sulphur, letting the molten sulphur rise above the water, and pumping the sulphur up. Stockholding executives like Louis Severance were awash by then in dividend money, and often started new companies on the side. With Rockefeller's brother Frank, another investor, and Louis Severance as treasurer, Frasch started the Union Sulphur Company. Severance loaned Frasch an able young man from his office to go down to the huge sulphur deposits lying beneath Bayou Choupique, in southwest Louisiana, to try the new method out. There were technical problems to solve at first, but basically Frasch's idea worked just as planned. Before long the company was bringing up fifty tons of pure sulphur a day. The Frasch method had obvious cost advantages over digging mine shafts; super-heating the necessary water, however, used large amounts of fuel. Frasch's men burned all the available firewood nearby and had to buy more. Fuel costs made the process run in the red. Finally Louis Severance told the superintendent to pack everything up for an indefinite shutdown and return to Cleveland. The process was abandoned as a complete commercial failure.

Then drillers struck oil at Spindletop, Texas, about sixty miles from the Union Sulphur works at Bayou Choupique. With plentiful cheap oil nearby for fuel, the Union Sulphur Company resumed operation. Soon it was mining hundreds of thousands of tons of sulphur a year. Its sole rights to Frasch's mining patent made it the leading producer of sulphur in the world and the founder of the American sulphur-mining industry. America stopped importing sulphur and began to export it, driving the Sicilian economy into a panic. Louis Severance had retired from Standard Oil by then. He added millions from sulphur to the $8 million he already had from oil.

Severance and his children lived in Cleveland, near enough to attend most important events of the Benedict family. The Severance and Benedict cousins followed each other's progress through schools and into marriage. People in Norwalk knew the Severances were visiting when they saw Louis's private railroad car parked on a siding by the depot. In March of 1885 Louis came to Norwalk for the funeral of David's only son. Fred Benedict was eighteen, a student at Kenyon, when he got a sore throat which became bronchitis and then a fatal pneumonia. Fred had been his father's pride, the only chance of carrying on Platt Benedict's name. "Never in the history of the city has there been deeper sorrow," said the *Reflector*; the grief of the family was "almost uncontrollable." A granddaughter later said that David never really got over it. He continued to work at his drugstore into his sixties and then retired. His hair and beard turned white. He developed angina and could not do as much, which irritated him, as did the worry and watchfulness of his family. In 1901, at the age of sixty-seven, he had a heart attack and died.

Louis Severance became a local and international philanthropist.

He gave money to the YMCA, Oberlin College, and Western Reserve University. The College of Wooster, in Wooster, Ohio, burned down in 1901, and almost by himself he gave enough to rebuild it. He served on the councils of the Presbyterian Church and as vice-moderator of the Presbyterian General Assembly in 1904. A lot of his money went to Presbyterian missions in India, Japan, and Korea. In Seoul there was a hospital and a medical college named after him. (Severance Hospital still exists in Seoul; the medical college has merged with another school.) During 1907 and 1908 he took a trip around the world to inspect Presbyterian missions. The trip happened to coincide with an antitrust lawsuit filed in Ohio against Standard Oil of Ohio, one of many such suits at that time which finally led to the break-up of the Standard Oil Trust. My father often told me that Louis Severance carried the account books he had kept as treasurer with him on his trip abroad so investigators couldn't find them. Severance opposed college fraternities and believed them to be un-Christian. Later in his life he became involved in a controversy at Wooster College when he said he would not give the school any more money unless it outlawed fraternities and sororities; it did. In 1913 he fell ill while visiting his son John's office at the Arcade Building in Cleveland. He died soon after.

John Severance had made money on his own, in linseed oil, salt, and banking. John's sister, Elizabeth, was married to Dr. Dudley P. Allen, a prominent Cleveland physician. John and Elizabeth were Louis's only surviving children. Not long after Louis Severance died, John began to build an estate on rolling land east of the Cleveland city limits. The house included carved wood door moldings, a conservatory with an organ, and a gallery featuring a bronze replica of Verrocchio's fountain from the Palazzo Vecchio in Florence. Both John and his sister became philanthropists and figures in Cleveland society. In 1915, perhaps remembering a wish of their father's, perhaps on their own, John and Elizabeth set up a trust fund for their country cousins—David Benedict's daughters Mary, Hattie, Agnes, Fannie, Lillie, and Suzan. The fund was called the Norwalk Trust. Lillie Benedict Wickham collected her share of the trust income until her death in 1942, when it was divided among her three surviving children, Cora, Fred, and Anne Belle. At Cora's death in 1985, her share was divided between her surviving sons, David and Louis. When David died, his share was divided among my brother, my two sisters, and me. Now, because of a family affection 130 years old, and because of a fortune made in oil and sulphur pumped from the ground and used up generations ago, I receive, twice a year, a check for about $370.

•

Simeon Frazier lived in Columbus, Indiana, after his brief term in the army, and he went back to work for the Jamestown, Madison, & Indianapolis Railroad. Soon he was transferred to Madison, Indiana. Harry Edwin, my great-grandfather, was born there in 1868. Simeon and Sarah had four other children, Flora, Ella, Charles, and Alvin. In 1873 the J,M&I transferred him to Indianapolis, a city important to the Disciples of Christ Church. Indiana was said to have more members of the Disciples of Christ per square mile than any other state, and the most prominent lived in Indianapolis. The Disciples movement by now had begun to age, and it was running into problems. The fact that the Disciples rejected creeds, ecclesiastical organization, and central authority of any kind made it hard for the church to define just what it was. Disciples had always agreed most easily on those religious ideas they did not like, but after a while that was not enough. To strengthen their church, the Disciples had founded a university on the north side of Indianapolis. First they called it North Western Christian University, then changed the name to Butler University. If the Disciples in Indiana had any hierarchy, it was in the group that ran Butler. In 1876, Simeon was elected to the university's board of trustees and became the board's secretary.

Butler had a lot of support among Disciples and for a while was the wealthiest institution west of the Alleghenies. Its directors wanted to make it the great university of the Midwest. It began to expand, absorbing two Indianapolis medical schools which had faculty members who were not Disciples. Many Disciples became alarmed at this, so the board passed a resolution saying that in the future all Butler employees must be members of the church. Simeon voted in favor of the resolution. The newspapers said the real purpose of the resolution was to get rid of certain faculty members, among them David Starr Jordan, a former pupil of Agassiz and a popular professor of natural history known for his liberal theological views. In the controversy that followed, the resolution was rescinded but the board grew to include more members of the Disciples Church. The university lost face, but the Disciples were mollified. David Jordan left the same year for a position at Indiana University; later he would be the first president of Stanford. Butler endured, prospered, and did not become the great university of the Midwest.

The Disciples movement kept looking for new ways to grow without being too organized about it. Lack of any real central authority meant that individual congregations had a lot of power and that many congregations were run by small groups of older deacons who didn't want to do anything new. To get around this, many younger Disciples became involved in the church's Sunday school. For years, the Sunday-school movement kept the Disciples Church alive. Many churches had a large attendance of children and parents for Sunday-school classes but only a small group for regular services. Disciples from churches all over the state got together for annual summer meetings of the Indiana Christian Sunday School Association. These meetings lasted several days and included picnics and cultural events as well as preaching and religious instruction.

Among the crazes which swept America at about this time was a craze for culture. Public art museums opened in many cities, symphony orchestras were founded, people began to subscribe to magazines and to read more than just the Bible. Middle-class families bought pianos; the post-Civil War generation was the first in which large numbers took piano lessons. In 1874 an Ohio businessman and a Methodist minister founded an institution called the Chautauqua, a cultural gathering in the summer featuring lectures, informal classes in various subjects, and group discussions of books. Chautauquas drew great crowds all over, particularly in the East and Midwest. Thousands of men and women participated for the first time in intellectual life and talked and listened at round tables on topics like Milton, or Geology, or Temperance, or the Relations of Science and Religion; newspaper writers said Chautauqua was an Indian name meaning "talked to death." In Indiana, partly because of the success of the summer Sunday-school meeting, partly to give the church a new focus, the Disciples decided to organize their own Chautauqua.

They called it the Bethany Park Assembly. It was held on a rural forty-acre tract about thirty miles southwest of Indianapolis. Bethany Park first opened in 1884, for about two weeks in August, and assemblies of two or three weeks took place there every July or August for many years after. Disciples came from all over Indiana and elsewhere, and the park soon included the many summer cottages they built, as well as a hotel with a wide veranda, lawns, a lake, a boathouse, a sanitarium with mineral baths, a Disciples publishing company, and a 2,000-seat tabernacle with excellent acoustics. The gatherings often had days devoted to a special theme, such as Children's Day, or Christian Endeavor Day, for the young people in the Christian Endeavor movement, or Tourists' Day, at which non-Disciples were welcome. Visitors to Bethany Park rowed on the lake, picnicked, attended classes in vocal and instrumental music, watched stereopticon slide shows of photos of the Holy Land, and saw demonstrations of new inventions like the phonograph. In the tabernacle they heard lectures on such topics as "Are Preachers Fools?" and "James A. Garfield" (one of the most famous Disciples). Evangelical ministers, Disciple and non-, spoke, as did a variety of preachers who also whistled or sang. The assemblies heard hymns, like "Bringing in the Sheaves," written by the singing-evangelist Disciple, Knowles Shaw. In 1886 a big attraction was Indiana-born Lew Wallace, who read selected chapters from his *Ben-Hur* and lectured on "Turkey and the Turks." He had recently returned from serving as ambassador to Turkey, where as a favor to Standard Oil he had persuaded the Sultan to lift a ban on American kerosene.

Simeon Frazier worked to make Bethany Park a success; aside from his job and his family, it was the main accomplishment of his life. With Bethany Park his devotion to the Disciples movement and his knowledge of train timetables meshed. A short obituary of him in the *Christian Standard*, the Disciples' newspaper, says, "From its inception he was one of the active promoters of Bethany Park Assembly, and did more than almost any other man to carry forward that enterprise." The only piece of writing by him which I have been able to find appeared in the *Christian Standard* of July 27, 1895. It is a timetable for the Indianapolis & Vincennes Railroad—departures and arrivals for trains between those cities, intermediate points, and Bethany Park. Beneath the timetable appears a note:

Nos. 1, 2, 4, 5, 6, 7, 11 and 20 run daily. Nos. 9, 10, 15 and 16 run on Sundays only. Connections with other lines are made at Indianapolis, Martinsville, Gosport, Worthington, and Vincennes. Persons at Evansville and points south of there, purchase tickets at Evansville over E.&T.H., via Vincennes . . . [etc.] Be sure and get through round-trip tickets when you start, and don't fail to start.

S . F R A Z I E R , Sec.

B E T H A N Y P A R K , July 16.

Simeon died in Indianapolis in 1907. Among the several Disciples ministers assisting at his funeral was Jabez Hall, an associate of Alexander Campbell who had nursed that founder of the Disciples movement in the final days of his life. The Bethany Park Assembly began to lose attendance to rival summer encampments like the one at Fountain Park in Remington, Indiana. Some Disciples complained that Bethany Park put too much emphasis on culture and not enough on church business. Some disliked church festivals, instrumental choir music, choir singing, and other kinds of organized participation so much that they split from the Disciples and formed their own church. By 1927 the grounds at Bethany Park were in disrepair and the buildings were falling down. A beautification project improved the park in the thirties, but attendance at encampments continued to drop. The church tried to raise money to fix up the park again in 1951, but a fire in 1952 destroyed the hotel and other buildings. In 1954 the church sold most of the public buildings that survived.

When I was in Indiana a while ago, I decided to find Bethany Park. The map showed a town called Bethany near where the park used to be. As I drove up through southern Indiana I saw other church encampments set back among the trees, Methodist Bible camps and Baptist youth retreats, white board cottages in rows beyond white gates. Looking for Bethany I had to get off and on a four-lane highway wide as an airport runway. I asked at various warehouse-like buildings with multiacre parking lots where nobody had heard of Bethany Park. Finally I took a road that led down into a hollow, and I saw a sign that said BETHANY. There were cottages and narrow roads and a little hill and then a place where the road became a turnaround. I got out. A man with a baseball cap and blank spaces alternating between his front teeth was painting a porch. I asked where Bethany Park was and he said, "You're lookin' right at it."

He gestured to where the hotel used to be and the lake. He said, "The tabanacle used to set down there." I thanked him and went down

a trail through some overgrowth next to broken concrete stairs. A few
pieces of concrete under the grass showed where the tabernacle's seats
might have been. Larger broken slabs suggested the stage from which
the preachers had whistled and sung. Here and there I found worn
letters in the concrete, or a star symbol; the ruin was open to the sky.
Nearby, cottages ringed the edge of what used to be the lake, now a
hummocky meadow. I walked out on it, and water, not enough to
boat on, came through my running shoes. Stands of cattails marked
the wetter spots. To likely places on the margin I added boathouse,
hotel, sanitarium. A dam remained, wild rosebushes growing from its
cracks, and a dry spillway full of pieces of timber. At one side of the
former lake I climbed an incline to railroad tracks which appeared
active, but I could find no trace of the station from which eight or ten
trains a day used to depart during encampments. In a piece of lawn
between cottages stood a flagpole and a broken fountain with the same
star insignia. On a wall I saw a worn sign:

Welcome to Bethany

Religious   Literary

Scientific   Fellowship

The American Way

Though it was late spring, I saw nobody outdoors except for the
man painting. I walked down narrow roads past log cabins with wind
chimes and hummingbird feeders hanging from the porches. Some
cottages had stand-up swimming pools in the back yard. A few Shar-
Pei dogs were strolling around loose. Much of the land on or near the
Bethany Park site is now taken up by a junkyard for imported cars.
Beyond a corrugated plastic fence rusted a UN of auto bodies. A pile
of wooden pallets, some broken, leaned on the fence, and a trailer
made of a cut-off pickup truck had tilted onto its hitch. The trailer
was full of tires. A plastic soft-drink-cup cap with a plastic straw still
stuck through the hole lay on the driveway. By the locked gate, a sign
advertised foreign car parts and said this was the largest import dis-
mantler in Indiana.

•

O.A.S. Hursh delivered his first original oration in the chapel of
Heidelberg College on a Friday in October 1869. His subject: "Popular

Ignorance." He had turned twenty-three earlier that year. "Did not break down but felt very awkward," he noted in his diary. On a Friday in January 1870, he delivered his third oration, "The Unity of the System of Nature," to a large audience of students, professors, and visitors. Many had no doubt come to hear the speaker who followed him, the famous Dr. Dio Lewis of Boston. Of Dr. Lewis's speech, O.A.S. Hursh wrote:

[He] gave us a very entertaining and instructive lecture on health & the culture of the voice, in which he incidentally referred to my oration, and passed quite a compliment on it . . . He said: "It is like a *pyramid*, regularly built and nicely finished. One can easily remember such productions . . . on account of the methodical arrangement &c. But his *voice* was *bad* &c."

Dr. Lewis went from that criticism, presumably, to theories about the proper culture of the voice, and then to his laws of health, which O.A.S. Hursh also recorded:

Sit upright, *Stand erect*, and *walk* in a *soldier-like* manner. [Lewis's] contemplated book of four pages and and only four words: *Chin close to neck.*

Dio Lewis has been thoroughly forgotten, for someone who was so widely known. Lewis was a fitness guru, possibly the first American to gain fame and money with a system of exercise—his "New Gymnastics," which required no apparatus and encouraged the participation of women. Lewis's system (largely borrowed from someone else, in this case two Germans, as many exercise systems seem to be) taught free movement, group calisthenics, baton passing, and beanbag tossing. Lewis was said to have invented the beanbag. He also advocated exercise to the music of drums, piano, violin, and especially hand organ, foreshadowing aerobics and the dance workout tape. His illustrated book of exercises came out in 1862, and soon people as far away as Russia were doing them. He emphasized correct carriage of the body and said that keeping the chin close to the neck would bring everything else in line. A person who carried twenty pounds of sand in a sheepskin bag on the head for half an hour every morning and evening would attain the grace of the water carriers of Greece, he believed. He also regarded heavy dresses and restrictive undergarments as a life-sapping vice and favored loose-fitting

Garibaldi-style clothing for women. For reasons of morality and health
he taught strict temperance in drinking alcohol. Early in his career
he had been a temperance lecturer, but gave that up during years
when interest in temperance faded.

Lewis ran a girls' school, edited a weekly health newsletter, and
wrote books. Mainly, he traveled and lectured. In 1873 he returned
to Ohio to give a lecture in the music hall of Hillsboro, a town in the
south-central part of the state. Perhaps he had sensed a change in the
public mood; in any event, his topic this time was temperance. He
told the audience that, when he was a boy, his father had been a
terrible drunkard, and his mother, Delecta Barbour Lewis, finally
went to the saloon where his father drank and she knelt in front of it
and prayed, which act so affected the saloonkeeper that he closed up
permanently. Lewis's lecture, and this story in particular, ignited the
women of Hillsboro. That night a hundred or more of them organized
themselves into groups, and the next morning they marched to the
saloons, drugstores, and hotels of Hillsboro. The women knelt outside
on the stone steps, prayed, sang hymns; they stayed all day and relieved each other in shifts. A Hillsboro druggist filed suit against them
for damaging his business, local newspapers covered the story, and
soon women in other Ohio towns were organizing into groups and
marching on saloons.

In Washington, Ohio, where Lewis spoke next, praying bands
knelt on the ground and held temperance vigils through the coldest
day of the winter. A saloonkeeper got an injunction to keep the women
off his property; they prayed for the lawyer who served it, moved off
as far as they had to, and shone a locomotive headlight at the saloon
door. Bands of "Singing Sisters," as the newspapers called them,
marched in Waynesville, Morrow, Ripley, Lebanon, Athens, Mc-
Arthur, Logan, Lancaster, Greenville, and Norwalk. In some towns,
like New Lisbon and Mount Sterling, the liquor sellers capitulated.
Individual women whose lives liquor had made especially miserable
were delegated to smash in the heads of the barrels, and S. S. Block's
Common Whiskey and Quick's Best Whiskey and Detweiler's Black
Mariah flowed in the streets. At other places barkeeps' wives flung
pails of dirty dishwater at the women and cursed them, while drunkards mocked them with blasphemous prayers. In New Vienna, praying
women were drenched with beer by one Van Pelt, "the wickedest
man in Ohio," owner of a saloon called the Dead Fall. The women

did not retreat and after days of praying induced Van Pelt to abandon the trade. He afterward went over to their side and joined Dr. Lewis on the temperance platform, delivering speeches which moved audiences to tears despite what a Cincinnati paper described as his "horrid grammar."

Lewis did not think that praying bands would be as effective in cities as in towns, but women marched on liquor sellers in cities anyway. Mobs confronted them in Chicago and Cleveland, spitting at them and sometimes hitting and kicking. Police arrested some of the women for creating a public nuisance. In Pittsburgh, people threw pepper at them and burned sulphur under the sidewalk gratings where they knelt. In Dayton, four saloons closed down, which left 302 to go. The movement, by now named the Women's Crusade, drew on moral fervor left over from the abolition movement. In parts of Ohio people were said to be as excited as they had been when the Confederates fired on Fort Sumter. Prayer bands adapted Civil War songs to their new cause, like "A School on Every Hill" ("No saloon down in the valley, but a school on every hill/ . . . As we go marching on") to the tune of "The Battle Hymn of the Republic," or "We're Coming, Father Lewis." Lewis said that the hymn "Nearer, My God, to Thee," should be the keynote of the campaign.

Supporters of the Women's Crusade were encouraged by reports that praying bands had begun to organize in other parts of the country and even in the British Isles. Pro-temperance newspapers said the movement showed no sign of slowing down, but in fact it was over by spring, 1874. Lewis had hoped that morality-minded Easterners and New Englanders would join the cause, but few did, and the Women's Crusade remained mostly an Ohio phenomenon. Saloons were as popular as ever, and many that had closed reopened. The women of temperance gave second thought to their cause and decided they needed a bigger organization and longer-range tactics. In April 1874, a group founded the Women's Christian Temperance Union, which would grow to a membership of hundreds of thousands and great political power. The WCTU held its first meeting in Cleveland in November. Some years later, other temperance reformers founded what would become the most powerful temperance group of all, the Anti-Saloon League, in Oberlin. Ohio became the center of the temperance movement and of the campaign for legal prohibition which grew from it.

Dio Lewis gave up other lecture engagements to lead the Women's Crusade in Ohio, and after it had tapered off returned to the hotel-with-Turkish-baths he ran in Boston. Lewis never believed in prohibition, preferring "moral suasion" as the most effective weapon against the drunkard and the liquor seller. That idea lost fashion among temperance forces, especially after its failure in Ohio, and later when Lewis lectured he got into arguments with prohibitionists. He did not think selling whiskey was as bad as stealing a horse, and prohibitionists said it was worse. The WCTU changed from a policy of moral suasion to a prohibition stance in 1879. Lewis remained one of the WCTU's heroes despite his insistence that prohibition was tyranny. Lewis sold his hotel, moved to California, suffered a stroke, moved back to Massachusetts, opened a sanitarium, and began to publish a magazine, *Dio Lewis's Monthly for Jolly Folks*. He sold his sanitarium, moved to New York City, moved to Long Island, built a steam-heated hennery and began to raise chickens, lectured on gymnastic training at Martha's Vineyard, and moved to Yonkers. He incorporated ideas about temperance into his over-all program of diet and health designed to cure the main weakness of the American character, which he identified as "nervous irritability." In Yonkers, he hurt his leg while horseback riding, developed erysipelas (a streptococcus infection) in the injury, and died in May 1886. He was sixty-three; those who knew him said the real cause of death came from overwork.

O.A.S. Hursh belonged to the Independent Order of Good Templars, an organization which promoted temperance and good works. His wife and daughters joined the WCTU. They not only disapproved of drinking, they thought a person should not live too close to a saloon. O.A.S. Hursh's son, Osie, was raised to keep his distance from people in the liquor trade; he regretted that a fellow band member worked as a distiller by day. In Indiana, Simeon Frazier would have felt the same. His church usually refused fellowship to people who made, sold, or drank liquor, and strict temperance became an unofficial tenet of the Disciples of Christ. The Norwalk *Reflector* supported temperance and the Women's Crusade, when Norwalk women marched on saloons and held temperance prayer meetings in the Methodist church every afternoon for weeks at a time. A leader of the movement in Norwalk was Charles Wickham's wife, Emma. A hundred and twenty years ago, every ancestor I know of either believed strongly in temperance or said nothing for the record against it.

C H A P T E R   9

CHARLES WICKHAM came home from the war in July of 1865. By
August, he had resumed his law practice and was selling life insurance
for the Lumberman's Insurance Company of Chicago. He and Emma
had two young children, Charles Jr. and Grace. In November of 1866
Emma gave birth to another boy, Louis. In 1868 Emma wrote a letter
to her brother, away at college:

> Dear Brother Sam:
>   I received your letter of January 31st a little over a week
> ago. I suppose when you wrote it you had no idea I would ever
> answer it, at least not so soon as this. Well I thought I would
> surprise you.

Lotus Lilies, painted by my grandmother's uncle, Charles C. Curran, in 1888. When it was
shown at the Académie Julian in Paris in 1890, a French critic wrote, "M. Curran has given
me a fierce desire to go for a boat trip in the middle of the LOTUS LILIES OF LAKE
ERIE, UNITED STATES OF AMERICA in the company of the charming women who
boat there so placidly" *(Courtesy the Daniel J. Terra Museum of American Art)*

Mary has just gone from here having spent the afternoon
with me. How am I ever going to let her go so far away; it makes
me sick to think of it.

I have no girl yet, but get along very well with my work. My
health was never much better than it is now. I have had two girls
engaged this week, but neither of them came to time; the last
one wouldn't come because I wanted her to stay home once in a
while with the children and let me go to church. Verily girls are
getting on their high heels. I have some little trials, but I guess I
am as happy as it is the lot of most people to be . . .

There comes a faint cry from my bedroom. What business
has Louis trespassing on my time I wonder. I must go and give
him a drink . . . [He] grows very cunning. He tries very hard to
talk, and says a good many words. The other day Gracie was saying "blind man"; and he looked up and said "blind man" . . .
[When] Gracie said "Mama Louie has got a dirty nose" he took
up his dress and wiped it and went on with his play.

Charlie talks a good deal about going with Mary to Arizona
when she goes back . . . She was telling him one day that he
must learn all he could for maybe there would be some little
heathen children there and they would have a Sunday school and
he would have to be a teacher. "Well," said he, "they'll have to
know something themselves for I don't know much to teach
them." . . . One day I was reading him a story about a naughty
boy, suddenly he said very earnestly, "That's just like me."

I suppose you will write to me very soon again. If my letter
is not very interesting, I go out so little and am so taken up by
home cares that I have little news to tell you in my letters. That
God may bless you and keep you and make you a Christian is my
daily prayer.

Emma's health was indeed sound; she would live another fifty-
one years. Sam would graduate from college and eventually return to
Norwalk and become a law partner of her husband. Mary, her sister,
would spend many years at posts in Arizona and elsewhere in the
West with her husband, army lieutenant John Q. Adams. Charles Jr.'s
estimation of himself proved to be sort of true; if not a "naughty boy,"
he was by most accounts a disappointment in later life, moving from

one occupation to another and failing at business enterprises from which his family had to bail him out. Grace grew up, went to a young woman's seminary, and married Charles C. Curran, a painter of a school sometimes called American Impressionism; he painted her often, and her face may be seen in a number of museums. Louis, the fourteen-month-old baby crying for his mother and wiping his nose on his dress, was my great-grandfather.

Young children of both sexes wore dresses back then. An early photo of Louis shows him in a military-style tunic belted at the waist and buttoned diagonally from right shoulder to left hem. He also wears white stockings and black ankle-strap shoes, the kind little girls today wear to parties. He has let someone neatly comb his hair, and he sits at ease with legs crossed on a tasseled couch in a photography studio in Norwalk; evidently he enjoyed dressing well from an early age. Of his childhood he remembered especially the thick, scratchy woolen underwear his mother made him put on from ankle to neck, October through May. He tried to take it off whenever he could. His brother Charlie and his uncle Frank Wickham, both about six years older than he, taught him to swim by throwing him into the east branch of the Huron River, and after that he was a good swimmer. In the spring Norwalk Creek would overflow cornfields and meadows, and Louis and his friend Fred Benedict and other boys would skip school, walk upstream about a mile or so, take off all their clothes, and float downstream with the fast-moving floodwater, sometimes knocking against submerged fenceposts on the way. The creek would carry them almost to the center of town; then they would walk back to their clothes naked, dodging from tree to tree.

Norwalk was a smaller town when Louis was young than it became even thirty years later. Lamplighters lit the gas streetlamps at dusk in winter and extinguished them at nine-thirty. Frederick Wickham, Louis's grandfather, served as the town's mayor, and every night before he went to bed he would try doors on Main Street and check at the police station. One July night about nine o'clock a six-year-old boy disappeared from his home, and the town's church bells rang an alarm, and citizens turned out to look for him. The boy was found at a relative's house south of Norwalk, nine miles away. Norwalk got fresh produce from the farms around it; when the roads were too muddy for wagons, the townspeople knew they would do without eggs and milk for a while. In May, when they saw that the pastures were green and fat, they imagined the yellow-grass butter they would be eating soon. Big stands of woods grew nearby, with plenty of game—squirrels, rabbits, partridge, quail, woodcock, and sometimes passenger pigeons. The pigeons had not yet become extinct and flew over in great numbers in early spring. Louis hunted the woods occasionally without much success, using a double-barreled muzzle-loading shotgun his grandfather had given him. The gun was so big he had to set the butt on the ground and stand on a stump to load it. Once, he was hunting with a friend and the friend's gun went off by accident and the charge passed by him about six inches away.

Louis's parents had lost a child to measles during the war, and he later thought that may have been why they hated to let him out of their sight. Whatever the reason, they took him and not the older children with them on long trips. When he was seven he accompanied them on a trip of almost five months, which he would remember the rest of his life. He and his parents left Norwalk on June 1, went by train to Chicago, saw new buildings rising on blocks burned by the Great Fire of 1871, and then went on to Salina, Kansas. They stayed in Salina two weeks visiting Louis's grandfather Wildman, who had moved there a few years before. From Salina they crossed the Great Plains on the Union Pacific Railroad. Louis saw Indians and buffalo —the year was 1874, the Sioux and Cheyenne had not yet been conquered, George Custer lived, and buffalo were still numerous enough along the route that passengers sometimes shot them from the trains.

Louis and his parents stopped at a hotel in Denver and took a scenic excursion up Clear Creek Canyon on a railroad that crept and wound along the canyon sides. Then they went back to Denver, on to Cheyenne, and continued west over the Union Pacific–Central Pacific. They rode the train for four nights and four and a half days, across deserts and mountains. They got off in Sacramento, took another train to Redding, then traveled 115 miles to the mining town of Yreka by stagecoach. The stage rocked so much they felt seasick, and the dust poured in and covered them. The wagon track ascended heights from which they looked down on the tops of pines thousands of feet below—"Truly *wonderful!*" Charles Wickham wrote to his family in Norwalk. His wife was perhaps four months pregnant at the time. Her

brother-in-law, Lieutenant Adams, met them at the Yreka stage station. The next day they set out with him in a spring wagon on another
115-mile journey over mountains, to Fort Klamath, the post where
he and Mary lived.

Along the way, the lieutenant pointed out to them sites of interest
from the war with the Modoc Indians the year before. Conflict between
the Modocs and the whites had begun when the California gold rush
overran Indian lands, and proceeded through removal of the Indians
to a reservation, return of the Indians, attempted reremoval, skirmishing, warfare, murder of settlers, murder of peace commissioners,
eventual defeat of the Modocs, and the hanging of four leaders, including the famous Captain Jack. From a signal post Lieutenant Adams
had observed the meeting at which Captain Jack and others shot and
killed an army general and a Methodist minister of the peace commission, and he sent the first news of the murders. The army held,
tried, and hanged the Modocs at Fort Klamath; Lieutenant Adams
took as souvenirs a piece of the rope and a lock of Captain Jack's hair.

Louis and his parents found the climate at the fort cool and the
water from the mountain springs the clearest they had ever seen. They
went horseback riding for miles along mountain meadows that
stretched beyond the fort. Louis liked meeting the soldiers and talking
to them. He and his father did a lot of fishing. He later said the fish
were so hungry he had to hide behind a tree to bait his hook. His
father wrote home describing the fish he caught in the Williamson
River when he went with a big party of soldiers, wives, children, and
a cook tent for a fish fry. Charles fly-fished for the first time in his life
and caught rainbow trout by the score. One day he caught fifty-six.
Many were between three and five pounds, and a companion caught
a rainbow eleven and a quarter pounds. Charles's largest was six
pounds; it stripped line off in bursts that made the reel sing, it jumped
and came sailing through the air toward him so he had to scramble
up the bank reeling in slack, it jumped again four or five feet above
the surface, it sounded and gave violent tugs, it sulked on the bottom
and refused to budge, and then it did everything all over again.

The Wickhams stayed at the fort for perhaps a month. When they
started home, the wagon Emma was riding on the way to Yreka hit a
rock and overturned, throwing her to the ground. Louis had been
riding behind with some soldiers who were being mustered out and

had drunk whiskey along the way. They managed to stop their mules just short of the wagon. When Lieutenant Adams saw how drunk the soldiers were, he used profanity Louis had never heard before. Emma, by now five months pregnant, was knocked unconscious. The men righted the wagon and laid Emma in it and took her to a cabin nearby, where she remained unconscious for three days. When she could travel the family went on, eventually arriving in San Francisco, where they boarded a steamer for the Isthmus of Panama. They reached the isthmus, crossed it, boarded another steamer, sailed to New York City, and went from there to Norwalk by train.

They got back to Norwalk on the twentieth of October, and on November 27 Emma had her baby, a boy the family named Winthrop. She would have two more children, Romeyn and Mary Grace (Mayno). Of the six Wickham children, Winthrop would be the runaway. Perhaps because of his travels while in the womb, he liked to roam the town. Louis, eight years his senior, often had the job of tracking him down at suppertime. Once, when Winthrop was about six, he sprained his knee while running up some planks against a fence, and he was laid up for a long spell. Another time he was run over by a hay wagon on West Main Street; somehow he rolled into a depression in the road and the wheels passed over him and left him unhurt. His mother made him a harness that fastened in back where he couldn't reach and tied it to a fifty-foot clothesline and tied the clothesline to a sweet-apple tree in the side yard; Winthrop got his black spaniel, Curly, to chew the line until it was frayed enough to break. One morning Winthrop did not show up for breakfast and the family went looking for him. His father finally found him at the passenger station of the Lake Shore & Michigan Southern Railway, sitting on the cowcatcher of a waiting westbound train.

Louis's other jobs around the house were chopping wood for the kitchen stove and milking the family cow. One fall with the help of a cousin he chopped up a large woodpile and earned enough money to go to Cleveland and sit in the gallery of the Euclid Avenue Opera House for a performance of *The Roman Gladiator*. He did not like milking, and the family's first cow gave ten quarts mornings and evenings. Louis was happy when she kicked over the milk pail and he didn't have to carry the full amount up to the house. The cow was always jumping over fences and getting stuck halfway over, and Louis secretly hoped she would suffer some accident and die. One winter he bought two piglets and kept them in a corner of the barn and fed them out of her corn, oats, and bran. His father noticed the increase in feed bills, found out about the pigs, and let Louis keep them. Louis sold the pigs for twenty dollars in the spring.

Charles Wickham became prosecuting attorney of Huron County. One of his first convictions came against a traveling peddler named Bennett Scop, accused of murdering and robbing another peddler. Scop, a Polish Jew who claimed to have served in the Tsar's cavalry, never stopped saying he was innocent. The county hanged him in Norwalk a few months after the verdict, and buried him in a shirt on the front of which he had written the names of everyone who had been kind to him. Charles ran for Congress as a Republican in 1878 and lost, but in 1880 he was elected judge of the Court of Common Pleas. He presided over cases of forgery, selling liquor on Election Day, selling silverware without a license, assault, assault with intent to rape, arson, seduction, placing obstructions on railroad tracks, and first-degree murder. A man from a neighboring town was found guilty of murdering his wife with an ax; Charles called this "one of the most cruel and relentless crimes in criminal annals," and sentenced him to hang. As one of the town's leading Republicans, Charles took part in the torchlight parades which the party held on evenings around election time. In 1886 he ran for Congress, made campaign speeches which were "applauded to the echo" (according to his father's newspaper), and defeated a Democrat named Bristor. During his first term as representative from Ohio's fourteenth district he became friends with the representative from the nineteenth, another former prosecuting attorney named William McKinley.

Louis attended the Norwalk grammar school, its sand playground marked with holes and rings made by kids playing marbles. He spent a lot of time with Fred Benedict, and doubtless knew Fred's younger sister, Lillie. He and Fred and other boys swam in a deep place in Norwalk Creek, into which emptied the refuse from a brewery and the sewer from the St. Charles Hotel, suffering no ill effects aside from the bloodsuckers they had to pull off their arms and legs sometimes. He loved circuses; a Barnum circus that came to town when he was fourteen advertised a "wild" Zulu girl *only seven months in this country* sitting on a platform and reading the New York *Ledger*.

Frederick A. Wildman, Charles P. Wickham, and Charles's daughter Mayno on the porch of the Wickham farmhouse on the outskirts of Norwalk. The photo probably dates from the 1890s; Frederick Wildman died in 1899

Emily Jane Wickham in front of the Wickham farmhouse. A lawn occupies the site today. Nothing in the photo remains but the maple tree in the foreground

Every Christmas he and his family joined sixty or seventy other relatives and in-laws at the home of his grandparents Frederick and Lucy Wickham. The little kids would wait upstairs while the adults ate Christmas dinner downstairs, but the kids became so obstreperous, yelling and pushing each others downstairs, that after a number of Christmases it was decided to feed the kids first. The teenagers would wait on the little ones, then sit down with the grownups. Afterward relatives who lived in town would head home, stuffed, while the dozens who had come from farther away found places to sleep at Frederick and Lucy's.

When Louis went to Norwalk High School, clever things to say among his peers included the phrases "I should blush to murmur" and "That's a horse on me!" Perhaps Louis did not get good enough marks, perhaps the school did not provide the courses he needed; in any event, when he was seventeen his parents sent him to the preparatory school of Adelbert College, in Hudson. (Today it is called Western Reserve Academy; my brothers and I went there.) He later said that he was kicked out for borrowing two anvils from a local farmer, setting one anvil on the floor of a building on campus, filling the anvil's hardy hole with gunpowder, raising the second anvil above the first anvil with a rope, dropping the second anvil, and causing an explosion that blew out windows. The school impounded the anvils, and Louis got caught when the farmer showed up to reclaim them. Whether or not the story is true, Louis was still enrolled in March of 1885, when Fred Benedict died. The *Reflector* noted that Louis had returned from Hudson for the funeral. He and five other young friends of Fred served as pallbearers.

The next fall, Louis left Norwalk on the Wheeling & Lake Erie Railroad on his way East to enter the freshman class at Princeton. His class ('89) would produce doctors, career diplomats, a president of the Goodyear Rubber Company, a famous Catskill trout fisherman, and many Presbyterian ministers. (Of one, the Class Record would later note: "He has a remarkable collection of Sunday school equipment of every kind.") A single Japanese name turns up among the 150 or so members of the class; none of the rest appears to be anything other than Wasp. First term, Louis took Latin (Livy, Latin Composition), Greek (Xenophon, and the *Iliad*, Books XVI, XVIII, and XXII), algebra, geometry (Todhunter's Euclid), and English (Elementary Discourse, Diction, and Sentences). He got the equivalent of C's and D's, for a low C average. Later he could recall no work of his in college that did him much good. He enjoyed browsing about the library and talking with classmates Bob Speer and Bill Jenney. At the end of the year his average had slipped to D; at the end of the next year it was even lower, with failing grades in math, French, and biology; and near-failing in Latin, Greek, and English. He left Princeton in November of his junior year and did not return. The family later said he had been kicked out for stealing an exam to help a roommate. The college gradebooks do show a stolen paper on his record, in a course on Horace and Cicero, but that was during his freshman year.

After Princeton Louis went to Washington, D.C., probably to work as an aide to his father in Congress. There he also studied law on his own. In October of 1889 he joined his father's law firm as junior partner and began to practice in Norwalk.

●

Lillie Benedict did not go to college. She attended Norwalk High School and lived in her family's house at 80 East Seminary Street. The death of her brother Fred devastated her, and perhaps caused her to become closer to Fred's friend Louis Wickham. She was nearly two years younger than Louis and had known him most of her life. On August 9, 1892, she and Louis were married in the Episcopal church in Norwalk. The church was decorated with green vines and plants against a background of white, the maid of honor wore a gown of pale green crepe, and the bride wore white crepe and carried a large bouquet of white roses. A Princeton friend of Louis's, William "Boogus" Chase, served as best man. The six bridesmaids wore white dotted muslin trimmed with ribbons and lace, and carried bouquets of fern leaves and pond lilies.

The pond lilies were flowers of the American lotus, which blooms in summer on a nearby Lake Erie estuary called Old Woman Creek. The lotus lily is large and of a yellowish-ivory color, and it grows on a stalk above the surface of the water. It looks a lot like the lotus in ancient Egyptian friezes. Lotus lilies seem to have been a common accessory in summer weddings in Norwalk back then. Charles Curran married Louis's sister Grace in the summer of 1888, and that same year he did a painting of two young women in a rowboat on Old Woman creek gathering lotus lilies. The painting, *Lotus Lilies*, is perhaps his best-known. The women, eyes downcast, sit beneath a green parasol; one wears a flowered bonnet, the other a white straw boater. The woman in the bonnet holds five or six lilies in her lap, with more heaped at her feet in the bottom of the rowboat, which has oarlock holes but no oars. The woman in the straw hat reaches from the boat for another lily. Two men approach in a boat in the far background, and beyond them light from the lake spills around the trees. Curran did many paintings which identified women with flowers. Critics have seen a reactionary purpose in this, an attempt to rebut new ideas of the independence of women by portraying them as flowerlike, decorative, passive. *Lotus Lilies* hangs in the Terra Museum of American Art in Chicago. I had not seen any political content in it at all until I heard it is the favorite painting of former First Lady Nancy Reagan.

Freshwater estuaries are rare, and so in 1970 Ohio and the federal government made Old Woman Creek a nature and research preserve. Now when the lotus lilies are in bloom the creek still looks much the same as when Curran painted it in 1888. One afternoon in late July I went there, looked at the reproduction of *Lotus Lilies* in the visitor center, and walked down to the creek. The muck along the shore was a byway of raccoon tracks. Something had left piles of wild cherrystone scat on fallen logs. Light coming through leaves tinted spiderwebs green. On the other side an egret high-stepped through the shallows, moving its snaky neck. I waded into the painting, disturbing slicks of duckweed. Curran's idyll had not prepared me for what a mess everything was. The leaves of the lotus faced toward the sun. They were large, round, and concave; on their long stalks they looked like umbrellas blown inside out. The understory was a litter of lily petals, dead stalks, and wrecked old leaves decomposing on the water's surface. Spiderwebs hung everywhere. The *Lotus Lilies* ladies may have been passive and flowerlike, but clearly they were not afraid of spiders. I smelled a lily and looked inside. Louis and Lillie's wedding was a big society event in Norwalk, and the church was crowded. The bridesmaids emerged from the vestry room, marched slowly down the aisle to the vestibule, joined the bride and maid of honor, and followed the four ushers back up the aisle to the altar. Lotus lilies, I now saw, are sticky on the inside, with a seedpod as big as a showerhead and dozens of long, antenna-like stamens—which, in the bridesmaids' bouquets, probably trembled.

•

Louis and Lillie had their first child, Suzan, the following June. Two years later, they had Cora. Louis settled down to life as an "ordinary country lawyer," he wrote to his college alumni magazine. He dreamed of lawsuits involving thousands of dollars, or of murder cases where he would surprise witnesses with clever questions and the judge with the depth of his legal knowledge, but his actual victories were more mundane. One morning he had a big stack of flannel cakes for breakfast and fed the leftovers to the family dog. He went to the courthouse and was speaking for the defense before the judge and jury when the dog walked in, stopped by his feet, and threw up. Louis made a remark about the dog and the case for the prosecution that got a laugh.

He put on some weight, but remained long and lanky. He smoked Sweet Caporal cigarettes and stood angled back in a way that made you notice his shoes. His children remembered him as a good father who liked to do things. At bedtime he read them poems by Eugene Field in a clear, dramatic voice. After they got old enough for the circus he always took a day off when it came to town so he could go with them. In the mid-nineties his father, his father-in-law David Benedict, and two other relatives bought several acres of Lake Erie waterfront and built cottages. They called the property Oak Bluff because of the red oaks that grew there; Charles Curran painted Louis, Lillie, and the baby Suzan sitting beneath the oaks with the lake beyond. At first Louis and Lillie had no cottage of their own, and stayed in the Benedict cottage or pitched tents. A few years later Louis built a cottage with a legal-fee windfall of five hundred dollars. The children stayed there with their mother for weeks at a time in the summer, playing on the wide beach, fishing, harvesting wild rice in Cranberry Creek, picking pink hibiscus. Louis rode up from Norwalk on the electric railway nearly every evening after work and then walked two miles to the cottage from the nearest stop. A grocery wagon drawn by a team of horses came twice a week, and an ice wagon delivered blocks packed in straw and sawdust. From the bluff the family could watch the occasional sailboats that passed or the sidewheel steamboats that ran between cities on the lake. Louis wore a boater and a white linen suit, even when he took children fishing with cane poles for perch and sunfish in Old Woman Creek.

Louis's runaway brother, Winthrop, fulfilled the auguries of his youth and went West almost as soon as he was old enough. He had a degree in mining engineering and a young wife, Blanche Woodward, of Norwalk. He worked in a mining camp in Ely, Nevada, which he thought too rough for Blanche, so she stayed in Denver, where she knew people. In 1901 she was pregnant with their first child. Diabetes ran in the Woodward family, and back then there was no insulin. At the birth of her baby Blanche went into shock and convulsions, and then died of kidney failure. Winthrop received word in Ely. He wired the news to his father, adding, "I am heartbroken." Louis took the train from Norwalk to Denver to help Winthrop bring Blanche's body and the baby home. A nurse accompanied them, although a relative wrote, "Lou would be as careful and tender a nurse as most women."

Louis and Lillie had two more children—Fred, named for her brother, and Anne Belle. Relatives say Lillie also had abortions, a practice not unknown even in small-town Ohio a hundred years ago, to judge from newspaper reports of unidentified fetuses turning up in culverts and trash barrels around town. Lillie owned many rental properties, no doubt inherited from her father. Collecting rents the first of the month took her around the county and introduced her to all kinds of people. She worried especially about the families in Norwalk's Negro neighborhood. She often said that of all she was thankful for, she was most thankful she hadn't been born black. Her children grew up. Fred would be as tall as his father and much heavier. Fred, Louis, and at least one of the girls snored loudly. Lillie slept in a bedroom by herself, with a bottle of whiskey in a bureau drawer nearby. When the family stayed up at the lake, the cottage with its thin walls resounded at night with snores.

Louis became county prosecutor. Other lawyers of the Huron County Bar Association liked him and assumed he would one day become a judge as his father had. The family moved from Benedict Avenue to West Main Street. Cora met Ray Frazier and fell in love, and they began their long engagement. In 1918 Suzan came home for Cora's wedding, fell ill with appendicitis, died. The family left no record of their grief, except for a large portrait of Suzan which Charles Curran painted the next year. It shows Suzan in a light-pink strapless gown, seated with her hands in her lap holding a bouquet of roses. It used to hang on Louis and Lillie's living-room wall; now it hangs on mine.

Great-grandfather Louis W. Wickham as a child (inset), and later in life. At left he is on the lawn of his house in Norwalk in about 1916 with his son Fred, wife Lillie, and daughters Anne Belle, Suzan, and Cora. At right he stands with unidentified man, possibly Cleveland political boss Maurice Maschke

A parade on Sunday School Day in Norwalk about 1910. Cora holds the reins in the pony cart

Around the turn of the century, in country towns everywhere, a person who wanted a drink would have found it harder and harder to get one. The Women's Crusade had faded away, but the movement for legal prohibition grew, schools instructed students in the evils of alcohol, prohibition amendments began to come up for discussion in Congress, Mrs. Rutherford B. Hayes banished intoxicating liquors from the White House during her husband's administration ("The water flowed like champagne," said a foreign ambassador), and at the death of Frances Willard, president and moving spirit of the Women's Christian Temperance Union, four states declared her birthday a school holiday. Prohibition was basically a battle of the rural districts against the cities. Its supporters tended to be country Protestants— Baptists, Presbyterians, Methodists, and Disciples of Christ. It expressed a dislike many country people had for Catholics, wine- and beer-drinking foreigners, ethnic types, and godless cities; for a while forces for prohibition included the Ku Klux Klan.

Early temperance and prohibition groups had been Republican, but the Anti-Saloon League aided prohibition candidates regardless of party. The league's counsel and legislative officer, Wayne B. Wheeler, became the most powerful Washington lobbyist in history. The league and other groups worked for prohibition laws at every level, and by 1913 more than half the population was living under some kind of prohibition. Liquor taxes had provided as much as two-thirds of the revenue of the federal government, so in the same year anti-liquor votes put the Sixteenth Amendment through Congress and the state legislatures, it made legal a national income tax, removing a big obstacle to national prohibition. In 1918 Congress passed a constitutional amendment prohibiting the manufacture, sale, and transportation of intoxicating beverages. The amendment, the eighteenth, received the required number of state ratifications by January 16, 1919. It went into effect a year later, at one minute past midnight, January 16, 1920. Country churches celebrated the event with midnight prayer services; in Chicago someone hijacked a truckload of whiskey.

Prohibition said nothing about purchase, possession, or consumption of alcoholic beverages. You could make apple cider, leave it in your garage to harden, and get drunk on it in your parlor without breaking any law. No law could do anything about what happened chemically to fruit juices if left to sit. Of course, putting additives in the juice or otherwise treating it would constitute manufacture, a crime. Prohibition brought the thrill of lawbreaking to millions who had never really done it before, and gave other law-abiding people opportunity for defeating the purpose of the law. On September 30, 1920, an item appeared in a Norwalk newspaper:

> NORWALK'S CELLARS EVIDENTLY
> WILL BE WELL-STOCKED
> Norwalk's cellars will contain more intoxi-
> cants this fall than at any time in the history
> of the city. This prediction has been made
> by more than one observer.
>
> In many homes, the entire family has
> been put at work making wine or home brew.
> Grapes, elderberries, and other fruits are
> being used in great abundance, according to
> reports.

At about the same time, two strange characters began to be seen in and near Norwalk—in the local poolroom, at a dance pavilion on the lake, in a tourist cottage at a lake resort called Mitiwanga. One was a handsome and dapper man of forty-three who went by the name Mail Pouch; his real name was Charles Fulton. His partner, a boy of fourteen who called himself Lucky Strike, came from Pittsburgh and had been known as Herman Sell. Mail Pouch and Lucky Strike knew how to smoke cigarettes, play pool, sing, and entertain the flashier of the small-town boys. Mail Pouch came from England and spoke with an accent; both he and Lucky Strike had charm. Sometimes they made money by carving lake stones into cameos and watch fobs for fraternity men in Ohio college towns. Also, they bootlegged. Like anyone else with the price of a newspaper, they knew about the homemade beer and wine in the cellars of Norwalk. Young men they became friendly with learned that Mail Pouch and Lucky Strike would pay for any of the beer or wine they could get. That fall, Norwalk teenagers began jimmying doors and popping hinges and stealing liquor from their neighbors' cellars.

Petty crime in general seemed to be up in Norwalk. People came out from stores to find that the blankets left on the hoods of their cars had disappeared. Items were taken from the shelves of the department store. Someone stole two pistols from the historical museum. The railroad station, the laundry, the telegraph office all reported thefts. Three boys and three girls were suspended from the high school for staying in the building after hours, ringing the school bell, and cutting capers. Many people did not notice at first that beer and wine were missing from their cellars. Then one night a sixteen-year-old Norwalk boy named Kenneth Hakes entered the chapel of St. Paul's Episcopal Church for the purpose of stealing Communion wine. The rector, C. S. Gross, caught him, and although Hakes had no wine in his possession, he told the rector what he had intended. The rector called the police. When they questioned the boy, he told about Lucky Strike and Mail Pouch and the cellar burglaries.

At this, the town became unglued. Hakes and the boys he implicated were all from good Norwalk families. A mass meeting was held at the Episcopal church on the problem of teenage delinquency. A probate judge addressed assemblies at the junior high and high schools and reminded students of crimes they could be sent to the reformatory for, such as smoking cigarettes (if under eighteen) or wandering about the streets at night. The mayor said delinquency was the parents' fault, that in the country town he grew up in parents knew where their children were at night, and that in his opinion Norwalk should pass an ordinance against poolrooms because of the deviltry hatched there. People said it was the fault of the recent Great War. People said it was the fault of too much freedom with automobiles, or of the lake resorts, which instilled in youth "a strange, callow and perverted philosophy of life." The Wickham family no longer owned the *Reflector*, having sold it in 1913 to R. C. Snyder, who published another Norwalk paper called the *Evening Herald* and merged the two into the *Reflector-Herald*. R. C. Snyder took out after the "boy thieves," listing their names and crimes in front-page stories with big headlines. He had himself been among their victims: sherry wine was stolen from his cellar the previous October on a night when he and his wife were attending a touring opera company's production of *Carmen*.

As a third-generation parishioner whose great-grandfather had founded the church, Lillie Wickham carried some influence at St. Paul's. She and Louis were friends with Rev. Gross. He had baptized their youngest child, and my father, their first grandchild. Lillie believed the church should be lenient with Kenneth Hakes. He had not actually done anything but enter the church, he had confessed, he was contrite, he had no previous misdeeds, and he was only sixteen. R. C. Snyder and his wife also belonged to the church, and they disagreed. Lillie was known to get into feuds, and she did not avoid this one. She called Snyder a whited sepulchre ("Woe unto you, scribes and Pharisees, hypocrites! for ye are like unto whited sepulchres, which indeed appear beautiful outward, but are within full of dead men's bones, and of all uncleanness." Matt. 23:27), a remark which apparently tore it.

Charges against Hakes were not dropped. He pleaded guilty to attempted robbery and was sentenced to a term at the Lancaster Reformatory. A day or two after the sentencing he disappeared, leaving his parents a note which said he had gone to Cleveland to join the navy.

The police had put out an alert for Mail Pouch and Lucky Strike. They caught Mail Pouch in Columbus and brought him back to Norwalk for trial. Lucky Strike was apprehended soon after. Bail for both was a thousand dollars, which they could not make. After some weeks in jail they came to trial. Mail Pouch was convicted of selling liquor and grand larceny, and he received a sentence of one to seven years in the state penitentiary. Lucky Strike was convicted of grand larceny. Although R. C. Snyder's newspaper wanted all the Norwalk boys charged in the burglaries to get the same treatment as Kenneth Hakes, none of the ten or so was sentenced to the reformatory. Perhaps the judge thought he had been too hard on Hakes; he released all the boys on bench parole. They were not to drink, gamble, or go around with bad companions. Stories about the boy thieves slipped from the front page and disappeared.

Some months later, a Huron County judge named Stephen M. Young died unexpectedly during an operation in Cleveland. Louis had been a friend of his and helped to carry his coffin. After the funeral, political and other organizations in the county sent petitions to the governor suggesting names for Judge Young's replacement. Young had been judge of the Court of Common Pleas. Louis wanted the job. He received the endorsement of the county bar association, and although there were other candidates, he and his friends thought he would get it. R. C. Snyder and the *Reflector-Herald* had a history of strong support for the governor, whose name was Harry Davis. The paper had endorsed Davis at election time, praised his administration, and ran an eight-part series of articles with the governor's byline, along with a large front-page picture of him. According to an account passed down from Lillie, Snyder and his wife held a grudge against her for the Hakes incident. In revenge, Lillie said, Snyder called his friend the governor and persuaded him to give the judgeship to someone else. The governor chose a local attorney and former prosecutor named Joseph R. McKnight. The story in the *Reflector-Herald* began, "Good evening, Judge McKnight!"

Louis was fifty-five at the time. Wisely or not, he had spent much of his life anticipating his rise to the bench his father had once held. People in town felt bad for him. The Kiwanis Club elected him president the week after the governor's announcement, but Lillie was not consoled. She said, "I will never live in this town again." Within a few months Louis had accepted a position with a law firm in Cleveland. Of the children, only Anne Belle was still at home. Louis and Lillie and Anne Belle soon moved to Cleveland to an apartment on Lancashire Boulevard. Both Louis and Lillie had spent their whole lives in Norwalk. Lillie had never lived anywhere else. Her family's association with the town went back more than a century, his family's nearly as long. They never returned to Norwalk for longer than a visit until they died.

For the Wickhams, leaving Norwalk meant a change in class. Norwalk was not nearly as big or rich as Cleveland, but it had history and influence and respectability, and in Norwalk the Wickhams were somebody. When they left they gave up being country gentry and became upper-middle-class professionals like many others. In Norwalk they had owned an ample brick house on Main Street, in Cleveland they always rented. Perhaps the change made them nervous. They relied on their rich cousin, Elizabeth Severance Allen, to help them get established in the city. Anne Belle, a teenager then, paid special attention to Cousin Elizabeth and partly thanks to her became a Cleveland society deb herself. When Elizabeth died she left a lot of money to Anne Belle. In general, our family has always liked to think that social classes mattered little and that we were more or less the same as everybody else; but Anne Belle knew better. After Norwalk, our status would depend mainly on education and the kinds of jobs we had, and each generation would have to renew the credentials on its own. Perhaps because of the experience of losing Norwalk as a girl, Anne Belle saw the shakiness of this arrangement and decided the best direction for her to go was up.

Also, the move attached the family more closely to the Episcopal Church. Louis, formerly a Presbyterian, had joined it when he married Lillie. After leaving Norwalk they still brought grandchildren to St. Paul's to be baptized, and eventually some of the grandchildren brought their children there. For decades St. Paul's would remain the family's "real" church, the one for weddings and funerals, and because of its influence the Wickhams and their descendants remained Episcopals (as much as they were anything). No doubt they also liked the Episcopal Church because of what its snobby undertones said about the class to which they thought they belonged.

•

In Cleveland, Louis went to work for the firm of Reed, Meals, Orgill, and Maschke, which later became Orgill, Maschke, and Wickham. Their offices were in a building downtown. His partner Maurice Maschke, a German Jew, had recently replaced reform mayor Tom Johnson as the most powerful political boss in the city. Maschke organized the Polish, Russian, Hungarian, Italian, and Negro millworkers of Cleveland into a political force which he controlled for twenty years. Cleveland was a growing city then—the Forest City, the Fountain City—its steel and oil and coal businesses bringing it millions. In 1920 the Cleveland Indians won the World Series, beating the Brooklyn Robins. In 1927 Cleveland built the second-tallest building in the world, the Terminal Tower, a skyscraper only a little shorter than the Woolworth Building in New York. Louis went to the office five days a week and wrote briefs and tried cases on appeal in the upper courts. Sometimes he wrote political speeches for Maurice Maschke. Relatives who knew him in the thirties say he spent a lot of time drinking and playing whist with friends in the lobby of the Olmsted Hotel.

He and Lillie still summered at their cottage on the lake. They moved the cottage to a new location down the bluff; my uncle, asleep in an upstairs bedroom at the time, woke to find the house moving across the lawn. At a spot convenient to the road they built a three-car garage, a low, gravel-floored shed wide enough to fit their new Ford sedan. They also bought a house in Fort Lauderdale, Florida. They chose one small enough to discourage visitors and filled its yard with tropical plants, Florida cherry trees, orange trees, kumquat trees. Louis continued to work for his law firm into his seventies. He wrote to his college alumni magazine: "I have had no honors or degrees conferred, having earned or deserved none." He and Lillie began to spend seven months a year in Florida. The older they got, the more they dreaded the Ohio winters.

They were in Fort Lauderdale in 1941, when the Japanese bombed Pearl Harbor. Lillie wrote her daughter Cora a letter. She had been thinking of the families of the boys killed at Pearl Harbor and on Guam. She told Cora to give her sons a good Christmas but to take care of herself, and she ended:

Even I sometimes think I would enjoy a chance to kill a Jap or a German. Isn't that awful for an old woman like me? I look at my revolver and really imagine I could use it if a chance came. None will but war brutalizes even people like me.

Lillie was seventy-three. At least two of her sisters had lost their minds in old age. Aunt Hattie told people that she had begun to grow new teeth to replace the ones she'd lost. Aunt Mary (Mame) mistook young relatives for contemporaries of hers long since dead. The Benedict sisters lived on in the house at 80 East Seminary as nutty old ladies of Norwalk. Lillie feared her mind was going, too, although her family noticed no symptoms. She said she didn't want people to come around and stare at her, the way they did to Hattie. When she and Louis returned from Fort Lauderdale that spring, she went for a ride with her new son-in-law, Anne Belle's husband, and talked about how unhappy she was. She said that Louis didn't listen to her. He had been sick all winter, and she said it was hard taking care of a demanding old man.

One morning soon after, twelve-year-old Fannie Moses was asleep in the front bedroom of her family's cottage just up the bluff from the Wickhams' when she heard Louis outside calling for her mother, Agnes. "He came to us because there was nobody else on the bluff," she says. "It was June 1 and most of the cottages were still closed. "He said, 'Aggie! Aggie!' I will never forget the agony in his voice." Aggie dressed and went with him to his cottage. In the dimly lit garage, beneath the low ceiling beams where Louis stored the shutters and the cane fishing poles, on the seat of their '41 Ford, Lillie was dead. She had run a gardening hose from the exhaust pipe through the car window. Aggie turned off the ignition. Louis said, "If she'd told me she was going I'd have gone with her."

Her first granddaughter and namesake, Ellen, was to be christened some days later. Louis wrote a letter for Ellen explaining why her grandmother had killed herself. A grandson, my uncle Louis, happened to be home by himself when the newspaper called, and he felt guilty for years afterward because he hadn't known her real name to give for the obituary. The family said they understood what Lillie had done and did not blame her, but in later years they never mentioned it. Rev. C. S. Gross performed the funeral at St. Paul's Episcopal in Norwalk. Lillie was buried in Woodlawn Cemetery in the town she once left for good, in the Benedict plot, near her mother and her father and her brother and her great-grandfather Platt, whose skull she had examined as a child.

Louis was very lonely without her. He sold the house in Fort Lauderdale and wintered there in the Hotel Broward instead. In the warmer months he visited his son and daughters or returned to his cottage on the lake. He liked to sit on the pier on a folding chair. Now he rarely fished or went out in a boat. He spent a lot of time on the porch listening to the radio, usually to broadcasts of Cleveland Indian games. He wrote reminiscences of his childhood to entertain his invalid grandson, Teddy, and when another grandson, Duke, stayed at the cottage, Louis wrote a daily newsletter reporting on what Duke and a playmate did. He also made up long adventure stories about a pair of monkeys named Jocko and Mungo, and typed the stories and cut out pictures of monkeys for illustration and stapled the pages into books for Duke. He often did an imitation of a sheep for Ellen, and she gave him the nickname Baa. He could sing only two songs— "Onward, Christian Soldiers" and another one that just went "Shipoo shi-poo." His grandchildren said they preferred him to their parents. Ellen threw crying fits and fell into a decline when he took a trip to California or left for Fort Lauderdale in the winter.

In 1951 I was born, his first great-grandchild. His second, my cousin Libby, came soon after me. When we were christened, he gave us each a $25 U.S. savings bond and a note. My note said:

> Dear Sandy:
> To-day you will have been christened
> In the old Church in Norwalk
> Where so many of your ancestors
> Have been christened, confirmed, Married
> And lived happily ever after.
>
> This little gift I have for you—
> May it remind you of the day—
> And, perchance, will serve,
> When it comes due,
> To buy a fishing rod and reel,
> Or something you may better like.

He no longer had his apartment but lived mostly with daughter Anne Belle and her family. He grew thinner and thinner. He still got around all right, still dressed well, and seldom was without his bow tie. When he went to Florida he needed someone to drive him there and back. He broke his arm. His sister Mayno came from California to visit him, and Anne Belle and Cora worried privately that something would happen to Mayno and then they'd have two old people to take care of. His vision began to blur, and in 1954 he underwent cataract operations. He convalesced in a bedroom with the shades drawn at Anne Belle's.

I visited him there. My grandmother or my parents must have brought me. He was lying on a bed listening to the baseball game on the radio. The long, thin old man, and the drawn shades, and the sound of the baseball game in the gloom are my second-earliest memory. I sat by the bed, and I'm sure I talked; I was a chatty three-year-old. I remember a feeling of pride that I was allowed to do this. I did not understand baseball but I knew that the team was the Indians, and I liked Indians. Now I know that he was listening to Cleveland play the New York Giants in the 1954 World Series, a historic event. Cleveland had won more games than any other team in American League history that year and lost to the Giants in four straight. This was the Series in which the Giants' Willie Mays made his famous over-the-shoulder catch of the drive hit by Vic Wertz. The Indians have not been in a World Series since.

Louis died that fall and was buried next to Lillie. He was almost eighty-eight. I have a photograph of Libby and me in sailor suits playing at his feet in a front yard, but all I remember of him is listening to the ball game. I thought he was wonderful. I enjoyed being around him, little as I was and little as we could do together. He gave off a kind of elegant gentle warmth is the best explanation I can offer. He was born the year after the Civil War ended, and I was a Second World War baby-boomer, and I would never know anyone from farther back in time.

CHAPTER 10

HUDSON, WHERE I GREW UP, is an older town than Norwalk. It is about fifty-seven miles east of Norwalk in the old Western Reserve, and farther from the lake. People from Connecticut founded it in 1799. When glaciers covered much of northern Ohio, the land around Norwalk lay under a body of meltwater at the edge of a glacier, and then under an early version of Lake Erie. Much of the land around Norwalk is flat, like Indiana or Illinois prairie. The land around Hudson is higher and lay under the glacier itself. Glaciers came and went several times, the most recent departing about 12,000 years ago. When we studied glaciers in an Ohio history class in grade school, I imagined our glacier receding smoothly, like a sheet pulled off a new car. Actually, glaciers can move forward, but they don't back up, they melt in place. Most likely, the glacier above Hudson softened, began to trickle underneath; rocks on its surface absorbed sunlight and melted tunnels into it; it rotted, it dwindled, it dripped, it ticked; then it

A hill on Stow Road in Hudson Township, not far from our house

dropped a pile of the sand and rocks it had been carrying around for centuries onto the ground in a heap. Hudson's landscape was hundreds of these little heaps, hills rarely big enough to sled down, a random arrangement made by gravity and smoothed by weather and time.

In town, the blocks of the sidewalks conformed to the rises and dips as best they could, tilting this way and that. Walking in the landscape was like finding a step where you hadn't expected one or not finding one where you had. Driveways tended to take unpredictable dips which would scrape your car's rear fender as you were backing out; lawns had sudden drop-offs where a lawnmower would cut down to the dirt and try to skid away. Fog pooled in the dips and not in the rises, so that, driving on foggy mornings, you went in and out of fog as your car bounced on its shock absorbers. The water table was near the surface, and many low spots became puddles wriggling with punctuation marks of tadpoles in the spring, or swampy places which eventually linked up to each other and to bankless creeks flowing slowly toward northern Ohio rivers as black and oily as roads.

In bad weather the rises and dips writhed under your tires and sometimes slipped away from the car entirely, and your headlights suddenly shone up into the trees, and an enormous possibility opened before you like a tear. My father said you could tell an upcoming dip in the road from the brown patch on the pavement made by drops of oil jiggled loose from cars' oil pans. The Ohio Turnpike cut through the hills and rode on columns above the dips and swampy places. Past the turnpike bridge on the road to our house from town was a dip just right for giving you a funny feeling in the pit of your stomach as you drove over it. Other kids on the school bus and I used to sit in the very back and raise our legs and whoop at that dip. A neighbor of ours came speeding out of town in his glass-bodied Corvette and sailed off the road there late one night, and the car threw him into a cornfield unhurt—an escape which annoyed my father when I reminded him of it. He believed strongly in seat belts and always wore his. Before seat belts were required by law, he installed them in both our cars.

Hudson was a village surrounded by farms and second-growth forests. A coal millionaire who had grown up there gave the town money in 1907 on the condition that it agree to certain restorations and improvements, such as burying electric and telephone wires underground and planting Dutch elm trees along the streets. He also specified that the town allow no store to sell liquor stronger than beer (a rule later overlooked) and added a brick clock tower to the town green which stands today. We lived not in the village but two and a half miles from it, in a new housing development in the township. Our address was 7603 Sugarbush Trail. An abandoned maple sugar mill had occupied the site before. Kids used to play in the sugar mill, and teenagers drank beer there and wrote on the walls; some of them were angry when the developers burned it down. Sugarbush Trail was actually a street of graded dirt paved with slag, in a grid of other streets called Deerpath, Huntington Road, Woodbridge Road, and Pioneer Trail. Alongside the streets ran shallow ditches. Most of the lots were still undeveloped and covered with trees. From Cleveland, before we moved, my mother wrote her mother: "It's a brand new house . . . Oh, it's going to be beautiful. It's out in the country and up on a knoll." The knoll was a glacial hill, a rise of sand and gravel slightly higher than others in the neighborhood.

My father said we would live there for twenty years, and some of us did. The house, a boxy colonial, had wood siding painted white, green shutters, four bedrooms, two baths upstairs and a half-bath downstairs, a two-car garage, a cedar closet, a basement, and a "housewife's planning desk" built into one wall of the kitchen. The newly varnished and sanded hardwood floors made good runways to slide on in stocking feet, but our parents always stopped my brother Dave and my sister Suzan and me from doing that, so we wouldn't wear out our socks. (Fritz was a baby then, and Maggie hadn't been born.) Also, we were supposed to stay out of the back yard, which was full of poison ivy, and not scrape the still-soft latex paint from the walls with our fingernails. Dave and I slept in one bedroom, Sue in another, and Fritz in a bassinet in my parents' room. The bedroom that would be his they kept empty and unheated, with the grates from the furnace vents closed. For a while there was nothing much in that room but my father's sea chest from the navy, a baby scale, a dismantled bed frame, and a few slow-moving wasps on the floor.

•

From our back windows we could see no other houses, and no lights at night. Once, a hunter came from the woods into our back yard. The trees—elms, maples, ashes, beeches—all stood at about the same height, with the slightly weedy quality of second-growth.

Whoever had cleared the land originally had left no big trees, and it still looked like a shaved cat starting to grow back its hair. Agricultural relics—crushed sap buckets, wagon springs, unidentifiable galvanized junk, cow bones—poked here and there from the woods floor. Rusty lengths of barbed wire disappeared slowly into encroaching tree trunks. People who lived in rural townships like this began to move away after the Civil War. The wave of settlement that opened the trans-Allegheny wilderness, cleared it, covered it with small farms, and filled it with towns crested after 1860. Before, 85 percent of Americans lived in rural areas; after, fewer and fewer lived on farms, and more and more in cities. This shift made some state governments worry that the rural districts would soon be depopulated; committees were appointed to study the problem. In Ohio, more than half the state's townships lost population from 1880 to 1900. Townships like Hudson which were farther than ten miles from a city would lose the most. Horses went to the cities, too, to pull carriages and omnibuses and streetcars. Farmers who stayed grew more oats to feed them, while abandoned farms went back to woodlands.

Cities attracted ambitious young people just as the wilderness had half a century before. New machinery like the self-binding harvester and the adjustable harrow and the grain separator reduced the numbers needed to farm; medical advances like the understanding of bacterial sources of disease and improved water and sewer systems made cities safer to live in. Among the many inventions or innovations of the period were the apartment building, steam heat, the hydraulic elevator, and the automatic fire sprinkler. New York City and Brooklyn opened the Brooklyn Bridge, the longest suspension bridge in the world, across the East River in 1883, St. Louis built the Eads Bridge over the Mississippi, Kansas City spanned the Missouri. Improvements in the dynamo made possible electric streetlights and streetcars. A discovery of natural beds of pitch on the island of Trinidad produced more asphalt paving; Washington, D.C., and Buffalo became the best-paved cities in the world. Cities had better stores and hospitals and schools, and city children went to class more days in a year than country children, who took time off for harvesting and planting. People in the dozen or more large American cities at the turn of the century could do things Americans had not been able to do before—go to a symphony orchestra concert, read a book from a public library, see paintings in a public art museum, take their children to a playground, buy a variety of newspapers and magazines, watch a major league baseball game.

America had more miles of railroad track than the rest of the world put together, and railroads made cities their hubs. The increase in passenger service brought customers to the new great hotels—the Palmer House in Chicago, and the Waldorf, the Clarendon, and the St. Nicholas (where Midwesterners usually stayed) in New York. Industries moved nearer to the good land and water transport at St. Louis and Pittsburg and Philadelphia and elsewhere, so the workers followed. The second half of the nineteenth century in America was about making money, and the cities were where it was made. In 1800, fewer than 4 percent of the population lived in big cities; by 1890, 28 percent did. Chicago grew from half a million people to over a million between 1880 and 1900, Minneapolis–St. Paul tripled in size. When New York annexed Brooklyn it grew to 3.5 million. In northeastern Ohio, between 1850 and 1900, the city of Akron went from about 3,000 to about 43,000, Youngstown from nothing to about 45,000, and Cleveland from about 20,000 to about 405,000.

A historian of the Disciples of Christ says that the church was not prepared for the rural-to-urban population shift, and lost many members as a result. In general, most Protestant denominations had this problem. The multiplying sects of the Protestant faith were made for the open country. Protestants emphasized the individual believer and the individual congregation, so their churches had trouble coming up with the larger-scale organization which cities required. Many churches believed in evangelism as a tenet of faith and as a way of getting new members, but the millions of recent city immigrants from Europe tended to be Catholics and Jews who were hard to evangelize. Members of Protestant Churches in the city often were from families which had been in America longer and had more money, and the Episcopalian and Presbyterian communions in particular came to be thought of as rich men's churches. Protestants had always defined themselves partly in terms of what they were not—Roman Catholics—but as the nation became more populous and complicated and fast-moving, the list of what they weren't expanded. Many said they also weren't liquor drinkers, evolutionists, vaudeville-show-goers, Sabbath breakers, tobacco users, jewelry wearers, lottery-ticket buyers. They feared the foreign influence in America and said that non-Protestants had no understanding of democracy. Some Protestants took up the new Social Gospel, which preached the improvement of poor people's lives materially as well as spiritually, but in general the Protestant Churches did not encourage trade unionism, racial justice, the feminist movement, or interdenominational unity. The Protestant Churches saw the future coming and didn't like it. Their narrow-mindedness was a big part of what had driven people from the country to the city in the first place.

The cities' boom years continued until about 1915. People from the countryside—Americans, and immigrants from rural parts of Europe as well—came to the cities, stayed a generation or two. Then, in growing numbers, they began to leave. Maybe some of them still remembered farming and wanted to own, if not a farm, a piece of land again. Maybe they had had enough of living in a row house or in a building with other families, or agreed with the English idea that a cottage surrounded by a yard made the best dwelling for a family. Maybe they wanted to get away from crime and noise and pollution and corruption and radical politics. Maybe they hoped never again to see city neighbors of certain racial or religious groups they couldn't stand. Maybe they just weren't city people. Whatever the reason, they moved to the cities' fringes, usually farther along the streetcar or interurban railroad lines, where the expense of commuting kept other people away. Between 1920 and 1930 the suburbs of larger cities all over America grew twice as fast as the cities' cores.

The three big population shifts in American history since 1800 have been the frontier movement West, the move from the country to the cities, and the move to the suburbs. My family and almost everyone I knew until I was about twenty-five were part of the third move. The third move depended on cars. By 1920 cars had become cheap enough that most middle-class people could own one, and could choose houses in the suburbs farther than the standard mile or so from the commuter station. Henry Ford, the man most responsible for making these cars available, prophesied, "The city is doomed." States spent millions on new highways and abandoned public transportation. Towns on the frontier often had been built by a single church or sect; suburban towns usually were for just one class, and almost always for just one race. Designers of suburbs encouraged suburban towns to write restrictive ownership covenants saying (for example) that no blacks or Jews could buy. The Federal Housing Administration preferred suburban single-family homes in all-white neighborhoods for its loan guarantees and made it possible for a first-time home buyer to get a loan with a 10 percent down payment, instead of the 30 percent required in the past. Buying a house in the suburbs sometimes was cheaper than renting a city apartment.

The suburban trend paused for the Second World War. After the war, when construction supplies and labor reappeared, it started up again. White people left the cities by the millions, filling places in the Midwest like Bloomfield Hills and Shaker Heights and the various River Oaks and Park Forests and Oak Groves, and the Levittowns of the East, and Westchester County, and Shawnee Mission near Kansas City, and greater Los Angeles, and hundreds of suburbs more. Where we lived, nearly every lot in the development was filled by the time I was a teenager. Behind the house, where there had been only trees, we could soon see many lights at night and hear our neighbors' voices when they argued. The smells of my childhood are the smells of cut lumber and wet mud and drying cement, and the sounds are hammering, chain saws, and bulldozers. In the evenings our father would take us kids on a walk to look at the houses that were going up, and we would climb around on them and have sword fights with scantlings and throw mudballs and dig in the piles of sand. Always in some corner of the houses would be a few upended ten-gallon cans of caulking compound the carpenters had sat on while having lunch, and the crumpled wax paper and cigarette packs they'd left behind.

By 1970, more Americans lived in suburbs than in rural places or cities. By 1980, America was a suburban nation; 40 percent of the population, nearly 100 million people, lived in suburban areas, which often stretched so far it was hard to say what they were suburbs of. Cities like Chicago and St. Louis began to export used bricks to make patios. Industry now moved more by truck and car and electronic impulse than by water or mail, so it could relocate to the suburbs, too. Suburban manufacturing grew to about two-thirds of the nation's total, and suburban shopping centers accounted for two-thirds of the retail trade.

In the countryside around Hudson, development first took the likely sites, the higher ground, and then moved on to the wetter places.

Freeway extensions built close to the town made it easier to commute from there, and in the seventies a real-estate company responsible for the success of several upscale suburbs of Cleveland began the largest development project ever in Hudson. Hundreds more houses, some the size of airplane hangars, went up in the township, and people bought them. Cars filled the narrow roads, one of the few parts of the town that had stayed the same; every evening a traffic jam began to grow north and south along Main Street and out of sight. Bulldozers crawled everywhere on the sold farmland, but they were in their twilight. When I was a kid, bulldozers did the early work at the construction sites, and bulldozer tracks led across the bare yards, notched the tar-and-gravel roads, and scored the sandy glacial mud to ingots. The glaciers that had made the landscape were, in a sense, natural bulldozers, so the environment they left behind proved ideal for mechanical ones. D-4 Caterpillar 'dozers pushed the rises down into the soggy dips, erased the hilly corrugations, and smoothed the ancient glacial debris like cake batter. Today the bulldozers are fewer, and much of the previous landscape is gone, replaced by acres as smooth and green and even as a developer could want.

•

In high school and after, my friends and I drove around in cars a lot. On a summer evening I would sit on my front stoop waiting for Jimmy or Kent to come by and pick me up—I usually was passenger, not driver—and then we would pick up some other kids, and then we would ride for hours around Hudson, to neighboring towns, to Cleveland, to the highway sprawl north of Akron, to the shopping malls, to dirt roads in the country, to houses of kids whose parents we knew weren't home. One night we put 300 miles on Jimmy's (father's) Cougar. Many people in town recognized us by sight, and sometimes when we waved, an adult would look back at us in the big car not our own with an expression of helpless exasperation. We always listened to the car radio, which we called "listening to tunes." I still use that expression today. We called driving around "cruising": cruising and listening to tunes. Sometimes when the song on the radio was right and the place in the road and the color of the sky and the smell of the cigarette smoke of the girl sitting next to me all came together in a certain way, I would feel an emotion which was a mile wide, but which turned out later to be only an inch deep.

Hudson is about an eleven-hour drive from Brooklyn. If I leave home in the morning I get there at dusk or dark. I stop again at Merino's Beer & Wine and talk to Rich or sometimes to his customers. (Charlie, a plumber who has lived in Hudson for years: "This used to be a nice town, but the real-estate companies ruined it, puttin' up all these half-million-dollar houses on half-acres of property. I don't even drive on Route 91 no more, the traffic's so bad. Used to be, downtown was a hardware store, a clothing store, a feed store, a grocery store. Nowadays, when you go downtown, what're you gonna buy? A house! That's all you *can* buy. Only kind of store left downtown anymore is real-estate offices.") Then I walk across the street to the town green, by the old town hall, where my family used to be in plays and my mother used to direct plays, and I stand in the dark and drink beer and watch the traffic jam sort itself out, and I dance around a little bit, and I say, "Baby, I'm going to witch you, I'm going to woo you! Baby, I'm going to kiss you awake!" I used to walk in Hudson at night sometimes and feel like every front lawn was my own front lawn and every grownup was my father or mother and every girl was my girl-friend and I could sleep on any porch and open any door without knocking. Now I stand in the dark by the traffic jam in the town I no longer know and an emotion comes over me and I say, "Baby, I am your heart!"

After a while I walk to the Reserve Inn and have a good dinner for the price of a cab ride in New York. I get in the car and go to a motel by the turnpike and register. I lie on the bed and watch TV or talk on the phone until the traffic has eased up. By this time it is usually pretty late. Then I go for a drive, to the places we used to, in Hudson and beyond. Like me, most of the people I knew have moved away. Almost no one lives in the same house as when I was a kid. I look at the houses, and I think:

She was in my fifth-grade class and one winter day I was walking home without any gloves on and she saw me, put on gloves, came out her side door, knocked me down, and washed my face with snow. She grew up to be smart and shy.

I danced with her at the Episcopal church square dance one night and liked her a lot. Her mother liked me, but she didn't. She later became a hippie and went with older guys and got pregnant or something.

She and I and some other kids ran in the smoke and flames when the farmers were burning off their pastures along Middleton Road in early spring, and later we roughhoused and I pinned her to her front lawn under my sooty knees. She inherited a restaurant in Spain.

She was the prettiest girl in town in 1967. She died in a building collapse in New York City.

Taking the SAT tests for college he got so nervous he chewed the buttons off both his shirt cuffs. His mother had no hair and wore a wig and penciled on her eyebrows. The family moved away.

She wore cut-off blue jeans so short you could see the white ends of the pants pockets underneath. She became a jeweler and married a jeweler.

He once slammed another kid and me together, knocking me unconscious, when we called him a hood. He became a first lieutenant in the Marine Corps and died in Vietnam.

He—the kid I was slammed against—married a popular daytime-television star. I follow his family's progress in the soap-opera fan magazines.

She stood by the lockers outside the cafeteria at a high-school dance, her hips cocked like a fist.

She wore white knee-high vinyl boots the time we sat on the hood of a car in the parking lot behind the academy football field and watched the northern lights. She moved to New York and became an actor and appeared as a mom in a cough-syrup commercial on TV.

She sat on her front porch on hot afternoons reading, holding her long hair up off the back of her neck with one hand. When we went out together, she decided she didn't like me because I was such a drip around her friends. She told me, "This is what you do—you stand."

He moved to Washington, D.C., and got a job at the Pentagon doing research for a colonel who holds the world record for sit-ups.

She wore tight blue jeans with a seam separation at the hip joint, on the side. A friend of mine who went with her said that sometimes she made his brain so inflamed he could look up and see his forehead. She works for an advertising company out West somewhere.

She liked horses and looked kind of like a horse, and we used to whinny at her. She got a fatal illness in her twenties.

She was sixteen or seventeen, and I was twelve or thirteen, and her grandmother was my piano teacher, and one day I was sitting in the parlor waiting for my piano lesson, and she was upstairs singing "It's in His Kiss" ("The Shoop Shoop Song") as loud as she could, and the mailman came and went at the front door, and she ran downstairs, singing, to get the mail, and she was wearing nothing but glasses and bikini underpants, and my piano teacher appeared and screamed, "Renee, there's a boy here!" and Renee stopped and looked right at me for a long moment, and I looked at her, and then she turned and went back upstairs.

The stripes on the seat of her bathing suit, like longitude lines on a globe. That tight Mickey Mouse T-shirt.

She and I used to sit on the grass and talk and smoke cigarettes and pick the vein structures from broad-leafed weeds.

One summer at the Ice Cream Social she slid her bare arm around my bare arm to hold my hand. She married a man named (can this be right?) Bill Shrunk.

I kissed her, holding her against the chain-link fence behind the elementary school. She became a therapeutic masseuse in New York with her own portable table and towels.

He teased me and I got two big kids to hold him and I slugged him in the stomach. His teacher came to my classroom and complained, but I was in so good with my teacher that nothing happened. He later became a tour guide in Hawaii.

He was the most talented kid in town. I admired and envied him. He could act, sing, play guitar, draw, play basketball and baseball. He was funny and had straight brown hair he could fling easily back from his face. I remember riding with him in his Mustang and discussing the new TV series *Batman*. He killed himself, people said for love of an older woman he met during a production at the local little theater.

She teased me and another kid for being nerds. She married a man not from Hudson who became obsessed with the town and collected its stories and personalities like baseball cards and now probably knows more about it than anyone.

She put her tan bare feet with coral-polish-painted toenails on the dashboard and bumped her heels in time to the radio. She got sick from something she sprayed on trees while working for a landscaping company and moved to Atlanta and moved to Buffalo and got married.

He used to say he'd drunk so much beer he could piss a pound of foam.

He marked up a friend of mine with a Magic Marker for giving him the finger.

When we were little we used to make fun of him, basically because his family was poor. The yard of his house was so full of iron junk it appeared to be magnetized. He got into trouble for stealing returnable bottles from a neighbor's garage. Years later I ran into him with his wife and baby in town, and he said he had joined the circus.

To her senior prom she wore a gown made of dyed bedsheets. She became a newscaster in Florida and shot herself to death on live television.

She sat by the Hockey Pond on a still night and dangled her feet in the water, and a while later the ripples made the streetlight on the opposite side of the pond waver. She pushed me into the pond and thought that was hysterically funny. I thought it was funny, too. She moved away.

He used to pick me up when I was hitchhiking, and even though he was almost at his house, he would give me a ride all the way to my house. He became an Episcopal priest.

She was a dental hygienist and we flirted so much while she was cleaning my teeth that the dentist yelled at us. She married a guy named Steve and divorced him and married another guy named Steve.

When she was about eight years old she took off all her clothes and tried to slide down a laundry chute and got stuck and called for help and wouldn't let her stepbrother pull her out because then he'd see her without any clothes on. She married a man who made a lot of money doing computer graphics for TV and now she does computer graphics, too.

She and I went to a golf course late one night and took off our shoes and ran across the fairway, and the moon was so bright that when we looked back we could see our footprints far behind us in the dew. She liked me but I didn't know it, and I liked her but I didn't know it. I was always saying upsetting and competitive things to her. She went to college and became a museum curator and moved to California and married the son of the discoverer of a polio vaccine.

By this time I am singing along with the radio and rocking back and forth in the seat and hitting the heel of my hand against the steering wheel. Here and there I see the blue glow of TVs through the windows; most people in Hudson are in bed. I coast down Oviatt Street, pause in front of 80 North Oviatt. Her locker was near mine in sixth grade, and one day I asked her for her telephone number, and she said she didn't know it, and I said, "You must be pretty dumb not to know your own telephone number." Her family had just moved to town, which was why she didn't. In eighth grade at a dance at the high school I asked her if she would sneak out of her house later and climb the town water tower with me, and she said yes, and I went home and snuck out of my bedroom and walked back to town and threw pebbles at that window, the one above the door to the right, but she didn't wake up, so I climbed the water tower by myself. The summer after tenth grade I saw her at a dance talking to a guy I believed I was cooler than, and I started talking to her, and the guy disappeared, and I walked her to her house, and we talked some more. I started to come around her house in the evenings. My dad let me drive his Corvair. Everybody said I would have a girlfriend as soon as I got my driver's license, and they were right. I got my license on July 6 and she and I started going together July 19. That evening I drove by her house, and her little brother saw me and ran inside, and then she came out. She had told him to sit out front and watch for me. I had some cigars in the glove compartment that belonged to a friend, and I asked her if she wanted to walk with me to his house to return them. We went via the playing fields and the open fields behind the high school. On our way back, I took her hand. She was wearing a kind of loose madras dress with a tear in the side. It was just past sunset. I heard voices and I said, "Is that somebody coming?" We stopped and looked across the fields and she said she didn't think so. I said, "In that case—" and turned and kissed her. Her head turned quickly to me and her hair swung between us and her tongue pushed into my mouth through strands of hair. She pushed her hair back behind her ear and we kissed again. We saw each other every day we could for the rest of the summer. At night we used to say we were going for a walk and then lie down in the long grass behind the garage where her father never mowed. We went together all the next school year, broke up in the spring, and continued breaking up and getting back together for about nine years. She was engaged to marry someone else in college, returned to town, and got back with me. Finally, after a lot more happened, she married my childhood friend Kent. They had two kids and moved to Boulder, Colorado, and divorced. She lives in Boulder and is a licensed nurse. Her name then was Susie, later it became Susan.

I turn right on Aurora Street, heading toward our old house. My father never liked her. Maybe he was afraid I would marry too young and get stuck in Hudson; I know he thought he was stuck in Hudson himself. The speed limit on Aurora Street, from the clock tower all the way to the town limit, has been 25 mph for as long as I remember. My father never drove one mile over the speed limit on this street. He maintained an unvaried 25 the whole way, both hands on the steering wheel, both eyes on the road, never a glance at the would-be speeders cooling their heels behind him. It made no difference how late we were for something, how in a hurry I was. People in town dreaded the sight of his car up ahead when they turned onto Aurora. At night, if one of the streetlights happened to be out, he would slow down while passing underneath it. Naturally, when I began to drive, I drove much faster, and got a speeding ticket on Aurora Street, and wrecked a car he was fond of when I missed a turn and rolled twice and ended up in a ditch by the Little League baseball field. Nobody got hurt (Susie was with me), and he had the car fixed, but it was never the same. The rear suspension was shot. Now I usually don't like to drive fast myself, and I annoy other drivers by poking along. Tonight I drive 25 or slower out Aurora.

I continue to Stow Road, and up the hill to Woodbridge Road. The corner of Stow and Woodbridge is where I rolled the car. When I ran home and told my father what I'd done, he went into his room and cried. But once the car had been towed back to our house and he was checking the engine for damage, he cheered right up; he always liked a good technical problem. I turn onto our street and creep up it so slowly that if anybody is watching at this hour they will wonder what I am doing. Our house looks like a mansion to me now. The driveway is paved—ours was gravel—and the landscaping is more elaborate, with shrubs and plantings and a lawn trimmed at the edges. We never trimmed the lawn. When we first moved in, we didn't even have a lawn. My father thought it would be better to plant rye grass. We had a field of four-foot-high rye in front of our house for a year or more. My father used to cut it with a scythe. Somebody is probably asleep in a bed in my old room. I could just pull into the drive, go through the side door, up the stairs, into my room, into the bed. My father was so glad to move from this house. He took the buyer all over it and cheerfully pointed out everything that didn't work or needed repair. The buyer began fixing the place up before we'd even moved and he quickly sold it for more than he'd paid. My father used to paint the outside of the house every few years, he dug up the septic tank and the leach bed from time to time, he fooled with the driveway and the furnace and the pump and the washing machines. My mother was less sure about moving. She wanted what he wanted.

The truth is, being in Hudson often fills me with anxiety. Feelings rise up, an internal tantrum of them. Sometimes memories cause me one long, unrelieved wince after the next. One reason I prefer to think about Norwalk is that it is familiar but not as personally confusing. My later memories of Hudson are mostly sad. I remember getting into the car to drive home from the hospital after Fritz died. My mother sat in front and we kids in back, our number now permanently reduced by one, and my father, in the driver's seat, took his leather gloves from under the visor and put them on, carefully pulling each finger to. I thought it was remarkable that he could do that after his son had just died. He bought Fritz a plot in Markillie Cemetery in Hudson, and at the same time bought two plots adjoining it. Why two? Why not six, or none? Maybe he couldn't bear to think of his son there alone without some of us to keep him company. Maybe he knew that the end of Fritz's life meant in some way the end of his, and of my mother's.

I am ready to go back to the motel. I choose a route from our old house that leads past the cemetery. I don't look to right or left; I am fast-forwarding through Hudson now. A song that I like comes on the radio and I turn it up so loud that the sound vibrates the dash and distorts in my ears and fits around me like armor. I am roaring and hollering, on general principles, but I can hardly hear myself. I come down Route 91, streetlights flickering through the windshield, and the cemetery approaches on the right. The gates are locked. Houses have built all around the grounds, back-yard decks now overlook the graves. As I drive by I shout out to my parents and my brother.

C H A P T E R   1 1

MY FATHER USED TO SAY, gloomy-joking, that he may have
been young but he never was a child. He was born in November of
1919 at his grandparents' house in Norwalk, where his mother had
returned to have her first baby. A local doctor delivered him, assisted
by a black woman about his mother's age who had worked for his
grandparents for years. Her name was Dorothea Geneva Cleopatra
Anna Maude Carmen Butler, a fact which he sometimes told people,
perhaps in resentment at having no middle name himself. His parents
named him David. His mother called him Davy, and his father called
him Pete or Bud. They had him baptized at about seven months old
at St. Paul's Church in Norwalk. The church was celebrating its centennial at the time, and it held a pageant on the lawn. Church members
portrayed the characters Adventure, Courage, Unrest, and Spiritual
Hunger. The last of these acted upon the hero, Platt Benedict, to
found a church. Louis Wickham, wearing some of Platt's actual clothes,

My father in his football letter sweater, at sixteen, with his brother Teddy

portrayed him. Afterward the congregation went into the church to see the baptism of my father, the latest of the line.

When David was four he assisted at another Norwalk ceremony —the unveiling of a portrait of his great-grandfather Judge Charles P. Wickham, at the Huron County Courthouse. Before a full courtroom of relatives and jurists from around the state David unveiled the portrait painted by the judge's son-in-law Charles C. Curran. The artist had declared this work his masterpiece. There were many speeches, through which my father probably sat in a lap and fidgeted. The judge, "quite overcome" according to the newspaper, thanked everyone for this honor. Charles Wickham was now a small, thin veteran, eighty-eight years old, with a round, bald head and a walrus mustache and a skinny neck above the black cape he often wore. The next year, as a result of being hit by a car, he died, and David's mother did not take David to the funeral and regretted it.

In a photo album his mother kept David is a towheaded, serious little boy. Sometimes he smiles, provisionally. In the only picture in which he looks completely happy he is swimming, shoulder deep in the lake. His mother liked children old enough to do useful chores and carry on conversations. She had no interest in cuteness or baby talk, and may have subscribed to the idea then current that showing young children too much affection would spoil them. In many pictures David seems to be waiting for someone to pick him up and give him a hug. In others he looks worried. His mother's sister Anne Belle, twelve years his senior, had been present at his birth and regarded him as her favorite, and he liked to be with her. When she and other Cleveland society girls posed for a newspaper fashion ad, he stood at her side, unsmiling, in a coat with fur collar and cuffs. It hurt her that he wasn't nicer to her when he got older. She sometimes said she couldn't believe that such a sweet boy grew up to be such a disagreeable man.

At an early age he knew he wanted to be a chemist. His aunt Peg remembers her sisters buying him a chemistry set when he was six. They forgot about it until Christmas Eve, and they called the store owner, whom they knew, and he had somebody bring it to their house. When Anne Belle returned from the Grand Tour of Europe which Cousin Elizabeth Severance Allen sent her on, she brought David a toy deep-sea diver on a rubber hose. The diver surfaced or submerged when you squeezed a ball. Anne Belle said she got it for him because he was the scientist in the family; this made his younger brother Louis jealous, and he pushed David in the goldfish pond as David was trying the diver out. David's mother always said he came up with seaweed on his eyebrows. One Christmas he asked for an electric train, and the night before went downstairs in the dark to the Christmas tree and stepped on the track in his bare feet and was thrilled to feel a tingle from the third rail. He learned how to take the engines apart and fix them. He was doing routine repairs on a train when his father came up behind him and watched for a while and then said, "It's fun to watch a real professional work." David was very flattered but didn't let on. In his life, that would become one of his terms of highest praise: *professional*.

He was almost ten years old when the stock market crashed. Later he did not say simply that he grew up in the Depression; it was always the *depths* of the Depression. The sight of people standing in lines scared him. Money would be the only subject he would never joke about. His father worked at the steel mill almost every day and sometimes took trips to other cities in the Midwest to inspect and buy scrap iron. Nonferrous metals mixed in with the scrap—coils of copper, say, in an old generator—were the banes of his father's life. His parents argued about money but never were completely without it. His mother raised chickens in a shed out back and kept or sold the eggs. If she butchered a chicken and hung it on the trellis to drain and the dog got to it, she might still cook and serve the parts that weren't torn up. Economies learned then never left them. She couldn't stand to see scraps on a plate go to waste. If you wouldn't eat them, she often would. She made her grandchildren finish the milk in the bottom of their cereal bowls. My father learned to clean his plate. As a kid I marveled at how he left his plate so clean you almost didn't have to wash it.

When David was eleven, his mother had her third child, Teddy. The congenital defect from which Teddy suffered, a malformation of a chamber of the heart, could be corrected by surgery today. David and Louis didn't know at first how sick Teddy was. Louis remembers the day his father sat them down and told them. Worry about Teddy would consume most of the remaining time and attention their parents had. The boys had to be quiet around Teddy and never roughhouse.

Teddy's condition caused him to react to cow's milk, so the family bought a goat. In the evening David had to put her in the shed and milk her. She would drag him around and kick and sometimes butt.

The goat's name was Grandmaw, and she provided the family with a favorite story. One afternoon David's mother was about to leave the children with a babysitter and was giving last-minute instructions. Going out the door she remembered the goat and said to the baby-sitter, "If Grandmaw bellers, just spray her with the flytox." The babysitter's eyes widened: "Oh, is she upstairs?"

Bay Village, where David grew up, looks the way it sounds. Its sky is high and often full of fast-moving clouds brighter on the un-dersides with light reflected from the lake. Light from the lake peers over the treeline well in from the shore; sometimes a flock of gulls billows above the community like a bedsheet. Much of the Bay Village shoreline is high slate cliffs which muddy brown waves pushed by the prevailing westerlies hit at an angle, in a sequence of high, show-stopping kicks. Storms from the lake knock down trees and powerlines in the fall and pile up snowdrifts in the winter. Summers can be calm and blue for weeks at a time. In the twenties and thirties, Bay Village was a streetcar suburb. The Lake Shore Electric Railway, which people called the interurban, ran all the way from Cleveland to Toledo, more or less along the shore, and through Bay Village. People along the route described where they lived in terms of the interurban's num-bered stops. For many years David's family lived in a gambrel-roofed house on Lake Road by Stop 19.

David had a paper route delivering the Cleveland *News* on his bicycle. Once somebody stole the bicycle. Louis remembers the relief on his brother's face when their father walked in the back door and said the police had found it. David liked to read Howard Pyle adven-ture tales, and sea stories like Stevenson's *Captains Courageous* or Verne's *Mysterious Island*. His mother read and recited poetry, all of which rhymed and scanned; she had no sympathy for any that did not. His father explained technical curiosities to him, such as why some people could pick up radio station KDKA from Pittsburgh on their downspouts or how an Edison vacuum tube worked. His father also became interested in the new theory of relativity and described it to him. David spent a lot of time by himself, working in the little chemistry lab he set up in his room or walking on Stop 19 Beach across the street. He looked for lucky stones—small flat bones from the head of a fish called a sheepshead, with a mark on one side like the letter L—and he skipped smooth pieces of shale across the water and watched the freighters and sailboats with binoculars. Louis sometimes came to the beach, too. The brothers did not walk together, though each could tell where the other was from the sound of feet rattling the stones.

My father went to Bay Village Elementary School, but later did not mention any friends or teachers from it. His mother worked for the school board and sometimes got involved in school board disputes; perhaps this caused him to be singled out or teased. For high school he went to Parkview, which people called Bay High. Of his high-school years he usually spoke with the same bleak brevity he applied to the rest of his childhood. He had bad skin, he didn't know how to talk to girls, he was not popular, he felt so awkward socially that he had to devise special strategies to approach people. A scrapbook he kept during his junior year—1935–36—gives a cheerier view. He had a part in the junior class production of *Fixing It for Father*. He played Professor John Risdon, the father. His football team went undefeated and won the championships of the west side. He started out at left guard although he weighed only 140 pounds; he looks resolute in his leather helmet in the team picture. His classmates elected him a delegate to Buckeye Boys' State, the mock legislature sponsored by the American Legion in Columbus. There he was elected clerk of the assembly and kept records of such hypothetical legislation as the Much-more Anti-Dust Bill. His name turns up from time to time in the session minutes, usually moving to strike an amendment or adjourn.

He graduated from high school in 1937 and went to Oberlin College in the fall. In 1938 he began a diary with these entries:

January 1   Saturday   Grandfather Frazier died in aft—Dad went to Akron right away—they called up and said he was sick—later said he died—

January 2   Dad home from Akron 1700—

January 3   up 0930— Took mom's car in to be serviced—rental battery—got my watch—left for Akron 1100—Grandfather's funeral 1600— Everyone stood it very well—bus to Oberlin after . . .

In small, hard-to-read handwriting he made brief notes about his classes, a student who had an epileptic fit in chemistry, the time he and a confederate trapped some guys in a dorm room by screwing their door shut, Hitler's invasion of Czechoslovakia; and women he square-danced with or sat next to at supper. The entry for February 15, 1939, reads, "Boxing a little   Hard—I smacked Horvath."

Theodore S. Horvath, '41, a sociology major, now is a retired minister living in Wayne, Pennsylvania. I found his telephone number and called him. He did not remember the incident, though he said it must have been in Phys. Ed. class. He was sure there had been no animosity involved; he said, "I did not know him at all well." He suggested I call Phil Swartz, former captain of the football team. Phil Swartz, who lives in Poughkeepsie, said, "I knew your dad, but not real well. He was basically kind of quiet." Many people I talked to said they did not know my father well. People who might have known more—his roommate, his chemistry professor, his friend James Moser—have died or disappeared.

He saw a lot of movies at Oberlin, and kept a record of them— *Boy Meets Girl* ("very funny"), *Men With Wings* ("good"), *Submarine Patrol* ("lousy"), *Destry Rides Again* ("OK"), *Confessions of a Nazi Spy* ("lousy!"), *Lost Horizon* ("very good"), *Bringing Up Baby* ("OK"). A favorite movie star was Deanna Durbin in *Mad About Music* ("good even second time"). She plays a fatherless boarding-school girl whose mother is a glamorous young actress who cannot reveal that she has a daughter for fear of ruining her career. To replace her, Deanna Durbin invents an explorer father who goes on safaris to Africa and, in fear of being found out by her classmates, persuades a handsome stranger to play the part. After many complications he meets the famous actress and they hold hands as Deanna Durbin sings. Deanna Durbin's well-scrubbed peppiness reminds me of my mother; perhaps my father felt the same.

David won letters at Oberlin in football and track. In football he played left guard and cut his forehead in practice one day when he pulled the wrong way on a sweep and ran into the right guard head-on. He used to talk with pride about what a bad player he was and how bad the team was. He claimed to have played on the last team the University of Chicago ever beat before it gave up football for good. Actually, Oberlin had a winning record (4–3) his senior year. In track he ran the sprints—the 100-yard dash, the 220, the quarter-mile, and the relays. On several occasions he ran the 100 in ten seconds flat. I saw him run only once in my life. We were on vacation in California and he was strolling along the beach in his usual legs-apart seafaring gait, with his arms crossed, thinking about something, and suddenly a big wave came up farther than the rest. He saw it at the last minute and turned and ran full speed. I had never seen his arms and legs move so fast—he was like a different person.

At Oberlin he earned money for tuition by washing dormitory windows, clearing tables, and doing dishes. In the summer his father got him a job at the steel mill shoveling coal into a blast furnace. He would dig shovelfuls from the heap, turn to the furnace door, and heave them in while turning quickly away from the heat. One day he stepped into quicklime, which got down his workboots and burned his ankles and scarred them. Other summers he worked as a lifeguard at Huntington Beach in Bay Village. He was a sandy-haired young man with sloping shoulders, strong, skinny legs, and skin that reacted to sun almost like photographic paper. He put zinc oxide on his large nose, he wore sunglasses, he covered himself with suntan lotion, but he sometimes still burned in overlooked places like the tops of his feet. Apparently he never had to save anybody, but he was a watchful sort and busy days like the Fourth of July nearly drove him crazy. His diary recounts problems he had on the job yelling at "wise guys" and keeping track of "families of Dagoes." Some days the lake was so rough he had to close the beach. On slow afternoons he talked to girls and sat around.

He took history, English, math, calculus, religion, philosophy, and chemistry courses at Oberlin. He studied hard and sometimes drank Cokes or coffee to stay awake at exam time. Problems with certain courses worried him sick. His chemistry teacher, Dr. Holmes, later told his brother what a thorough and independent worker he had been. A note in his diary reads: "Lathrop told me I am #3 in Org[anic chemistry], ½ point behind Halpern—cream that final!" He graduated cum laude in chemistry in 1941.

After Oberlin he went to Stanford University for graduate school, and became completely happy for the first time ever. He drove out to California with a friend, seeing Mt. Rushmore and climbing to the top, sleeping in the desert, hitting the bars in Reno. It gave him a thrill to write *Palo Alto, Calif.*, for his return address on letters home. In later years he always pronounced "Palo Alto" with an inflection that made it sound like heaven. He rode his bike with no hands among the eucalyptus and royal palms in the sunshine and wondered why anybody lived in Ohio. At a graduate-student boardinghouse run by a German lady called Mrs. B. he roomed with a fellow chemist named Harold Kirkby, who would be the only friend from his past he later stayed in touch with or spoke of with affection. Kirkby had graduated from Harvard in 1940, and claimed to have been seated alphabetically next to classmate John F. Kennedy at graduation. The two appear on facing pages in the 1940 Harvard yearbook. Kennedy's hair was wavier then, and he wore it combed up. Kirkby had a smooth, childlike face, with prominent lips, which he used to emphasize his favorite phrases, such as "*Sacré bleuuuuu!*" He weighed only 110 pounds. He looked so young that Palo Alto bartenders sometimes refused to serve him.

That fall David did not play football for the first time since freshman year in high school, and he missed it. He remembered the sound of cleats on the sidewalk by the gym, and stopping to take a buckeye husk off a cleat, and seeing beads of rainwater balanced on a leaf of clover inches from his nose during calisthenics, and looking at the campus upside down during neck bridges, and the locker-room shower that turned scalding hot when a toilet flushed in the adjoining bathroom, and the different way the air tasted when he was tired. He went to Stanford football games and sat in the card section, holding up a little piece of the Stanford Indian or the Golden Bear of California during card stunts.

He taught two undergraduate sections in chemistry, for a starting salary of $500 a year. Tuition and expenses (not including books) would come to over $700, he informed his parents. For extra money he worked in the dining hall and tutored. He wrote that they had no idea how stupid the average Stanford freshman was. He rarely dated and did not go home for vacations; he could not afford to. He studied organic chemistry with Professor C. R. Noller, a tall, heavyset man who looked like a prizefighter and who expected students to be at their lab tables by eight in the morning. Among colleagues David liked to be regarded as a dour Scot. "We called him Friendly Face, for obvious reasons," recalled one. In the big third-floor lab in the chemistry building on Palm Drive, David and other grad students did

experiments involving echinocystic acid, a substance found in certain
California tubers. Echinocystic acid interested Professor Noller because it belonged to the same family of compounds as some sex hor-
mones but possessed characteristics unexplained by existing pictures
of its molecular structure. David tried to figure out what the structure
could be. Back then chemists in general paid less attention to safety;
the grad students often used their Bunsen burners without hoods and
dispensed fumes and started minor fires and burned themselves and
their clothes with corrosives. For fun they played softball—physical
chemists against organic chemists—and flew kites on the lawn behind
the building and sometimes made cocktails of ethanol poured over ice
in a beaker, with a glass stirring rod for a swizzle stick.

His grandmother Lillie killed herself at the end of his first year.
His father wrote to tell him, and he wrote back that he was proud of
her. He added that he prayed if he ever thought his mind was going
he would have the courage to do the same thing.

The start of World War II made grad school even more exciting.
Like many worriers, David felt a certain joy and relief at disasters not
of his own making. He had a special student deferment from the draft
and did not give it up to enlist. He joined a civilian air defense organization and studied airplane profiles and spent hours after dark
looking for enemy planes from a fire tower in the hills above Palo Alto.
He disapproved of people talking loosely about ships they saw go
through the Golden Gate or horsing around with the fire buckets of
sand in the dorms. The war brought lots of people to San Francisco.
To his mother he described Market Street on a Saturday night:

It's like a carnival of some sort. There are soldiers and sailors of every Allied
nation and beggars and tramps and gyp salesmen and ladies of the street and
gypsy singers and admirals. The stores are doing all the business they can
handle and every tattooing shop has sailors lined up outside and the bars are
packed and you can't get near the penny arcades and every street car has
customers on the cowcatcher and the doors of the buses won't close and the
lines waiting for the movies extend 50 yards six abreast. What a town!

He decided to apply for a commission in the navy before his
deferment expired, but changed his mind. Then he may have heard
from his draft board; he wrote to his mother asking her to send by air

mail special delivery an affidavit stating his place of birth, so he could submit his navy application: "I have a feeling I may start walking in the infantry at almost any moment." The army had taken over much of the Stanford campus, and now his students were all soldiers. Air-raid warnings and blackouts continued. People studied by flashlight in their closets and threw blackout parties in windowless rooms. Grad students in the sciences arrived and left all the time. Some disappeared into secret government projects and were not heard from again until the end of the war. David finished writing his thesis for his Ph.D. and passed his oral examination. His navy application went through. In June of 1944 he received a commission as an ensign in the U.S. Naval Reserve. He shipped his belongings back to Ohio. Donna Co-sulich, a chemist in the same graduate program, remembers a party just before he left: "The whole gang was breaking up, we were all sort of separating at that point. We didn't know what would happen but we knew this was the last of something. We'd had this posh life in this absolutely gorgeous place where you never even locked your bicycle, and the world was in flames. A bunch of us went up to the fire tower where Dave watched for planes and we talked until late. I remember I was sad he was going away."

David reported to an officers' candidate school in Tucson, Arizona, in July, and was assigned a bunk in an air-conditioned barracks with about 800 men. Many were recent college graduates in engineering or law. The trainees did a mild amount of drill and took classes in navigation, military and naval fundamentals, gunnery, and seaman-ship. In camp they followed a relaxed uniform code, but had to dress to regulation for trips to town. The Tucson Chamber of Commerce threw fancy balls with individually chaperoned women in Tucson's best hotel. After two months of school he went back to Ohio on leave and then took a train to San Francisco en route to the *Guadalcanal*, the ship to which he had been assigned. He stood in line at the commandant's office in San Francisco, and when his turn came the WAVE in charge made a number of calls and disappeared and after a while returned with the news that the *Guadalcanal* was in the Atlantic. He was sent back across the country by Pullman car, seven nights and days to Norfolk, Virginia, where he found the ship and went aboard.

The *Guadalcanal* was a small aircraft carrier of 12,000 tons which had been converted from a merchant ship since the war. Earlier that year it had been part of a task force which surprised a German U-505 submarine off the Cape Verde Islands, hit her with depth charges, and captured her with fifty-eight sailors including her captain. The *Guadalcanal* had then towed the prize, one of the few subs captured in the war, to a base in Bermuda. David set sail in mid-September and was assigned to the gunnery department. He also stood one four-hour watch a day as junior officer of the deck, in charge of the ship's steering and speed. The ship cruised in fair weather through waters of a fantastic blue he had never seen anywhere before. From his station on the flight deck he looked down into the water at the shadow of the ship slipping through the depths. A large school of porpoises played alongside, sleek and shiny and graceful. Flying fish shot out of the ocean up ahead in panic.

The *Guadalcanal* had been out of port about a month when it ran into a hurricane off Cape Hatteras. Censorship prevented David from mentioning it in his letters home, but the ship's on-board newsletter, *Scuttlebutt*, described the winds of nearly 83 miles an hour which made raindrops sting the skin like BB shot, and the bulkhead plates on the hangar deck booming, and the sound of heavy equipment falling in the innards of the ship, and the rainbows and rain squalls in the sky, and the sea whipped to foam like snow. The ship ran a hundred miles before the storm, pitching and rolling as fifty-foot-high walls of water rose up behind and chased and passed her. Much of the time nothing could be seen of the escorts but the tops of their masts. The hurricane with no name—hurricanes weren't given names back then—continued to the coast of Florida, where it drowned eleven men.

On this cruise the *Guadalcanal* saw no action. David would not encounter an armed enemy in his two years' service. Perhaps the closest he or his officer acquaintances would come was at the commissioned officers' golf club in Norfolk; one of the fairways paralleled a fence around a camp for prisoners of war, who obligingly threw mishit golf balls back to them. But David did spend almost twenty months at sea in the North Atlantic, a war zone, and the Germans were there somewhere, too. He stood night watches in immediate command of a ship carrying a thousand men or more. He adjusted well to life at sea, quickly learned new duties as communications officer, and felt that now he had become an adult. He went home on his first leave and arrived at the door in uniform. When his mother, who had some friends over for bridge, said, "Oh, Davy, come in and let the girls see your sailor suit!" he was deeply hurt and offended.

David learned to recognize the sounds of lots of different kinds of aircraft on the *Guadalcanal*, and wrote to Louis describing them. ("The bearcats sound like Greyhound buses with broken spark plugs.") He liked to watch flight exercises and saw many crash landings. One afternoon a group of student pilots went up to try carrier landings for the first time; the Wildcat fighter planes circled as the ship turned into the wind, and then they began to come in. They bounced off the deck, they ignored wave-offs, they crashed into a structure called the island. The men on deck were diving for cover at the first sign of trouble. A plane caught the cable and bounced back hard; after the crash they saw the plane on the deck upside down, with the pilot's glassed-in cockpit smashed flat. An officer in charge grabbed a bullhorn and shouted, "Get up! Get him out of there!" A crowd came running and began frantically trying to lift the plane, until they noticed the dazed pilot himself lifting along with everybody else. He had simply unstrapped his harness and slipped out of the wreck unobserved right after he hit. David saw pilots unbuckle their harnesses and walk away from worse crashes. Later he said this was how he came to believe in seat belts.

He had been in the navy for less than a year when the war ended in Europe. Soon after came Hiroshima and the end of the war with Japan. He remained at sea, with brief stints in the shore patrol in Jacksonville, Florida. He received a promotion, to lieutenant (junior grade). Toward the end of his two-year tour of duty the navy transferred him to the Pacific. He took a train to San Francisco, flew by navy DC-4 to Honolulu, laid over two days, and continued by DC-4 to Guam. He slept in the back of the plane on mailbags, which were like sacks of cordwood. The plane stopped at Johnston Island, little more than a landing strip and a serviceman sitting at a desk talking to himself, and Kwajalein, where the plane developed a fuel leak. The sun went down during the eight-hour flight from Kwajalein to Guam. David sat up forward and looked out the pilot's window at the pink-tinted cumulus clouds against sky the color of aluminum over the black Pacific. The sun disappeared below the clouds and the west became red, then purple, then a fading glow in which a single brightening planet rose. Then there was nothing but the planet and the black sea. He looked back into the cabin at the lights farther aft, and his pupils contracted, and when he turned again to the pilot's window all he saw was his own reflection. He landed on Guam in the dark, reported to the bachelor officers' quarters across the street from the airport, found a bed in a Quonset hut, put sheets on the mattress, sprayed the bed thoroughly with DDT, and went to sleep.

At Guam he boarded his new ship, a big black aircraft carrier called the *Boxer*. She weighed 37,000 tons, was as long as three football fields, and carried almost a hundred planes. She was bound for China, he rejoiced to learn; he would waste none of his hoarded Kodachrome on the boring scenery of Guam. He had only about two months left in his enlistment, a fact which may have increased his natural tendency to smart remarks and insubordination, such as saying "Okay" instead of "Aye, aye, sir!" "This is practically a sightseeing luxury cruise for me," he wrote to his brother Louis. To his brother Teddy, confined in Lakeside Hospital for a long series of tests, he sent many-page letters describing the Chinese on sampans sorting through pails of kitchen refuse lowered over the *Boxer*'s side, and the rickshaw trip he took all around Hong Kong behind a barefoot puller, and the Finnish woman in the Tsingtao PX with eyes the blue of newly turned steel.

In mid-June 1946 he returned to Guam and started for the States on the destroyer *Atlanta*. To a fellow officer from the *Guadalcanal* he wrote that the cruise to China had been "among the most wonderful months of my life." He received his discharge at the Great Lakes Naval Station in July, and arrived home a civilian in time for the Fourth.

•

While in the navy David heard from Stanford that he had been awarded his chemistry Ph.D. On a leave visit home late in 1945 he walked into the offices of Standard Oil of Ohio, in Cleveland, and asked if there were any jobs. He got an interview with the company's small chemical research department. As part of the interview he was given a psychological test which included the question "What is your ultimate ambition in life?" In the space provided he wrote, "To drink up all the beer in the world." Dr. Everett C. Hughes, head of the research department then, recalls, "I thought that was a good answer from a guy in uniform who had just walked in off a battleship. We were trying to get inventive people. I believed we would get an invention from him." Dr. Hughes wrote David a letter offering a position as senior research associate at a salary of $330 a month. David took the job, the only one he would have for the rest of his life, and started work on July 15, 1946.

Standard Oil of Ohio, called Sohio, was one of the companies formed by the court-ordered breakup of Rockefeller's giant Standard Oil Trust. Other fragments included Standard of New Jersey (now Exxon), Standard of New York (later Socony-Vacuum, now Mobil), Chesebrough (now Chesebrough-Ponds), Borne-Scrymser (now Borne Chemical), and South Penn Oil (now Pennzoil United). Sohio became an independent oil company marketing and refining oil in Ohio; legal restrictions kept it from marketing under its own name outside the state. It had no crude oil production, as the Ohio oil fields had dried up long ago, and no oil pipelines, and an antiquated plant designed originally to produce kerosene. Competition from companies with better crude supplies almost put it out of business in the 1920s. In 1928 the company got a new president, W. Trevor Holliday, a man who kept a bust of himself on his desk. Holliday reduced gasoline prices to recover Sohio's lost market share, cut distribution costs, and improved profits generally. Soon after he came, the company set up a department of chemical research, a field it had neglected, evidently, since the days of Herman Frasch. Sohio researchers set about trying to remove mercaptans from gasoline to make it smell not as bad, and looking for chemical inhibitors to keep it from forming gummy deposits on copper engine parts. Eventually the company received patents for processes to solve both problems. Everett "Doc" Hughes took over as research director in 1942. He is a big, broad-faced man whose eyebrows seem perpetually raised in a look of happy anticipation, as if he is about to open a present. He put David to work trying to devise a better lubricating oil for use on metal-cutting lathes. Such oils, called cutting oils, are poured over the piece in the lathe to make cutting easier. Here again the problem had partly to do with smell; some of the cutting oils smelled so bad that neighbors blocks away from the research lab complained. In a shed behind the lab David turned thousand-dollar "logs" of solid steel in a big lathe and began pouring

My father in the late 1940s

various oils on them and chipping and gouging them and observing the results.

He lived with his family in the new house his parents had built across Lake Road and a distance west from their old one. The new house had the lake in the back yard. Ray and Cora had gone through all kinds of problems trying to get the house built; just starting it took the whole war. Their friends could not understand why Ray insisted on a floor plan that could be divided into two independent living units. Ray had begun to worry about his health, and about what would happen to Teddy if he and Cora weren't around. He wanted a house that Teddy could live in while renting part of it to a tenant to pay its upkeep. Ray did not tell his friends this. Getting materials and workmen was so difficult that months went by without much progress. The family sold its other house and had to move out and board with relatives, which upset them, especially Teddy, a smart boy who probably understood that this was all really for him. They moved in not long before David got out of the navy.

Ray and Cora had talked to heart specialists at the Cleveland Clinic about a new operation described as "an almost sure cure" for Teddy's condition. They considered the risks and benefits for a couple of years, discussing it also with David, Louis, and Teddy, and finally decided to go ahead with the operation. A surgeon at Johns Hopkins Medical Center in Baltimore was to perform it. Ray and Cora drove Teddy to Baltimore in October of 1948. After giving him a few days to rest from the trip, the doctor operated. Teddy came out of surgery and seemed fine; he was no longer blue. But one day soon after, he sat up in his hospital bed, thanked his mother for giving him a wonderful life, collapsed, and died.

This is probably the main reason David did not like to remember his childhood—all those years of hoping, all those battles with the goat, and Teddy died anyway. Ray's sister Peg says that Ray felt so guilty about the decision to operate that he headed into a decline which Cora could not get him out of no matter how she tried. Worry about Teddy may have distracted David from what he wanted now in his own life: marriage and children. He took a while to look for a wife. He had no car—he was one of many on waiting lists to buy a new car after the war—but his mother let him borrow hers. He dated women from work, but decided he didn't want to marry a chemist. He went to church, but did not meet the kind of women he was interested in there. He decided that women he liked might be involved in the theater, so he went to the community theater in the neighboring town of Lakewood and tried out for a part in their production of *I Remember Mama*.

C H A P T E R 1 2

GROWING UP, PEGGY HURSH was so close to her parents she felt sometimes as if they were all different parts of the same person. Her father, Osie, and her mother, Flora, liked children in general, and were crazy about her. She filled years that would otherwise have been lonely for them after her older brothers and sister had moved away. She had friends, but liked best to do things with her parents. She went on vacations with them every summer, to Petoskey, Michigan, and to Canada, and to cabins on the shore of Lake Erie. She and her mother sometimes took baths together, even when Peggy was a teenager. They rarely missed a basketball game at East Tech High School, where Osie taught. They sat in the bleachers and he took tickets and kept the game clock. Tech had begun as an industrial-arts school on the east side of Cleveland with an almost-all-white student body, but recently more black students had begun to attend. Jesse

My mother in an ad for a now-defunct Cleveland department store. The ad appeared on the back of a program for the Lakewood Little Theater, 1949–50

Owens, the world's fastest human at the 1936 Olympics in Berlin, had graduated from Tech a few years before. The school's mascot is the scarab, a dung-rolling beetle sacred to the ancient Egyptians. The school had a cheer which went:

> Go back! Go back! Go back to your school!
> You tried to beat the scarabs, so you must be a fool!

Flora spoke baby and toddler; whenever she saw a child under the age of about six she would talk to it as if it and she were the only ones there. This embarrassed Peggy. Children responded, and Flora's nursery school was so popular she limited its enrollment, reluctantly. Some parents brought children to her house early in the morning and some didn't pick them up until after supper. Flora stayed up late making costumes—twenty-two squirrel suits, for example—for the plays she put on with the children once or twice a year. Peggy helped her. Osie still woke up earliest in the house and fixed himself a bowl of oatmeal. He had become a soft-spoken man who turned in the cycle of days like a gear. His personality ranged from merry to stern, with a broad band of equanimity in between. His stern aspect had been perfected through years of disciplining high-school boys; it was Germanic, dark, lowering, and, to Peggy, convincing. She always took seriously what teachers said and replayed in her mind comments they made about her. She did her homework, starred in plays, helped edit the yearbook, and graduated first in her high school class.

Her parents expected it would be hard for them when she finally went to college, and it was. Osie asked her to write her mother as often as she could. They splurged on long-distance calls to her, and when her mother heard her voice she nearly cried—it sounded as if Peggy was just next door. Flora looked forward to the package of laundry which Peggy sent home every week, and she carefully washed and ironed it, and sent it back with presents—a package of jujubes, a new sweater—for her and something for her roommate. Not long after Peggy left, Osie received a letter from the Stephens College dean saying that Peggy showed poor or incomplete work in several of her courses. Her parents wrote to her immediately. They feared she was trying to take on too much. Osie told her to drop piano and dancing, and that she needed an ironclad budget of her time. Flora added that it was hard to make the sacrifices they had to if she didn't do her part.

The money Flora sent her to spend, enclosed in the laundry box, came from what she was able to save from nursery school and baby-sitting, often in quarters and dimes. Paying for college took almost all the extra they had. But during Peggy's first term, the war started and there wasn't much to buy anyway. Stores stopped carrying two-way-stretch panty girdles, because of the rubber. Flora also could not find embroidered identification tapes for clothes, Baker's bitter chocolate, apricots, or standing rib roasts. Peggy asked her to buy her a pair of white rubber boots; Flora hunted the stores in Cleveland, set her daughters-in-law searching in Michigan and Boston, and made inquiries by mail, all without luck. Osie had trouble getting non-highway-use gasoline and sometimes could not run the lawnmower. Kleenex, coffee, shoes, sugar, and stationery all became hard to find. "You just have no idea how different it is to shop now," Flora wrote her daughter.

They wanted Peggy to come home for vacations, if possible. One Christmas vacation she was asked to be maid of honor at her roommate's wedding in West Virginia, but the expense of the trip and of the bridesmaid dress, on top of the loss of seeing her, seemed too much to Flora. Peggy decided not to go. Her parents sometimes consulted with her about young men she was seeing. Flora suggested that a young man Peggy liked had been rather indifferent to her and that the right man would love her more than anything in the world. They worried about the boardinghouse she lived in after college when she taught school in Sidney, New York—whether it was entirely safe and whether she could make herself healthful breakfasts there. They were glad when she moved back home. The school in Cleveland where she got her next job was near enough to East Tech that she could ride to work and back with her father.

Peggy's success as a director and an actress pleased them, as long as it remained local. The summer she tried her luck at acting in New York they fretted not to hear more from her; Peggy did not, apparently, tell them about her romance with the sculptor. But they faithfully attended openings of high-school plays she directed in Cleveland and sent congratulatory telegrams and baskets of snapdragons to her dressing room when she starred in productions at the Lakewood Little Theater. Sometimes she called herself an old maid—she was only in

Peggy Hursh with her parents

Peggy in costume, perhaps after an elementary-school play

her twenties yet, but the parts she played tended to be wives and mothers. She seems to have owned the part of Vinnie, the mother in the Lindsay-Crouse adaptations of Clarence Day's *Life with Father* and *Life with Mother*, and played her many times. Critics called her Vinnie "dainty and maternal," "timid and placating," "winsome, wily," and "winsomely sweet." Probably she portrayed mothers so convincingly because of her familiarity with her own.

•

She had known David Frazier her whole life. Her mother had sometimes worked for his mother, helping with children's parties and taking care of Teddy. When David was a senior, he signed her high-school yearbook, along with most of the rest of the class. They met again at the Lakewood Little Theater when he was twenty-nine and she was twenty-seven and both had parts in *I Remember Mama*. David was cast as Dr. Johnson. His first lines were "How do you do, sir?" and "We must get her to a hospital. At once. We'll have to operate." (I can see how he got the part. Those are good lines for him.) Peggy played the woman with whom a reprobate uncle is keeping company. She had few lines and was supposed to project quiet dignity. *I Remember Mama*, an adaptation of Kathryn Forbes's reminiscences of her Norwegian-immigrant childhood, was one of several plays about middle-class families which became popular around the Second World War. These plays featured overbearing elders disguised as lovable eccentrics; jokes about maids; mischievous, lovable children; and happy endings. Today they seem like proto-sitcoms.

Sometime during the fall or spring theater season, 1948–49, David and Peggy began to date. The following summer Peggy joined a company of Cleveland actors who had been hired to put on plays at a summer theater in Malden Bridge, New York. She went there in June. While she was away, she and David wrote to each other:

[June 27]

Dear Dave,

Hello—you! Who are you? Where'd you come from and *now* where've you gone—damn it!

I miss you, Dave. I miss you. I can't quite understand it, but I do. I really hope you've been *very* lonely.

Dave, the playhouse is beautiful, very simple, but well-

equipped. The setting is scenically all that could be asked. I like
the company. I have a small part in the first show, but, gee, I
want a *huge* part—gaudy. I want to be completely and thoroughly the actress this summer.

I'm living in a cabin right in the woods—loads of bugs, spiders, flies, mosquitoes, *everything*. I keep telling myself I'm not
at all afraid of them. Now if I could believe it.

Tomorrow, I'm going in swimming in the nude in the creek
above the dam—*alone*. Why do I tell you? Really—I don't know
—darling. There's a lot I don't know. Tell me, will you, but more
important—*write*.

[June 30]

Dear Peggy,

Got your very nice letter this afternoon—did you enjoy your
swim . . . alone? Very unsafe to swim alone, they tell me. Must
take a practical, pessimistic view of these things . . .

You want to know about me? Well, there was a strong movement afoot in the Lakewood Police force to toss me in the clink
last night. Long story. Seems like Lake Avenue is closed between
West Blvd and 117th St. . . . At the corner of 117th and Edge-
water was some sort of confusing barricade—and a rather confused cop. As I filtered through, I remarked rather
conversationally to the cop, "You sure have things fouled (sic) up
here, don't you?" Then I drove on in my sedate way. I stopped
for the light by the Lake Shore Hotel and there was a roar beside
me and there was the cop on his motorcycle . . . What burned
the guy most was I was totally unrepentant. Well, we talked for
quite a while, things becoming more relaxed and friendly as we
proceeded. Finally, we parted friends . . .

[July 8]

Dear Dave,

I shall really try to make my letters more factual in the future. It's difficult, though. Even in all this excitement and in the
happiness I feel I remember those lovely moments. Do you? I
find it hard to believe you do. It seems unreal. Dave, make it
real again—for another moment. Come to see me. We have an

extra room for visitors. Besides, there's another good reason. I've been given a marvellous part. I'm playing the mother, Lavinia, in "Another Part of the Forest" July 20th through the 24th. Next week we're giving "The Imaginary Invalid" by Molière. I'm in that, too—playing the shrewish wife, Beline. No! It's not type casting! Well, all of it is very exciting. It's the biggest thrill I've ever had—well, almost, but, after all, you're not around.

The opening last night was wonderful—very successful for which I'm grateful.

Dave, the next one will be factual. I must end this—entrance coming up—I'm Mrs. Pringle.

I loved your letter—glad you weren't arrested.

[July 12]

Dear Peggy,

. . . Glad to hear you've got a good part in "Forest." Week end of 23–24 July, you say? Well, the gods willing, I shall drive up and see how you do it. Expect me before, but not much before, curtain time on Saturday, July 23. By the way, where *is* Malden Bridge? . . .

Dropped in at the new drug store at Eddie Knoll's center the other day. Said I to the gent behind the counter, "How ya fixed fur vanilla cones?" Said he, "Pretty good," and he brewed one up for me, but before he handed it to me he wrapped it in wax paper. "Hey," I says, "Howinell am I gonna eat it like that?" and without batting an eye he came back, "Oh, I thought you wanted to take it to your kid out in the car." I felt very flattered. Nice idea. Need some help, though. Any volunteers?

[July 19]

Dear Dave,

Hurray! I'm so glad that, God willing, you're coming next weekend. I really miss you, man!

. . . Should I find a place for you to stay? Yes, I guess I'd better.

Honestly! The circles I'm dancing! Playing the "Shrew" in "Invalid" at night and rehearsing Lavinia frantically during the day. Oh, what a whirl of lines I'm in! I'm only afraid I'm going to do "Invalid" with a southern accent.

I'm a very good volunteer, Dave, very good indeed.

Let me know when! I can't wait!

[July 19]

Dear Peggy,

Just a few words to let you know I've been doing a little checking and I find that Malden Bridge is too far away for one week end's driving. Therefore I'll take the night train each way and I s'pose I'll be drifting in about noon or thereabouts . . .

Had a wonderful time sailing last weekend. Went out right after dinner on Friday night—not much wind then, but there was a beautiful sunset and I sort of drifted around and watched the stars come out as the sky got darker and the lights came on in Cleveland. About the time it got really dark the wind started to come up and I started to move right along. I sailed a few miles off Cleveland—it was a funny, godlike sort of feeling, cruising absolutely silently, unseen, alone, just a little way from the great city. There was a baseball game on and the stadium was all lit up. After the game was over the stadium lights went out and I sailed back to the mass of flickering lights from the swarm of fishermen off Rocky River. I ghosted around among them for a while, but the wind was coming up all the time and soon the fishermen started to go in and about two I found myself alone in a world of black water and unseen spray and ominous, threatening, impersonal wind. I turned towards the two green lights that mark the Rocky River harbor and roared along on top of the cresting waves until the big, white beacon loomed beside me in the dark and I was safely inside the breakwall.

See you soon, lovely lady . . .

[July 28]

Dear Peggy—

As this will attest, I got home safely after our wonderful weekend. You may be sure it's one I'll never forget. Always losing things, weren't we? The whole thing was wonderful and I'll never have any regrets no matter how it all turns out.

After you left me on Monday I walked around town and determined that there wasn't a single movie in town that I cared to see. So I eased into the bar of the Hotel Ten Eck (that isn't the name, is it?) and had four beers in a row and discussed the eternal verities and the baseball scores with the bartender—then I staggered into the street and wandered around for a while and drank four chocolate milk shakes and finally, feeling fine, I wandered into the station, found my train, got on and in, and woke up in Cleveland . . .

I love you very much . . .

[August 3]

Dear Peggy,

Haven't heard from you since my wonderful week-end in Malden. What's the matter? trying to get rid of me?

All proceeds peacefully here. Had the grand opening of the new Kroger store up by your place. They gave out free orchids. So did the new Linder-Davis store downtown, for that matter. Haven't been in either place but the people who have say that they're quite the nuts . . .

"Everything happens for the best in this, the best of all possible worlds," was written as satire, but in our case it's true. Don't worry or get upset—everything will turn out wonderfully no matter what.

[August 5]

Dear Dave,

I miss you! I'm sorry I haven't written, but I think of you always!

Mother and Dad are coming this week-end.

No news.

[August 11]

Dear Dave,

I'm sorry, darling, to be so long. I guess you take advantage of the people you love. Really, though, enough is enough! Let's face it! I'm exhausted! It's all my own fault, and I've firmly resolved to be sensible from now on.

I've been worried, too. I'd hate to rush you into anything. You know that, Dave. I've been upset. That worry at last has left, and darling, now you don't have to marry me. Think of that! Feel the freedom in the air. Actually, Dave, I don't believe I would have minded, although it certainly wouldn't be the ideal way to begin. I love children and I want them! I intend to be a good mother!

Well! That's that!

I wish you could have seen the show this week—"Goodby Again"—sophisticated comedy. I had the role of a wife who desired to rekindle an old flame—much fun. This one you should have seen because I wore beautiful clothes and could try to be young and lovely . . .

Well, Dave, now you can go out and celebrate with a big tall glass of beer and some nice bachelor talk with the bartender.

[August 12]

Dear Peggy—

Just got your note. Certainly was brief, wasn't it? Why don't you sit down right now and write me a long letter. Tell me about the shows and the weather and Tink and Stu and Polly. It will probably do you good and I know it'll do me lots of good . . .

The sailing has been good. I sailed most of Friday night—it was quiet and calm and there was a big full moon and occasionally I'd see another sailboat, white and ghostly and vague and absolutely soundless in the moonlight. There were hundreds of fishermen with their intense blue-white lanterns and a few stars and a warm, steady, friendly wind. Wonderful.

Then on Saturday I was out again. As I went out there was a slight off-shore breeze, but that very quickly died, and by 12:30 I was drifting around becalmed and wishing I had the energy to paddle back in. Then all at once a north east wind started and by 1:00—one half hour later—there was so much wind I almost had more than I could handle. I sailed straight out until I was almost out of sight of land and then I turned and rushed back right down-wind, rolling along on top of the feathering waves . . .

Please don't get worried or upset—we've got a wonderful future . . .

[August 27]

Dear Dave,

I'm worried! Why haven't I heard from you? Did I say something? Please let me know! I hope you've just been busy. I hope I didn't say the wrong thing. I so often do. It's an impulse I should curb, I know . . .

I love you, Dave. Don't worry me like this!

[August 29]

Dear Peggy—

I'm sorry I haven't written—really I've been busy. I've been learning a special brand of higher mathematics known as "mathematical statistics"— Don't let it fool you—it isn't the "statistics" most people think of . . .

[September 11]

Dear Dave,

It was wonderful to talk to you. Are you *very* annoyed? I don't know what to say. It's just been an unbelievably rugged summer, and the only way I got through it was by concentrating on nothing but what I was doing. But it's been exciting, too, because now I can believe one of the dreams of my life. I believe now that I can act. And I don't want to give up the theatre *ever*. I don't believe I could. However, that doesn't mean the glittering stars of Broadway.

Because one thing that has sustained me is the thought of my love for you and the miracle of your saying that you love me. And I don't want to give you up, Dave . . .

Darling, please miss me! Wait for me! Love me!

Peggy came home, then left for Yale School of Drama—too late for fall term, as it turned out. While she waited in a hotel in New Haven to learn if she could attend, she wrote to David that she was really lonely and that not even he was a bulwark for her because he wasn't sure that he wanted her. When Yale told her to try again next term, she went back to Ohio without regret. David meanwhile had been trying to persuade his company to send him to the Institute of Nuclear Studies at Oak Ridge, Tennessee, so he could learn how to trace chemicals using radioactive isotopes, and in January he went for a three-week course.

[January 5]

Dear Peggy,

Here I am at Oak Ridge—and what a town! All government, of course, though there are privately operated stores and restaurants, etc. There is absolutely nothing to do here outside of working hours—except a couple of movie houses showing Bob Hope & westerns & such. Apparently the natives have to stay home & amuse themselves, and the town shows it—you never saw so many children—the place just crawls with them. There aren't even any bars or beer parlors . . .

How goes "Life with Mother"? Making money hand over fist? What's the hot gossip around the theater?

[January 11]

Dear Dave,

. . . Yes, there's lots of gossip around the theater *and* village lately. There's the incredible rumor that Peggy Hursh is going to marry Dave Frazier. Upsetting, isn't it? People, it seems, are always cornering Mother. Poor thing! She doesn't know what to say, but you can see she'd like to pretend it was true about her popular—but unmarried (unsuccessful) daughter. She asks me what to say—and is it true? Of course, I tell her truthfully that I know *nothing* . . .

You see, Dave, I don't agree with you. I don't believe you should go through life with a long face and pessimistic views. I think it's ridiculous to say it's necessary. I don't believe in unhappiness—I don't want to be—but I am. This confounded longing in me won't be still! It's always been there in the background, but now it's tom-toms beating my brains out so I can't think straight anymore. I've said No! and I don't know why. No reason I can think of seems good enough. Forgive me, Dave. I miss you.

They were married about three months later in the Presbyterian church in Lakewood. David's brother Louis served as best man, and the maid of honor was a woman who had played the cook in *Life with Father*. David thought it would be funny to pay the minister in change; he and Louis gave him a heap of pennies they pulled from their pants pockets. A reception at Flora and Osie's followed the ceremony. The newlyweds moved to an apartment on Cedar Road in Cleveland Heights. They did not go on a honeymoon until Peggy's teaching had ended for the summer, when they took a long car trip to Quebec. By then Peggy was pregnant. At the birth of their first child, me, David was so excited he couldn't remember his address to give the Western Union agent when he telegraphed his parents in Florida. He invited the man from the diaper service to stay to dinner, but the man declined, saying he had seen new fathers before. Peggy's parents sent her roses in the hospital, and Flora finished the baby bunting she had been sewing. She spent days helping with the baby after Peggy came home. As my mother would often tell me, she was happier then than she had ever been in her life.

PEOPLE OF Flora and Osie Hursh's generation and circumstances tended to disapprove of serving food from its original container at the dinner table. Even at breakfast, people like them usually poured the milk or cream into pitchers first. They apologized for gifts wrapped at the store and cakes made from mixes. They called the refrigerator the icebox and air conditioners coolers and sherbet "sherbert." They did not want to be poor, and they weren't so sure about being rich, either; they believed certain things were too cheap for them and certain things too fancy, too "utterly smart." The list of words they would not say or write was long and included swear words, "shut up," and slang expressions. Their children generally swore more than they did, and their children's children a lot more. The Sabbath became secular during their lifetime. The sight of stores open on Sunday continued to surprise them. They kept a family Bible in a prominent

Osie and Flora Hursh's Ford, parked outside the first place they stayed in Tucson when they moved there in 1952

spot in the living room and were careful not to set anything on top of it. They attended church and took it for granted that they believed in God, usually without giving the matter much thought. They talked about religion less, in general, than their parents and grandparents had.

At bedtime, they wound clocks. On Saturdays they weeded their driveways and varnished their front doors and stained their fences. They covered solid walnut bedsteads with coats of enamel paint which a later generation would strip and sandpaper away. In the mornings they set empty bottles on the back porch for the milkman, with some coins for the next delivery. They used Sloan's liniment for rheumatism and camphorated oil rubs for colds and witch hazel for soreness and bruises. When very hungry, they might say, "My stomach's been thinking my throat's cut!" When faced with a complicated problem, they put on their thinking caps. They listened to programs over the radio—*The Cities' Service Orchestra* and *Doctor I.Q.* and *Search for Tomorrow*. They collected glassware. They thought of themselves as fair, but often held secret dislikes against blacks, Jews, people who were not intelligent, fat people, foreigners, Southerners, Catholics, Indians (both kinds), and Mexicans. They said there were nice people everywhere in the world.

When thirsty, they drank water, which they sometimes called "Adam's ale." They were middle-aged before they tasted a hamburger or a milkshake and old before they had pizza. They read the *Ladies' Home Journal* or *The Saturday Evening Post* and recommended darling stories they saw there. At Christmas they gave and received gift cartons of cigarettes. On a Saturday night they made popcorn balls and invited friends or relatives over to help. They used things up, even return-address labels with their own names misspelled. They said, "Use it up, wear it out, make it do, or do without." During the Depression they wore their good clothes sparingly and took care of and mended them until they were beyond repair. (Today, a business suit from the thirties is a rare find.) Those who had jobs considered themselves lucky, and were shy about asking for a raise.

Osie Hursh taught school in Ohio until he was seventy-one years old—from 1904 to 1952. During his twenty years at East Tech he also taught shop mathematics in night school. He was in good health when he retired, but Flora was not. Overwork had aggravated a bronchial

condition that ran in her family, and she suffered from spells of bronchitis and pleurisy that kept her bedridden—"bedfast"—for days. Her
doctor recommended a drier climate. Osie had wanted to travel since
he was young but never had been able to manage more than a few
weeks' trip in the summer. Now, with their last child married and
him pensioned and free, he decided they should go to Tucson, Arizona.
Flora did not want to, but she agreed. He said they would stay for
the winter, maybe longer. They started out by car in September 1952,
leaving their house just as it was—food still in the cupboards, beds
made. By the time they reached Tennessee, Flora had developed a
rash which prevented her from sitting up and caused her hands to
swell. A doctor they saw in Nashville said it was an allergic reaction
to an ointment she was using. Osie liked the scenery more and more
the farther west they went on Route 66, but Flora suffered in the
heat. She ate nothing the whole way, drinking only some distilled
water, orange juice, medicine, and tea. Osie found them a motel cabin
with kitchen on North Stone Avenue in Tucson. The air conditioning
made her cough and the sun bothered her rash. She lay on the bed
under cold compresses and wept with homesickness.

Cora Frazier rented their house in Bay Village for them and sent
them the checks each month. Osie thought Tucson was perfect. He
told Flora he dreamed of buying a house big enough for all their
children and grandchildren to visit. Flora could not believe he was
making plans as if they were both about thirty years old. He looked
for teaching jobs and quickly found one at a private school in the
Catalina foothills. Flora spent days alone. Occasionally the woman
who owned the motel looked in on her, and the minister of Trinity
Presbyterian Church, where Osie had begun to go, paid a call. Flora
did not like the unvaried sunshine—no rain fell for months after they
arrived. Laundry hung up to dry was stone dry in half an hour. Flora
said she had deceived her raincoat and umbrella by bringing them
along. Even water from the faucet did not seem wet enough to her.
Sometimes in the evenings Osie took her for drives through unfinished
housing tracts in the desert. She thought the empty sand streets and
the little gardens around the houses looked so hopeless.

Tucson, a Spanish town originally built on an Indian pueblo, is
about sixty-five miles from the Mexican border in southeastern Arizona. In 1950 the city's population was about 45,500. Midwestern

retirees had begun to move there, and people with lung and other medical problems. Tucson had acquired a state university, a large Southern Pacific Railroad station in mission style, a training camp for a pro baseball team (the Cleveland Indians, as it happened), and a nearby air force base. It also would have a high rate of divorce, murder, and suicide. When Flora and Osie arrived, the city was without a television station. Television had come to most American cities of any size by then, but people in Tucson received only one signal, faintly, from Phoenix.

Early in 1953, a TV station, KOPO, announced it would soon begin to broadcast in Tucson. Local appliance dealers stocked up on the latest Stromberg-Carlson, Packard-Bell, Dumont, Philco, and Motorola television sets. People began to raise big aerials all over town; now, in the developments of one-story adobes, there was something taller than the saguaro cactus. A newspaper ad showed a man holding out his suspenders with pride as a uniformed technician crouched on his roof to install an antenna and a woman in the foreground clapped her hands in delight. Another ad showed father, mother, and children leaning forward in their chairs and holding hands as they looked at the television screen: "The 'good old days' are here again, when the family gathered around in the living room to have fun together. In city after city, it has been proved that the modern miracle of television weaves stronger family ties, provides a new center of interest for all . . ."

KOPO, Channel 13, first went on the air on a Saturday at four in the afternoon. People crowded in the small studio and the appliance stores, or watched the opening ceremonies at home. Live, the mayor snipped a blue ribbon while dignitaries including a senator, the county supervisor, and the city manager looked on. On a screen in the background a slide projector showed scenes from around the country—the Santa Anita Racetrack, in California, and the New York City skyline at night. A sponsor asked permission to kiss his wife, for the first live TV kiss ever in Tucson. Then came a feature film, *Texas, Brooklyn and Heaven*, starring Guy Madison and Diana Lynn. After it ended the station signed off. Regular weekday programming would be from 4:00 in the afternoon to 11:10 at night, with short news broadcasts, movies, miscellaneous half-hour shows, and hours of professional wrestling. "Tucsonans seemed to be under the spell of TV," said the Arizona *Daily Star*. It pronounced the reception excellent.

Peggy wrote her mother and told her she should just decide to *like* Tucson, by gum. Flora began to put on some weight and soon was up to eighty-six pounds. She went to Trinity Church with Osie, and a woman there invited her to a get-together called a Circle Meeting at the home of a church member. Flora met a lot of women at Circle, and she played the piano, and everybody made a fuss over her, and she began to feel better about Tucson. Flora had babysat for me often—I called her Barbar, and Osie Ha-ha—and my mother later told me that I used to get so excited whenever I saw Barbar coming up the stairs to our apartment that I almost jumped out of my mother's arms. I missed my grandparents when they left. I repeated "Tucson, Arizona" and "far away." Flora and Peggy thought of each other constantly, and sometimes talked by long-distance telephone while my father timed the calls with a stopwatch.

In March 1953 we went to Tucson for a visit. My mother sent a special-delivery letter to say we were coming, and Flora was so happy she ran to tell first the motel owner, who squeezed her hands tightly, and then her bachelor friend in the cabin across the courtyard, who gave her some sweet peas from his garden. We took the train from Cleveland. I had just turned two. My earliest memory is of riding the train to or from Tucson on that trip: I am sitting on the floor between the seats and crayoning in a Bugs Bunny coloring book. My mother remembered the orange trees along the station platform blooming and the warm, fragrant air when she stepped down. I was so glad to see my grandmother I told her all about changing trains in Chicago and the engineer I had met. We talked and talked. My parents and I stayed at the motel in a cabin next to Flora and Osie's. My father took us for drives in their car to places in the desert where Flora and Osie had never gone. We went with them to church and ate dinner after at the oddly named Panda Steak House. One day we drove several hours to see the Grand Canyon. I got out of the car, walked to the edge of the canyon, and said, "It's nothing but a big hole." We visited Old Tucson, a Western movie set outside town, and I sat on a pony while my grandfather steadied me. My father found the building where he had attended officers' training school. My mother shopped with delight in supermarkets bigger than any she knew in Cleveland.

Osie and Flora sold their house in Bay Village (with Cora Frazier's help) and bought an adobe house a little smaller than Osie had dreamed of in a development in Tucson. Their new back yard was paloverde bushes and pincushion cactus and devil's coachwhip and desert stretching all the way to the Catalina Mountains. Osie fenced a plot in back and planted prickly pear, arborvitae, roses, a fig tree, and a tree that grew lemons as big as grapefruit. The private school where he taught went bankrupt, and he looked for work for months before finding a job doing the books at a company that installed air conditioners. My parents would drive us to Tucson often for visits—sometimes two trips in a year. They took turns with the driving, but my father did most of it. In good weather they could leave Cleveland after dinner on a Friday night and arrive in Tucson Sunday night or Monday morning. They liked to drive straight through. Once we reached the plains I would lean over the front seat, count jackrabbits running in the headlights, and watch for the first mountains to appear on the horizon. The last hundred miles to Tucson were the hardest to wait.

Osie and Flora also bought a big television. Theirs was the first generation to have TV to watch in old age. None of our other relatives owned one yet. My father refused to buy us a TV; he said we would never be one of those families eating from trays around it. When I wanted to watch *The Mickey Mouse Club*, I had to go to a neighbor's house. Part of the fun of our trips to Tucson was watching TV—or "televiewing," as my grandparents called it at first. My father could not object to something that kept my grandmother company as she reclined on the living-room couch under the afghan her daughter-in-law Lydia had knitted. On holidays when she was not well enough to attend church, she watched services on TV. I liked to watch her favorite programs with her, especially *The Lawrence Welk Show*. She always called the show's singing Lennon Sisters "my girls," and I was much older before I realized that the Lennon Sisters had not gone to her nursery school, were not somehow related to her, and in fact had no connection to her at all. With my grandfather I watched *Gunsmoke* and *The Saturday Night Fights*. A large black-and-white TV picture still looks pretty to me.

•

My father told a colleague at his lab that he intended to have six children. The year after I was born my mother had a baby boy who was born blue and lived less than two days. I believe this event may be the source of a chronic guilt I feel, and of the early-morning dread that I have somehow committed a crime in my sleep. Could I, at eighteen months, have been angry at the approach of a rival, and then horrified at my power to make the rival go away? When my mother became pregnant again, I used to startle her and my father by saying, ominously, "Now the problem's coming!" They had no idea what I meant. In 1953 they had a healthy boy, David. On their wedding anniversary in 1955 they had a daughter, Suzan—their fourth child in five years. Because of a problem with my mother's Rh-negative blood, Suzan needed a transfusion, but soon was fine. In 1957 they had Fritz, who also needed a transfusion but was also fine. Meanwhile, they had moved from the apartment in Cleveland Heights to a house nearby, and then to the house in Hudson. In 1958 they had their last child, Margaret, called Maggie.

My father, to forestall people who might refer to himself as "big David" and to my brother as "little David," called my brother "big Dave." The hospital kept Dave a while for observation after his birth because of the Rh problem, and when he finally came home he began to nurse immediately and looked at his mother with beady brown eyes as if to say, "Well, where've *you* been?" My parents and especially my grandmother Flora soon began to compare Dave unfavorably to me. Flora had a leaning toward private alliances and intrigue; she had moved to Tucson by the time Dave was born and did not see much of him as a baby, and perhaps she secretly shared my jealousy of this newcomer. In any case, she was nicer to me than to him. To make up for her, my father sometimes paid special attention to Dave and left me out. Dave liked to get into things, to turn on switches and pull plugs and topple Christmas trees. I remember the way his eyes widened and his mouth got long the time he stuck a spoon handle into an electric socket. My parents took to keeping objects on shelves out of his reach, and he began to carry a chair around with him to help him climb. I was always tattling on him. I used to say to my mother, "Dave's up to his mechanical tricks again!" When my mother caught me slapping him, I said, "How can I discipline this child if I can't hit him?"

Once, the lady who had bought our house in Cleveland Heights hired some men to make a small addition to it, and Dave and I were playing on a pile of dirt surrounded by a low row of bricks there, and I pushed him off the pile of dirt onto the bricks and he cut his head open. A black workman named Zeke saw what happened, and he said

I had to tell my parents. I took Dave inside and told my mother he had fallen, which she readily believed—he was always getting banged up. After Dave had gone to the hospital, I came outside and Zeke was still there. He asked if I had told my parents the truth, and I said I had, and he said, "No, you didn't." In my twenties I told my mother this story and she became retroactively angry at me.

When Suzan was born, my father, who had had only brothers and sons until then, said it seemed slightly indecent to have a girl in the family. Suzan's deep blue eyes and blond hair and fair skin went well with the blue, yellow, white, and lacy pink dresses Flora hand-stitched, happy to sew for a girl baby again. Suzan did not much like to be picked up or handled, and she frowned and fussed when her mother put Dave in the baby carriage with her. One of her first phrases was "Oh, dear!" She and I both played with Dave more than with each other. She argued fiercely when Dave teased her, and would not go along with made-up things he said. Usually she insisted upon the literal. In nursery school her teachers noticed how well she could draw, especially pictures of real events and people.

After the birth of Fritz, my father was too impatient to wait for elevators and bounded up five flights of stairs twice a day to visit him and my mother in the hospital. Fritz's problems with the Rh blood condition were worse than the other children's, and he stayed in the hospital longer. When he finally went home, a nurse who had seen many Rh babies told my mother she had never known any to suffer permanent harm. By now the number of us children had begun to confuse friends and relatives, who had trouble keeping us straight. Our parents were constantly counting heads and taking roll. At a trip to the beach they left Fritz too long uncovered in the shade and he got a sunburn. Afterward they called him "Fritz, the Sunburned Baby." He was the most active of all their babies, so wiggly my mother could hardly dress him sometimes. He became a swift crawler and walked before he was one. He got into more than Dave ever did— climbing stairs, playing in the toilet, taking the phone off the hook, tearing magazines, throwing blocks. He loved to devil Suzan. If told to stop some act of mischief, he would continue, meanwhile shaking his head vigorously to show he knew he was doing wrong. When he was three his mother asked him what he wanted for his next birthday; he said he wanted to be a man.

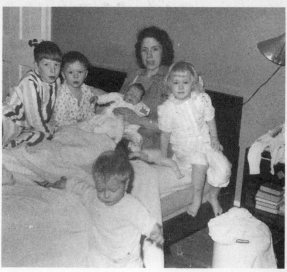

(left) My mother with me in 1951; (right) me, Dave, my mother, Suzan, and Fritz in 1958. Maggie, just born, is at center

(left) A picture I took of my brothers and sisters standing on the front lawn in Hudson; (right) in our parents' bedroom, about 1962

At the birth of their sixth and last child, Maggie, my father joked that they would call it Quits. Margaret Kathryn, named for my mother, was eighteen months younger than Fritz. She would be the closest to my mother of all of us. She talked early and could soon hold her own in arguments. She and Fritz used to argue, "*My* mommy!" "No, *my* mommy!" "No, *my* mommy!" If people tended to notice Maggie more than the middle children, they also thought of her as the littlest, which she could not stand. For Halloween when she was two she told her mother she wanted to be a tiger. Suzan asked if she wouldn't rather be an angel. Maggie said she wanted to be a tiger, and she began to cry. Her mother made her a tiger costume complete with ears and tail which she wore for months. My father's nickname for her was Tiger.

From a certain point of view, we were five towheaded children, a set in graduated sizes. Sandy-Davy-Suzy-Fritz-Maggie. Our parents, who had grown up without siblings close to them in age, seemed to enjoy the "howling mob," as they sometimes called us. Nearly everyone they knew with children had three, many had four or five. The houses that sprang up around us in Hudson filled with big families like ours. But from another point of view, we kids were random people who happened to be related. Our similarities could be seen on the surface, but our differences were unknown, possibly enormous, and not, we suspected, the ones our parents used to distinguish us. We struggled and fought and threw tantrums and misbehaved to find out what the true differences might be. Now when I talk to my brother and sisters about those years, it is as if each of us grew up in a different family.

•

We were raised according to Dr. Benjamin Spock's *Baby and Child Care*, and our mother even took a course from Dr. Spock himself at Western Reserve University in Cleveland. The course was called Child Management. She thought Dr. Spock was very nice and very funny. He told the students that women should breast-feed their babies and not worry about social attitudes which disapproved. This pleased my mother, because she had been breast-feeding all along. Our father said if she failed the course they'd take her children away. She got an A. She felt better in those years than she ever had, despite all the work of three, four, and then five children; she was "*bursting* in good health and spirits," she told her mother, and eager to clean her house as thoroughly as her mother had cleaned. Daily tasks bored her, and she generally let some go for a while, then took care of a month's worth in a day or two. Often she awarded her attention in the same way, deferring it to some future moment and turning off in the meantime. Suzan, when she was two, used to follow her around saying, "Yisten! Mommy! You're not yistening!"

She saved her best efforts for the embellishments—baking twenty-two pounds of fruitcake or 130 gingerbread men at Christmas, canning dozens of jars of black-raspberry jelly, cleaning enough tiny wild strawberries so we could have them over ice cream at dinner. Because of her experience in the theater she knew how to make costumes and did new ones for us every Halloween. She made Dave a devil's costume of red satin, with a black satin cape lined with red, and she made me a one-eyed, one-horned, flying purple people-eater (a character from a then-current novelty song). Other years I was Captain Hook, Sherlock Holmes, and a rajah with turban and yellow silk pants. Dave was a crook and a Roman soldier, Sue was a ballerina and a mermaid and an angel, Maggie a flower, Fritz a policeman. She often stayed up all night and did not finish the sewing until just before we headed out the door. Most of the other kids in our school were ghosts—a bedsheet with two holes for eyes—or hoboes, with faces blackened with cork and bandannas knotted on a stick. Our teachers would take us around to other classes and show us off.

Some years I had three birthday parties—one at school, one at home for friends, and one at home for family. She arranged parties with treasure hunts and games and picnics and trips to see movies like *Spartacus* and *My Darling Clementine*. In second grade I told her that I wanted a birthday cake with no cake, just solid chocolate icing. She had trouble getting that much icing to stand up in the shape of a cake, so finally she put it in a big bowl. Then she iced the top of the chocolate icing with pink icing saying "Happy Birthday." Friends who came to my party agreed that an icing cake sounded like a good idea. We were surprised to find out how difficult a large slice of chocolate icing is to eat.

Household crises in those years seemed to happen when my father was away at scientific conventions. In June of 1953 he told my mother by long-distance phone what to do if the tornado approaching Cleveland from the west got too close; she loaded the car with food, jugs of water, and money, and then waited by my crib in case she had to grab me and escape. The tornado knocked down buildings and killed people on the other side of the city, not near us. He was in the Poconos at a gathering of the American Association for the Advancement of Science when I fell off the swing set in the back yard and broke my arm. She called my aunt and a babysitter and a cleaning lady to look after the younger kids—Fritz was six weeks old—but could not reach anyone. Finally she called a friend who was having a dinner party but came anyway. I remember the black rubber anesthesia mask and the smell of the ether and the clean white plaster on my arm. My father was in New Orleans to give a paper when Suzan complained of a pain in her lower right abdomen and my mother couldn't get a doctor out to the house and finally a doctor told her it sounded like appendicitis and she had to rush Suzan to the hospital. Suzan winced and said "Ouch" at every step as my mother carried her to the car. I stayed home and looked after the rest of us. I called Mrs. Beck, the lady across the street, and she came and made us dinner.

After Maggie was born my mother began to be in plays again. The first time she auditioned for a part at the Hudson Players onlookers broke into spontaneous applause. She appeared there as Bunny in *The Desk Set* and Nell in *The Gazebo*. She also directed a production of *A Man for All Seasons* which a few people in town still talk about today. When Maggie started school my mother decided to take courses toward her master's degree in drama at Kent State University, about twelve miles away. There she got the part of Lady Macbeth in a production on the main stage. This *Macbeth* was as jinxed as most versions of the play seem to be; my mother fell into the orchestra pit during a rehearsal of her sleepwalking scene, and another time a wrench fell from the flies and hit her on the shoulder. She put years of cleaning up after kids into the "Out, damned spot" speech. I saw the show with Dave and Suzan. I remember especially her lines about snatching the smiling infant from her breast and bashing its brains out. She said that playing Lady Macbeth was some of the best fun she'd ever had.

My parents may have died at a younger age than many people, but they probably spent as much time awake as anyone. My father used to lie awake at night by the hour. I knew that if I knocked on their bedroom door at three in the morning his voice would answer immediately, unblurred by sleep, level as water. And if I went downstairs, perhaps I'd see a light and find my mother at her sewing machine surrounded by scraps as she worked on fourteen Russian-townsfolk costumes for a production of *The Inspector General*. Lack of sleep often caused her to nod off when lulls came in her day. Her head would tilt to the side, right itself, tilt to the other side. This happened regularly when she was driving, but she never hit anything and she never got stopped by the police. She went through life in the aura of the good student, the one nobody had to worry about. She believed that whatever she was working on would succeed, even if it seemed late or disorganized, and that the more she did, the more she could do. She had always felt lucky, protected. Ever since childhood she had believed that bad things could happen to other people, but never to her or her family.

•

When we lived in Cleveland Heights my father used to walk the half mile or so from our house down the hill to his research lab on Cornell Road, waving off colleagues who slowed to offer him a ride. When the lab moved to a new building in a suburb and we moved to Hudson, my father drove to work in various off-brand foreign cars— "lawnmowers with roofs," a colleague called them. My mother made him Hawaiian shirts in bright abstract patterns and he took to wearing them winter and summer. He almost never wore a coat. Even on the snowiest day he left for work with nothing over his Hawaiian shirt but his little car. The new lab had plenty of room for the staff of over a hundred scientists, technicians, and others. A high-ceilinged room near my father's office held car and truck engines mounted on columns. The engines ran at high speed day and night, testing oils and fuels. In another room was a sealed chamber mounted on tracks on the floor and ceiling, for experiments which might blow up. (Things occasionally blew up at the lab.) My father roamed the halls a lot; he said he did his best thinking while walking. Then he would return to his desk and pull out its small sliding shelf and sit with his feet up on it. When people asked me what my father did for a living I said that he sat with his feet on his desk.

He had toys in his office—red and white plastic tops, gyroscopes, box kites made of balsa and thread and tissue. A white lab coat hung in a corner, and there were cabinets of small stoppered bottles and cylindrical glass jars labeled in his neat printing. Sometimes he would take an eye dropper, adjust his hot plate to the proper temperature, set the hotplate on the floor, and drip nitroglycerin onto it while standing on his desk. Each drop made a bang like a shotgun. The Sohio lab was the sort of place where you could do that. Doc Hughes ran it loosely and wanted people to have fun. He hired many young scientists just out of college, women as well as men. Staffers set up an informal lab band which played Glenn Miller and show tunes after hours. He also let staffers use lab facilities to work on their cars, a pastime of my father's, who liked to fool not only with his own rickety Lloyd but with almost any disabled car he saw. People around the lab said if you wanted to talk to Dave Frazier, just go out to the parking lot and lift the hood of your car. When the Russians launched Sputnik, two scientists at the lab built a radio dish to track it. People often stayed through the night to listen for the satellite when it passed in its orbit above. The men could not hear the approaching echo quite as soon as the women, who could pick out the higher frequency better. For a while, before the government was making public what it knew about satellites, the Sohio lab was the only source of tracking data in the United States.

My father soon preferred the mathematics of his job to the chemistry. (Doc Hughes says he thinks my father forgot his chemistry while he was in the navy.) His cutting-oil experiments had left him with a thick file of data and not much way to make sense of it. He began to think of better methods of setting up experiments and interpreting results, inspired by Paul Gerhard Hoel's *Introduction to Mathematical Statistics*, a book of his brother's he found lying around his mother's house. He made special note of the section titled "Statistical Design of Experiments," which discussed how experiments could be made more sensitive and efficient using statistical techniques. With a colleague he designed and carried out an experiment comparing the rates of consumption of two motor oils. This turned out so well that he soon was designing more statistical experiments and giving advice on statistical design to other researchers. He taught a course at the lab called Strategies of Experimentation, which most people there took at one time or another. His former colleagues remember him as a proselytizer for statistics who helped to change the way experiments were done

Photo from a newspaper story about the Sohio research laboratory. Dad uses a laboratory engine for an experiment with motor oils

AAAS JULY 23, '51
NEW HAMPTON, N.H.

ACHBER
LACONIA,
N.H.

Dad makes himself conspicuous at a convention of the American Association for the Advancement of Science

not only at Sohio but elsewhere. Many of the papers he gave at scientific conventions had to do with the statistical design of experiments.

Recently I read *Introduction to Mathematical Statistics*, as well as some other books my father learned from, including *Statistical Methods Applied to Experiments in Agriculture and Biology*, by George W. Snedecor. Or rather, I paged through them, mostly without comprehension. The experience reminded me how dull I was at science and math at school, and how afraid of my father's mind I felt sometimes. The only sentences I was sure I understood in the book by Snedecor—the standard text in the course my father taught—were in the introduction:

In searching the unknown for new truths there is mystery, there is adventure, there is the thrill of discovery. As most of us know, also, there are grinding routine and disappointment. Research is a hard mistress, but her rewards bring satisfactions that few of us would forgo.

Then the book headed off into thickets of random sampling, chisquares, standard deviation, and calculus equations the size of paragraphs.

Studies of statistics led my father to operations research, a discipline with claims of being a science developed in England during the Second World War for analyzing mostly military problems—patterns of carpet bombing, for example—and later applied to large and complicated human systems like governments or industries. Operations research, or OR, wanted to quantify the supposedly unquantifiable by using an over-all approach to problems, including ones of human behavior. From operations research he moved to studies in cybernetics, another new science, which has to do with comparisons between electrical or mechanical systems and the human brain.

What these studies offered him, I see now, was a cosmology. Statistics served him at his job, and in ways not related to it. He used them to compare Korean War casualty figures from the local paper and government sources (he concluded the government had to be underreporting the U.S. total), and baseball scores (the games were not being fixed, he decided), and the growth rates of children (mine went way down when the second baby died), and the times at a trotting track across the street from his lab. Statistics went with him everywhere, a flowering of the greater faith people had in science back then. Reading the statistics textbooks published in the late 1940s and early 1950s I came across many words—"alternatives," "options," "choices," "values," "parameters," "channels of communication," "relationship," "attitude," "interaction," "bonding"—of such persuasive magic that they have since entered areas of life far from the science in which they began. I think that, for my father, statistics were a way to explain the complicated postwar world in inclusive, neutral terms, without the old Calvinist insistence on good and evil, saved and damned.

In the early days of computers, my father was one of the few people at the lab not to be afraid of them. With a computer he could practice his religion of statistics more easily than with pencil and paper or adding machine. In the forties, he and his brother talked at length about the ENIAC, the pioneer computer built by the navy and declassified after the war. Its components were vacuum tubes; the transistor had not then been invented. From the first my father pushed Sohio to buy computers and use them in their business. He and another researcher wrote what may have been the first linear program for running a refinery. Doc Hughes says that back then he sent anyone who had a computer question at the lab to him. In the early fifties Sohio did buy a computer, a Bendix G-15, but because management did not think it should be for research staff only, the company housed it in the main office downtown. Researchers had to work there at night, after the accounting staff had finished with it for the day. The Bendix G-15 was nearly the size of a studio apartment. To fix it, technicians crawled around inside.

One afternoon when I was four or five, I crossed the street in front of our house in Cleveland Heights on my own and by myself, something I was never supposed to do. I stood on the smooth green of the opposite lawn with a feeling of adventure and of being-where-one-was-not-allowed. My babysitter, Alice, spotted me out the front window and ran across and grabbed me by the hand and hustled me back; she was angry and, I imagine, scared at what could have happened. When my mother came home she sent me to my bedroom and said that when my father came home he would spank me. I lay in fear in the top bunk, on the bed frame between the mattress and the wall, calculating whether his arm could reach me there. I was pretty sure it could not. Dusk fell. I heard my father come home. I heard his steps on the living-room floor; they stopped, then proceeded up the stairs. He had large feet. They came down the hall, into my room. His arm stretched across the bed. I saw that I had been wrong—it reached me easily. But instead of grabbing, he lifted me out of bed, spoke gently, put my shoes on me, took me downstairs to the car. We got a hamburger and a Coke someplace. Then he took me downtown and showed me the new Bendix computer. It was in a room with windows which ran all the way along one side, a wide-screen view of the industrial flats of Cleveland—steel mills and smokestacks and refinery towers scattered with lights, and here and there a tall, wavering flare burning off petroleum wastes. The computer took up another wall of technical-looking switches and slots and gauges which all seemed to lean forward into the room. If what my father wanted me to learn from the experience had to do with computers, he failed; I never understood them, and am writing this on a manual typewriter. But if he wanted to show me the connection between love and boldness, he succeeded. When I remember that evening I still feel happy, lucky, and brave.

For a while, Sohio kept its research goals modest. A company vice president who oversaw research and development said that if the department did nothing but inform the company of what was then current in petroleum technology elsewhere, that was enough. But naturally a young and patent-hungry group of the kind Doc Hughes had assembled wanted to do more. A research supervisor under Hughes named Frank Veatch got the idea of taking light refinery gases, by-products of gasoline refining which were plentiful and hard to market, and making something with them. He thought Sohio could invent processes to take gases like propane and convert them chemically to monomers—materials from which plastics and other products could be made.

The basic process would involve partial combustion of a hydrocarbon over a catalyst. Instead of simply burning the hydrocarbon—propane, say—all the way, to the usual end products of carbon dioxide, water, and energy, oxidation would be controlled in a reactor. There, at high temperatures, a limited amount of oxygen could combine with the hydrocarbon in a reaction aided and spread around by the catalyst. What you would end up with, ideally, would be a product combining molecules of hydrocarbon, oxygen, and (in some cases) catalyst. Key to the whole process was the catalyst. A catalyst encourages a chemical reaction without necessarily taking part in it. Catalysts are wild cards, often mysterious in their operation, and sort of like spices in cooking. Discovering good ones for certain reactions can be hit-or-miss.

Starting in 1953, Veatch and co-workers experimented with reactions between propane and mineral oxides. At this stage Veatch was using the oxides as well as air to provide the oxygen for the reaction. Reactions between propane and two oxides in particular produced small amounts of acetone, propionaldehyde, and aliphatic acids. However, the company was not interested in these products; a consultant they hired said that such products had little value and would be hard to sell. The company gave Veatch six weeks to try to come up with a more promising result. Researchers began to try other hydrocarbons in reaction with the two oxides which had worked the best with propane. One of the hydrocarbons they tried was propylene, a light gasoline by-product in such ready supply that the company had more than it could dispose of as agricultural fuel and sometimes burned the excess in flares at the refinery. A test of propylene run through the reactor over vanadium pentoxide produced a small amount of acrolein. This liquid, whose name comes from its sharp, tear-producing smell, can be made into some useful plastics and resins. The company allowed Veatch's project to continue.

For the next few years, a number of Sohio researchers worked on improving the propylene-to-acrolein reaction. Along the way they tried many oxidants and catalysts, and began to run the reaction solely on free molecular oxygen in the air. Eventually they found a catalyst, bismuth phosphomolybdate, which produced a conversion of propylene to acrolein at a level of 40 percent. This discovery, which no one had ever made before, caused them to look harder at possible derivatives of acrolein valuable enough to justify the construction of a large manufacturing plant. Most promising of these derivatives was acrylonitrile, a raw material for fibers, polymerized rubber, hard plastics, and plastic flim; at that time most acrylonitrile was being made from acetylene by a costly multistep process. Veatch assigned a recent Ph.D. graduate from Purdue named Jim Idol the job of finding a reaction sequence to make acrolein into acrylonitrile.

My father did not himself work directly on Veatch's acrolein or acrylonitrile projects. He consulted with project researchers often, helping them design and interpret experiments and work out the math of the reactions. At an important moment, he and another researcher came up with new pressures and rates of flow to double the acrolein yield; Veatch told them they had saved the project. Jim Idol says that he sat in my father's office by the hour discussing reaction mechanisms. Idol had the advantage of coming to the project at a later moment and seeing it from the outside. He soon achieved results making acrolein into acrylic acid, a step on the way to acrylonitrile, and he found an effective catalyst for the reaction. He also knew that researchers at Allied Chemical had been able to make a small amount of acrylonitrile by combining acrolein, air, and ammonia. What the Allied researchers didn't have, he guessed, were catalysts as good as Sohio's. Using the catalyst that had worked for acrolein-to-acrylic acid, he fed acrolein, air, and ammonia into the reactor and produced acrylonitrile. Then he had an inspiration, one as simple as the research leading to this moment had been complex. Rather than using acrolein as the feed, he would start with propylene and take the reaction sequence all the way to acrylonitrile in one step. He hooked a cylinder of propylene, another of fertilizer-grade ammonia, and another of compressed air to a reactor charged with the bismuth phosphomolybdate catalyst. He went to a meeting and told his assistant to come and get him if anything happened. In a little while she burst into the meeting shouting, "It worked! It worked!" They had produced acrylonitrile in a 10 to 15 percent yield.

When Frank Veatch heard the news, he fired off a Roman candle in celebration, burning holes in his office ceiling. More work would be required to improve the acrylonitrile yield. But now his team could make a valuable plastics raw material from cheap and plentiful substances using a simple method known to no one else in the world. The company began to plan the construction of an acrylonitrile plant capable of producing about 50 million pounds a year—at the time, total world production was about 160 million pounds. Sohio asked Dow Chemical to go in on the plant with them, but Dow turned them down. Dow and other chemical companies said the process would not produce acrylonitrile of sufficient purity. The plant, built in Lima, Ohio, was on-line and operating within four years of Idol's discovery. American Cyanamid, a large acrylonitrile producer, tried to put Sohio out of business by cutting its own acrylonitrile price in half. Sohio met the price and made money at it.

Eventually American Cyanamid had to buy a license to the Sohio acrylonitrile patent, as did Monsanto, Goodrich, Du Pont, and chemical companies all over the world. Fibers spun from acrylonitrile are among the most heat-retentive of all artificial fibers, and the Soviet Union and China, with large populations to keep warm, bought acrylonitrile licenses from Sohio. Doc Hughes says the Soviet Union paid Sohio the $15 million license fee in gold. World production of acrylonitrile soon rose to billions of pounds a year, most of it produced by the Sohio method. Acrylonitrile found uses in high-impact plastics in telephones, football helmets, and cars. It became a component of oil-resistant rubber and plastic food packaging. Sohio built other acrylonitrile plants and improved its first plant so it could produce nearly 90 million pounds a year. At Lima, the company disposed of process wastes—ammonium sulphate, tar, and other effluents—by injecting them into porous rock formations thousands of feet underground. Today the Environmental Protection Agency lists the Lima plants as the worst producers of deep-well hazardous waste injections in the state. Ohio is one of the worst states for release of toxic chemicals in the nation. Wastes from the acrylonitrile process contribute to making the company which now owns Sohio the tenth-worst toxic polluter in the nation.

From licensing the patent and making the product, Sohio had earned between half a billion and a billion with acrylonitrile by about 1970—estimates vary. The company decided to use surplus cash from that and other ventures to solve the problem of sparse oil reserves it had suffered from ever since the breakup of Rockefeller's Standard Oil. It began a project in partnership with British Petroleum, Ltd., to develop oil fields discovered on the North Slope of Alaska. British Petroleum owned the leases; Sohio, with other partners, would build the pipeline.

The inventors of the acrylonitrile process became famous, in chemical engineering circles at least. Jim Idol appeared on the cover of *Chemical & Engineering News*. A photo inside showed the main members of the acrylonitrile team: Jim Callahan, Ernie Milberger, Idol, Frank Veatch, and Gordon Cross. In the photo they stand relaxed and happy, still young, their hair greased and combed back in early-sixties style, pens in the pockets of their white shirts. Later, Callahan and Veatch would be elected to the Ohio Inventors Hall of Fame. My father was as proud of his part in acrylonitrile as of anything he ever did; a lot of people from the lab felt the same. They took a refinery by-product so plentiful it had to be burned off, and they transfigured it. They took a flame and made it into a football helmet.

•

By 1956, Osie and Flora had so many friends in Tucson that they rated an article in the newspaper to announce their fiftieth wedding anniversary, and Trinity Church held a reception for them. Flora pinned on a corsage for her first-ever airplane ride, back to Cleveland for the celebration my mother had arranged. All Flora's children and nearly all their grandchildren came. Flora and Osie stayed at my other grandmother's cottage on the lake. I was five, and held Flora's hand tightly, jealous of everybody. In those years, their lives, and ours, revolved around our trips to Tucson. Flora would bake us cookies and strudels and lemon pies from their lemons, and the gooey breakfast rolls my father liked. Osie would lay in some Blatz beer for my father to have first thing when we arrived. "Thank you, Professor," my father would say when Osie offered one to him; then he would sit back on the couch with right ankle propped on left knee and drink with road-weary satisfaction. And after we had left, Flora would talk Osie to sleep at night recounting details of our visit. Funny expressions we kids used entered their daily speech. She would find socks we had left behind, and things of theirs we had played with and misplaced. The discovery of the missing bathtub plug in her sewing-machine-table drawer almost made her cry, she missed us so.

Their neighborhood was getting built up. Weeks passed when all Flora heard outside was construction machinery; the house filled with dust. Tucson began work on a new high school nearby. One year Flora heard the bulldozers, and the next she heard the boys on the football team shouting during workouts. She retained her attraction for children. Kids who moved to the neighborhood got to know her, and walked right into her house and back to her bedroom sometimes. She sunned herself on a lawn chair in the back yard listening to the call of mourning doves, as hollow and breathy as a person blowing over the mouth of a bottle. Kids with butch haircuts played around her in their sunsuits, barefoot, pounding on Indian drums made from coffee tins covered at the ends with pieces of inner tube. I made friends with some of these kids when we visited. (Where is Rusty Long today?) Once I was playing with a girl named Kim, running around and chasing and banging doors, and we locked ourselves out of the house. My mother had gone shopping with Flora and Osie, and my father was in the front yard with the other kids flying one of his little balsa-and-tissue kites so high the kite string seemed to be ascending on its own. I ran to tell him, and he said that no one had a key to the house, that we would never get back in. He said that my grandparents would just have to find another house. I protested that it was Kim who had slammed the door, not me. My father said that when I was with a girl, anything she did I was responsible for. I looked in the window at my grandparents' belongings, preserved there now forever. I remember the paperweight in the shape of a scarab beetle, a memento of East Tech, sitting on my grandfather's desk in a blue, eternal twilight.

I liked Tucson better than anyplace. I hunted for garnets in the gravel sidewalks on my grandparents' street, helped my grandfather in his cactus garden with little gardening tools just for me, set fire to the lawn by accident while playing with matches, and told my brothers and sisters that a certain type of cactus would jump at them if they got too close. With my father I walked all over, hustling to keep up with his stride. On the campus of the University of Arizona was a locomotive engine you could climb on at the historical museum, which also had an Indian mummy, Apache shirts made of printed flour sacks, and an exhibit of fossilized mammoth bones with paleo-Indian stone projectile points still stuck in them. (The bones and the points were replicas, I later learned.) My father knew somebody in the university's chemistry department, and he showed me around its laboratory. Then he asked if I wanted to go to the student union. I did not know what a student union was, and replied that I did not want to go to another smelly laboratory. He said that he had intended to buy me some ice cream, but now he wouldn't. Mouth set, he took me back to my grandparents'.

Sometimes I sat by Flora on her bed and examined what was on her night table—her teapot of plain hot water, her bottles of pills, her book of crossword puzzles. I liked to touch her face and feel its looseness and wrinkles. At night a patch of moonlight lay on the coverlet, and during the day the sun crossed the room from the paintings of horses by my cousin Elise on the walls to the photo of Uncle John on the bureau. We played with paper dolls and looked at a lot of magazines. *Arizona Highways* had the prettiest pictures, usually of blooming cacti and buttes and scenery unoccupied by people. She could not stand Jackie Kennedy and always made a sour face when she came across her picture in *Life*. My mother later told me that her mother would have preferred that she, Peggy, had married the President.

Flora's health improved during her first years in Tucson, but then it slowly declined. She went to the dentist for partial sets of false teeth and for fillings for the few bottom teeth she had left; she thought it silly to spend so much money on an old lady. Friends they had made began to fall ill and drop away. A woman who had talked Flora's head off about her children and grandchildren and how they couldn't afford to visit called Flora on a Thursday about plans for the coming week, and on Saturday morning at 6 a.m. the woman's husband called to say she was dead. Flora finally met the children and grandchildren at the funeral; the husband sold the house and went back to Cleveland with his wife's ashes next to him on the car seat. Flora began to spend so much time in bed with pleurisy and colitis that she wore out pajamas and bathrobes. A woman she knew who ran the snack bar at the colored American Legion came to the house to do her hair. Flora said the new hairdo made her look like Liszt. After a long sick spell she finally got up and saw herself in the mirror. She could not believe she had once been that young girl everybody called Floss.

Some people—teachers, especially—get along best with children of a certain age. Flora's gift was for preschoolers, and as I grew, she and I knew less and less how to have fun together. I didn't like to sit around inside. I used to say, "Barbar, let's *do* something!" Also, as other siblings followed me and provided competition, the special attention she showed me made me feel proud and guilty, an uncomfortable combination. When we visited she sometimes wanted to spend more time with me than I did with her, and that made me feel guilty, too. She said she wished she could be "Barbar" again, and not a bothersome old granny. One year we arrived at the house in Tucson to find nobody home. My mother was scared. It turned out that Flora had been taken to the hospital with dehydration. When she came back she looked thinner than ever. After a few days' visit we continued on from Tucson to Los Angeles, where my father had to attend a convention. My mother told Flora that we might just drop him off and come back, but then we found a motel we liked in Pasadena, and went to the beach and to Disneyland, and sort of forgot about Tucson. We returned to Ohio via San Francisco and a northern route. Disappointed and hurt, Flora mailed us the presents she had bought for when she expected to see us again.

Trouble with her heart weakened her so she could not even write letters for weeks at a time. She was not well enough to attend church from June to October 1959, and did not put on a dress all that summer. Osie had quit working for the York Refrigeration Company; Flora aired out his closet, happy that he would no longer be bringing home all that office cigar smoke in his clothes. She always had the most sensitive nose. He began to substitute-teach, receiving his accreditation at age seventy-eight, which officials told him was a record for the state of Arizona. He stayed at home more, but still spent some days working and some evenings at church choir practice. She lay in bed and composed letters to Peggy and her other children in her head. After we visited at Christmas in 1959, she felt so low she feared she would not be around for Bill and Ginny's visit in June. She went outside only twice between October of 1960 and May of 1961. Her son John made a special visit to see her. She sent me a wristwatch, my mother said, to remember her by. She managed to make a pair of Raggedy Ann and Raggedy Andy dolls for Maggie; my mother said they were so precious she could hardly bear to let Maggie play with them. In 1961 we drove to Tuscon as soon as school let out for the summer. Afterward Flora wrote us a letter:

My Dear Ones,
This is a very lonely place since you went away. It was so wonderful to see you all again—and I was so very sad that I could not do *anything* for you. How I *longed* to—I sit here on the couch seeing Maggie's little *hands*—and her bobbing curls—and dancing—trying to do it like Suzan— They are such darlings both of them—and Davy and Fritz banging in and out—you know it has been too quiet around here all Winter—and Sandy I know, was disappointed with his Barbar—but Barbar was very pleased with him—he has learned many things— In my heart I kept

thinking prehaps I'll never see them again—and my Peggy who
brought so much joy to us . . . and given us so much pleasure
every time you came. What a wonderful family you have. God
bless you all—I am so sorry Maggie had to have measles—but so
glad you got home all safe and sound— I wish I could bake you a
birthday cake—as good as our 55th wedding cake!—daddy has to
do all the shopping now—and I hope it will be OK. I tried to tell
him just what to get—but he is not such a good shopper as you
are—by the way—I'll have to send Mrs. Carr out for Father's
Day—Dad likes his shirts and pajamas so much. Dad taught several days this week— We have had lovely weather—*so much*
love and "thankyoualls" and how I wish I could *see* you—

Always lovingly,
Mother & Barbar

She died the next month. I came home from day camp and my
mother was in the kitchen, her nose red from crying. I had avoided
thinking about my grandmother, and somehow believed her death
could not really happen. I ran to some woods up the street and climbed
a tree and cried. I felt additionally sad because this interrupted the
summer, and I did not know how long my sadness would last. She
was buried in Tiffin next to her mother-in-law, who had never liked
her, in a casket so much bigger and sturdier than she was. The wind
blew hard the day of the funeral, and the lake at my other grandmother's house, where we went afterward, was muddy and rough.

Osie stayed in Tucson for a while, then sold his house and moved
in with Uncle John and Aunt Lydia. He often caught himself saying,
when something interesting happened, "Well, now I'll have to tell
Mother about *that*." He told Fritz he had done all the growing he
was going to, and now he was settling, like a full sack when you shake
it. He died of a stroke in 1964. From his lifetime of work, he left an
estate of about thirteen thousand dollars.

IN THE SUMMERS, when we weren't away on trips, we spent almost every Sunday at my grandmother Cora's cottage on Lake Erie. We skipped church between Memorial Day and Labor Day. Soon after Sunday breakfast my parents would load the station wagon with bathing suits, towels, vest-style life preservers, the wicker picnic basket, casseroles of food Grandmother had told Mom to bring, my fishing rod and tackle box, parts to my father's little sailboat. Some of us kids would sit in the car for a long time before everything was ready. Then we would head west, most often via the turnpike, where we looked from the side windows at ourselves reflected bulgingly in the chrome hubcaps of trucks we passed. Each new stage of the journey had a higher level of anticipation. Finally we would pass Cranberry Creek and the old cemetery, take a right onto the dead-end road which had washed into the lake years before, and turn immediately at a break in an Osage-orange hedge into my grandmother's drive.

Fishing at sunset from the pier at Grandmother's cottage on Lake Erie

If we pulled up next to Uncle Louis and Aunt Evie's station wagon, we cheered, because that meant our cousins Libby, Cindy, Louis, and Annie were already there. Those of us who had put on bathing suits beforehand hopped out onto the lawn—it was so moist and green, a real lawn, not just mowed weeds like parts of our own lawn, Grandmother could make anything grow—and ran across it to the stone steps leading down the bluff to the beach. We were not supposed to run down these steps and so walked fast on the balls of our feet, shouting to let our cousins know we were here. The steps ended at a worn path which made the rest of the distance to the beach in a single switchback, worn deep at the turn. We ran across the beach, past Aunt Evie who had already started a driftwood fire to cook hot dogs, and splashed into the lake.

Lake Erie can be so rough and cold and windswept you'd think the glaciers left just last week. It is so shallow the bottom often gets churned up and whitecaps turn the color of café-au-lait. Its waves don't roll, as on larger bodies of water, they bounce and vault, and can swamp even big boats. It has fooled and drowned many people. But when it is calm, as happens often in the summer, it is like the world's biggest swimming hole. Its shallowness causes it to warm quickly, and by July it is usually in the low seventies, a refreshing coolness after the sun. The sand bottom is fluted into little ridges which flatten underfoot like icing. You can float on your back and practice the crawl and breaststroke without waves splashing in your face. On calm days some of us even brought bars of soap down to the lake and took baths. Waves on such days were so mild as to be hardly waves at all, curling on the brown and purple sand like toes. Passing motorboats left wakes you could see heading shoreward a half mile away until they finally landed on the slate pebbles at the beach's edge with a sound like setting down a sack of change.

Grandmother's beach stretched thirty or forty feet from the base of the bluff to the water. A long concrete pier extended far enough from the west side of the beach that we could jump from it into the water without getting hurt—although we were not allowed to jump from it. A partly sunken crib of logs filled with big rocks enclosed the beach at the eastern end. We boy cousins built forts of driftwood twigs and sand, manned them with plastic soldiers, and then blasted them with stones. In addition to the large, devastating stones, I liked to throw handfuls of small pebbles, which peppered the sand walls with a bird-shot effect. We dug tunnels from opposite directions until our fingers met underground. The girl cousins drew outlines of dream houses in the sand, with kitchen and living room and patio and bathroom all only a little smaller than actual size. When they went back into the water they were careful to leave their beach towels where they belonged, inside the lines of the bathroom.

Sometimes we played with our older cousin Jimmy Moses, whose family lived down the bluff. Jimmy's mother was a first cousin of our grandmother's, on the Benedict side. He stood over six feet tall and played college football; I remember him as something I used to climb on, like my bunk bed. Waist-deep in the lake he would toss us in the air, one after another, until he had to get out and sit on the pier and rest. I regarded him as a hero, and he actually was. On a winter night in 1950, Jimmy was skating on the lake with a group of other kids when the ice broke off and began drifting away on an offshore breeze. Jimmy stripped to his shorts and swam a quarter mile through darkness in 33-degree water back to shore, then ran to get help. By the time rescuers reached the kids, they had drifted out over a mile and waves were beginning to break over the ice. My grandmother talked of many relatives she admired, but Jimmy was the only one with a framed recent newspaper clipping hanging on the cottage wall. He won medals and awards, and walked in a halo of heroism from then on.

Mornings and evenings, I fished from my grandmother's pier and other piers up and down the beach. I searched between the seats of our car for change to spend at the fishing tackle shop at Hayes's Marina at the mouth of Cranberry Creek, or asked my parents for the money. The tackle shop, in a converted two-car garage at an end of Art Hayes's house, had a horse trough full of minnows swirling in the turbulence of the little outboard motor which aerated it, a glass counter of knives and reels and lures, a refrigerator with sodas and paper cartons of nightcrawlers, and a mounted pike with a yellow-red-and-black Flatfish lure dangling from its jaw. I bought a red-and-white plastic cone about two inches long and an imitation minnow with white plastic hair for a tail and a body of white plastic tube painted red at the head, a black dot inside a white dot for an eye. I tied the cone to the end of my line, and tied the minnow from line trailing from a ring in the narrow end of the cone. When you reeled in quickly, the cone splashed and bubbled, attracting fish to hit at the minnow.

This rig was designed for white bass. Sometimes on calm summer evenings schools of white bass moved in to shore chasing bait, roiling the surface and splashing by the end of the pier, and I would get so excited I lost coordination and messed up my casts and created maddening backlashes in my reel. After a good cast I reeled in; the cone bubbled; a white bass flared at the lure; the cone suddenly submerged; then the sensation was sort of like flying a kite underwater, as the broad little fish swam and darted and tried to get away. When the school was thick enough, I could sometimes tie two lures to the cone and reel in two fish at a cast. Some evenings I caught a dozen or more. I gutted and scaled them on the pier, my knife making a gritty scraping on the concrete as I cut through the heads. Grandmother dredged the fish in cornmeal batter and fried them for breakfast.

I stood on the pier and cast endlessly even when the white bass weren't running, using lures and worms. Once I was casting a multicolored spoon marked in a fish-scale pattern and I hooked a sheepshead of about two pounds—the biggest fish I had ever caught. Sheepshead, also called freshwater drum, are regarded as trash fish on the order of carp, but I did not know that. I put the sheepshead on my stringer and carried him along the beach showing him off. Then I decided Jimmy Moses might like to see him, and ran up the bluff to Jimmy's house, and from there to Cousin Dave and Anne's. I came back to Grandmother's pier still carrying the fish. As I stood admiring him further, he peed. My mother and Aunt Evie felt sorry for him and said I should let him go. He had met most of the family and had been out of the water for twenty minutes or so. I took him off the stringer and put him back in the lake, and he slowly swam away.

Grandmother had a rule that kids could not go in the house until they had rinsed all the sand from their feet. We stepped through a flower bed of wood chips to a hard-to-turn-on, spiderwebby spigot attached to a garden hose. The water from the hose always was bitter cold as we hopped from foot to foot on the soggy grass. Grandmother had bought out her brother's and sister's shares in the cottage after her father died and had redecorated it herself, and she did not want it full of sand. Her authority underlay the whole place. She outranked her sons, and could reduce her daughters-in-law to a level not far above us kids. She had survived the long-term illness and sudden death of a child and the decline and death of her husband, and she knew her strength, and she was generous with it and merry. She

Grandmother in the living room of the cottage on Lake Erie. On her face is an expression she wore when reciting poetry

Dad and Grandmother in lawn chairs on the bluff by the cottage

Dad in his sailboat on the lake

wanted us to call her Grandmother, and we did; she would never have stood for anything as unofficial as "Barbar." She had great skill at planning fun events—entertaining us cousins at the cottage in pairs for a week at a time and taking us to a nearby amusement park. (How happy and grown-up Libby and I felt on the Sunday evening at the beginning of our week, after our families had gone home and we sat on the bluff with Grandmother in the twilight and listened to the waves!)

To hail someone from a distance, Grandmother trilled "Yooooo-hooooo!" like an old-time country wife. I remember her you-hooing us up from the beach for meals, or standing on the bluff with one hand shading her eyes and the other holding her skirt from blowing as she scanned the horizon for the red sail of my father's boat. He used to try her by sailing out of sight and staying away for hours. It was sort of a game with him to see if he could get her to call the Coast Guard. The mood at the cottage remained unsettled until we finally saw the tiny red sail again, growing larger from the direction of Canada.

At the end of the day, if the weather was good, we ate dinner on the bluff. The adults sat on folding chairs and the children at a small white table. Grandmother and Mom and Aunt Evie brought out the food—cold baked ham, baked beans made by Grandmother in an ancient crock, potato salad, sliced fresh tomatoes, sweet corn on the cob. For dessert we had brownies, cake, watermelon. The setting sun sent racing stripes of yellow across the lawn. At dusk the kids caught fireflies, visited relatives down the bluff, picked up smoldering sticks from the fire and threw them out over the water to see the sparks. Rafts of seagulls took off with a sound like spreading applause. The lake stayed warm longer than the land; after sunset an offshore breeze would begin to blow.

Recently I finished some research at the Norwalk Library on a late-summer evening and decided to drive up to the lake. I parked at the public beach by Old Woman Creek, a distance west of where Grandmother used to live. The wind had died but the waves still pounded in, rolling over the shadows in their crests and then spreading out in brightness across the smooth sand. I startled a heron from the mouth of the creek, and he turned his body nearly sideways as he ascended with creaking flaps of his cape-like wings. Long uneven Vs of seagulls coasted out to far water on the breeze high above and became too small to see, and more gulls followed, flight after flight. The top half of the red sun went below the horizon. All at once I had a memory of my father that pushed past more recent memories of him as old and confused and sick. I saw him at an hour like this, his wet T-shirt still clinging to him from his long sail, his few hairs mussed across his sunburned head, his legs white and wiry. He says, "C'mon, Sandy, let's go," and I help him bring up the life jackets and other paraphernalia left on the beach. He doesn't want anything to wash away during the night. Then I grab the chrome-steel handle on the bow of his sailboat, and he takes the stern, and we carry the boat up the beach. I step backward carefully in the sand, I feel for the path up the bluff, we turn the boat bottom-up there in the weeds. He gathers the mast and boom and sail and wraps them together with the lines and unlocks the little boathouse and stores them. He checks the beach again to make sure nothing is forgotten, and we climb the steps. The sky over the lake is still light, but under the oaks on the bluff the darkness is almost full. Mom and Aunt Evie are walking in and out of the lighted house, putting away the folding chairs. My father goes upstairs and changes into dry clothes in a stuffy, still-hot bedroom. He takes his navy wristwatch from inside the toe of his shoe and puts on his shoes. He and my mother round us up and stow us in the car. Some of us fuss—we don't want to go. My father makes sure he's got everybody. He starts the car and backs carefully out of the drive.

•

Biologists say that the Lake Erie basin used to be one of the richest ecosystems on earth. The lake's clear, mostly shallow waters produced an abundance of plant and animal life, especially fish. Even today, Lake Erie produces ten times more fish per unit of area than any other of the Great Lakes. Before settlement its inflowing rivers and marshes and reefs and shoals provided good spawning grounds. Travelers who tried to cross the mouth of the Sandusky River in the early 1800s reported that the fords were so thick with white bass and pickerel they had to be shooed away from the horses' feet. Large sturgeon existed in numbers which made them a nuisance fish; steamboats sometimes burned their oil-rich bodies for fuel. Lake Erie whitefish and blue walleye were table delicacies. Other plentiful categories included lake trout, freshwater herring, sauger, pike, black bass, smallmouth bass. The fish ate smaller fish, frogs, ducklings, turtles, mayflies, and minnows. The insects and minnows ate plankton. Fish-eating birds from eagles and ospreys down to sanderlings thrived along the shore.

When I was a boy, more dead fish than the surviving scavengers could eat washed up on the beach all the time. On Grandmother's beach and along the sand in either direction as far as we could see, dead fish sometimes lay in white windrows. Certain Lake Erie fish like the pike or smallmouth bass I never caught but only saw dead on the shore. Grandmother issued us kids small shovels and gardening trowels and set us to burying fish in the sand.

I wondered why the lake at Grandmother's was always muddy, but farther east, in Pennsylvania and New York State, it was clear. The reason has to do with runoff and siltation. In the mid-1800s settlers drained the Black Swamp, which had covered hundreds of square miles near the Maumee River in northwest Ohio, and they made the land into farms. Also, they drained many marshes along the lake's edge. Fewer trees to hold the soil, bigger expanses of farmland, and fewer swamps meant that thousands of tons of silt began to wash into the lake every year from rivers at its western end. (At the lake's eastern end the land is rockier, less productive of silt.) In general, the Lake Erie basin turned out to be as good for farms and industries as it had been for wildlife. The same advantages of location that caused John D. Rockefeller to start his oil business in Cleveland attracted other industries, notably steel. Boats loaded with ore from the Mesabi iron ore deposits at the western end of Lake Superior entered Cleveland harbor and docked in the Cuyahoga River at steel mills fired by coal brought up by rail from mines in southern Ohio or western Pennsylvania. Along with raw materials and energy, industry needed water. It takes about 113,000 gallons of water to make a ton of steel; like my grandfather, the lake worked in the steel mills. An oil refinery can use about 8 million gallons a day for once-through water cooling; like my father, the lake worked for Standard Oil.

By the early 1900s, factories making cars, rubber, paint, glass, salt, chemicals, and paper had grown in lakefront cities from Toledo, Ohio, to Buffalo, New York. To the north, Detroit, Michigan, poured wastes into the Detroit River, which drains into the lake. Instead of building waste-treatment plants, many municipalities along the lake used it to dispose of sewage. The population of the Lake Erie basin went from about 3 million in 1900 to about 8.5 million in 1950. By 1960, bacteria-laden wastes contaminated about a third of the shoreline in the United States some or all of the time. Along with sewage and warm wastewater from industrial cooling, the cities along the lake added toxic chemicals—manufacturing by-products like mercury, cadmium, and lead. Agricultural silt that washed into the lake often carried pesticides like carbon tetrachloride and DDT. Table-salt refining industries like Diamond Shamrock in Painesville, Ohio, released large amounts of calcium chloride and other salts. Runoff rich in fertilizer contributed unionized ammonia and phosphorus. Steel mills dumped thousands of gallons of sulphuric acid. Effluents from paper mills in Erie, Pennsylvania, fouled nearby beaches with foam and smell for miles.

During the Second World War, as a result of shortages of lye and animal fats, soap manufacturers began to experiment with synthetic washing compounds of sodium and hydrocarbons. These "soapless soaps," as manufacturers called them before people got used to the word "detergent," cleaned cotton and lighter fabrics as effectively as soap flakes, and unlike soap, they worked well in mineral-rich, or "hard," water. Later, manufacturers improved the detergents' cleaning power by adding phosphate "builders" to them. The phosphates neutralized the minerals in the water, helped to lift mineral compounds left in fabrics from previous washings, and kept the dirt in suspension longer. Synthetic detergents with phosphate builders could clean almost any kind of fabric, and the fact that they worked well in hard water made them appealing to suburbanites, whose houses often had hard-water wells. Manufacturers believed that housewives wanted detergents to foam, and so added foaming agents. On busy wash days, sewage-treatment plants began to disappear under mountains of synthetic detergent foam. Detergent-laden rinse water ended up as household sewage, which in the Lake Erie basin generally ended up in the lake.

In all the time my family spent at Grandmother's cottage, I don't recall anyone talking about pollution. My father, grandmother, and other relatives were people of strong opinions on many subjects, but apparently not on that. I was a child and assumed the lake was as it had always been. I did not reflect much on the dead fish we buried, or the fish we saw swimming upside down in circles, or the decline in the numbers of white bass, or the ear infections I got in the summers, or the rainbows of oil slicks on the water, or the livid green the water sometimes turned on sunny days or after a rain. The grownups must have noticed that the lake was sick. Maybe they thought that if it got too bad they would just spend their weekends someplace else. Maybe they had some idea what had gone wrong but thought—as anyone would, as I would—they could do nothing about it.

By the mid-1960s, parts of Lake Erie had become so dirty as to be unfit for body contact. The harbors of Toledo, Buffalo, and Cleveland were filled with septic sludge, scum, bacterial contamination, and floating wastes of many kinds. In Cleveland, the Cuyahoga River leading into the lake was so clogged with oil and debris it contained no visible life at all, not even the bottom-dwelling sludge worm *Tubifex tubifex*, which feeds on waste and can live without oxygen for weeks at a time. The dark brown Cuyahoga ran to the lake channelized and inert, enlivened sometimes by gas bubbles rising from decomposing matter or by wind ripples which glittered without allure. From all the industrial cities discharges of heavy metals, pesticides, and other chemicals had reached levels of concentration which showed up in the fatty tissues of fish. Concentrations of PCBs, toxic chemicals suspected of causing birth defects, became dangerously high and began to be found in the milk of nursing mothers. Levels of toxicity increased as you went up the food chain, with fish-eating birds showing some of the more serious effects—weakened eggshells leading to a low rate of chick survival, and physical deformation. But of all the lake's problems, pollution from synthetic detergents turned out to be the worst. The new synthetic detergents cleaned well, reduced rinsing and elbow grease, and soon took over the household-cleaning market. Brand names like Dreft, Glim, Savex, Swerl, Sail, Scoop, Soilax, Tish, Breeze, Spic and Span, Dick-A-Doo, Fab, and Sudz filled supermarket shelves, and eventually the lake. What finally did in Lake Erie during the 1960s was the washing machine: the lake strangled because of Tide, it choked because of All.

Simply put, certain kinds of plankton in the lake needed phosphorus for their biochemistries, and detergent wastes gave them much more of it. Between 1940 and 1970 the amount of phosphorus going into the lake tripled. Along with phosphorus from fertilizer runoff, the amount from detergent wastes made the lake a nutrient-rich breeding ground for non-diatomic plankton and blue-green algae. On warm, sunny days the lake began to experience "algae blooms"—immense growths of algae that sometimes colored the water to the horizon. In the eastern part of the state, where the shoreline is rocky, the nutrients encouraged a seaweed called cladophora, which grows in long strands from rocks and then breaks off and washes ashore and overwhelms beaches with its odor of decaying protein. Throughout the lake, algae bloomed and died and fell to the bottom. In the lake's broad, shallow central part, decomposition of dead algae used so much oxygen as to make the water at the bottom devoid of oxygen for long periods at a time. During the day, oxygen released by the algae's photosynthesis compensated for what was lost by decomposition. But on dark days, and at night, rotting algae consumed more oxygen than living algae produced. And when the weather was calm, the lake did not receive atmospheric oxygen from the aerating action of the waves. On those calm summer nights I loved as a boy, the lake was actually suffocating to death.

In 1968 a federal water pollution report said that almost 7,000 square kilometers of Lake Erie were "devoid of oxygen in the hypolimnion" (the lowest stratum of water, beneath the surface and the thermocline). Divers who studied the bottom of the lake's central basin in the summer of 1970 found it covered with a mat of decaying algae two to three centimeters thick. The bottom was black, with here and there a dead smelt. The anoxic water stank of sulphides, and held no life other than anaerobic bacteria. Further examination showed that in the anoxic conditions of the lake bottom, chemical reactions had begun which would not have been possible in oxygenated water. Insoluble phosphate compounds—inert phosphorous salts which had sunk into the sediments—now became soluble and released their phosphorus. During the summer, the anoxic central basin of the lake now actually produced more phosphorus than waste-treatment plants and other sources were putting in. Journalists called Lake Erie dead, a description not far from the truth.

To add insult, the Cuyahoga River caught on fire. One afternoon, hydrocarbon wastes ignited by sparks burned so fiercely on the river's surface as to damage steel bridges and destroy wooden trestles spanning it in Cleveland's industrial flats.

Cleveland itself was not doing well in those years. It is hard to say just when the city's decline began. Some might point to September and October of 1954, with the humiliating defeat of the Indians in the World Series, followed by the trial of Dr. Sam Sheppard for the murder of his wife—a sensational and mishandled trial which became the most famous of the decade. Or maybe to 1955, when the Terminal Tower, the city's tallest building, formerly the second-tallest building in the world, lost its distinction as the second-tallest in the world outside New York to a new skyscraper in Poland. In 1964, Boston's Prudential Building became the second-tallest in the United States outside New York, and before long a dozen American cities, including Detroit and Pittsburgh, had skyscrapers taller than the Terminal Tower. The Sears Tower, in Chicago, rose twice as high. The Terminal Tower slid farther and farther down the list of tallest buildings, until it was just barely in the top one hundred, remaining (until recently) the tallest in Cleveland. Meanwhile, more white Clevelanders moved from the city to the suburbs, taking with them tax revenues and the money that they used to spend in downtown stores. Black Clevelanders, kept out of most suburbs by unfair loan practices, discriminatory real-estate agents, restrictive homeowners' covenants, and lack of money, stayed in city neighborhoods which decayed like teeth. In 1966, riots in Cleveland's mostly black Hough Area burned to the ground many blocks which were never rebuilt. Crime and drugs got worse. A father was stabbed to death downtown while waiting in line to take his children to see Santa Claus. Many industries closed or moved away. By the time I left Ohio to go to college, Cleveland had become sort of a national joke. People used it as a symbol of the falling-apart cities of the industrial Northeast, now sometimes called the Rustbelt. Mid-level comedians made fun of Cleveland on television talk shows. I made fun of it myself to entertain new friends at my East Coast college. Probably the real reasons for the decline of Cleveland—a city whose industries had helped win several wars, a destination of emigrants from the South and Midwest and East and Eastern Europe, site of hundreds of churches and temples, birthplace of one of the nation's great fortunes, home of universities and museums and a world-famous hospital and symphony orchestra—are many and complicated. Probably the reasons involve international economics and large-scale social change. Certainly, sitting on the shores of a polluted lake by the mouth of a river that caught on fire did not help.

In the late sixties, the United States and Canada set up the International Lake Erie Water Pollution Board to study the lake's problems. The board concluded that phosphorus loading had a lot to do with depleting the lake's oxygen, and recommended that the amount of phosphorus going into the lake be reduced at once. An organization representing the detergent makers argued that carbon, not phosphorus, was to blame. A lengthy debate followed, which the detergent makers lost. In 1972 President Nixon and Prime Minister Trudeau signed the Great Lakes Water Quality Agreement. It called for a reduction in phosphorus loading by more than a third within four years, programs for controlling other kinds of pollution including toxic metals and oil, money for an international commission to monitor water quality, and more than $7.25 billion for construction and improvement of sewage-treatment plants in communities around the lake. By the late seventies, plastic tampon dispensers and other sewage wastes no longer washed up regularly on Cleveland's beaches. The lakewater was declared safe for body contact, except in Cleveland harbor. Concentrations of phosphorus went down and algae growth decreased. The lake's fish-growing power reestablished itself. The walleyed pike, a popular game fish, multiplied in numbers from about 3 million to about 90 million in a few years, and Lake Erie walleye-fishing guides began to advertise during fishing season, and a professional fisherman sold how-to videotapes of himself catching big walleyes along the shore not far from downtown Cleveland.

People talked with pride about how clean the lake was and how well it had recovered. Coincidentally, the idea of Cleveland as a national joke began to fade and the city began to revive. Concentrations of mercury and other heavy metals in fish decreased, then leveled off; scientists said that a lot of toxic substances remained in the lake's sediments and would continue to enter the food cycle whenever rough water stirred up the bottom. New sewage-treatment facilities could handle only a certain volume, and during heavy rainstorms the excess flowed untreated to the lake. Platforms drilling for natural gas and oil were built along the lake's Canadian side. Occasionally they experienced spills. Power companies added new plants to the ones already encircling the lake. The power plants put in millions of gallons of warmed water, and killed more fish by impingement at their intakes than all the sportfishermen in the lake caught. The Water Quality

Agreement of 1972 had said nothing about shore erosion or the lake's problem of siltation. The lake level rose several feet in the seventies and eighties, washing away much lakefront property. Nobody seemed to know why. Heavy siltation continued, especially at the western end of the lake. Pesticides, phosphorus, nitrates, and other agricultural pollutants came with the silt. PCBs continued to enter the lake from the air, through windborne dust. These chemicals are especially slow to break down, and persist in the sediments. Levels of PCBs in some game fish are still high. The Ohio Department of Health recommends that people eat most species of Lake Erie fish less often than once a week, and that children and women of childbearing age eat Lake Erie fish only every once in a while. And yet, without doubt, the lake is cleaner than it was.

•

Grandmother, like her parents before her, preferred to spend the winters someplace warmer than the Lake Erie shore. After Ray died, she went with her father to Fort Lauderdale, and after he died she began to winter in Key West. She had been there before, in the thirties and forties, on the only vacation Ray ever took. Henry Flagler, after making millions from Standard Oil, spent some of his fortune developing Key West into a resort. He financed construction of an ambitious overseas railroad to the island and talked up the resort in his home state, persuading many Ohioans to visit. Grandmother lived in the Old Town section in courtyard apartments she rented from a native Key West woman who became a friend. The friend knew many of the island's literary residents and invited her to dinner parties. At least once Grandmother sat next to Tennessee Williams and entertained the childless playwright with photographs of us grandchildren. Later, when Williams ran into her on the street, he would say, warily, "You're the one with all the grandchildren."

In 1967 Grandmother decided to live in Key West year round. She looked for someone to buy the cottage; none of her family wanted it, so she sold it to a neighbor. Early in the summer of that year she threw a party at the cottage for us, our cousins, and other relatives. The party was in honor of her sister Anne Belle's daughter, Ellen, and Ellen's new husband, Peter. The fact that Peter was Jewish had upset Anne Belle, who declined to give the couple a party herself. Ellen and Peter and all us younger cousins played Wiffle ball on the lawn. Peter hit a line drive which smacked Ellen in the face—a bad omen. After the game we changed into our party clothes for dinner. Peter wore a coat and tie. In the photographs you can see how polite he was being. I wore a madras shirt, and my cousin Libby a brightly colored pants suit. My father wore a glowing Hawaiian shirt to match his sunburn. Grandmother made a special new punch she had just learned about in Key West. It was called the Key West Rattler—a frothy orange beverage containing lots of rum. I took two Seven-Up cans and poured out the contents and filled the cans with punch when no grownups were looking and gave one can to Libby and drank the other myself. A strange, winey, drunk feeling rose through my sinuses to the top of my head. The evening twilight became garish. People were talking loudly and laughing, always just past the corner of my eye—by now the party had spread across the lawn. Peter, an assistant professor of theoretical physics, remarked to my father that, in his opinion, chemistry was just cooking. The girls gathered around Peter and laughed at things he said. Libby was laughing especially hard. After a while she and I went down to the beach. We lay on the sand and began to make out, but then some guys passing by yelled wise-cracks, so we climbed a white wooden staircase up the bluff and stopped at a little bench on a landing halfway and continued to make out there. Libby began to feel dizzy, then sick. By now it was dark. We walked back along the bluff to Grandmother's. The mortar shell of the punch bowl had detonated on the party, scattering it. Grand-mother's bedroom light was off; she had gone to bed. I remember a body or two passed out on the lawn. I couldn't find my father, and my mother was in a cottage down the bluff with the younger kids. Libby went to bed. Ever the tattletale, I found Cousin Ellen and confessed to her all that Libby and I had done. It took Ellen a while to grasp that we had not done much—she couldn't understand why I was confessing. Her reaction disappointed me, and I told no one else.

Grandmother moved to Key West in the fall. Uncle Louis had taken a job in New York City and moved his family to Rowayton, Connecticut. I never fished in Lake Erie again. For ten years I did not even return to Oak Bluff to see relatives or look at Grandmother's old house. I told Grandmother that I wished she hadn't sold it, and she answered that there was nothing else she could have done. She told me not to mourn for the cottage. She was always able to accept reality and move on, a skill which no doubt helped her to live for ninety years.

I still dream about the cottage often. It, and the Lake Erie shoreline, are the settings most common in my dreams. Sometimes I dream I am in a boat off the concrete-lined lakeshore of downtown Cleveland, with the lights of the Terminal Tower reflected in water so oily and dark as to be all chemicals. Sometimes I am leaning over a bluff looking at the lake far below; my father has somehow mistakenly driven a car off the edge, a pleasantly vacant Alzheimer's expression on his face; I watch the car fall for what seems like forever; I can just barely see my father get out the passenger-side door; the car hits the water and makes a cloud of mud, but I am not sure I see my father hit. Sometimes I am standing before the cottage chest-deep in chocolate-colored waves with café-au-lait crests slashing and sloshing along the bluffs; the beach I used to play on is underwater, the blocks of the pier are tumbled and broken and submerged; an El Greco sky rises overhead; the surge of the waves lifts me almost off my feet; a small powerboat vaults and plunges nearby; a fisherman holds a bent-double fishing rod trying to boat a walleye; cars speed past on the lakeshore highway; I am taking short steps, feeling with my feet, searching for where our beach used to be.

RELATIVES, AND OTHERS:

My father's brother Louis lives now in a suburb of Washington, D.C. He and Aunt Evie divorced years ago. In the late 1960s Louis joined a computer company; married the boss, Joan; and in 1970 had a son with her. After a subsidiary of IBM began offering a computer time-sharing system similar to theirs, Louis and Joan sued IBM and eventually won a settlement out of court. They divorced. Now he is married to Charleen, who used to be a nun and now works for Amtrak. He is retired. Recently I flew down to Washington on the shuttle to visit him. (If you don't think white guys run the country, just take the New York–to–Washington shuttle on a Monday morning—almost nobody on the plane was even slightly swarthy, let alone a darker color or female.) Louis is bald, blue-eyed, stocky. His wide smile can look seraphic or wicked; his smile, bald dome, and glasses are like lines in

Uncle Louis, Cousin Lane, Uncle John and Aunt Lydia, Uncle Bill and Aunt Ginny, Aunt Betty, Alice Cooper

one of those brushstroke caricatures you see hanging on the walls of cocktail lounges. In fact, during his days as a public-relations man long ago, a sketch artist did such a drawing of him. Louis has the Frazier skill (which missed me) at repairing and building things. He is often working on some long-range home improvement project. I think of him always in the vicinity of sawhorses and piles of lumber. When we were children and the cousins lived in a farmhouse west of Cleveland, Louis lowered an old barn out back by six feet or more. The job involved power saws, automobile jacks, and the cousins' roller skates. Later I asked him why he lowered the barn, and he replied that there was no need on that property for a barn of that height.

Louis was sitting in the living room when I arrived, among boxes of old papers and pictures he'd brought out to show me. He saw me through the window and without getting up gestured for me to come in. We talked from eleven in the morning until six in the evening. After we'd been talking for five or six hours I happened to think of the dreams I had about the cottage and asked if he ever had any himself. "I dream about the cottage every couple of weeks," he said. He showed me a number of dream paintings he had done on shirt cardboard at a time when he was living alone on Fourteenth Street in New York; the scenes—of the white dinghy on the beach as seen from the bluff, of oak trees with a lake horizon behind them—almost duplicated dreamscapes of my own. I asked him about details of specific dreams he'd had, but in trying to remember he began to hyperventilate and see spots before his eyes. The spots, which he had experienced before, resemble nineteenth-century military fortifications, and the syndrome is called Fortification Syndrome. As he explained it to me and described a magazine article he had read about it, he began to feel better.

Some of what Louis said:

"My relationship with your father was very 'taught'—I was the kid brother, and he was always teaching me, *always* teaching. He sits on my shoulder even today. I think of him whenever I do a truth table, for example. And a lot of the time I was resentful as hell. He and I talked about technical things or the sky or the weather—never about emotions or how we felt. He was still teaching even in his last days, when he'd lost his mind, when the teaching had become fanciful. I suppose I thought our father preferred him to me. You say Dad

wrote him letters in the navy—I'm sure my father never wrote me a
single letter. Dad was like Dave in that he liked to explain stuff but
wasn't much on emotion. There was an era where I was terrified of
my father. The specific thing I remember was I used to get yelled at
for getting into his tools. Dad had tools to fix anything. Also—item
—he was a horseplayer. I remember he came home one time and
reached in his pocket and plunked down enough cash to pay the taxes.
He traveled a lot, inspecting scrap. He followed the scrap-iron cycle
all around the Great Lakes, to Detroit and Chicago and Milwaukee
and Duluth. I sometimes wonder if he didn't enjoy the same kind of
pleasures traveling men enjoy. I have traveled myself, and I have
known very few traveling men who were not susceptible to pleasure.
He was a statistician like your father, he used statistics to figure the
charges in the blast furnaces. The furnaces ran day and night, and
Dad used to telephone from the house to find out how they were
running—he'd ask, "How's number one? How much wind has she
got?" He was a volatile guy. He and Mother would fight, sometimes
Mother would cry. But she always talked about him with absolute
devotion, the way your mother talked about Dave. Dad became the
assistant superintendent of blast furnaces, and his boss, the superintendent, was an alcoholic who Dad was always having to cover for.
Dad was this guy's enabler for years. We read *The Saturday Evening
Post* cover to cover every week—it was our TV, movies, everything
—and in one issue we read an article about alcoholism and Alcoholics
Anonymous; Mother and Dad started talking about getting his boss
to AA. But then the guy ran into an abutment of the Sixty-fifth Street
bridge, and Dad became superintendent. Dad worked and smoked
to the point where he developed malignant hypertension. He died of
uremic poisoning in his bed at 25720 Lake Road, that house he built
of concrete blocks made of blast furnace slag. I remember that when
Dad died I was surprised to feel pain—it was the first time I ever felt
real pain in my life.

"One Sunday afternoon when I was five Mother sat me down and
told me I was going to start kindergarten the next day and that I'd be
going by myself because she would be taking care of Teddy. So next
day at the appointed hour I walked to the school and presented myself
and said, 'I'm here for kindergarten.' The woman behind the desk
looked at the paper with my name and asked how I pronounced it

and I said Louis, and she said, 'Oh, no, you said it wrong—we'll call you Lewis." The system has been on my shit list ever since. I didn't even learn to read until the fifth grade. But I figured out how to deal with the system. When Mother got into controversies on the school board, teachers and other people would sometimes give me a hard time about her—I remember guys upbraiding me in front of a beer joint one day—and I learned to give it right back to the bastards. I learned if you make yourself unpleasant enough you can back most people down, and if you can't back 'em down, you can run like a hermit crab.

"I remember very clearly the day Grandmother killed herself—we drove down to the cottage and Mother had said Grandmother was dead, but she didn't say how it happened, and Aggie came up to us in a state of agitation and I figured out the situation for myself. If you see a suicide when you're a kid, one thing it teaches you is that suicide works. I loved Grandmother but I didn't feel anything when she died. Nobody cried at the funeral. It seemed as though the thing to do in that family was to take care of yourself. I know Grandfather had said that he would have gone with her, but I wonder if that wasn't just something you say at the time. I don't know how much attention he paid her. I think there was a lot of drinking and whoring around with his cronies in Cleveland. And sometimes when he and his buddies would come to the cottage they'd get in a boat and sit out on the reef and come back sloshed out of their fuckin' skulls. Every family needs a place where the men can go get drunk and pass out in the yard, and the cottage always served that purpose for us. There was always a lot of bootleg liquor in the neighborhood, especially at the roadhouse, Ruggles Beach, just east of the cottage. I used to go there and play the piano and get drunk and play grab-ass with the girls.

"Dave left home for California when I was sixteen. I'd been throwing his paper route for years by then, ever since he started football in high school, and I took over his front room under the gambrel roof after he left, and I set up a little chemistry lab like the one he'd had. I followed him in a lot of things, and I suppose we could have become closer if it weren't for my resentment and my damn determination to be competitive. He wrote us from Stanford about how wonderful it was out there, and at Mother's urging he looked into the possibility of my going there for undergrad right away, so I applied and I got

accepted. I left for California when I was just seventeen. My parents
put me on the westbound Nickel Plate Railroad and I walked to the
back platform and stood there and lit a cigarette as the train pulled
out, hoping they'd see me. I had a grand trip out—the train was full
of soldiers. When I got to Palo Alto I was quartered in a frat house,
and within two weeks I was going out drinking with the boys—I
remember after one time in particular lying on my belly at the Union
Pacific Station. At Stanford I started drinking heavily. I saw your father
from time to time. His roommate, Kirkby, did not like me hanging
around too much. Anybody Kirkby didn't like he called 'avenaceous,'
and at first I didn't know what avenaceous meant. It means having to
do with oats. A lot of beer drinking went on in the house where your
father lived. After two quarters at Stanford I joined the navy and got
into the V-12 program, an officers' training program. Then the navy
sent me to Oberlin, back in Ohio. For a while I thought I'd make a
career of the navy, and my biggest worry was what I would do when
I retired on half-pay at the age of thirty-five. I left the V-12 program,
was sent to boot camp, got discharged. Eventually I went to Kenyon
on the GI Bill. I joined the Kenyon Players—I played Walter Burns
to Paul Newman's Hildy Johnson in their production of *The Front
Page*. By that time Newman had already established his persona on
campus, beer bottle in hand. I joined a loose-knit group of nighttime
prowlers on trips to beer joints and roadhouses. One of these guys
was Ron Penfound, later 'Captain Penny' on a children's TV show in
Cleveland, and another was Olof Palme, later Premier of Sweden,
assassinated a while ago.

"After college I became a newspaper reporter, writing real estate
and public service stories for the *Cleveland Press*, a first and seminal
job for me, an exciting job. I did some crime reporting, too, although
it seemed the really good stories all happened on my day off. Meanwhile, your father had walked out of the navy and into the job at
Standard Oil. I suppose those years when we were both single and
living at home was as close, emotionally, as we ever got. I went sailing
a lot in his sailboat, his Comet, and one day I dropped the little
outboard motor off the back of it into Rocky River Harbor. I slipped
off the boat while holding it, actually, and didn't let it sink until I'd
nearly drowned. I told Dave I'd replace it, but I never did, and I still
feel bad about that. When your dad started acting in plays at the

theater in Lakewood I got involved there, too, doing walk-ons and helping build sets. He and your mom seemed perfect for each other from the beginning. I remember your mom from when I was a kid and she was Peggy Hursh, who used to direct junior-high plays and boss us around. I was your dad's best man, and he was mine when Ev and I married. I saw your mom in *Life with Father*, and it always seemed to me that your parents were acting that play in real life—they wanted to be Clarence and Vinnie Day, with a troop of kids with hair all the same color.

"When I was twenty-eight years old I went to one of the hotels in Cleveland for a real-estate press conference and I started drinking and woke up the next day in jail. Sergeant Roddy gave me back my wallet and let me go—he knew me from the crime beat—and I talked to some friends—I had about a dozen friends in AA by then—and decided that if they could quit, I could, too. I never went to a meeting because I didn't think AA was right for me. On my own I just quit drinking completely. I didn't have a drink from when I was twenty-eight until I was thirty-five. I left the *Press* and got a job doing PR for the Cleveland Health Museum, the most fun job I ever had. Then Gebhard, the museum director, fired me and I went to work doing international public relations for Goodyear. I traveled all over the world. God, it was marvelous. After just a few months I had evened the score with your father for his Pacific cruise in the navy. I would take a stack of twenties about this high and my passport and my plane ticket and just go—very exciting and heady work. And on one of these trips I took a drink.

"From then on I was drinking regularly again, regularly or in binges. I would say that in those days I was a disagreeable son of a bitch, wouldn't you? (As a matter of fact, I'm still disagreeable. I was disagreeable as recently as yesterday to a guy down the street—guy stripping a car in front of his house in a residential neighborhood.) I had a split personality for years. I kept a shell of alcohol around me, I floated in a fine impartiality that let me be difficult with people all the time. I used a lot of alcohol to take the twist out of my gut. Being angry was addictive, too—just as addictive as alcohol.

"I think your father ingested alcohol to the point where it affected his life in a negative way. I don't know that for sure, but I know *I* overused alcohol and I *think* he did. Finally one morning I woke up behind a 7-Eleven after a binge. You can always tell after a binge which side you slept on, because that's where the bruises are. I went home and slept until ten o'clock and at five that afternoon looked up Alcoholics Anonymous in the phone book—it took me a while to find it, I couldn't remember how to spell alcohol—and they sent a guy to get me, a great big guy, he'd been a captain of an aircraft carrier, and he took me to a meeting, and I haven't had a drink since. That's over fourteen years now.

"Alcohol simply isn't an issue with me. It doesn't have a place in my life because (a) I tend to get drunk and (b) it's very bad if you drink steadily; continued use of alcohol is bad for you physically, systemically. I get so much more out of living without alcohol. I used alcohol to turn off my skull, but that meant I could count on a lot of throwaway days, sometimes several lost days a week. Now I get so much more done without it. I've almost finished digging out under the house to put in some new rooms down there, I've been doing more work on my computer-generated light sculpture—I call it Cognisculpture, 'Art that appreciates *you*.' I can maintain outside friendships. Last year we had 123 people to the house for potluck to celebrate my birthday and retirement. As I look at it, how many machine cycles do you have between your ears? It's a finite number, like a fender stamper. How many seconds do you have in your consciousness in a lifetime? If I waste any on alcohol or hating someone, those are machine cycles I'm not going to get."

•

Cousin Lane Barton is my oldest relative, and the most distant one I still keep in touch with. Lane's grandfather was Will Wickham, Charles Wickham's brother and comrade in the Civil War. That makes him and my grandmother second cousins; I'm not sure what it makes him and me. Lane was born in 1899, and he hopes to survive until the year 2000, so as to be one of the few people in history to live in three centuries. He grew up in Norwalk, at 67 West Elm Street. His father owned a pharmacy and flower shop and wrote his own advertisements for the *Reflector*. Sometimes he tried to get people to buy by referring to how broke the Bartons were, which embarrassed Lane. Lane went through the Norwalk schools and to Kenyon College, where he graduated Phi Beta Kappa. He studied at Kenyon's Episcopalian divinity school, received his Bachelor of Divinity there in 1924, and was ordained a minister. In 1946 the Episcopal House of Bishops and House of Deputies elected him a bishop. He served for many years as bishop of the Missionary District of Eastern Oregon, and retired in 1968. He and his wife, Polly, moved to Vancouver, Washington. His cousins sometimes refer to him as "the bishop," or "the bish."

People over eighty can be hard to talk to on the telephone, but not Lane. At ninety-five he still has a ringing, from-the-pulpit voice which is exciting to listen to even when he has misheard the question. He is a person you can call every year on the same date, as another cousin of mine does, for example, on the afternoon of the Ohio State–Michigan football game, and he will be there. When I call, he always says, "Sandy! Glory be!" pronouncing "glory" so you can hear every letter in it. He never speaks ill of anyone; a relative who everyone else says was a bum he describes as "colorful." Practically anyone he mentions receives generous praise. He says he enjoys hearing from me because it reminds him of Cora, my grandmother. Often he suggests that I come out to visit, and a couple of summers ago I did.

Lane was in the yard of a modest colonial house on a tree-lined street cutting a cream-colored blossom from a rosebush when I drove up. He looked at me and said, "We're expecting a stranger." I hadn't seen him since I was a kid, and didn't recognize him without his collar. He does not look ninety-five. He is tall, blunt-faced, rawboned, with glasses, two hearing aids, and a wide smile. His silver hair is combed up and back in a clerical wave. He led me inside and introduced me to his son Lane Jr. and Lane's wife, June, who were visiting. June remarked that I had arrived on the tick of four. Then he brought me to a white-haired woman in a yellow dress half-reclining on pillows on a couch. He said, "I want you to meet my bride." To her he said, "Can you say hello to our cousin Sandy, dear? Of course you can't, you haven't spoken a word for eight years." His tone was factual, without bitterness. Polly suffered a stroke years ago and had been paralyzed since. This was the first I'd known of it. I said hello and she looked at me with bright eyes.

Lane poured me a big drink of bourbon-on-the-rocks and we sat in his study for a while and talked. He sipped from a faceted glass mug of straight bourbon. He kept saying, "It's so great to see you!" He showed me a black-and-white photo of Polly from when they were married, and it took me a moment to realize that stuck between the edge of the frame and the glass was a small color snapshot of my then-two-year-old daughter, Cora. He said, "How old are you? Thirty-nine? Oh, you're young. I can't even remember when I was thirty-nine. Now, you're David's son, and David's the one who died of Alzheimer's disease. I'm so sorry. I've got it, too, but I don't die! I just become so senile, I forget everything. I'm the senior surviving member not of the human race but of Kenyon College Class of '21—I don't have friends my age who can remind me of things anymore. I feel lonelier every time I open a piece of mail and discover that another friend has departed this life. Now your mother—grandmother, rather—grandmother Cora, oh, how I loved her. She was one of the loveliest creatures on this earth.

"Now, you wanted to talk about my grandfather, Will Wickham. He was a lovely, lovely man, and oh, how cruelly he suffered! The war deprived him of his hearing and ruined his dream of being a lawyer. Finally he couldn't even hear well enough to run a newspaper and so he had to leave Norwalk and get a job in the patent office in Washington, and Grandmother ran a wonderful boardinghouse there. I don't think he ever achieved what he'd hoped for. His brother Fred, who was in the Confederate prison camp at Andersonville, had it worst of all, and when he died at seventy the doctor said he guessed the war had taken twenty years off Fred's life. One time in Norwalk a tramp went into Fred's garden and started helping himself to the vegetables, and a neighbor told Fred, and instead of calling the police Fred took the man a basket and filled it full, because he'd learned what it was to be hungry during the Civil War.

"It was a miracle that the three elder Wickham boys, Charlie, Will, and Fred, came through the war alive. Charlie was unscathed. To me he was Uncle Charlie, and he was head and shoulders above anybody. My younger brother Charles Edwin died of septicemia in 1921 and was in and out of hospitals for four years before that, and one of the kindest and most thoughtful things Uncle Charlie ever did was to invite Charles Edwin into the courtroom to watch proceedings. My family were all Presbyterians, and when the time came for me to join the church, when I was about twelve, my mother went to Uncle Charlie and asked him to prepare me. So he walked me to the church and we sat down in a Sunday-school classroom and he talked about what it meant to be a Christian and a church member. I haven't the slightest idea what he said, but I sure was impressed that he took his time to speak his convictions about the Christian religion to me. And of course he was a sterling example of what a Christian should be. When he was upset, the strongest words he ever used were 'Thunder and guns!' But that Presbyterian church—gad, were they strict! They practically never cracked a smile, and the Episcopal church had a better choir, and a lot of my friends were in that choir. So I joined the choir, and fell in love with the Episcopal prayerbook. And eventually I went to Kenyon and became an Episcopalian. But, oh, I was a low-church Episcopalian, a rotten black Protestant, because of my Presbyterian background. If it was up to me I'd get rid of the incense and the robes and the bells and all that fancy business that the high-church Episcopalians do.

"There were ninety-one men at Kenyon when I went there, and the football team consisted of eleven men. We didn't have a single substitute. If the center got wounded, why, one of us had to take his place. But we were pretty formidable all the same—we had one fellow, Fat Warman, who they couldn't get britches big enough for and he played in coveralls. After I graduated I stayed on for a year and played as a ringer. In the First World War—this was before college—I joined an artillery brigade and went overseas on the *President Grant* with 6,000 men sent to replace troops who were coming home. The ship was infected with the Spanish influenza and 121 men caught it and died. I saw all these guys dying and being buried at sea and I said, 'I'm darned if I'm going to die,' and I didn't. I'd seen a lot by the time I decided to become a minister. When I got my Bachelor of Divinity, I'd already been helping the minister in charge at St. Mark's Episcopal in Shelby, Ohio, a tiny congregation, and I served there until 1927. From Shelby I went to Newark, Ohio, one of my most interesting ministries, because in '29 the Great Crash came and the poverty in Newark was so dreadful that children were fainting in schools for lack of nutrition. One of our parishioners, Mrs.—I'll Think Of Her Name In A Minute, It Doesn't Make Any Difference—Miller, Schaefer (her husband was a conductor on the B&O Railroad), anyway, she came to me and said we should set up a soup kitchen. She told me how we could do it and what it would cost and I said, 'Glory be! Glory be! It's time we got off our fannies!' You may have noticed that Episcopalians almost never go hungry—we introduced our congregation to the people who did, and we served hot meals to a lot of families in Newark. From Newark I went to Flint, Michigan, a buggy town, a car town, where I had the most prosperous of all my congregations. That church membership included the presidents of all four banks in town and three vice presidents of General Motors. I'm different from a lot of preachers in that I believe rich people have souls just like anybody else. And, gad, those folks in Flint were an active bunch. They wanted to start a social ministry in Flint and they wanted it right away. It was exciting—working with the state welfare board, helping auto workers that were in such distress. One out of four people in Flint was unemployed at the time. Then from Flint I went to Grace Church in Orange, New Jersey, and it was as dead as a dodo. The folks there didn't want to do anything and they wondered what was this upstart from Michigan doing. Grace Church made a patient man out of me. Then in '46 the powers that be elected me a bishop and I came out here. In Oregon most of the population is along the Pacific slope and two-thirds of the state is practically empty, the towns very small and the churches far apart. We lived in Bend, Oregon, and I drove all over the eastern part of the state—perfectly gorgeous driving, through beautiful forests, along glorious rivers—the Columbia, the Snake, the Deschutes. It was like being private chaplain to a national park. I was active in the House of Bishops for forty years, until 1986. I was well up in the echelons. Politically I stood pretty far over to the left. The church was so cruel when I was ordained—you couldn't take Communion if you'd been divorced, for example—and I belonged to the faction that wanted to make it more humane. I always said I was a liberal, but today I don't know just what that word means. I'm a liberal, but by gad, my bucket has a bottom."

Lane's son George and his family came over. Lane brought me into the living room and introduced me to everybody. Lane made a fuss over me and treated me as the guest of honor, which pleased me and made me worry that people would think I was a jerk. At one point Lane asked George to get up and give me a seat, and this made me feel so awkward that I remained standing and George and I conversed over the empty chair. During dinner I sat between the two Lanes, father and son. The bishop was at the head of the table and a woman who helped take care of Polly put her in a chair by the foot. All ten of us held hands as the bishop bowed his head and said grace and prayed for us. The rest of us let go of each other's hands and began to eat our seafood Newburg on rice with peas and tossed salad. George's daughter Mariniah held on to Polly's hand throughout the meal.

After dinner, the George Bartons got ready to leave. Everybody said good night to Polly, and she was put to bed. Lane went into the living room and sat in an armchair and talked to me and June and Lane Jr. Soon he leaned his head back and began to doze, snoring occasionally and then rousing himself. June and Lane Jr. told me about a book written by another bishop, a colleague and admirer of Lane Sr.'s, on the subject of rescuing Christianity from fundamentalism. All I had heard about that book was that it said St. Paul was homosexual. They told me it was about more than that, and definitely worth reading. The bishop woke up and announced he was going to bed. He shook my hand, thanked me for coming, and wished me a safe trip in a voice that boomed no less for his having just been asleep. He bid good night to Lane Jr. and June, and went off to bed.

The next year, I received a letter from Cousin Lane:

My dear Sandy & family:

It is my duty—a sad duty—to report to you that my bride of 68 years has joined the heavenly host.

It was a "blow" but after nine years of cruel paralysis Polly is now released, and since her release makes her happy, the least we can do is to be happy. To be sure we grieve and will miss her but it won't be long at my age before I join her.

Blessings on you & yours
Cousin Lane

My mother's brothers, Bill and John, live with their wives in a retirement community south of Tucson now. Uncle Bill and Aunt Ginny and Uncle John and Aunt Lydia had never seen my daughter or my sister's children, so we flew down for a visit. We all sat together on the DC-10—Maggie; her husband, John; her daughter, Lucy, age one; Suzan; her daughter, Caroline, one and a half; my wife, Jay; daughter Cora, two; and me. That was a mistake. The kids sort of flipped out. They were excited and they played and yelled and cried, we adults became nervous and kept getting up and walking them in

the aisles, and the family turmoil built and spread around our vicinity
on the plane. I was checking my watch every five minutes, then every
three, seeing how much remained of the flight during four and a half
hours of strangers looking daggers at us. When we landed in Dallas
to change planes, a woman passenger smiled a big, tight smile at us
and said, "I'm sure not going to miss *any* of you-all!" The flight from
Dallas to Tucson was better—Cora and Caroline slept, and John
calmed Lucy by reading to her from an in-flight catalogue of financial
self-help books. At Tucson the airport was empty and clean and quiet,
with a low sun coming through the windows. The children sped away
down the concourse like released trout. We picked up the rental cars
and the plastic-wrapped car seats and then headed for the motel. Jay
was happy at first, but when I turned out not to know where I was
going she got mad. Finally we all checked into our cabins at the Best
Western Ghost Ranch Lodge, a place I had chosen from a Chamber
of Commerce guide because of its "world-famous cactus garden." Night
had fallen, and the cacti were dramatically lit. Jay went to the motel
restaurant to order us some take-out and came back pleased with
herself because someone had asked the bartender for a Rusty Nail and
he hadn't known how to make a Rusty Nail and she had told him.
Finally we were all eating steak and drinking vodka gimlets and watching the kids play, and the anxiety of the flight began to wear off.

The next day we went to Bill and Ginny's for an early-afternoon
dinner. Their house is a prefabricated white double-wide with green
shutters in a hedged lot of raked ground and cacti, on a smoothly
paved street in the desert about thirty miles from Tucson. John and
Lydia live nearby and they came, too, and parked their Volvo well
up in the yard. John explained that in this community of 13,000 people
over the age of sixty-five, some are the sort of drivers liable to crash
into a car if it's left on the street. Seeing our aunts and uncles reminded
me of our mother, and seeing us probably did the same for them. She
would have been happy we were all together. We did not talk about
her much, however. Ginny had made lasagna weeks in advance, when
she first heard we were coming. There was a lot of it. At one point
Bill, eighty-three, turned to John, eighty-five, and said, "More lasagna, John?" and the way he said it, his gentleness and his formality,
brought tears to my eyes, it was so like my mother.

Another afternoon, at John and Lydia's, we drank some of the lavender-colored wine John makes from the fruit of the prickly-pear cactus. John has made wine for years, and sometimes wins prizes for it. He is a benign, sturdy man with a long face like the actor Max von Sydow's. The Depression thwarted his dream of becoming a doctor, so he got a Ph.D. in physiology. For much of his life he was a professor of radiation biology and biophysics at the University of Rochester. Aunt Lydia, who had just come back from Palm Sunday services, said that John never went to church and had never joined one. She said that because of his scientific training he could not accept the simultaneous humanity and divinity of Christ. John nodded in assent, half-ruefully, as if he wasn't proud of this but couldn't deny it. I think that if others of my relatives, especially my father, had examined their beliefs, they might have agreed with John. This was the first time I had ever heard anyone in my family speak about believing or not believing in God.

We did a lot in Tucson. At an exhibit advertising life-sized moving dinosaurs we paid, walked in the door, an eight-foot-long iguanadon lurched as if someone had suddenly released its parking brake, and our daughter sprinted from the museum. We drove to the Mission of San Xavier, south of the city, and to Tombstone, Arizona, and to the Mexican border town of Nogales. The kids could not get enough of the motel pool. I took walks—greater Tucson now has almost three-quarters of a million people, and mostly I found myself walking on car-thronged highways and across vast discount-store parking lots. The branches of trees in Tucson wave plastic shopping bags they have caught by the handles, just like trees in New York. The peaks of the Catalina Mountains now horripilate with antennae. The house where my grandparents used to live has a high brick wall around it, as do many houses in the neighborhood. Our cousins John and Mary (Bill and Ginny's son and daughter) live in Tucson, and we had a big Mexican dinner with them and their spouses and kids and parents and in-laws and friends. Cousin John had hoped that he and I would get a chance to talk, but except for a short conversation at his house we didn't, really, and he was disappointed and I felt responsible for that and bad.

But things just got so confused. None of us from New York knew our way around Tucson, so whenever we went anywhere I would have to call somebody for directions and then write out additional sets for

Maggie's car and Suzan's car. Even with that we got lost. The keys to Suzan's car disappeared and she had to call the rental company to bring duplicates. Maggie's daughter came down with an ear infection and Maggie and John spent a night sitting with her in the emergency room. Uncle John and Aunt Lydia are members of Tucson's Sonora Desert Museum and wanted to take us there one afternoon. The kids liked the museum, but after an hour or so began to tire. Uncle John then wanted to take us to Furr's Cafeteria for lunch. He and Suzan went to the exit to wait for the rest of us. Maggie got separated from everybody and hunted all over the grounds for us for half an hour or more. Aunt Lydia sat in the aviary waiting for Uncle John. Cora threw a fit. Jay and I got to the exit with the squalling Cora and told him Lydia was in the aviary, but when he went there she had left. He went looking for her, she came to the exit, and I went to look for him. Finally we all were in our cars. Discussion of where to go continued. Were the kids too tired for a restaurant? Yes, probably. I was running back and forth in the parking lot relaying the discussion to family members in the various cars. We decided to go back to the motel. As we turned in the motel drive, we saw Lydia and John go sailing by.

In fifteen minutes they came back with cold cuts and bread and potato salad and beer. We all sat in the patio behind our cabin and ate and felt a lot better. Afterward, John and Lydia went home. The kids wanted to go swimming, so Jay and Suzan took them to the pool. I sat by myself with my feet up and watched a bird run across the patio fence with a wad of monofilament line in its mouth and I reflected that life was not so bad, confusion gets sorted out in the end. I strolled to the pool to watch the children swim. At my arm a voice said, "*Sandy?*" It was Susie, my high-school girlfriend.

I was so stunned I did almost nothing. I had to force myself to talk, as a silence of this length bordered on rudeness. I would have hooted in derision at a coincidence like this happening in a soap opera. She said they'd been coming to this motel for seven or eight years. They, also, had chosen it for the world-famous cactus garden. She was with her two children and a friend. She and Kent had recently divorced, and she had cut off almost all her hair. She said she hoped nothing like a divorce ever happened to me.

People sometimes regret that they never sat down with their grandmother or other relative and recorded that person's stories while they still could. The problem is that generally when you're with such a relative you're in the middle of a family event, with all its emotion and tensions and confusion, and kids and dogs running around. You are *in* life, not reflecting on it. After I left Tucson my uncles and aunts all wrote me. Bill and John sent recollections of my mother; Bill sent me diaries of O.A.S. Hursh's he had found, John sent me boxes of correspondence between Flora and Osie. Lydia writes long, detailed letters, Ginny writes short ones, and I write back. About certain subjects we talk more easily in the mail.

•

My mother's sister, Betty, married a man from Columbia, South Carolina, named Dan McLean. Uncle Dan wore his trousers high on his waist and his gray fedora tilted back on his head. His round face leans toward the camera in family group photos, smiling in a way that belies the dislike some of his in-laws had for him, and probably he for some of them. He and Betty quarreled with Flora and Osie in the forties and moved South. When they returned for Flora and Osie's fiftieth wedding anniversary in 1956, Betty was apprehensive of more arguments. None happened; Betty wrote my mother afterward that it was good Dan had been able to spend the days fishing with my cousin and me. Dan loved to fish. I watched him on my grandmother's pier and wanted to try it. He took time with us, although the string-with-a-rock-tied-to-the-end-of-it he first rigged for me (I was only five) looked so unpromising that I asked for a cane pole with a line and a real hook and worm. Photographs show us standing on the pier, content and male, fishing poles in hand.

In 1958 Betty and Dan again came North to visit. My mother made a lunch buffet at our house for them and Aunt Ginny and Uncle Bill. My father generally avoided events like this, but he attended, too. As we were sitting at the table Uncle Dan began to tell a story about a Negro foreman at work—Dan was an accountant at a stone quarry. The story had to do with an injury suffered by this foreman, and how everybody at the quarry had taken up a collection for him. Dan pronounced the word Negro "nigra." My father objected and said something like "Why don't you call him what he is?" Dan said, "Well, that's what they are, isn't it—niggers?" My father said, "No, seriously, Dan, we don't talk like that in this house." Dan said, "Well, come on, Betty, let's go." Betty made no move to rise, and Dan walked out the front door and zoomed his car down the drive. Our house was still new then, and raw, without curtains in the front window or grass along the walk. Dan's departure through it made that part of the house look scary and dangerous to me for a while. Betty left later with Bill and Ginny. My father spent the rest of the afternoon in his bedroom with the door closed; displays of anger upset him more than he let on. Betty visited us again—I remember her sewing the hem of my sister's wedding dress hours before the wedding while my sister stood in the dress on the dining-room table—but Dan never did. I never fished with him again. I saw him only once more, in a hospital, when we had stopped to visit on our way to Florida.

I drove down to see Betty a while ago. She was still in the same big ranch house in a Columbia suburb where she and Dan had moved some years before he died. I swerved on my way into Columbia to follow the road the 55th Ohio had taken with Sherman's army in 1864, burning and destroying, on a march they later called "That Smoky March." "The dry pine-trees flared like giant torches," wrote the 55th's chronicler. Today the road is lined with pine trees, auto-parts places, and video stores. When I arrived at Betty's and told her I'd followed the Union Army route, she added, "They burned the State House in Columbia." Her tone was mild but accusatory; life has given her a Southern accent and point of view. She has white hair and dark eyes, and looks a lot like my mother and grandmother. She inherited Flora's skill at baking. My mother could never get the lebkuchen she made from Betty's recipe to taste as good as the lebkuchen Betty sent us each Christmas, and she suspected her of purposely leaving out some key ingredient or step.

In letters, Betty repeats words and sentences; I had thought that was by coincidence or mistake, but it is a style. As we talked she said, "That was a long time ago . . . it's been a long time . . . it's been a while," over and over, a sort of refrain. She said she didn't really know my mother, that she used to play with my mother like a doll. She told me a lot I had never heard before about Aunts Alice and Elinor and Grace, and about Grandmother Hursh, who she said contributed to the death of O.A.S. Hursh (see p. 3) by not calling a doctor for him in time. The life she and her brothers had led before my mother was born sounded better than what came after—their father worked hard, but he didn't let it bother him any; he built a little cottage on the lake in Bay Village near Stop 23 on the interurban, and Flora and the children spent the summers there and sometimes part of the fall; Osie took them on drives and Flora made made them picnics. But after Peggy was born, the family sold the cottage for practically nothing. It just about killed the kids not to go out there anymore, but Flora said she couldn't manage in a cottage with a little baby. Flora had worked worked hard before Peggy was born, but really knocked herself out after. She used to jump up and run every time Peggy cried.

As a girl, Betty liked to visit her grandmother Hursh in Tiffin. She used to ride down by herself on the train. After she graduated from high school she went to Heidelberg College, and boarded in a little room at the Hurshes' house. Grandmother could be a selfish person sometimes, but she was good to Betty. Betty became close to her aunt Grace, but thought her aunt Alice was peculiar and head-strong. She saw little of Aunt Elinor, who was gone much of the time. Betty got her diploma ("*dee*-ploma") in 1932. She met Dan McLean not long after, at the Presbyterian church in Lakewood. Dan's father had been transferred to Cleveland, via Pittsburgh, by the railroad he worked for. Dan and Betty married in 1936. Dan hated the weather up North, as did his parents; he never could get used to snow. And everybody they knew in Bay Village played bridge, which he never did like. It just about killed Betty's parents when she and Dan moved South. Dan was glad to be back where he could hunt and fish in good weather for more of the year.

Through the window Betty pointed out her camellia bushes, some of them pink and some of them almost a red, which she cultivated at her old house and which Dan dug up and moved to their new house himself with the help of the company truck and a colored man. She talked a lot about her son, Bill, and about the many jobs he worked to help put himself through medical school, and the long hours he works in his practice, and the help he gives her keeping up the house now that Dan's gone. Even before, Bill was better at repairs and yardwork than Dan, who preferred fishing. She mentioned that after graduation from medical school Bill had been stationed in Antarctica by the navy; "You know that Bill was in the Antarctic," she remen-tioned several times with pride. She talked about her daughter Elise's kids and Bill's kids, and about vacations they take at the Atlantic shore, and about Elise's husband, Jim, a dentist. And about Dan's background, his grandparents and his parents, and about the places he liked to fish, and about how Dan's mother always said he used to fish with a string in a bucket when he was a baby, and about the friends Dan fished with, and about the hundreds of friends he'd had. I asked her if she remembered the long-ago incident at our house between Dan and my father. Betty said she did. She leaned back in her chair and looked away and thought for a while. Then she said, "Dan was the type that he never met anybody that he didn't know them and talked to them and enjoyed it."

●

Starting in 1942, a woman named Willie Johnson used to come from East Cleveland to Bay Village every other week to help Flora with the cleaning and ironing. Flora pronounced her "really a *good* cleaner and ironer," so she must have been. She had rheumatic knees, and some days she moaned as she walked, and some weeks she didn't come in at all. My mother was away at college, but Willie took a fancy to her picture and used to talk to it affectionately as she cleaned. Sometimes Willie brought her daughter, Alice. As a cleaner and ironer, Alice was at least her mother's equal. My mother referred to Alice as a "whiz" and a "whirlwind." After my mother married, Alice and Willie sometimes worked for her.

In the summer of 1958—just a week or so after my father's argument with Uncle Dan, as it happened—our parents left us with Alice and took a trip to New Hampshire. My father was to give a paper at a scientific convention there; they had never taken a trip without us before. They gave Alice money and the keys to my father's car and told her she was in charge. She brought her kids, Gail and Ronald, to our house to play, and we visited at her house in Cleveland. She cleaned our whole house, including the basement and garage and all the cupboards and closets. Davy took a special liking to her and followed her around. He, Suzan, and Fritz all came down with the measles, and she nursed them. She drove us in the car with her when she shopped in Hudson. Black people were rare in Hudson, and the locals probably stared. Davy told her that a neighbor boy had said something mean about her.

One day the mailman came to the end of our driveway and I started out the door to get the mail. Alice told me not to, that she would get it herself. I argued with her. Maybe I even became upset;

I enjoyed getting the mail. Some kids were playing in a yard across the street. Alice asked, "Are you afraid your friends might see me because you're ashamed of the color of my skin?" I don't know exactly why I answered as I did—I was just seven, the incident with Uncle Dan had confused me, I was angry at my parents for leaving, I wanted to hurt Alice so our parents couldn't leave us with her again. Or, more simply, I was willing to exploit a weakness to get my own way. I said, "Yes," and went for the mail myself. At this, Alice, who had done all my parents or anyone could have asked of her, fell into despair. She spent the days until my parents returned ironing, and singing as she ironed:

> O Lord, though I done my best,
> Ain't done enough to fulfill your request.

Our parents found all us kids in wonderful shape on their return, the house spotless, the measles healed, and Alice in despair. My father sat me down on the steps to the back bathroom and told me I had done a bad thing. Afterward, Alice worked for us less often; the long drive from Cleveland was the reason my parents gave. My mother found women to help clean who didn't have to travel so far.

Alice lives now in Cleveland Heights. My mother had kept a phone number for her in an address book, and on an afternoon when I was in the area I gave her a call. She had not seen me in at least thirty years. I explained that I was the kid she used to take care of, Sandy. She said, "Uh-huh." A pause followed. Then she said, "I liked Davy." I told her my father was dead, which she had known, and that my mother was, too, which she hadn't. I asked if I could come and see her, and she agreed. When she met me at the side door of her frame house on a street off Cedar Road, she looked almost as I remembered. In her seventies, she remains unwrinkled; her mother lived to be 102. She is a long-limbed woman with a sleepy-shrewd expression, and she smokes king-size menthol cigarettes in a way that calls attention to the angles of her shoulders and elbows and forearms. She said, "You look just like your daddy. You got that hair. It's thinnin' out some."

We sat in her living room. I told her about myself and my brother and sisters and what we were all doing now, and that I was a writer and had written books and had even been on television. She looked without enthusiasm at my sneakers, blue jeans, and plaid shirt and asked, "Tell me, when you go on TV . . . do you wear a suit?" Then she said, "Your daddy didn't care about dressin', neither. I used to tease your mother, I used to say, 'There ain't nothin' wrong with David, honey, he's just homely and raggedy.' He had that one blue suit, wash 'n' wear—this was when wash 'n' wear first came in—and we used to wash that blue suit and hang it up and then pretty soon we'd be washin' it again. He'd wear that suit and them big shoes—I believe he had a size-13 foot. The day David and Peggy married, Mother and I worked at the reception, and Miz Hursh be cookin' everything—that woman could *bake*, and *sew* like you wouldn't believe—and everybody was sayin' what a handsome guy this David was, and when Peggy walked in with him I thought she should be with someone else. But he had a brain, now. I asked Peggy, 'Why is he *Doctor* Frazier?' I knew he wasn't no medical doctor. Peggy set down and start explainin'; she said, 'He's the kind of doctor that's a scientist, he works for the Standard Oil.' I said, 'He don't pump gas.' She said, 'He's mixin' up the combustion that makes the gas *go*.' She was crazy about that David, she had him and that was good enough for her. She had a navy-blue suit, an all-occasion suit, and she'd wear black pump shoes winter and summer and just change accessories. I never knew her to wear a hat. She didn't like to dress, and David didn't like to dress. She just wanted everything to be common and everybody to have fun.

"Your daddy wouldn't never let nobody say a bad word about the Negroes. He th'owed Peggy's brother-in-law out the house for talkin' against the Negroes. When he was sick and he had that nurse takin' care of him, I called to their apartment one day and the nurse answered the phone and she was tryin' to tell me how nice your mother and he was and I said, 'Don't tell *me*, I know 'em, and I knew the generation *before* them.' My mother started workin' in Bay Village in '39, '40. She came up North from Milan, Georgia, in '28, stayed in Cleveland awhile, went back, and moved to Cleveland for good in '37. First person she worked for in Bay Village was Miz Richards, and after them she worked for Hustieners, Sharpes, Robinsons. You know how thick the houses were out there. Pretty soon everybody was wantin' her. They loved her in Bay Village. Mother always was a hard worker. In

Milan everybody called Mother Aint Coot. Down there she worked mainly for a family called McRanie. She had took care of the daddy, W. D. McRanie, when he was a little boy, and her mother took care of his father's family, and her mother's mother took care of his father's father's family. Down in Milan today there's still old white folks who know me as Aint Coot's Alice.

"I still go down to Milan every once in a while. I'll drive down there in a couple of weeks with my oldest daughter, Shirley. I don't believe you know Shirley. She was born in 1938, and she's spiritual, she's psychic. She's a minister now, in a church called the I Believe in Miracles Church. She's a secretary in the principal's office at East Tech High School, where your granddaddy used to teach. It ain't nothin' like it used to be—somebody shot a machine gun through the office window the other day. Now, you did know my son, Ronald. How old are you? Well, Ronald's forty-four. He was workin' in a store and the man wouldn't give him benefits so he quit. Now he's working as a substance-abuse counselor. He's not married. He has a real nice girlfriend, but she comes in his apartment and he don't even like to see her set her coat on a chair. He has an '83 car, but you'd think it's new, he's wipin' on it all the time."

I asked after Alice's other daughter, Gail. Gail is older than I am; I used to play dodge ball with her and Ronald in our basement. Alice took a drag on her cigarette, ashed it, and gave me a direct look. "Gail. Is in prison," she said. "She had a man she was livin' with and he beat her up—black men are bad about hittin' women—and the court says she shot him, she says she didn't. He was shot and he died. She'll be getting out soon—she's at North East Pre-release Center on East Thirtieth Street downtown. She didn't have no record, either, she'd been workin' fourteen years at Lincoln Electric.

"Now the one I loved in your family was Davy. I just loved that boy. He is the sweetest of you-all. He would talk to me while I worked, his mouth goin' like a clapper. He was at my feet all the time. He watched, but he never done no cleanin' himself. He didn't like things changed, he wanted me to leave everything just the way they was. That was the only thing I could get on Davy's nerves about. He used to use the word 'I guess.' You'd ask him a question and he'd answer, real slow, 'I g-u-e-s-s . . .' That time I came out to take care of you-all when your mother and daddy went on that trip, and you-all got the measles, I didn't think it was serious—it wasn't, you'd had that globulin medicine—but I didn't want to worry your mother when she called, so I didn't mention that you-all was sick. But Davy, he got on the phone and he said to her, 'Everything's all right, Mommy.' Then he said to me, 'Is it, Alice?' That made her know something was wrong. I had to tell her about the measles then."

Working up my nerve, I asked Alice if she remembered the incident with the mail. She didn't; I began to fill in the details. Then suddenly her glance sharpened. "God, I had forgot that!" she said. "Yes, you did do that. I remember those neighbor boys, they told Davy the Negroes had taken over his father's house. And you wanted to go out and get the mail, and I didn't want you to, 'cause it might have got misplaced. Your parents were people that received important mail. And you wouldn't let me get it. I do remember that."

"I know it was a long time ago, but I apologize," I said.

"Oh well, I knew you wasn't raised that way. You wasn't mean. You was just off readin' the newspaper."

She fixed us lunch—Campbell's beef barley soup, tuna-fish sandwiches, and glasses of milk. A disabled war veteran who boards with her joined us. He did not say a word. "I didn't see much of you-all, or your mother and daddy neither, for a long long time," she said. "We was livin' in an apartment on East Eighty-third, and my husband, Walter, died of a heart attack at the dining-room table at the age of fifty-seven. I had to raise three children all myself. I put 'em all through private school, Catholic school. I had a store over on Seventy-ninth and Holton and I did Stocks and Bonds—that's a numbers game that's based on the Stock Exchange from New York—it's illegal—and I also had a café and sold hamburgers and candies and ice cream to the kids. We were close to four school districts. I did that for many years. Then when Mother got too old to look after herself I took care of her. I took care of Mother for the last fifteen years of her life.

"Your mother called me when Sandy died—I mean, when Fritz died—and when your parents moved to the apartment in Lakewood she called me to come and clean a few times. I knew your daddy was gettin' sick, and I asked her if she needed someone to take care of him. She said she did, and I told her I could do it. But she said she couldn't hire me because I didn't have no nursing degree and the *in*surance wouldn't pay unless I did. I nursed Mother all those years,

I take care of disabled veterans in my home, I know about takin' care of people. But I don't have that paper. Nowadays if you black won't nobody talk to you if you don't have that paper, that diploma. Even in your own race people don't act like they used to. People love you for what you can do, not for *you*. All this talkin' about education and degrees and diplomas is just an excuse for not havin' to know the person. Down South, everybody knew you, and you knew who the good ones was. There's some nice white people down there, but the bad overpowers 'em. And up here, white people pat you on the back, but all they care about is your work. Used to be there wasn't no diploma between you and them. Used to be, you got to know someone you worked for, and after a while sometimes you loved 'em. And if they loved you, they loved you, and if you was in trouble, they was in trouble, too. Now they just want to know what paper you got. You can't get started the way you used to."

CHAPTER 16

WHEN FRITZ WAS BORN, and he and my mother had not yet come home from the hospital, Willie stayed with us during the days. My father bought us foods different from what we usually ate—large garlicky sausages, mainly. Grandmother commented on the way we strolled around the house eating them with our hands. One weekend she took me to stay with her at the cottage. The upstairs bedroom had no heat, so I slept in her bed in the downstairs bedroom with her. At night I listened to her loud snore; she claimed she heard me say in my sleep, "I will! I will! I will eat everything that is put before me!" She had planned to take me to the woods to hunt for plants with her and was irked at my parents' forgetting to provide me with over-shoes. She took me to a shoe store and bought me a pair. The month was early May, and the woods damp and chilly. We found many fiddlehead ferns and jack-in-the-pulpits, which we dug up and put in cardboard boxes without tops in the trunk of her car. The dogwood

Fritz at about age ten

trees were in bloom, luminous as night-lights in the drizzly overcast. We brought the plants back to the cottage and transplanted them on the bluff, among rocks she had put there to hold the soil. The plants later flourished, and Grandmother often reminded me that I had helped get them. The light green of ferns and the white of dogwood and the interior of a jack-in-the-pulpit always made me think of when Fritz was born.

We moved to Hudson the same year. My parents put Dave and me in bunk beds in a front bedroom. Suzan had the room next to my parents, across from the bathroom. When Maggie came along, she and Suzan shared that room. Fritz slept in the back bedroom by himself from about age two until he was seven or eight, when it was decided that I, now a teenager, should have a room of my own. Then he and I switched. We kids often slept with each other in various beds, especially on important nights like Christmas and Easter. "Sleeping around," our father called it. In the evenings he read us stories, usually in Dave's and my room. One night I leaned over too far and fell out of the top bunk and landed headfirst on his foot. After the stories we knelt with our mother by the side of the bed and said the Lord's Prayer, and another prayer asking God to bless us, our parents, grandparents, Uncle Louis and Aunt Evie, and cousins, and (without naming them) everyone else we loved.

The branches of an ash tree scraped the window across from our beds. For a while that window scared Dave; "The window *looks* at me," he said. On a little rise across the street was the Gellatlys' house. Pete Gellatly, my age, often got better grades than I did, and the sight of his bedroom light still on after I was in bed made me worry that he was studying later and harder than I had. By moving to the other window in our room, I could change perspective just enough to see the glow of the light above their garage without the glare of the light itself, and in the glow, on winter nights, I could see how hard the snow was coming down. I wanted it to snow all night so we wouldn't have school.

Mornings began with the sound of my father clearing his throat, and then the grinding of the hand-cranked coffee grinder in the kitchen below our room. A little later the springs on the garage door twanged as it went up, and my father's car started, idled, and bounced down the drive. Then we kids dressed and had breakfast and walked to the end of the street to wait for the school bus. Our bus, Bus 8, came from up the hill, and when we first spotted it, the boys left their lunchboxes in a cluster and began running the opposite way up Sugarbush Trail to see who could get the farthest up the street and then back in time to catch the bus. This game annoyed the bus driver, Mr. Hartz, and sometimes he drove off quickly and made us sprint to the next bus stop. "Hartzy" smoked cigars and unfiltered cigarettes, and every Christmas the children on his route gave him cigarettes in gift cartons with bells and ribbons printed on them. He made a big pile of them in the front of the bus by the gearshift lever.

The bus dropped us off in the village, at the fenced gravel playground by the elementary school. We played and chased around for a few minutes until the bell rang. Along the top of the two-story brick building ran a border engraved with a verse from "God Bless America": "Confirm thy soul in self-control, thy liberty in law." During the school year the windows were covered with seasonal decorations; once, as a reward for something, I was allowed to paint a Christmas decoration on the high window by a stairwell, applying red tempera to the glass, slowly reddening the winter light. We took off coats and boots in a coat hall at one end of the classroom. When the day was over, how exciting to find a note from a girlfriend folded into a triangle in the coat pocket! We played outside again until the buses arrived, then lined up by bus number and boarded single-file through an opening in the playground fence. On the return trip we were usually rowdier, and Hartzy would fix us with fierce glances in the long, rectangular rearview mirror. If that didn't work, he would pull over and unhook the leather strop from its place on the dash. Sometimes he would stare steadily at one of us as he made his way down the aisle, then suddenly and unexpectedly turn and whack another. He dropped us not at our street where he had picked us up but at a farther intersection on the paved road. From there we walked, stopping sometimes in winter to tunnel in drifts along the snow fences.

I played with Kent, Don, A.C., Pete, and Pete's brother Dave, called Sweetie. My brother Dave played with Don's brother Jim. Suzan and Maggie played with Pete's little sisters, Lisa and Wendy, and with A.C.'s sisters, Linda and Julie, and with the girl next door, Betsy, called Boo Boo. Fritz sometimes tagged along with Maggie and her friends, or played with Kent's brother Danny. In warm weather we boys played Wiffle ball, climbed beech trees and carved our names in them, dammed up the sewer ditches and sailed boats we'd made. Every March or April came the slaughter of the spring peeper frogs. I liked to fool with box traps I invented that never caught anything, and with those plastic rockets you half-filled with water and then pumped with air and fired. One of my favorite toys was a parachute inside a little plastic sphere spring-loaded to open when you threw it. Eventually it stuck high in a tree I couldn't climb. I lofted many stones at it, but never got it down.

In the fall, and even in the winter when snow was on the ground, we played touch football. In northern Ohio, people cared about football most, basketball second, and baseball a far third. We played almost every day after school at Kent's or Don's house, because they had more level front yards. We let the little kids, Fritz and Danny, play sometimes, but all they got to do was hike and block. When they complained in the huddle, we would use them in trick plays which seldom worked. We continued to meet for these games through high school, and even in college when we came home on vacations. By then some of the players had changed. At a game one winter in town, Fritz, a teenager then, caught the winning pass in the end zone. Still thinking of him as a little kid, we had neglected to guard him closely. The ball came in hard and straight with a solid *thunk* as he caught it against his sweater. I like to remember his teammates' surprised cheer, and the way he turned down the corners of his mouth in an attempt to be cool and not yell for joy himself. The moment is one of the few I can think of when I am certain he was happy.

So much of the time, he wasn't. From a difficult baby he grew into a vexed, vexatious kid. He started saying "No!" to everything when he was two. My parents ascribed this to the "terrible twos," but the phase didn't really stop. He argued with his brothers and sisters and screamed at his parents. He broke the glass in the cocktail table twice, once by kicking off his shoe, which flew through the air and landed on it heel first, and once by hitting it with a glass piggy bank. Our mother mentions often in letters to her parents how hard to control he was, how belligerent. Her father said that when Fritz got to elementary school and found himself challenged, he would probably calm down. But he was quiet and tractable in school. He could be sweet sometimes. Because he often went unnoticed, or got attention for being angry, a smile or flattering wisecrack from him was like a found dollar bill you'd forgotten you'd had.

He was the unpaired child among us five brothers and sisters, and the only one without a corresponding Frazier cousin. I played with Libby, Dave with Louis, Suzan with Cindy, and Maggie with Annie. Grandmother and my parents noted with regret that Fritz always had to make a third or play by himself. My father tried to remedy this by spending more time with Fritz, carrying him on his shoulders for long walks along the bluff in the evenings. Fritz had a wide mouth and a broad nose and blond, curly hair. An elderly cousin who lived near Grandmother asked us about the "tall, blond man" she sometimes saw walking by. One year, Grandmother decided to bring Fritz with her when she went on a tour of Central America. He was eight or nine, and he smiles wholeheartedly in a photograph taken at the ruin of a Mayan pyramid. Grandmother didn't know for sure why she had done this only for him and not for any of the rest of us. Later she was happy that she had, and understood better why.

•

We were a restless family. Dave and I walked the two and a half miles to town for the first time on a Sunday afternoon when I was eight years old and he was five. Our mother, rehearsing a play at the town hall, looked surprised when we showed up, but she did not get mad. Our parents would not allow us air rifles or bows and arrows or a television set, but rambling miles from home by ourselves was okay. I explored the woods—there were still woods in Hudson then—with Kent, and rode my bike to farm ponds to fish, and began to hitchhike when I was twelve or thirteen. In junior high, friends and I sometimes hitchhiked as far away as Akron. Once, Kent and I found a boat on the banks of Tinker's Creek, and we launched it on the muddy spring floodwaters, and the current jammed it under a low-lying branch, and it sank. Crushed against the thwarts, icy water rising around us, we thought we would drown. Every summer my father rented a camper trailer and hitched it to the back of our station wagon, and we spent weeks driving the western U.S. and Canada. Every year we got the same camper, and every year it smelled the same—of propane, of foam mattresses covered with plastic, of sour milk, of canvas. The camper tent folded out from the trailer, and Dad usually went inside the tent and snapped it together while I held it from the outside so it wouldn't collapse. Once, I became distracted and let go. When he disentangled himself and came out, he told me I didn't have the brains God gave a screwdriver.

Our parents folded the back seats of the station wagon down flat and put a thin mattress on top. We added pillows and blankets and personal items stashed in various corners, and all five of us kids rode back there, more or less in a heap. I liked the way-back, where I could look out the rear window at the stars. Half-asleep, head against the inside bulge of the gas tank, I could hear the nozzle of a hose going into the tank when we stopped, and the echoing splash of fuel. Once, I watched a hand embossed with oil in the fingerprints fumble with the gas cap and heard an expression I would not understand for several years. Once, during a long daytime haul somewhere out West, I noticed Dave grimacing in pain. I asked what was wrong. "I can't stop thinking about inclined plane!" he said. "It just keeps running through my mind, inclined *plane* inclined *plane* inclined *plane!*" Our mother set the picnic basket on the front seat and made us salami sandwiches and poured us cups of punch. Pretty soon the car would start to take on the raisin-y smell a vehicle gets when you live in it.

One summer we went to Alaska. Dad bought an extra spare tire and welded sheet metal under the gas tank; much of the Alaska Highway, the last 1,500 miles before Fairbanks, would be gravel road. We crossed into Canada at Lake of the Woods, stopped at the Canadian national parks of Banff and Jasper, and met the highway at Dawson Creek, British Columbia. The highway was loud, with stones pinging off the car and once in a while chipping the windshield, and it was dusty. I watched Fritz sleep as whitish road dust collected on his face. For much of a day we passed through a section of forest that had recently burned. A store where we had expected to buy supplies somewhere in the Yukon Territory was closed, so one afternoon lunch was scoops of chunky peanut butter served in individual paper cups. I had read a lot about fishing in Alaska and wanted to stop at almost every stream we crossed. Finally, well into Alaska, Dad pulled over, and I rigged my fly rod and put on a mosquito fly and began to catch grayling, a torpedo-shaped fish found in pure, cold streams. Grayling have a high dorsal fin like a sailfish and are easy to catch. Suddenly I heard Fritz shout. I ran along the rocky streambed, tumbling head-over-heels but somehow not breaking my rod. I thought he had fallen

On a cross-country trip, all of us kids in the back of the station wagon

Dave, in the foreground; beyond him, Fritz, in a bad mood

Suzan and Maggie

in. He was standing on the bank with the line from his little spinning rod fast to a northern pike nearly as big as he was. It didn't seem to know it was hooked and was just lolling there in a backwater. It hardly protested even when we hauled it out, and became excited only when we hit it on the head with rocks. We ate it for several camp dinners, spitting out its Y-shaped bones, and later in stews and sandwiches.

Our trips usually ended the same. We approached Hudson from the west on the Ohio Turnpike, passing spots that were more and more familiar—the exit to Norwalk, the exit by Grandmother's house, the long bridge across the Cuyahoga River Valley, the high arched bridge just before the exit for Route 8 and Hudson. Then we would drive through town, out Aurora Street at 25 miles per hour, up our street, into our drive. In the moment after Dad turned off the car, while it was still making its cooling-off clicks and sighs, and a sudden sense of deflation settled around us, he would turn to Mom and take her by the hand and say, "Well, we did it." They would look at each other and smile.

The afternoon we got back from Alaska, Dad and I unfolded the camper tent in the yard to air it out. As soon as I went to bed that night, I climbed out my window and walked into town to see what my friends had been up to while I was gone. I met a few of them and we skulked around all night. A big storm came up, which we spent sitting on a car in somebody's unlocked garage. I got home just before dawn. At breakfast Dad said to me, "When that storm hit last night I almost woke you to help me take down the camper. But then I just did it myself. I decided, what the heck, let him sleep."

•

Most evenings we all ate dinner together at the big oval table in the dining room. Dad would sit down, take his napkin from the steel napkin ring somebody had made for him in the navy, lift his glass of red table wine, and propose a toast, which my mother, lifting her glass, echoed. After Dad had taken perhaps three bites, he almost always sat back, sighed, and said, "I didn't know how hungry I was." Often he remarked to my mother, "This is unusually good tonight— did you do something different with it?" and she always said no, it was just the same. She made Swiss steak with mashed potatoes, sauer-kraut and pork, salmon croquettes with cream sauce, chicken and dumplings, liver and onions, and (the least popular) creamed chipped beef on toast. Salad, often with a pinkish sauce made of mayonnaise and catsup, came with the main course. For dessert we generally had instant pudding or homemade cookies and candies. Boys sat on one side of the table and girls on the other. Maggie and I sat at the end by Mom, Dave and Sue by Dad, and Fritz, odd man out again, between Dave and me. As his dinnertime tantrums progressed, our parents tried to pacify him by moving his place next to Mom, then next to Dad.

After dinner Mom rinsed the dishes and put them in the dishwasher. Dad sometimes helped. One of our few chores was to clear the table; Dad told me not to stack the plates together because that got the bottoms dirty, and they only washed the tops. Dad then sat in the living room and read *Scientific American* and *The New Yorker*, ripping out the cardboard subscription inserts and stuffing them between the cushions of the couch without taking his eyes from the page. Sometimes an article in *The New Yorker*—Capote's "In Cold Blood," for example—fascinated him so much he could not wait for the issue with the next installment to arrive in the mail and gained a day or two by buying it at a newsstand. As the dishwasher began to run, our mother joined him and did schoolwork. While studying for her master's degree she wrote essays, and a play based on the life of Edgar Allan Poe, which she submitted for her thesis. After she had begun to teach at Revere High School in nearby Bath Township, she always had papers to grade. Dad sometimes sat up late with her when grades were due and helped with the averaging. Many nights he kept a fire going in the fireplace, feeding it newspapers, magazines, used wrapping paper, kitchen scraps, out-of-date textbooks, and firewood from the stack in the garage only when nothing else could be found.

Some evenings Mom or Dad left after dinner for play rehearsal. When I was in the fourth grade both Dad and I got parts in *Nude with Violin*, by Noël Coward, at the town hall. The plot involves a painter who has fooled people into thinking that terrible abstracts done by amateurs are actually great art he has done himself. I had only a few lines but "stomped about the stage like a young Hitler," according to a reviewer. Dad played a cynical magazine photographer. I got to stay up late, sit on the town hall fire escape between entrances, drink Cokes, and go to school the next morning with greasepaint still in my hairline. I liked the smoky, sweaty, makeup-y way my T-shirt always smelled when I took it off for bed. At the dress rehearsal, when we practiced our curtain call, Dad refused to bow. The director kidded him, trying to make him relent. Dad told the director that he did not bow. Every night at curtain call he came out and stood straight while the rest of us bowed.

I see now that Dad was becoming more unhappy in those years. He had been ready to leave Sohio in the late fifties but put off serious search for another job until all us kids had reached school age. Then he began to write to colleges in California, many of which replied that he was too old or too well qualified for the assistant professorships they had to offer. His letters of application grew more animated as he tried to sell himself. To us, he talked about Hudson in angrier and scarier terms; of a local private swimming club, he said, "What do you think would happen if a Negro tried to go there? Would they kill him?" He was not wrong about the general racist mood in the air. A neighbor from up the street came to our door one evening circulating a petition to keep a black family who had bid on a house in the development from moving in. I remember Dad dismissing him with a full-armed, biblical gesture, but actually the encounter was so quick it left no time for that. The man sort of ricocheted out the door. In the late sixties Dad applied to teach at a college in Istanbul, Turkey, and nearly had the job, until the college decided it couldn't afford to move a big family all that way. With anger and bitterness, Dad told us the news one evening at dinner. To me, he added, "Now you can stay in your precious Hudson."

● Among the many thousand photographs my parents left behind is a group of eight which I have looked at over and over. They were taken in or just before March of 1967, the developer's date in the left-hand margin. They show the interior of several rooms of our house—kitchen, living room, parents' study, parents' bedroom—on a sunny day. Each room is seen from two different angles. What makes the pictures unusual is that they contain no people. The views have a cold, remote quality, like the part of a movie seen through the eyes of the stalker. The rooms are in full, lived-in dishevelment. Dishes soak in the sink, the dishwasher door lies open. A waffle iron on a counter suggests Sunday morning, when we often had waffles for breakfast. Was the family at church, all except for the photographer? I had forgotten that cookie jar shaped like a Christmas tree, and that

Candid interior shots of the house in 1967: parents' study, living room, kitchen, parents' bedroom. Dad hung his trousers on the closet door every night; perhaps he intended this photo as a self-portrait

aloe plant growing in the piece of white coral. In the living room, behind the worn couch, is an open magazine on the rug by the heating vent; I used to lie there in the warm air and read. Mom's big leather-and-weave purse, the one she often brought home student papers in, rests on her desk. The desk was made of a dark wood which had a spicy smell, I recall. By the desk is an overflowing wicker basket of laundry. Very few of the books in the bookcase are straight up and down. My favorite pictures are of their bedroom. From one angle you can see Dad's toolbox in the corner, tools spilling from it, and their bureau with the edge of the mirror where they always stuck adhesive tags saying "Hi, my name is DAVE." The other angle shows their mussed bed, with an inside-out girdle on the bedspread and Dad's trousers hanging from the corner of the closet door. The photographer must have been my father. Is the view of the trousers on the door a self-portrait? What caused the photographer to take these pictures— whimsy, journalistic curiosity, desire to try out a new camera? I think the purpose was darker: something on the order of "Look what I've gotten myself into."

·

Dave [to me, recently, on the telephone]: "Fritz and I started skiing together when he was seven or eight and I was twelve or thirteen. He was my skiing partner, one of the people I skied with the most. At first we'd just go over to Adolph's Hill. Later we began to try the bigger slopes like Boston Mills Ski Area, near Akron. He didn't live long enough to ski many places out of Ohio. I think the only place he went out of state was Peek'n Peak, in western New York. Fritz was a very good skier. I was four years older and so had a head start on him, but pretty soon he was skiing some of the same terrain I was. We used to talk about the Bone God. That was what got you if you overreached yourself. After we fell we'd say we had tempted the Bone God. Our parents bought him Kneissel skis—good skis, from an Austrian ski-making family—and one time he was going over a mogul and he fell and ripped the toe of the binding out of the ski. He grew so fast there for a while and got so big and strong; probably the bindings had been fitted for a younger boy. I remember that he was just crushed about that. When we got home Dad consoled him and said he'd fix it, and he did, the way Dad was able to do. He carefully drilled a couple of holes and fitted the bindings back in with epoxy. Fritz was delighted, absolutely. I'm sure with all of us in school at the time they wouldn't have had the money to buy him new skis. I loved skiing with Fritz. One of the saddest things about his death for me was not having somebody to ski with."

Suzan [also on the telephone]: "Considering what a difficult boy Fritz was, he never really did anything that you could call bad. He did bite one of the Sturtevant girls once, and it was like a big scandal and they made a big deal out of it, but in my opinion, biting one of them was not a serious crime."

Maggie [also on the telephone]: "Fritz always used to tell me he hated me: 'I-hate-you-I-hate-you-I-hate-you!' Finally it got to be so expected, I would be like 'Yeah, yeah, yeah.' "

Dave: "He and I loved to play around with Dad's stuff—with his calculator and his graph paper and his binoculars and his shortwave radio—and we loved to play in Dad's car. We would pretend to drive, we fooled with the levers and the knobs. Dad had a Heathkit radio in that car and one time we pushed in the cigarette lighter and got it glowing red hot and we pushed it against the plastic tuning knobs and melted them. We totally deformed the knobs. Dad was furious, and Fritz got blamed, but I'm sure I at least instigated it."

Suzan: "He and Maggie used to pass the time by fighting. I got tired of fighting with him. I was nineteen months older than he was and for a while I could overpower him. Then he got a little too big. That was an unfortunate moment."

Dave: "I remember watching *Johnny Quest* with him on TV, and playing with that Tonka Toy airport baggage handler set. When Dad was making model planes, which was a hobby of his for a while, all kinds of doping chemicals and really volatile airplane fuel found its way into Fritz's and my room. We had this little glass ashtray and we used to pour doping chemicals or airplane fuel into it and light it. It would go up like *poof!* From what we know now about carcinogenesis, I wonder if breathing those chemicals wasn't proximate cause for his illness."

Maggie: "He ate raw hot dogs all the time and I always wondered about that, if that didn't have something to do with his getting sick."

Suzan: "He had a paper route that didn't exactly work out. Dogs were a major problem, everybody where we lived had dogs and they let them run. It was like leash laws were too Communist or something.

He got bit by a dog and then I think there were places he wouldn't go."

Maggie: "I remember discovering a huge pile of *Plain Dealer*s in the woods by the Wearys' house, and then I knew why everybody was complaining they weren't getting their papers."

Dave: "When he was a baby Dad used to call him Toddler, and that drove him crazy when he got older. Dad was still calling him that when he was nine or ten."

Suzan: "He wasn't such a bad guy when he got older."

Dave: "He and I used to fight about mowing the lawn. We were supposed to mow the lawn because Mom was afraid if Dad did it he'd get a heart attack. That meant that you had to run and take the mower away from Dad when you heard him start it down in the garage, or he would just stubbornly go ahead and do it himself, and Mom would reproach you. Fritz and I hated to hear that mower start. We always fought about whose turn it was."

Maggie: "I remember that Fritz had a lot of friends. He hung out with the most popular kids when we were in junior high, and I think he ran for some office. He was very opposed to the war in Vietnam. He and his gang organized a strike where we all walked out of our classes one afternoon to protest the war."

Suzan: "He took a lot of LSD one time at Blossom Music Center when he went there with Dave and me. Dave got scared and took him home right away and left me there by myself without a ride."

Maggie: "When they came home I was watching TV and Fritz was so scared. I had no idea what he was going through. He lay down on top of me. I told him to wake up Mom and tell her he had taken acid. He went to their bedroom and woke her, and she was incredibly nice to him; nobody yelled at him. Also, he wasn't afraid to tell them, which was sort of brave. I would have been afraid, and if they found out, I think I'd've gotten in trouble. He had a certain way about him."

Suzan: "He got along really well with girls. I remember my friends Beth and Kathy said he was cute. He had a pretty girlfriend named Natalie."

Maggie: "Natalie was really really really nice. Lots of girls wanted to go with him. For a while he dated a girl with a bad reputation and I thought he shouldn't do that. But after he died I hoped she had been as promiscuous as I had heard."

•

Unlike many people my age I read about in magazines and newspapers, I was not basically a loner in high school. I wanted to be part of the in-group of popular kids, and when I couldn't attain that, I settled for a lesser group. I did what I had to to be accepted, often showing off by trying to be funny, sometimes going far enough to embarrass myself, sometimes hurting kids even more unsure of themselves than I. I sweated with nervousness, soaking my short-sleeved madras shirts. In seventh grade I was in a second-tier, sort of nerdy group, but in eighth grade I made it up to the first group, composed mostly of good-looking kids and basketball stars. I also wanted the approval of adults, and did my homework frantically in the evenings. In ninth grade I switched from the public school to Western Reserve Academy, which back then accepted only boys and charged a tuition of about $1,400 for day students like me. Most students at the Academy, as people called it, boarded there. Students and teachers (called masters) wore coats and ties to classes six days a week, to meals, to morning chapel services, to vespers services on Sunday evenings.

I had good teachers in Latin, French, and English. I liked to translate Latin. We read several books of the *Aeneid*, Cicero's letters and orations, Caesar (something like "The Gauls being in retreat, our cavalry were able to kill a great many of them at no risk to themselves"). Senior year we read lyric poetry so dirty the teacher could find no standard textbook of it and gave us assignments on sheets he had mimeographed. In an English class, a young teacher took apart an essay by a classmate with a cold thoroughness which scared me memorably. I got good grades. One term during my junior year when the grades came in the mail I tore open the envelope and was so happy I danced all over the downstairs. In the fall I played football, and in the spring I ran sprints and relays on the track team. When Susie and I were going together, I spent all my spare time with her. I graduated in 1969.

Dave entered the Academy two years after I did, and Fritz four years after Dave. They both liked the school but sometimes got tired of teachers comparing us and confusing one of us with another. Freshman year, Fritz took an English class in which the teacher believed the students should write all the time. My mother saved a folder of his essays:

Sandy is sure a jerk. I'm sitting here trying to do free writing which is really a pain in the neck. As Donnelly is breathing down my neck I can't think of anything to write. Thank God Mr. Donnelly was later than I was. I really messed up those preliminary grades About five more minutes I had better start reading more of the Odyssey I wish Mr. Baker would call off Hebrew Heritage on Saturday considering just three people will be there. This just isn't coming like it usually does It's probably because I'm not letting it come I wonder whether I should go up to Laurel this weekend well for a second I thought we were going to stop but good old Mr. Donnelly keep it going. Well now that Mr. Donnelly left I can get down to loafing I wish Riedal would shut up . . .

The Idea originally was a good thing "Fast to show our concern for the Pakistan refugees." I said it started as a good idea. But soon after-wards it became a status-seeking thing. You were considered "out" or stupid if you didn't sign up. Even the setting was wrong. At a small private school how many people would be able to go without food for a day when they haven't even known hunger for more than a minute That is when ever we are hungry we are but a few steps away from something to eat. But when it was over it did serve a good purpose

The out line of the hockey pond was very evident as it had just snowed and the water wasn't frozen so the snow was like a white frame around a black picture. The pine trees on the south side of the pond were especially beautiful. The branches were bent down with two days accumulation of snow on them. Then it began to snow again. The snow would come down and melt in the pond. The trees on the north west side were laden with snow as well. On the other side of these trees was a drift which made the trees seem a lot smaller than they are in reality. At the places where the branches joined together the snow also built up.

Sitting under the table holding hands was a definate experience. The first thing I noticed was the extreme reaction when Mr. Donnelly said for every-body to hold hands. This is a typical response to make to the prospect of having to touch an other male. This inhibition is Lacking in most of the girls I know. This is not to say that the girls are queer but they don't have the same inhibitions.

It began with him staying up late at nights. Then before long he was taking long walks at night. These were all the steps that led to my brother's relapse from his emotional break-down. We all had our speculation as to how this came about although we all kept our ideas to ourselves. I thought it was because my parents forced him into doing something when he was in his hair trigger mental state. There's no way I can explain the anguish he went through. But one time I walked in the room and his face was contorted in the most anguish Look I ever seen

Boy I really don't want to run again today it's such a pain in the neck just constant run Wonder what Mitch did with my doughnuts I'm so hungry Saturday night was allright but I wish I hadn't had to get up the next morning what time is it I'm so sick of school right now esbesally Latin & Eng that chaple assembly sure was phony Wonder how much more I'll have to write this sure is tiring . . .

The brother in anguish Fritz described could have been either Dave or me. We both had spells like that, he more than I. There were many alarms in the night. For college I went to Harvard, a place I knew little about and chose mainly for the cachet and the challenge of getting in. I had never seen it; our family, in all its travels, almost never headed east. The school was too big, and I could not make even a small part of it revolve around me. I read Zap Comix by the hour, hitchhiked with a friend at midnight out to Walden Pond, and flew to Coe College in Cedar Rapids, Iowa, to visit Susie. A guy in the house she sometimes stayed in got drunk and tried to kill himself and left a large pool of blood under his kitchen table and a smell of blood and booze in the hall. She and I broke up again. When the Ohio National Guard shot four students at Kent State University in the spring, I was annoyed that the first time something exciting happened near my home I hadn't been there. I joined the thousands of other people running from police in the riots in Cambridge that followed. Cops hit people with clubs and shot tear gas. Kids wearing motorcycle goggles picked up the gas canisters and threw them back. I ran into a kid who had been first in my high-school class; he told me he was with the Yale dynamite team and had set the trash-can fires in Harvard Square.

I worked two nights a week at a Sunoco gas station on Route 2 in Cambridge, out by Fresh Pond Plaza. One night a Portuguese tow-truck driver named Carl smashed seventeen new-car windshields at the dealership next door because he or perhaps someone he knew had bought a lemon there. Carl gave me a ride back to the dorm in the tow truck and took a revolver from his glove compartment and said if anyone said he'd done it they would wind up in a ditch. One summer and part of another I worked at a ranch in Wyoming and hitchhiked back and forth from Ohio several times. Police in a small town in Nebraska took me into the station and searched my luggage and scared me and let me go. In Iowa a driver of escort cars for wide loads told me that he liked girls but the best blow job he had ever gotten had been from a guy. In the ranch owner's living room I listened to the national draft-lottery drawing on the radio; my birthday was drawn number 187, pretty much guaranteeing I would not be drafted for Vietnam.

Over the years, some men in my family had served in the military, some had not. Even in Charlie Wickham's generation many stayed out of the Civil War. The next generation had no major wars to fight, so none of my great-grandfathers served. My grandfather spent his army hitch in the States during the First World War. My father joined the navy in 1944, after the Second World War was winding down. When Vietnam came along, I had a student deferment and never worried that I might have to go. Nobody I knew well went to Vietnam. A friend four years older than I dropped out of college and soon received an induction notice; on the day he was supposed to report, his father, a lawyer of some clout, got him deferred. Once in the checkout line of the Harvard bookstore I ran into an acquaintance from Hudson who told me apologetically that he had just enlisted in the Marines. I could not understand why anybody would do such a thing. The idea of serving my country had not crossed my mind.

•

Sophomore year I went out with a black girl, and when she broke up with me at the beginning of junior year, I fell into kind of a tailspin and began to think about dying and couldn't sleep and had nightmares when I was awake: for example, I imagined I was looking at the Hockey Pond (the one Fritz described, it's on the Academy campus) and the water was moving in a gentle swell, and I knew I'd been watching the swell all my life, and then I looked more closely into the water and saw that its motion was caused by the tail fin of an enormous shark which was swimming back and forth, as if pacing in a cage. The night-mares made me afraid to be alone. I checked myself into the college infirmary, where they gave me a gown and locked up my clothes. I stayed for four days, over a Columbus Day weekend, eating the good food and taking a green-and-black pill. Afterward I began to see a psychiatrist, who told me I had had an anxiety attack. I felt better hearing the term.

Back in Hudson, over Christmas vacation, I flipped out again. When I tried to sleep, anxiety would surge through me just as I nodded off. One night I thought I was going to choke to death on my tongue. I came fully awake in a panic and dressed and walked around the block a number of times. I thought if I was tireder I could go to sleep, but I only got more jumpy. I cut some ham from the Christmas leftovers in the refrigerator and made a sandwich, but was too con-scious of my throat to swallow. I woke up Mom and Dad. He walked around the block with me and tried to comfort me, but instead said odd, overdramatic things like "Well, this is the beginning of our new life together," which had the opposite effect. I tried to sleep again and insisted that Mom sit by my bed to make sure I did not choke. When I finally did sleep, she called our doctor in Hudson. He refused to see me but prescribed Valium over the phone. I took Valium pills the rest of the vacation, but my anxiety had begun to recede the moment my parents became upset. This technique had worked well all my life: I would cause my parents to absorb my unhappiness, then immediately feel less unhappy myself. My problems became smaller once I had made my mother worry and cry. I returned to college in an upbeat mood. The psychiatrist suggested that maybe what was bothering me would take longer than a Christmas vacation to work out.

•

With a friend I hitchhiked up to Nova Scotia during midterm break in February. We stayed with hippie friends of his who were trying to farm near Yarmouth on hills above the Bay of Fundy. From Yarmouth we took a nighttime ferry back to Maine. The bay had iced over, and the ferry started its engines, creaked, strained, and suddenly sent a crack shooting through the pale ice far into the darkness. Just after we got back to Cambridge I was sitting on the bed in my dormitory room. The dusty black telephone rang on the floor under my bed. As I was lifting the receiver to my ear, as I heard the silence before my mother spoke, I knew the news was disaster.

Fritz was in the hospital, she said. He had been unconscious for a time but now was conscious again. The doctors said he had a kind of leukemia called lymphosarcoma. Her voice took on the quiet, past-tense, reportorial tone which it would use often during the rest of her life. He had not been feeling well, she had brought him to see Dr. Smith, Dr. Smith had done a routine physical, he had noticed Fritz's blood pressure was unusually high, he retested the pressure to be sure, he took a count of white blood cells, the count was very high. The dead white cells in the kidney, as my mother understood, had caused the elevated pressure. Dr. Smith said Fritz should go to the hospital right away. In the hospital Fritz collapsed and lost conscious-ness. He had had surgery, radiation, chemotherapy. But now the crisis had passed. The doctors had said something optimistic, I forget what.

I packed a suitcase, took a shower, washed my hair. In those days I often did not use a comb and so did not own one. I decided I should comb my hair, and without knocking went into my roommate's bed-room to borrow his comb. He was in bed with a woman. They looked at me with shock and indignation. I took the subway to the airport and bought an airplane ticket with a check and flew to Cleveland and took a taxi to Mount Sinai Hospital. In a downstairs corridor I ran into my father, who hugged me so hard he lifted me off my feet. He took me to Fritz, in the intensive care unit. On the way we met my mother. She kissed and hugged me and said Fritz was much better. Neither of them prepared me for what I would see. Fritz's lips were turned back and whitish and cracked, his teeth had dark lines between them, his skin was yellow and marked with purple and yellow-blue marks like bruises, he had lost a lot of hair. I shook his hand, which was big and bony, an old person's hand. IV tubes went into taped-up bruises on both arms. His hospital identification tag looped around his thin wrist. He smiled happily and we talked as he tried to eat a hospital meal, forcing his lips with difficulty around the drinking straw. I re-member we discussed Heisenberg's uncertainty principle, something he had just learned about in school.

Everyone was cheery—Fritz was conscious, he was talking, the doctors had said he might be able to go home soon. He had made friends with a pretty young nurse named Georgine, called George. A lot of friends came to visit. I tried to tell funny stories about college and the gas station. I felt like a hero, completely healthy and strong. The friend I had hitchhiked to Nova Scotia with appeared. Now he was riding freights around the country. He told how a trainman had tried to kick him off a train and had ended up giving him his sack lunch. During visiting hours we were a lively group. The hospital moved Fritz from intensive care to a private room.

The family had rallied, and Fritz had rallied. I went back to Cambridge with a feeling of accomplishment. Fritz came home from the hospital and returned to school. He had to take all kinds of medicine and go to a clinic for radiation therapy. He lost the rest of his hair and Mom bought him a wig. I sent a long, rambling letter on a cassette tape for him to listen to as he lay immobile for a spinal tap. He wrote me a letter telling about his new classes at school, and an Irish setter puppy he wanted to get, and the trouble he was having sleeping. He added, "I feel terrible." He said that Maggie was showing more and more signs of maturity, and that he could really say that he loved her. He said that he had decided to go to Harvard for college. Not long after he got out of the hospital, to my alarm, my parents bought him a ticket to come visit me. I met him at the airport, showed him the campus, introduced him to my friends. I had begun to write for the college humor magazine, *The Harvard Lampoon*, by then, and he and I went to a dinner at the Lampoon building and he had a few beers. One afternoon in my dorm room he spent a long time rewinding an audiocassette tape that had gotten all pulled out and tangled. He took a long walk around Cambridge by himself. Later I thought often about that walk, and wondered what he had seen and what he had thought about.

He remained out of the hospital for weeks, maybe months. My mother kept track hopefully of how long it had been. The doctors said that the disease was in remission. The family held its breath. One day he got a nosebleed that would not stop. My mother called the doctor and he said to bring Fritz into the hospital. Maggie came home from a school event, and the lady across the street saw her arrive and came out and told her where Fritz and my parents had gone. She invited Maggie in and made her a snack, but Maggie was too worried to eat. She went home and saw a little trail of blood leading to the car's empty spot in the garage. Fritz recovered, came home, then went back into the hospital again. Mom visited him every chance she could, but he spent a lot of time alone. Friends who had visited him at the beginning stopped coming, with the exception of Natalie, Gwil, and Becky. Fritz made friends with other patients, especially with tough kids who had broken legs or arms in car wrecks. But these friends soon got better and left. George, the nurse, often looked in on him, telling him stories about an elderly Cleveland TV personality she was taking care of, and how difficult it was to get the TV personality to sit on the bedpan. Suzan sketched him, other patients, and various hospital scenes. Mom bought him a tape player and he listened to rock music—"Aqualung" and "Thick as a Brick," by Jethro Tull.

Dave, in college then in St. Louis, made several visits home during the spring. At semester end in May he left college and decided not to return there. He got a job at a restaurant in Hudson. In July, suffering emotional and physical problems that included walking pneumonia, he wound up in the hospital himself. The doctors put him on a medical floor, then transferred him to a psychiatric unit. Fritz became ill with another relapse, and our parents then had two children at Mount Sinai. Dave got out of the hospital and decided to stay home that fall and help Mom and Dad. In the mornings he would drive Mom to her school, then drive to the hospital, spend the day with Fritz, drive Suzan and Maggie home from the girls' school they attended in Cleveland, pick Mom up at her school, and drive back to Mount Sinai.

A tumor doctors found at the base of Fritz's skull required much radiation. For accuracy, the technicians drew lines on his scalp with marker. Fritz wore his wig—a woman's wig which Mom had cut down to medium length—without embarrassment. At home he tried to eat dinner with the family, but sometimes had to leave the table and throw up. He joked about throwing up, and about his doctors, and about the tedium of the back-and-forth trips to Cleveland. Once a movie-soundtrack song called "Fred Is Dead" came on the car radio. "What a coincidence," Fritz said. He enrolled in classes for his sophomore year at the Academy and worked at assignments friends brought him. He liked math and drama and anthropology. Dad rigged up a wire-and-pulley arrangement from Fritz's bedside to a bell in our parents' room. Often Fritz was too tired to do much. He lay on the

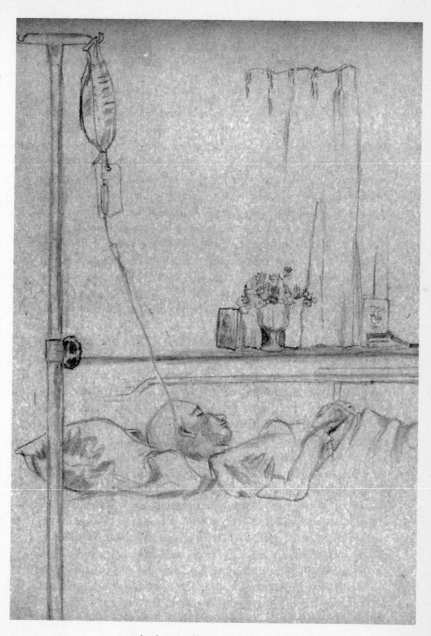

A sketch Suzan did of Fritz in the hospital

couch in the family room and looked out the sliding glass doors at the back yard. He seldom complained or got angry. He wrote our parents a poem about how much he loved them. On a walk in the fall with an Academy teacher, he said that days like this one made a person glad to be alive.

•

At college I had begun to hang around the *Lampoon* building almost full-time. I met a guy a year younger than I from Joliet, Illinois, named Jim Downey, who was so funny it was like falling in love. With other guys and a few women we hung out at the building and thought up funny ideas. We discovered that we all found the same things funny, after years of being sort of submerged at Harvard, and the experience was such a rush, I never laughed so hard. We published issues of the *Lampoon* and parody issues of other college publications. We did pranks. In late spring we elected new members and invented initiation rites to use on them. After school was out in June I stayed on in Cambridge with other *Lampoon* members, and we wrote a parody of *Cosmopolitan* magazine. The issue featured a nude center-fold of Henry Kissinger—a composite photograph, done to specifi-cation by a studio in New York, of the diplomat and emissary to China stretched full-length on a panda-bearskin rug. A New York publishing company distributed the parody nationwide and hired publicity people to promote it. We appeared on many radio and television shows. I was scheduled to go on *The Tonight Show* and even did a pre-interview over the phone with one of the show's writers. I asked him how he liked his job and he said he couldn't do it without Valium, and I was pleased I knew what Valium was. I flew to California, but then the show canceled my appearance, lucky for me. I did appear on a daytime TV talk show out of New York hosted by Barbara Walters on which I blurted unfunny comments and looked at my hands.

I went home seldom. On a visit in the summer I did the imitation of my father which caused Fritz to tell me I had no compassion. On another occasion I stayed only a day or two and then hitchhiked to Illinois to visit friends. I wrote Fritz from school and talked to him on the phone. Each time he went back in the hospital they gave him a new number. I did not go to Ohio for Thanksgiving weekend that fall. I had no plans, just stayed in the dorm. I attended the Harvard-Yale football game by myself and watched from the sidelines. A referee broke his leg and was carried past me on a stretcher, gray-faced, in shock; I had never seen an injured ref before. Thanksgiving Day I called home and spoke to everybody. Fritz was there. He asked if I remembered how he had rewound that tangled-up cassette tape when he visited me. This was the last conversation he and I had.

In early December my mother called to say that Fritz was back in the hospital and that I should come right away. I walked over to the *Lampoon* building. A woman I knew and liked was there by herself in the delft-tiled kitchen. I told her my brother was going to die. She said, "Maybe he's just going home." I said, "But it's such a big house." She told me to go to the TV room upstairs. I thought she intended to join me for further comforting; I went and waited, but she didn't appear. I opened the TV room door, where I found she had posted a DO NOT DISTURB sign. She was gone. I made some calls, packed, flew to Cleveland, took a cab to Mount Sinai.

I received no happy welcome this time. Mom hugged me, Dad shook my hand. Fritz lay in a bed by the window; the other bed in the room was empty. The curtain partition had been pulled partway around his bed. He was on his back breathing heavily into a clear plastic oxygen mask, chin pointed almost at the ceiling. The lights had been turned down low. Mom said to him, "Sandy is here, honey. Sandy is here." I sat on his left side and took his hand. I held it for a while but got no sign of recognition or awareness. But when I went to let go, his hand tightened on mine. I didn't let go again for a long time after that, and when I finally did, I made sure Maggie was there to slide his hand into hers. His breathing fell into a rhythm and sounded almost like ordinary breathing. I left the room and stood for a while with my father in an empty waiting room with a view of the hospital parking lot. As we looked out over the cars, my father said, conversationally, "I always told your mother, 'We're gonna lose one of 'em.' "

We stood around Fritz's bed, all of us, and put our hands on his shoulders, on his arms. I was a little hesitant at first, but the rest of the family was used to touching him. We were crying a lot. All kinds of crazy thoughts ran through my mind. From my recent experience of writing humor in a group I had gotten the habit of noticing how people laughed—how much, and at what. Now I was noticing how people were crying. I was surprised that Suzan, usually a reticent girl, cried so hard. I found it easier to cry if I thought of a corny phrase, like "My little baby brother . . ." The nurses, not ones my family had come to know, left us alone. Occasionally they adjusted the oxygen mask or swabbed Fritz's mouth with Q-Tips, which they then put in a red waste container marked HAZARDOUS.

After a while the sound of his breathing changed. A tall nurse standing a few feet away gave him an appraising glance. She was just doing her job, but I held that glance against her. The breathing became rougher, shallower. Mom said to him, "Fritz, you had a good time. You and Sandy had a good time, and you and Davy had a good time, and you and Suzy had a good time, and you and Maggie had a good time." We stood around the bed and told him we loved him, in raised voices, as if through the windows of a departing car. His breathing became so shallow that his chest barely moved; then it didn't move at all; then all that was left was a muscle reflex moving in his yellowed neck; then that faded, too. The nurse came over and removed the oxygen mask and turned off the flow of oxygen from a switch on the wall. Darkness filled his open mouth.

Dad gestured to me to help, and he and Mom and I smoothed the tangled bedsheet and pulled it up. I thought we were going to pull it over his head, like in the movies. Instead, Mom and Dad raised the sheet as far as his chin, then folded it back double and tucked it around him. Dad went to the foot of the bed and stood for a moment. I did not know what he would do. Suddenly, with a big motion, he knelt. He bowed his head against the bed. We all knelt with him. He said the Lord's Prayer in a steady voice. Then he rose and patted Fritz lightly on the foot. "Good night, Fritz," he said.

I was in awe of my father then, and saw that he was a man and I was not, that he knew something and I knew almost nothing; and I was afraid I would never be a man like him.

We collected Fritz's clothes and belongings. In the closet we found a pile of girlie magazines. I hesitated over them, and my father said, "Oh, go ahead, take them, you know you want them," but the truth was, I didn't. We stood in the hall. Suddenly we heard sobs, and saw George, the nurse, being comforted in a group of nurses. Mom went back into Fritz's room. After a few minutes Maggie followed to get her. She was lying next to Fritz on the bed, holding him and crying and saying something to him. Then she and Maggie came out

and all of us took the elevator down to the parking lot, and we got in
the car and went home.

•

People don't know what to say. In fact, what people seem to say
most often about such a death is that they don't know what to say. In
the days and weeks that followed, I had to agree; grief at that stage
is mostly wordless. It provides, incidentally, a lens to view the character of friends and acquaintances. Some people have less to give you
than you expected, and some people more. The notion that might
have comforted my great-grandparents—that Fritz was now happy in
heaven—did not sound right on my lips or my friends', so there wasn't
much spiritual comfort to be had. But in my mind that did not exempt
people from trying to find some. I'm sure I scared my friends with
how much I wanted from them. The people I remember with love
were those who had no more to say than I did but who tried hard
anyway. Susie, Toni, Sarah; the headmaster at the Academy; my roommate; a guy I hardly knew named Mitch Karton; Bill, Tim, Don. Not
knowing what to say is different from saying nothing. A friend smiled
at me at the funeral in a way that made me remove myself from him;
a woman on the *Lampoon* smiled nervously as she told me how sorry
she was, and she and I became friends.

Fritz died on December 7. Our family didn't have much enthusiasm for the Christmas holiday that followed. Mom did hardly any
baking. The house looked as it had all that year—disorganized, un-
kempt, strange. When people are sick, housework flags. I remember
not even wanting to be indoors, preferring instead the snowy back
yard, the fields. One afternoon I was standing in the family room, by
the sliding glass doors. A pickup truck came up the driveway and
stopped and the door slammed. A moment or two later, Fritz's friend
Natalie knocked. I had never seen her before. She had dark eyes and
long dark hair. By herself she was carrying a large Christmas tree.
She had ridden on her horse to some woods near her house and cut
the tree and hauled it out to bring to us. She was ruddy-cheeked, still
in the rush of this idea, the idea of doing this for us. Some people are
better than you could ever imagine. I would be lucky if I did anything
in my life that meant as much to anyone as that tree did to me. I don't
know where Natalie is now; my brothers and sisters lost track of her.
She was a reminder that God is good.

C H A P T E R   1 7

I TELL MYSELF THIS STORY to explain what had happened to our faith:

We crossed the Atlantic to the wilderness of America. We thought we were building an earthly version of the kingdom of God. In the wilderness we would build a New Jerusalem, where people could live according to God's will and so be free. We thought the places we settled had a correspondence to heaven because of the holiness of this purpose. We likened our enterprise to a "city on a hill," which people everywhere could lift their eyes to and take hope from, a light to the world. Here we would be new people in a new land. Some of us believed that God's providence ordered the discovery of America to happen when it did so that the new religion—ours, the Protestant religion—could flourish here.

We believed then in a God few of us now can imagine. That God was the Almighty, maker of all things, vast, awesome, a being know-

A tent-meeting revival on the frontier (Courtesy New York Public Library)

able only through faith. That God made the whole world and saw that it was good. When we said we believed in predestination, we meant that every person's fate was in the hands of that God, that no person could hope to affect a fate willed by God. We believed we were not our own but God's. We believed that poverty, shipwreck, the suffering and death of a beloved child—all the misfortunes of life—were to be accepted with gratitude as signs of this God's will. We believed that yielding to this will was sweet. We believed in the holiness of the Sabbath perhaps more strongly than any Christians before. All those Sundays devoted to God poured ideas into our thoughts and visions. Some of us said we saw God and could talk about the experience without sounding insane. God spoke to some in a voice we heard inside ourselves or outside, and told us how to worship, how to live. God came to some as a sudden presence, a nearness, which filled us brimming with joy for hours at a time. Some saw angels and could describe them—the beating wings, the bright feet.

We argued among ourselves from the beginning. Our faith had always involved defiance and conflicting ideas about what true faith was not. We debated theology, we reproved each other, we rebuked and disfellowshipped and excommunicated each other, and worse. The more persuasive among us led followers into new sects and churches. Coming to this new place had itself been an act of defiance, of removal from the corruption of the old faith. Some said we had journeyed here out of Babylon. And here, when we disagreed beyond reconciliation, we simply divided up and moved again. We settled great parts of the country, sowed it with farms and towns, by dividing up and spreading out. In our tendency to division we resembled the Indian culture that preceded us here, the culture we destroyed.

We had the power to enslave Africans, and we used it. Along with people from European countries and some Africans, we participated in a trade that filled New World colonies with slaves. We and others brought so many that by the end of the eighteenth century more black people than whites, probably, had arrived in the New World. The passage killed Africans by the millions, slavery killed millions more. Some of us—my slave-trading ancestors of Newport, Rhode Island, for example—may have preferred to look away from the size of this crime. The Newport captains thought of themselves as superior to the average slavers, and belonged to a fellowship club which forbade gambling, drunkenness, and oaths. Ministers justified the trade by saying that it brought heathens from a godless land to a Christian one; that the Africans' loss of liberty was repaid by the gain of the Africans' souls.

We still thought of ourselves as Englishmen, and joined England's wars against the French. After France lost Canada and England began to hold us more tightly—taxing us, telling us who we could trade with, where we could live—some decided that we didn't need England anymore. Some of us fought a war against England, some didn't; England lost, and some (rich men, almost all) met to decide how to run our new country. The constitution they wrote included safeguards of freedom and property for people like us, and separation of church and state. By not instituting any church, we were responding to a fact of life, and to a society already more varied than we knew.

We thought a "multiplicity of sects" would promote religious freedom. The Protestant sects responded like deregulated businesses competing for market share, each trying to offer spiritual advantages the others didn't. In such an environment, an all-powerful God who predestined people's fates from birth proved a hard sell. It was hard to attract converts with the news that they might have already been condemned to hell. The idea that Christ's atonement applied to all, that man could effect his own salvation (John Wesley, Methodism) sold better. The balance between man and God, previously in God's favor, tipped toward man.

We converted by the ten thousands to Methodism and to Baptist and other churches, often at backwoods revival meetings. Because so many were lonely people living on little farms out in the woods, we brought a hunger for companionship to the religion. It became sort of a "cabin fever" religion. The revivals burned off months of solitary, stored-up, housebound energy, and produced a saviour who would also be a friend. Our Jesus was a personal saviour, a helper who would take a sinner by the hand. Camp-meeting religion spread westward through the wilderness with settlement, becoming in the process the most personal form of Christianity in the world.

At about that time, we began the debate over slavery, using biblical quotations to support pro and con. Some of us lived in parts of the country where debating about slavery was against state law. Some took the revivalist idea that man could reform himself to mean that he could also reform society and win salvation through usefulness to God; ergo, some said, we should work for the abolition of slavery. The most liberal of us came to favor immediate abolition, and the most conservative, extension of slavery to the frontier south and west and beyond. By the hundreds of thousands, we fought in the Civil War and, by the hundreds of thousands, died. And although those who fought for the North sang, in "The Battle Hymn of the Republic," "As He died to make men holy, let us die to make men free," most no doubt would have agreed with Lincoln that they fought to save the Union, not to end slavery. But opinion gave those who fought for the North credit for ending slavery, whatever the motive had been. Historians said that the nation had purged itself with suffering and blood. Remarkably, those who had fought to preserve slavery also got credit for their part in the suffering and blood.

After the war, in general we prospered. Most of us became middle-class, some wealthy, a few richer than nearly everyone in the world. We made world-changing inventions by the dozens, finished settling the continent, killed or Christianized the few Indians still in our way, hit strikes of precious metals and oil, quickly paid off the debts from the war. Ministers told us that God was rewarding us for our virtue, that making money was what He wanted us to do, that money was good. As we had always favored independent congregations, we had a lot to say about hiring and firing of ministers, and many ministers took care to preach what we wanted to hear. Most of us wanted a comforting religion, a personal saviour, a God of love not of wrath, racially segregated churches, and few reminders of those making less money than we were.

We thought of our country with a reverence close to that we offered our God. We believed God had specially favored our country, had made it strong to carry Christ and His teachings throughout the world. We called America the Redeemer Nation. We did missionary work overseas for reasons of evangelism and empire. As our optimism grew, our God dwindled further and became more man-sized, more the encouraging personal friend. This God cared about each individual person but not, evidently, about the problem of certain people as a group; not, for example, about the widespread lynching of blacks. Even the new Social Gospel generally overlooked the problems of blacks.

We tried to avoid thinking about aspects of modern life that might undermine our religion—theories of evolution and natural selection, geological discoveries about the age of the earth, evidence that the Bible was of human authorship. What our religion could not explain many of us rejected or ignored. And what about the growing cities, and the fact that our churches did not work as well there; and what about the millions of new non-Protestant immigrants, especially the Catholics, whose church we had always criticized and opposed? Many of us decided that the cities were bad and not worth worrying about, and that the true strength of the nation resided in the countryside. As for the Catholics, some of us decided to continue to oppose them; some joined organizations whose purpose was to keep Catholics and others down.

We were approaching the height of our power. We preached and legislated against vice and against private sexual practices we considered sinful. As we cared most about individual salvation, we paid closest attention to personal, private acts of sin. Some of us attacked the modern world in all its sinful forms. Nationally, we solved the immigration problem by passing laws to shut down most immigration. Some of us papered over the disputes that had always divided us by stating that we all, as white people, belonged to a superior race. For a while, two million or more of us belonged to the Ku Klux Klan. With near unanimity, we opposed the drinking of alcohol. When we found our spiritual force alone was not enough to save drunkards, we moved our attack to the occasion of sin, the liquor trade. After decades of trying, we made Prohibition national law.

When Prohibition failed, we—the white, mostly small-town Protestants, the "Protestant Establishment," so called only after the beginning of our decline—took it personally. Some of us sulked, said the country was going to hell, threw up our hands. Some of us retooled biblical prophecies about the approach of the millennium, a strong current in American Protestantism from the beginning, and said that certain events of modern history corresponded to events prophesied as signs of the earth's last days. The world would soon end in Armageddon, these people said; God's chosen would be transported to heaven to watch the destruction, billions would die, the earth would be renewed, and Christ would return to reign for a thousand years. Millennialist preachers began to multiply the way the sects used to, providing American Protestantism with its one new area of solid growth.

Many of us now got our religion mainly from the radio. The lonesome Jesus of the tent-meeting revivals translated well to radio and (later) television. Radio evangelists preached individual salvation and tended toward right-wing politics. Many Protestants of different denominations took up Christian fundamentalism, with its belief in the literal inerrancy of Scripture, the necessity of conversion experience, and same-body resurrection. Others of us questioned our faith, couldn't find answers, and replaced belief in God with belief in science. For some of us, Sundays suddenly free of religious obligation were bliss. A number of observers said Protestantism was in trouble. A popular Midwestern minister compared it to a vein of gold that had petered out. H. L. Mencken declared it "down with a wasting disease." Protestant theologians said that apparently the movement of the kingdom of God in America had come to a stop, that faith had dried up or been forgotten, that people should return to a God less sentimental and more mysterious and grand.

Then for a while everybody had enough to worry about, with the Depression and the war. Patriotism, a near-religion in itself by this time, took over. And afterward came the Cold War, when details of religion mattered less than the fact that you had one at all—seeing as the atheistic Communists did not. Many preachers had long opposed Communism, some so strongly that they even welcomed Hitler as a barrier against it, and the Protestant Churches remained anti-Communist after the war. Throngs of Protestants and former Protestants moved to the suburbs, prospered again, were happy with new things to buy and new money to buy with. Some joined country clubs for fun, and to set ourselves even farther from people we didn't want to be like. In numbers until then unmatched in American history we had children. We bought television sets and watched Western dramas, versions of our history largely stripped of unflattering details. Also in record numbers, we went back to organized religion. In surveys, most Americans identified themselves as Protestant, and gave a denomination, but in fact religion in those days was becoming more generic. Denominational differences were forgotten and former schisms healed as churches separated since the last century reunited. Millions of us read religious books about positive thinking and living with confidence and finding peace. The old questions of faith versus reason, God's will versus man's, remained unexplored. We wanted a religion of peace and serenity and noncontroversy and refuge from the world.

And in suburbs like country towns of a century before but with ever-less distance between them, in expanses of development radiating from and encircling falling-apart cities, in landscaped acres accessible almost only by car, in single-family houses built in a colonial style to suggest perhaps the Americanness of the people inside, in suburban families focused now on the unit of father-mother-and-children, in master bedrooms and living rooms and dens connected to the outside world mainly by technology, in closet top shelves stacked with boxes of old family papers and in bookcases of mostly forgotten books, the dream of America as the kingdom of God came to rest.

•

This, at any rate, is what occurred to me as I went through the papers in my parents' apartment, and afterward. Seen this way, history helps explain why, for example, the most common profession among my ancestors some generations ago was minister and the most common professions today involve computer math. Or why in marriages of ancestors 150 years ago I can find few who married outside their denomination, while in my generation we have spouses who are Catholic, Jewish, Italian, Greek, African, and same-faith marriages are the exception. Or why my parents toasted each other with glasses of wine at dinner instead of saying grace. Or why my father wouldn't let us have a television (he finally did relent, of course). Or why I collapsed in giggles at the altar rail during my first Communion at the Episcopal church in Hudson when I was thirteen. Or why our portion of doubt increased down the generations, my father doubting more than his grandfathers, who doubted more than their Civil War veteran fathers, who perhaps doubted more than old patriarchs like Platt Benedict, who from this distance seem to have doubted nothing at all; or why I have so much doubt myself.

Now that I have revised the past, I can approach parts of it that eluded me before: the books of Thoreau, for example. I could never understand why he didn't do more hunting and fishing, considering all the time he spent outdoors. Now I see that Thoreau came along at the moment in the nineteenth century when the Puritan God whose kingdom we would build gave way to a vaguer being, an "oversoul" diffused and distributed democratically in all things. A lot of Thoreau's ideas came from Transcendentalism, which began as a sect from the liberal wing of Unitarianism, which was itself a sect from New England Congregationalism, which descended from the original Puritan movement in England. Once I recast Thoreau as another nineteenth-century sectarian, I can whip right through *Walden* and other books by him. Thoreau was born in 1817, the same year as my great-great-grandmother Rebecca Warner. I now see figures in history in terms of my relatives, and vice versa—Abraham Lincoln was born the same year as my three-greats-grandfather Jonas Benedict; my great-grandfather O.A.S. Hursh lived and died in almost the same years as the outlaw Jesse James; my grandfather Ray was of the same generation as Hitler; the Italian writer Primo Levi had the same lifespan as my father, 1919–1987. Primo Levi got his degree in chemistry at the University of Milan two days after my father got his at Oberlin. My father went on to graduate school, Levi to the mountains with the partisans, capture, and Auschwitz.

If the background is loss of mission and religious decline, I can understand better why my father felt so strongly about the civil-rights movement of the fifties and sixties, why he identified with it and set his dislike of the place he lived in terms of it. Here at the tail end of the Protestant era in America, at a time when the faith had been inert for generations, when it had become personal and warm and boosterish, here all of a sudden were Protestants—the black churches and leaders of the civil-rights movement—with something real to protest. After generations of ministers preaching against the World's Fair being open on Sunday or the frequency of Hollywood divorces, here were ministers protesting an evil that most Americans knew well and participated in all the time, an evil that went back to the crime of slavery. Here again, after a long absence, was a God of judgment, a God of righteousness. Many Americans recognized that God, willingly or not, as the one they used to know.

I admired and feared my father's vehemence on civil rights, but I usually changed stations on the car radio whenever the news came on. Now I like to listen to the speeches of Martin Luther King, Jr. I read his collected speeches and interviews, and I've visited his Ebenezer Baptist Church in Atlanta and the memorial center nearby, where people eat their lunches on benches under the trees and look at his sarcophagus of light gray marble on its pedestal in a small reflecting pool. Every year on the holiday celebrating his birthday TV stations usually play only excerpts of his famous "I Have a Dream" speech. I prefer to replay the speech whole on a tape I have. At the beginning the speech is almost low-key, remarks on the occasion of the March on Washington of August 1963; you can hear the background noise of the immense crowd that did not know it was about to hear one of the greatest pieces of American oratory ever. King's voice builds as he talks of America's unfulfilled promise, of the necessity of a struggle of nonviolence and love, of the impossibility of stopping until justice is achieved. I get to my feet and begin to pace as he reaches the "I have a dream" part, as he talks about the sons of former slaves and the sons of former slave owners sitting down together at the table of brotherhood, as he talks about being judged not by color of skin but by content of character, as he runs the words "I have a dream" to the end of each paragraph. I am pacing quickly as he recites the verses to "America the Beautiful," as he says, ". . . from *every* mountainside, let freedom ring," as he says:

So let freedom ring from the prodigious hilltops of New Hampshire!
Let freedom ring from the mighty mountains of New York!
Let freedom ring from the heightening Alleghenies of Pennsylvania!
Let freedom ring from the snowcapped Rockies of Colorado!
Let freedom ring from the curvaceous slopes of California!
But not only that.
Let freedom ring from Stone Mountain of Georgia!
Let freedom ring from Lookout Mountain of Tennessee!
Let freedom ring from every hill and molehill of Mississippi, from ev-*ery*
    mountainside, let freedom ring!

And by now his voice is full-throated, wide-open, like a blues shout, and the crowd is cheering, breathless at what it is hearing, cheering well before the end in heightening excitement like at the National Anthem at a baseball game, and the sound in my head is even louder, and I've got both fists in the air, and I echo, "Prodigious hilltops! Heightening Alleghenies! Snowcapped Rockies! Curvaceous—*curvaceous*—slopes!" And I'm thinking about the Yankees and Confederates who fought near Stone Mountain in Georgia, and about the Yankees and Confederates who died at the Battle of Lookout Mountain in Tennessee. The speech is a poem, a history lesson, a landscape: "Every hill and molehill of Mississippi!" (hill and *mole*hill). Describing the speech later, what it was like to be there and to hear it, Coretta Scott King said, "At that moment it seemed as if the kingdom of God appeared."

In America, the kingdom of God has sometimes been imagined as a specific place: Boston, Massachusetts, or New Jerusalem, New York; or, with enough faith, the entire country from one end to the other. The speech is a compendium of American places, each lifted from the map and polished with the glow of justice, of freedom, each restored to the best dream of America; and to me, every place in the speech, every site in this coast-to-coast and Southern travelogue, is an America across the river and under the trees. Martin Luther King remembered that America had once been thought of as a promised land. He had the generosity to believe that it actually could be, that somehow it still was.

•

Clearly I prefer the old, wrathful American God to the modern, nice one. My reason is no doubt theologically unsound: I think the Almighty, predestining God is funnier. What an idea, creating souls just to condemn them to hell! What a pie-in-the-face to humanity! And for the few who are heavenbound, what a lucky break! I know that faith supposedly prepares the recipients of grace to receive it, but still, it seems as if a lot of luck (or grace) is involved. This God has managed to survive into the modern world in various disguises— for example, in the belief that the world is about to end. Armageddon is just another version of a wrathful God's anger at man's sinfulness, and the chosen who await the millennium another version of the Calvinist elect. I think the idea of predestination also resembles the now-traditional teenage idea of "cool." Cool, which came along some-time in mid-century, was like divine grace, something you either had or you didn't. It could not be explained. If you had to have it explained to you, you would never attain it. The idea of cool devastated lots of progressively educated, diligent kids. When it came to being cool, their good works availed them nothing. Their good works, if pursued without cool, only made them more uncool. A lot of them realized that no matter what they did they just weren't cool, and never would be. They were powerless before their fate.

I prefer the fierce, Calvinist God at times of great spiritual need, such as funerals. At a funeral, I want a God with a lot of definition and certainty and might, not a maybe-yes, maybe-no, I'm-OK-you're-OK kind of God. I want a tough God to stand up to the encroaching Hefty bag of death. You know the way in certain showers the shower curtain pushes up against you no matter how you try to keep it off? Death seems sort of like that to me. I want a God who blows that death clean away. But at less difficult times, I want a God who is all friendliness and understanding, who always agrees with me, who doesn't even have to forgive because He (She) knows I could have done only as I did.

I would like to see God myself, if only for the excitement of it. But I'm sure that's not the way it works. When my brother died, and when my parents died, I felt a sort of enormity right next to me, as if I were very near an unbreakable limitless vertical pane of glass that went all the way up to the sky and all the way through the earth. And people I knew so well, people almost exactly like me, were now on the other side of the pane, and I was still on this side. This feeling of enormity came at odd moments; not long after Fritz died, I was walking down our driveway on which snow had just fallen and I saw boot tracks leading down the drive in the snow, and I had a sudden awareness of how completely vanished Fritz was; and with that came a strong, wordless sense of the no-place he might have gone. One time I was in the park across the street in Brooklyn thinking about my father, and I passed by a pond, and a mallard duck flew up, and I saw how the shimmery blue-green of the duck's head reproduced the colors in the troughs of the ripples on the pond, and as the duck cleared the cattails and headed in a curving path over the trees, I saw the angles of white and blue-black and gray and brown in his tail feathers marking his path in a rapidly shifting Cubist sweep, and the angles were as neat and exact as if cut from colored paper with a razor, and I thought that those colors must have come from somewhere. Then I thought that my father had gone to wherever the colors on the duck came from.

•

Although the Reverend Jerry Falwell and the Nation of Islam and the Jehovah's Witnesses and TV shows and movies and environmental activists and Ronald Reagan have said that the world is going to end, it probably isn't—not soon, anyway. Based on past experience, the world's indefinite continuation seems the safer bet. All during the Cold War people lived with the scary and flattering idea that this might be the last generation on earth. The end of the world fit nicely with all kinds of heedless, fun behavior, and provided a way to explain and even enjoy bad developments in current events. More likely, instead of ending, the world will go on, getting better in some aspects and drastically worse in others. If we continue to act as if the future does not exist, when it does arrive it may be even worse than it would have been otherwise, and our children and grandchildren who will have to live in it will hate us.

In recent years, the present meant everything. The future was seen as threatened, the past as inconsequential. But without past and future, people had trouble defining what they believed. Belief is re-vision, each generation rewriting the beliefs of the generations before and passing along its version to the next. I think my parents' generation had little conscious idea what it believed. That generation went to church or temple on general principles because that's what families did, and it was busy having families. Belief wasn't something you really thought about or talked about, anyway. Belief and reason had parted company a long time before. When my generation reached the late teen years and early twenties, the age when Martin Luther and John Calvin and Joan of Arc and Joseph Smith and countless others began their ministries, we didn't have much to revise against. So we sort of pitched and yawed all over the place, spiritually. We tried all kinds of beliefs and disbeliefs, later discarding most of them in embar-rassment.

Now many people run in the other direction when the subject of religion comes up. If you asked people to provide a noun to go with the adjective "religious," many would probably say "fanatic." Talking about religion became, in some circles, the sign of a nut. But every-body believes in something; a lot of us just don't know what that something is. And if you don't know what you believe, someone else will always be glad to tell you. At the moment we are being told—by advertising, and by the powers that can pay for it—that we mainly believe in fear and greed.

A meaning I discovered among the relics in my parents' apartment is that meaning exists, but you have to look for it. Or rather, you *must* look for it, we are all obliged to look for it. Of all Stonewall Jackson's beliefs, the one I could subscribe to most easily is that keeping the Sabbath is important—not in the sense that you must never mail a letter on Sunday, but in the sense that every person should spend a certain amount of time thinking about what he or she believes. Because what you really believe in coincides with meaning in a larger sense, with meaning that connects to other people alive and dead and yet to be born. And the belief is there inside you, just like your preference for certain foods or music or hobbies, but deeper. You have to know what it is, because, first, if you don't someone else will enlist you in what they believe, and the next thing you know you've spent your life participating in confusion; and, second, because one day children, yours or someone else's, will ask what you believe, and if you don't know, that just leaves them more to figure out for themselves and less to react against or accept, and they'll have to unearth your beliefs before they can get started on their own. They might just take the short route and assume that our fear-and-greed advertising expressed all, in the deepest sense, we had inside us; and they might not be wrong.

From the beginning, America was an aspiration; and against odds, the aspiration is still out there. The people who founded the country came from a tradition of thinking about God and man and about how people best should live, a tradition more passionate then than it became or is today. And if the founding words about freedom and justice and equality were traduced the moment they came out of the speakers' mouths, traduced by crimes against people unlike the speakers themselves, still no fact of history tells us we cannot believe the aspiration. The words could not be unsaid; the aspiration, once brought into existence, existed. Because the country was based on it, the country could go beyond boundaries, could live in the minds of people far away. Its aspiration was set at large in the world. The dream of this country came from somewhere and is going somewhere. We came from somewhere and are going somewhere. We must pursue.

THE YEAR AFTER FRITZ DIED my parents decided they wanted
us all to do something different and special together for the Christmas
holidays and, not incidentally, spend them away from home. My
mother signed us up for a cruise chartered by members of the National
Education Association, to which she belonged. We flew from Cleveland to New York and there boarded a Spanish airline and flew to the
Canary Islands. All of the people on the tour were teachers or teachers'
relatives, a group inclined to nitpickiness and impromptu lectures.
Captive, sullen families stood in little knots around their particular
lecturer. We spent a few days in Las Palmas before boarding a ship
which would sail to Casablanca and other western Mediterranean
ports. One night—New Year's Eve?—our father took us out to dinner
where we sat at a large round table and drew many waiters. After
dinner my father ordered champagne for us all. The waiters brought
brandy snifters you could have raised goldfish in and filled them full

My father and my brother Dave in the mid-1980s

enough that several bottles were required, as my father watched with a pained expression. When we each had a glass, he lifted his for a toast; he had been planning this, I could see. He said, "Well, I guess we all know what the toast should be." I am sure that everyone at the table thought, as I did, that he was talking about Fritz. He held his glass up at nearly arm's length and said, in a ringing voice, "To . . . *acrylonitrile!*"

Our parents began to take long vacations to distant countries every year; except for Key West, closer destinations had worn out their appeal. On the surface, they showed little evidence of how Fritz's death had affected them. They didn't talk about it to us. It simply made no sense to them at all, they could not account for it, and they did not forgive it. They had done everything life had expected of them, and life had betrayed them. It had strayed so far into the debit column it could never get back to even. My mother saved some verses she wrote at the time:

> *Death hides in hesitation*
> *Death springs forth in spurts*
> *Death holds fresh pearls beyond price*
>   *on a string*
>   *draws into darkness*
> *Nothing out of black*
> *No calling back; no Proserpina*
> *For winter's cold and gray is all of*
>   *summer*
> *Feel shock*
> *Feel grief*
> *Feel anger!*
> *This should not be!*
> *Why must this be!*

In 1975, the year Fritz would have graduated from high school, our parents installed a memorial to him on the Academy campus. On a lawn behind the freshman dorm they had a local tree company plant a grove of three copper beech trees by a rock with a plaque. Grandmother, who knew about such things, said she thought the soil and the positioning would not be good for copper beeches, and she has turned out to be right. Twice now we have had to replace trees that died.

•

At my college graduation, at a cocktail party for members' parents at the *Lampoon*, Dad walked around with his latest camera and took pictures of the delft tile and the Great Hall and the stained-glass windows and the pool table. A woman I had a secret crush on, and who until that moment I had never thought might like me, introduced herself to him and said she had been hoping to meet him. He replied, "The world will end in our lifetime," and went on to describe upcoming famines and nuclear disasters as she backed away. My degree was in General Studies, and he said, on the subject of my prospects, "I just *wish* you would find *something* that you love to do!" He had often made this remark, which I took as criticism, and I replied, "That is the last time you will ever say that to me," so nastily that Maggie, who overheard, got angry. When I received my diploma he hugged me harder than he ever had. Right after the ceremony I threw my books in the trunk of the car and drove all night back to Ohio. A day or two later someone rear-ended the car, and the books, which I had neglected to remove, scattered on the road. I still have a few of them; the tire tracks and gravel holes look just the same.

I partied a lot with Hudson friends most of the summer. I had no job lined up. My psychiatrist had told me to apply for a job at *The New Yorker* magazine, so I did. A man there interviewed me but said they had too many Harvard graduates already. An editor of a magazine owned by *Playboy* in Chicago had written to the *Lampoon* asking if anyone there wanted to work for him. In August I wrote back and asked for a job. The magazine was sort of a copy of a French skin mag, and it aspired to sophistication. I wrote captions for photos of naked women (and some men) allegedly posed in places like Puerto Vallarta, Mexico, and the Reeperbahn District of Hamburg. After a few months I quit and lay on a mattress on the floor of my apartment in Chicago reading books and the latest issues of *The New Yorker*. The next year I went back to New York and again called the man who had interviewed me at *The New Yorker*, and he told me to come in and talk to the editor, Mr. Shawn. Mr. Shawn hired me to write short articles for the "Talk of the Town" department at $200 a week. My parents were more thrilled at this development than even I was. They came to New

York unannounced a few weeks after, and first thing in the morning Dad went by the magazine's offices and, not finding me there, strolled in anyway, introducing himself around and saying he was a lifelong *New Yorker* reader. He wanted to meet Mr. Shawn, but Shawn never got in much before eleven. He looked Shawn's desk over and chatted with Shawn's secretary. When I arrived later in the day the receptionist said, "Your, uh . . . *father* was here."

Dave enrolled at Kent State University and moved to a house with friends in Kent. He was in plays in local theaters, including *Once upon a Mattress*, in which he played the prince and Mom the queen. In the summers he worked for Sohio, driving the Sohio "Courtesy Car" and helping drivers of vehicles disabled on local roads. Suzan and Maggie also worked for Sohio, pumping gas at a service area on the turnpike. Suzan graduated from high school and spent a year traveling in Europe with a friend. Then she, too, enrolled at Kent. She applied for a transfer to Barnard College and Dave did not want her to go; he said he did not want to be left at Kent all by himself. But Barnard accepted her, and she moved to New York. Maggie was in a lot of plays at high schools and in the Cleveland Play House. For college she went first to Redlands, in California, but did not like being so far away from home. She came back to Hudson and worked for a while in a shoe store in a mall. Then she went to the University of Rochester, where she met a man from New York City named John Hayes. The year after she graduated they were married. Mom planned a big wedding for her, the youngest of us and the first to marry. As Maggie and my father prepared to march up the aisle, she looked at all the faces turning toward her and told him she was nervous. He said, "I was with you when you were born and I'm with you now."

•

Mom did not like to see her children leaving and the rooms of her house emptying out. Dave moved back home, and she fretted about his future, but really both she and Dad liked having him around. Friends of mine in Hudson often stopped by to visit them, to tell about their jobs and classes. For Maggie's last year in high school the family applied to the American Friends' Service to host a foreign exchange student for a year. The AFS sent them Tere, an Ecuadoran girl. Tere had learned little English before arrival, and Mom and Dad spent many evenings teaching it to her, reading her the homework assignments and sometimes acting pantomimes to explain hard-to-understand parts. Maggie had had more than enough siblings to compete with already, and she quickly got fed up with the whole business. She and Tere fought often, mostly silently.

On drives back and forth to her school, Mom thought about children. One fall evening the sky seemed to her "so tender like a mother waiting for the birth of either boy or girl with many shades of blue and pink." She listened to top-forty rock-and-roll on the radio and picked up slang from her students. Her father a half century before had picked up slang, too—his words were "snazzy" and "slick" and "putting up a bluff" and "hot diggity!" Hers were "flick" (as in to flick, or skip, school) and "freak out" and "uptight" and "awesome." Students helped her clean her house after school was out in June. Sometimes she took students out to dinner or invited them over and served paella and creamed chicken. One spring she took all twenty-nine students in her Advanced Placement English class to an amusement park. When she directed *The Diary of Anne Frank* for the school play, she and the cast spent two days and a night sealed up in the loft of a church building, keeping quiet for hours at a time to get an idea of what the Franks had gone through.

Parents sometimes complained about texts she assigned her students, and one year the administration took her AP classes away from her. One year a boy hit Mr. Wolski, the assistant principal, in the face with a cherry pie at a school assembly. A photographer for the yearbook got a picture so handily that the administration suspected the yearbook had been involved. One year she was reprimanded for unwittingly running a picture in the yearbook of a boy holding a bottle of champagne. Two years in a row the future mass murderer Jeffrey Dahmer snuck into the back row of the National Honor Society group photo. The yearbook staff noticed the interloper only when it was too late to retake the photo, and so blacked him out with marker.

She wrote me letters on her electric typewriter in an italic typeface which I came to think of as her handwriting. Often the letters were so affectionate they embarrassed me, and I was careful never to leave them lying around where friends might see. In those days I was locked in a more or less chronic depression and mope due to guilt at my good job and to resentment at having to take care of myself. She was always trying to cheer me up. She offered to come to New York and clean and paint my apartment. She enclosed simple dinner recipes, adding, "Do you have plates?" She sent me gifts and checks, and paid to have a bathroom installed in my new loft. In fact, she was a lot more depressed than I was. I paid small attention to her complaints of loneliness when Dad left on business trips and told her he was giving her practice at being a widow, when she eagerly planned family get-togethers, when she described a walk she took in the rain one Sunday as Dad watched a football game on TV: "I like a lonely walk in the rain, but being lonely is different when you're young than when you're old. When you're young everything is yet to be, but it will be." I did not think to remind her she was only fifty-five.

Dad's days passed in a routine of coffee in the morning, low-cholesterol sardine sandwiches at the lab for lunch, beers in the evening, dinner, and an early bed. He now got five or six weeks' paid vacation, and took them usually in July and August, when he and Mom went abroad, and at Christmas. Every fall came the cold day when he turned on the heater in the car for the first time since spring, and the dusty blast of heat always smelled the same. He worried about the house, about putting up and taking down the storm windows, mowing the grass, keeping the driveway plowed in winter. As he expected, moving to an apartment reduced his worries, but the few that remained—their cars, the price of Sohio stock, and the income taxes—were intense enough to make up the difference. The cars were in use all the time and one or another usually had a problem in the distributor or a squeaky brake shoe or a leaky radiator. Pride in his mechanical abilities interfered with his ever taking a car to someone else for repair. Sohio stock, of which he owned a number of shares, got him excited by going way up for a year or so; when it fell again, he saw poverty ahead. The income taxes always put him in an agitated depression, which began to build in March. He would wake in the night and review the figures and pace and clasp and unclasp his hands.

At work he told his friend Bill Fitzgibbons that his son had died, but added quickly that he didn't want to talk about it. His colleagues say that his interest in work declined after Fritz's death—"He lost his dynamic," according to one. As it happened, morale at the lab was low then in general. Many of the researchers believed that the lab's best days had passed. Doc Hughes retired in 1970. Sohio hired a management consulting firm to do an efficiency study of the lab, and efficiency experts followed researchers around with stopwatches and asked them how long it took to formulate a hypothesis. An efficiency report noted disapprovingly that many researchers spent a lot of time just sitting at their desks and thinking. The researchers rebelled, management overpowered them, and a vice president lost his job. Sohio spent billions building the Alaskan oil pipeline and lost billions more in the purchase of a copper-mining company, with the result that its partner, British Petroleum, Ltd., eventually ended up owning Sohio. BP's approach to research and development turned out to be controlling and secretive, and not encouraging toward "blue sky" research—research that showed no immediate promise of profit to the company. Statewide, BP replaced the red-white-and-blue Sohio emblem Ohioans had known for years with its yellow-and-green BP logo. BP trucks went to all the service stations and took every sign and poster and oil rack with the Sohio emblem, and the word "Sohio" disappeared from public view.

One year the company assigned Dad to teach a seven-week course in chemical engineering to a group of high-school seniors as part of its participation in a community program for minority students. He put a lot of effort into his lesson plan and hoped to teach the kids how to run chemical reactors and calculate flows and temperatures and make plastics on-site in the lab. The kids turned out to have so few skills that he had to pick simpler problems, like heating soup. They became bored far more easily than he had expected and, as he lectured, would put their heads on their desks periodically and go to sleep. (He noted that they never all fell asleep at the same time, however.) To end the class he had wanted to take them on the company jet to see the big acrylonitrile plants in Lima, Ohio, but higher-ups in the company said no. When the course was over no one in the program or the company thanked him. But at the program's graduation ceremony, the master of ceremonies, "a pert, tart, Afro-ed young woman" (he later wrote) who had been his best student, announced that she planned to go to college and study chemical engineering. He felt vindicated, triumphant.

•

He used to tell my mother what an old man he was. Sometimes he did a palsied pantomime, folding his shaking arms to his stomach and creaking, "I'm o-o-o-o-old!" He began to drive peculiarly, taking

wrong turns if Mom was in the car so that she always had to watch
and correct him. He drove with ever-greater circumspection and hesitation, and a speeding drunk ran into them from behind. Once, he
took the wheel mount of his Subaru apart to replace a brake shoe but
could not get the assembly back together, and had to give in and go
to a mechanic. He took his telescope apart and could not fix it and
put the parts in a box and stored it. The income taxes began to make
him so upset that he finally asked Dave to do them.

His fellow research associate Phil Fay, who had been at the lab
about as long as he, knew something was wrong when Dad went to
Fay for advice; before, Fay had always gone to him. Dad kept a
notebook to record progress in various research projects—adapting
the cutting oils he had worked on when he first came to the lab for
use as surfactants in oil-well drilling, or making bottles from a plastic
derivative of acrylonitrile—and his handwriting in the first entry,
September 29, 1981, is firm. But as days go by the handwriting wavers,
and there are entries like:

Why am I having trouble with Dave's Texas Inst Grade averager?
25 Jan 1982—WORKED IT OUT—OK!
I thought I had lost this notebook—I hadn't, but it might be better if I didn't
take it away from my desk.

The company wasn't sure what to do with him, and so put him in a
computer group at a different lab. The head of the group tried to get
more out of him, sending him many memos and telling him to get
counseling in assertiveness and communication skills. Phil Fay came
by to visit, sized up the situation, and persuaded an old friend to move
Dad to the friend's department. One afternoon Bill Fitzgibbons was
driving from work when he spotted Dad's Volkswagen diesel pulled
over on the shoulder of Interstate Highway 271. Dad had no idea
where he was, but recognized Fitzgibbons. Fitzgibbons pointed him
toward home and later called my mother. She listened silently as he
described the incident, and she did not want to hear more; Fitzgibbons
felt uncomfortable. Dad spent more and more time in the halls at the
lab. He dropped in on colleagues and began conversations, but then
became restless and walked away. His notebook entries grew frag-
mentary and hard to read. When he called colleagues on the phone,

he first wrote down in the notebook what he was going to say. Toward the end the notebook pages are mostly names written over and over in capital letters. On a later page he crossed out some names and phone numbers and wrote:

I am interested in BLEEDING of solid-liquids

The notebook ends in illegibility a page or two beyond.

With my mother's help, he worked out the details of his early retirement. In mid-1983, without farewell, he left the company where he had worked for thirty-seven years and began to spend his days in the apartment. Sometimes when Mom returned from errands or school she found that he had gotten out and was roaming the building. Sometimes neighbors made remarks. Mom hired a registered nurse named Naomi Taylor to be with him when she was gone. Dad and Naomi would take long walks in the mornings and stop at a coffee shop for lunch. Naomi usually dressed him in a warm coat and the Mao-style cap with the red star on the front he had picked up in China. She thought he looked cute in it. I left New York and moved to Montana, and passed through Cleveland from time to time headed east or west. I sat with him as he watched television or stared out their living-room windows at the lake and the sky, listing slowly to the side in his armchair. Once, a row of smaller clouds appeared in front of the dull gray overcast. "Looks like somebody came along and busted a bunch of holes in a slab of concrete with a jackhammer, doesn't it?" he said, and it sort of did. Once, I said something I thought was amusing at dinner and he suddenly snarled, "You're not helping a *bit!*" and I felt as bad as if I were a little kid. At my wedding in Bigfork, Montana, he flew out for the ceremony with my mother and brother and sisters. Worriedly, he kept telling my mother I was about to ask him for a large sum of money. He took pains to explain to Jay's father that he did not live there, at the motel in Montana, but in Ohio. Apropos of nothing, he told Suzan she looked like "a blonde on a binge." But after the ceremony, as we stood awkwardly in the church, he said, "Well, Sandy, we've come a long way together since the doctor held you up in the hospital for me to see." Once, I fell into a silent, unthinking rage at him for not anticipating how hard his illness would be on my mother and for not somehow sparing her. I shot him a dirty look, and he smiled back without resentment. Then he took off his hat and hit me a playful rap with it on the top of the head.

When he turned sixty-five later that year, he wrote his mother a letter—the last piece of writing by him that I have. It said, in part:

. . . thank you for the compliments on birthday #65. Actually it isn't too hard, is it? You just keep picking them up and putting them down.— . . . With regard to "Health" in "SOHIOLAND" There was one point I don't know if the parents knew about. It was "going out on the ice." Sometimes kids would go out so far they could hardly see land and then old John Eaton would come and stand up on the cliff and wave his arms and blow his whistle, and I don't think it helped a bit.

Grandmother often gave him and her other relatives advice. ("I received another hectoring letter from Grandmother today," Dave used to say.) Despite this I liked to write her and get letters from her. When I was broke and snowed in in Montana, she wrote me with a list of possible jobs I might take to support myself, and added that under no circumstances was I to accept a job on a shrimp boat, "for it is a living death!" I have followed this piece of advice, but in general I ignored her suggestions, sensible and otherwise. As Dad got sicker, her letters to him burgeoned with advice—he and Mom should go on a cruise and hold hands and recapture the magic of their marriage, he should stop drinking, he should eat hot homemade vegetable soup every day for lunch, he should cleanse his system of all medications, he should come and visit her. I think his reference to going out on the ice was a metaphor, a way of saying how far from her help he had already gone. She wrote me that his illness, along with the recent death of her sister Anne Belle, left her absolutely bereft. She took a plane up to Cleveland to make one last try at saving Dad, became ill on the flight, twisted an ankle, returned home, broke a wrist. She healed, but decided she'd had enough. She made plans to die. I did not believe she was serious. I called her at her senior citizens' home in Florida and she said that she couldn't talk on the phone, and that I should be a good boy. She died of a stroke a week or two later.

At her funeral Dad stood dazed and vacant, his eyes on my mother to see what he should do. Now he did not always recognize people. Sometimes he even asked her who she was, and she would say, "You know who I am, I'm Kate!" That winter she took him on a trip to

London, and he became angry at her and afraid she was trying to harm him as they stood waiting for the elevator in the lobby of the Forum Hotel. She managed to get him up to their room, but he continued to struggle and resist her, and finally she had to call an ambulance. He became more violent when he saw the ambulance men and hit one of them "in about the worst place you can hit a man," Mom said later. Dad stayed in a hospital in London under sedation for three weeks. After she had finally brought him back to Cleveland, she told me, "I guess our travels are over."

A grief that grows imperceptibly is perhaps harder than a quick and shocking one. Its increments are never unexpected or so great as to call forth a gush of tears; you just look up one day and sadness is everywhere. Dave and Mom and Naomi did the trying work of keeping up with the disease's sequence of indignities. For me, Dad was an absence that grew until it was a simple *fait accompli*. I do not remember any single moment of overwhelming grief. But one spring, fishing with a friend in the Catskills (I had now moved back to New York from Montana), I stood outside the cabin at night and tried to name constellations in the clear sky. I can reliably identify none but the Big Dipper. I asked my friend if he knew any more, and he said no. My father could have identified dozens of constellations. In Florida, he liked to walk on the dock and point a flashlight beam at the Southern Cross and others we didn't have up North. I went back in the cabin and fell asleep and dreamed that my father said, "Now I'm going to forget the constellations, one by one."

Acts like walking and eating became difficult for him. When food fell off his fork, he yelled at it. He lost weight. Mom had links removed from his metal watchband, but it still rattled around his dwindling wrist like a bracelet, and sometimes caught on objects and scraped him. His speech became hard to understand. In October 1987, at the time of the big stock-market plunge—an event which would have grimly interested him—he went into the hospital with pneumonia caused probably by aspirating food, or swallowing down the wrong throat. Soon after, a doctor told my mother that he might have to be put on a respirator or require a feeding tube through the wall of his stomach. On several occasions, even before he got sick, he had said he wanted never to be on life support. Reluctantly, she refused the respirator and the feeding tube.

Doctors told her he could not last much longer. She called for a minister from Trinity Episcopal Cathedral in Cleveland to come to the hospital. The church's dean, Reverend Williams, was unavailable, so the canon, thirty-four-year-old Reverend Ted Curtis, went instead. "I had never met your father," Rev. Curtis says. "I don't think I had ever seen him. I knew him only as a breathing person in the hospital. Your mother I did remember. She always sat in the back of the church behind the main pillar on the left, and she used to get in and out real fast—always raced away at the end of the service. I remembered her gray hair. In the hospital I got lost trying to find the room. Finally I found it—a strange room, long and narrow, with a window and mini-blinds at one end. Light was coming in the window, and the bed was cranked up real high, and he was propped up against the wall by the window and she was stroking his hair, and I saw the silhouette and I thought of the Virgin and Child—it was a very spiritual, holy sort of moment. I joined her at the head of the bed and we talked hushedly. Talking seemed difficult for her. I tried to include David in what we were saying. I asked her about your family and she asked me about me. I told her where I was born and that I come from an old military family and I went to Washington and Lee University and my mother's father was a navy doctor and that my father was a career air force officer and that I had just resigned my chaplain's commission in the army reserve as a protest against the military—she got all this and more out of me, I'm not sure quite how. Then she and I held hands and we touched your father and I offered prayers for a swift death and release, and I prayed for strength and courage for her. During the prayer your mother cried—prayer releases things in the psyche. Then I gave her a hug. She wasn't overly receptive. I did it probably more for me than for her. I gave her my calling card and wrote my home phone number. Later, on my way home in the car, I listened to WCLV, the classical music station. I wanted to think about the experience, to process it; I don't ever want experiences like that to become routine. He died a couple of days later."

Rev. Curtis conducted the funeral. Uncle Louis delivered a reminiscence eulogy and Dave recited a poem, the last line of which was "How frail the wand, but how profound the spell!" Later, at the graveside service in Hudson, people parked their cars in a line along the cemetery drive by the gravesite. Cousin Jimmy Moses was there, and friends from Hudson, and the director of the funeral home. Rev. Curtis read from the prayer book, and then we all said the Lord's Prayer. Then we hugged and cried. I hugged my uncle and my high-school track coach, both for the first time ever. My mother hugged my wife and told her she loved her. The people stood by their cars and my mother went down the line and thanked each of them for coming. She looked small and gray and, to me, great. My father's ashes in a small copper urn marked with a cross sat on a piece of all-weather carpet on the ground. The hole had been dug but was covered with a piece of plywood. I asked the funeral director if we should put the urn in the ground and he said, "I'll stay after everyone's left and burry it."

For an epitaph, I offer a maxim Dad used to use in the course in statistical design of experiments he taught at the lab. He always told his colleagues that when reviewing experimental data they should pay particular attention to the result they didn't expect. He told them never to throw out the outlyer, the crazy data point. He said it might be the most important result of the experiment, the breakthrough, the basis for a whole new invention. He had an affinity for the crazy data point because in a sense he was one himself; if you had a cluster of data points, he would always be the one far apart from the rest. He just was not like other people. "Never throw out the outlyer."

·

Mom's life continued almost as before. My sisters and Maggie's husband and my wife and I came back to Ohio for Thanksgiving because Mom seemed to want us to. We ate and drank to stupefaction. Mom was attentive, quiet, remote. Her actions had a quality of force-lessness, as if she was not performing them herself but only remembering their performance. She gave me Dad's watch and we went to the Cleveland jeweler she had always patronized to ask them to refit the band for me. A man at their downtown store took a quick look and flipped the watch back to her, saying they did not do such work. She held the spurned watch in her palm and looked from it to him, baffled; no one had ever been rude to her at Potter and Mellen before.

For Christmas she came to New York to visit us. Maggie, who had been to cooking school, made her a dinner of poached salmon with dill sauce and a raspberry torte. David Kwateng, Suzan's new husband, gave her a wicker picnic basket filled with many kinds of canned and dried gourmet foods. As she opened it and looked at the items inside one by one, he nervously brought from his pocket a pair of fingernail clippers and began to clip his nails; for me, at that moment he became a true relative. I had a party for her at my loft and invited friends and cousins and in-laws. She provided a lot of caviar for appetizers, and friends from Russia told me with surprise that it was good caviar. She found my loft chilly and kept her fur coat on part of the time. She talked to people I brought to meet her, never varying her quiet, as-if-memorized politeness. At more private moments I thought I saw in her some of Dad's later mannerisms—his look of wide-eyed apprehension, the slow, spooky turn of his head.

She decided that she wanted to go back to the Yale School of Drama—nearly forty years after her first attempt there—for her Ph.D. On the application she explained that she had hoped to get a Ph.D. before, but because of my father's love for travel had instead spent her free time in the summers on trips with him. She described his illness and its end, and said that now her "bitter freedom" gave her the opportunity to go back to school. For starters she took a short course in play directing at Yale in the summer, when her teaching and yearbook responsibilities were over. After the course she visited Maggie and Suzan in Brooklyn and then drove back to Ohio, passing right by on Canal Street without giving me a call. True, I was not home at the time, but Jay, now pregnant, was. Why wouldn't Mom at least stop by to say hello? This struck me as worrisome and peculiar.

A physical exam that summer pronounced her in good health. She could not account for her frequent bouts of nausea, or for her lack of appetite, but at a gathering at her nephew Ted's house she ate plenty of barbecue and felt fine and thought the problem had gone away. She began to prepare lessons for fall semester. At the end of August she attended the teachers' meeting as she had many times before. On August 30, the first day of classes, a feeling of illness and exhaustion came over her, until by afternoon she could scarcely stand. She excused herself in the middle of her senior drama class and rushed to the parking lot and got in her car and drove home. She called her doctor and said it seemed urgent, and drove straight to see him. On the way a policeman stopped her for going 45 in a 35-mile zone. She explained that she was sick, but he gave her a ticket anyway.

The doctor ordered a CAT scan, then a liver biopsy. A week or two passed, during which she felt worse and worse. On September 13 the doctor was supposed to give her the biopsy results. She waited all day by the phone. Just before dinner he called. From the medical fine print of his conversation emerged the fact that many malignant growths had been found on her liver. "Why isn't it ever good news?" she asked when she called to tell me. The next morning I called her doctor to say I hoped he would not keep her waiting like that again if he could help it, and to ask more about the disease. From the first mention of her name, I knew that he had already turned the page and moved on to problems less dire.

Meanwhile, Dave had fallen in love with a woman and moved in with her. Mom helped them plan their October wedding. Maggie went back to Ohio to stay in Mom's apartment and cook for her. She accompanied her on trips to doctors' waiting rooms and chemotherapy sessions. Mom could not sit up long enough to be in a pew at the wedding, but watched from a metal folding chair off to one side. Her sister Betty helped her home right after the vows. She came to the reception for a little while and sat on a couch with Betty and her brother John.

She and Maggie hired a nurse named Bernice Simons to help take care of her. Back in New York, I called Mom almost every evening and talked for ten or fifteen minutes. I sent her the bound galley proofs of a book I had written and Bernice read her the first few pages. She laughed at certain parts, but then became too tired to hear more. In mid-November Maggie called and said she thought I should come home. Jay was bedridden with all-day morning sickness, so I went by myself. Mom was lying flat on her back, eyes three-quarters closed, when I walked into the bedroom. The television flickered in a corner. I got myself a beer and came back and sat on the chaise by the bed. My stomach was so empty that the first cold sip showed me where it was. After a moment or two, I burped. Without opening her eyes, she said, "That sounds like Sandy."

Maggie called John and Suzan and told them they should come, too. They flew to Cleveland the next day. I called Jay. She was afraid she felt too bad to fly, but her mother drove her to the airport and helped her on the plane. In Cleveland she came off the plane in a wheelchair, face gray. But then she stood up and we walked slowly to the car. Mom was sitting up and alert when Jay arrived. Jay sat on the edge of the bed next to her and I put Mom's hand on Jay's stomach and the baby kicked and Mom felt the kick and smiled. She patted my hand and said, "You're great." For no real reason, I pretended I did not hear what she had said. She rolled her eyes in exasperation and gave up trying to tell me.

Talking was hard for her, and often she could not make herself understood. When we didn't know what she was saying, Maggie would lie down full length next to her and hold her and ask quietly to her face. She told me that Dave and I would be co-executors of her will; she said, "Don't fight." In the evenings we gave her medicines. She liked all of us to come around and hold her upright and help her take them. On Thanksgiving Day we set the table in her room and had dinner there. She ate nothing and dozed in the bed throughout the meal. The television in the corner of her room was on constantly. Once, not long after I arrived, I had tried to turn it off, but she roused herself and objected. Maggie told me that she really wanted it on.

For several nights, Maggie and Suzan stayed up with her, taking turns drowsing until Bernice arrived in the morning. Neither wanted to sit with her alone. Mom could not move to alter her position on the bed, and as she became uncomfortable her breathing would change to a sort of huffing, as if she were doing a lot of sit-ups. They would readjust her, turn her on her other side, and she would again breathe quietly for a while. The periods of strained breathing grew more frequent. After several nights with her, Maggie and Suzan were tired out. I told Maggie and Suzan that they should get a night's sleep and I would sit up with her by myself.

I took a blanket for my feet, and the book I had been reading for months—*Our Mutual Friend*—and leaned back on the chaise by her bed. She breathed quietly; I would not have to turn her for a while. The TV, sound kept as low as I dared without shutting it off entirely, held forth in the corner. Warm air from the vents by the window lifted the curtains and inflated them into the room. Then the air stopped and the curtains settled back down. Maggie looked in on us; she said she and Suzan would get up early to relieve me. She partway closed the door.

I was almost thirty-eight years old—maybe at the midpoint of my life, maybe not. On TV, sections of a movie about a muscleman in skins fighting horned cyclopses alternated with long stretches of commercials. I tried to read *Our Mutual Friend* but found myself bogged down in one of the sappy parts where I had been for weeks.

I turned sideways so as not to see the TV. Mom's breathing became a louder chuffing. It is hard work to die. I lifted her at the waist, shoulder, and leg, eased her onto her side. For a while the chuffing subsided. The curtains rose, then settled again. I wondered what she was seeing inside. Was it the pulsing, red-tinged, private darkness you see when you clench your eyes shut during a shampoo? Was it something shapeless, irregular, unseen, immaterial besides the pain? Was it nothing at all? The TV began to show newsmen and news-women. A shouted good-night conversation rose from the parking lot below—people leaving Pier W, a seafood place. She had watched me sleep, had driven with my father until dawn while we slept in the back of the car. Now I watched her.

My mother was bound elsewhere, soon she would be as gone as Fritz and my dad. On the bed, she was already on her way. The objects in the room, too, waited only for an approaching moment that would transport them. The bed itself would sail on like a raft after the raftsman has jumped off, and would beach in a different bedroom or a storage room somewhere. The pictures on the walls and the silver dollars in the sock drawer and the rug on the floor and the bifocals on the night table would disperse centrifugally as if flung. The chaise I rode would proceed feet first out the door. The curtains would inhale and exhale some more, then fold up and disappear. Everything was moving, even the darkness at the window, each instant becoming the next with an infinitesimal fading or brightening. I felt the motion under me and around me, touched its works, its sway. And just for this night, this long moment, the motion caused points to align; as if a hand could reach from a window of a speeding car and touch another hand in a window going the other way; as if the windows of many trains on parallel tracks fell into conjunction and you saw the faces of passengers in a line clear to the other side.

The TV began a show about a merman from an undersea kingdom. The merman swam strangely, with a jackknife motion of his legs. The commercials had grown more marginal and desperate. My mother was breathing hard again: *"Oh! Oh! Oh! Oh!"* I turned her on her back, with little effect, then to her other side. Her skin was tight with effort, her unconscious face intent. Now on TV old-time comedians in black and white were wandering in a garden maze. How many of these late hours had she spent averaging grades, sewing costumes, wrapping presents—in the middle of her family, but alone? I tried again to read, then kept my place with my finger and laid the book down.

Even in death, her face would show what a good woman she was. Tomorrow, or the next day, Dave and I would make phone calls, set up appointments, drive to the Johnson-Romito funeral home in Hudson, stop on the way for a middle-aged woman lying awake and sober in the right-hand lane of the Main Avenue Bridge; and after other cars also stopped, we would find the nearest pay phone and call a number copied from the clear-plastic-enclosed card pinned to the woman's coat, and I would hear Dave say to the person on the other end, "So how long ago did she move here from Indiana?" And we would be late for the meeting with the now-familiar undertaker, his name would be Bob, Mom and I had joked the year before that of course the person who buried you would be named Bob. We would have the familiar conversation with him, and he would list procedures and prices, and he would refer to the ashes as the "cremains," and he would bring us papers to sign, and I would sign without reading and Dave would read first and then sign.

We would stand where we had stood before, next to the cemetery drive, and people would gather by their cars near the small hole covered with plywood, and Ted Curtis would lead the prayers, and the wind would blow my hair across my face to stick in my tears, and I would not be able to free it for the urn in my hands. And in time we would come back to this apartment—it's in a tall building on the west side, and on top of the building is a large, lighted blue W, you can see it from the air when you fly over Cleveland—and we would sort her belongings and Dad's belongings, and I would take all the papers and all the small artifacts that suggested narrative, and I would make them into a book, a long streamer attached to her ankle to mark for a moment the spot where she had disappeared. And my daughter would be born, and Suzan's daughter and Maggie's daughter, and we would take them at the Feast of Pentecost to the Cathedral of St. John the Divine on 110th Street in Manhattan, and ministers would pour holy water into the font and a microphone would pick up the sound of the gurgling water and carry it through the high pillars of the cathedral, and Suzan's daughter would look cute and surprised with drops of baptismal water at the ends of her curls and the point of her nose catching the light, and Maggie's daughter would cry only a little, and my daughter when they lowered her to the font would cry nervously and when they lifted her up wet and the congregation applauded would react with outrage and surprise, and we would have a big party afterward at Maggie's with fried chicken and potato salad and African food and champagne and guests from all over, and Maggie would sit afterward in the party wreckage and say, "We did it," and I would feel a calm that lasted for days.

And I would overpay for a co-op apartment and carry a mortgage and fret about money just like my dad, he and my mother would accompany me through a life that would be much like theirs, and at every step I would compare myself especially to him, would judge if I was doing better or worse than he had done at being middle-class and putting kids through school and not terrorizing my family and staying between the lines while trying not to forget what it is I actually want to do. And unknown things would happen, and sooner or later I would die, too—I understood that now, clearly, the way you suddenly become aware of the sky and the diving board after the person in front of you has jumped—and my kids perhaps would see me off as I had seen my parents off, or perhaps not. And soon all the people who had accompanied me through life would be gone, too, and then even the people who had known us, and no one would remain on earth who had ever seen us, and those descended from us perhaps would know stories about us, perhaps once in a while they would pass by buildings where we had lived and they would mention that we had lived there. And then the stories would fade, and our graves would go untended, and the graves of those who had tended ours would go untended, and no one would guess what it had been like to wake before dawn in our breath-warmed bedrooms as the radiators clanked and our wives and husbands and children slept. And we would move from the nearer regions of the dead who are remembered into the farther regions of the forgotten, and on past those, into a space as white and big as the sky replicated forever. And all that would remain would be the love bravely expressed, and the moment when you danced and your heart danced with you.

Outside, dawn was approaching from western Pennsylvania. A bird sang; in a few minutes it would have enough light to fly. On TV, seated people in bright sport clothes talked about products. The room's curtains did their rise and fall. My mother breathed like a countdown. I turned her again, went back to the chaise. The building just to the east turned on the lights in its indoor-outdoor pool. Soon one of my sisters would be in to relieve me. Life was paying out like line.

Great-great-grandfather Simeon Frazier
(born 1832)

Great-grandfather Harry Edwin Frazier
(born 1868)

Grandfather Edwin Ray Frazier
(born 1891)

My father (born 1919)

Me (born 1951)

The Norwalk, Ohio, Public Library

C H A P T E R 1

3 Centuries begin on the year 1; 1900 was the last year of the nineteenth century, 1901 the first year of the twentieth. January 1, 1901, was a Tuesday. To judge from the newspapers, people in Ohio and Indiana did not take the day off.

3 My great-grandparents' addresses come from U.S. Census data for 1900 and 1910, and family sources. The census lists all residents, live-in servants included, at each address. The general appearance of the Harry E. Fraziers' neighborhood comes from *Baist's Property Atlas of the City of Indianapolis* (1899), a fire-insurance atlas on microfilm in the Indianapolis Public Library.

4 My great-aunts Alice and Grace Hursh's handwritten recollections of their father are my source for much of the information about O.A.S. Hursh. Biographical details about the man he was named for, Andreas Osiander (1498–1552), may be found in the *Encyclopaedia Britannica* (1973). Martin Luther's intervention as peacemaker in a bitter dispute between Andreas Osiander and a colleague over individual confession is discussed in *Luther and the Reformation*, by James MacKinnon (1962), Vol. IV, pp. 84–85. The name Osiander is a combination of the Greek ὅσιος, sacred or holy, and ἀνδρός, from the word for man. The meaning of the name Amariah comes from an index at the back of my King James Bible, and a list of biblical appearances by characters of that

name is in the *Dictionary of the Bible*, edited by James Hastings (1963). Other information about O.A.S. Hursh comes from his writings—sermons, an essay—found among my parents' papers, and from his diary, also found there. Details of his and Lizzie Chapman's wedding are taken from the Canton, Ohio, *Repository Republican* (December 26, 1873; January 2, 1874), which ran two short items about the marriage and spelled his name wrong both times. Another of his notebooks contained information about the building of the family's house in Tiffin; I am very grateful to my aunt and uncle, Bill and Virginia Hursh, for sending that notebook to me.

6 Information about and photos of the Harry E. Braziers come from my great-aunt Sarah Margaret Frazier Wallar (called Peg), to whom many thanks. One may trace Harry E. Frazier's employment history in Indianapolis in R. L. Polk & Co.'s *Indianapolis City Directory* from 1895 through 1903, which lists not only people's names and addresses but their jobs and whether they own or rent their homes. Written recollections by Peg's sisters Ruth and Dorothy provided additional data. The family's address in Norwalk, Ohio, comes from the *Norwalk City Directory* of 1909–10.

That publication, like most others I read about Norwalk, is in the Norwalk Public Library. I thank the library's then-director, Laureen Drapp, and librarians Maryellen Hamernik, Barbara Nutter, and Jean Beier for their kind assistance, and also for the lunch buffets they invited me to in the library's basement.

9 The fact that most Americans lived in rural places or small towns about a hundred years ago is found on the first page of Vol. X of *A History of American Life*. That volume, titled *The Rise of the City*, is by Arthur Meier Schlesinger (1933).

9 Details about Norwalk in 1900 come from the Norwalk *Daily Reflector*, from photographs, and from written reminiscences of my grandmother Cora Wickham Frazier and great-grandfather Louis Wickham.

An excellent source for life in Norwalk at the turn of the century is an unpublished typescript of nearly 300 pages which my distant cousin Winthrop W. Wickham wrote when he was in his eighties. He titled it *A Journal of Wickhams and Others 1324 to 19——* . . . Its first line is "Believe it or not, this is a revision of my original journal." Of all the family documents I read, Cousin Win's manuscript is my favorite. (Thanks to my uncle Louis Frazier for lending me his copy.) Cousin Win died in 1993, but I interviewed him at his home in Upland, California, in 1990. He was a retired surveyor, quiet, watchful, self-possessed, and God-fearing. Much of what he told me was of use in this book. My cousins Louis and Cindy Frazier, who both lived in Santa Monica then, set up the interview with Cousin Win for me, and Cindy, a writer herself, tape-recorded it. Many thanks to them both.

14 Most of what I know about the Bachmans comes from my uncle John Bachman Hursh, who talked to me about them and showed me letters and a family history his grandfather and grandmother had written. A trip I took to New Knoxville provided facts about the town and about Rev. Bachman's ministry at the First Reformed Church. Viola Katterheinrich, of New Knoxville, gave me additional information. Memories of Flora Bachman's girlhood are found in her letters.

16 Aunts Alice and Grace Hursh are again the source for details about the Hurshes in Tiffin. My aunt Betty McLean told me the story of Mrs. Hursh's interference in the romantic lives of her daughters, a story which Uncle Bill and Uncle John confirmed. The romance between Flora and Osie is portrayed in the letters they exchanged regularly between 1903 and 1906. I am grateful to Uncle John for finding these and other letters and sending them to me.

18 Cora Wickham Frazier recalled her girlhood in several typescripts she wrote, and in her letters. Additional information about Cora, Ray Frazier, and their wedding came from interviews with Uncle Louis and my father's cousin Ellen Harding Anderson.

22 Flora Hursh described details of housekeeping, her pregnancy, and the birth of my mother in letters to Grandmother Bachman, who by then had moved to the West Coast. The ledger book of Aunt Alice and Aunt Grace's household accounts turned up among my parents' papers. As soon as my mother went to college, she began to write her parents regularly; those letters, and a journal she kept at Stephens, are the sources for her college years. In none of the letters she wrote during her summer in New York does she mention her friendship or romance with the sculptor she met, although she saved letters he wrote to her. That as a young woman she feared ending up an old maid schoolteacher I infer from her writings, particularly an autobiographical note she included in an application to the Yale School of Drama near the end of her life.

CHAPTER 2

30 The article on potatoes mentioned is "The Incredible Potato," by R. E. Rhoades (*National Geographic*, May 1982, p. 688).

31 The article about the effect of a nuclear attack on Washington, D.C., is "Some Civil Defense Problems in the Nation's Capital Following Widespread Thermonuclear Attack," written by members of the Operations Research Office of Johns Hopkins University and presented in March of 1957 at the annual meeting of the Eastern College Science Conference at Georgetown University.

32 According to "The Amateur Scientist," by Jearl Walker (*Scientific American*, September 1977, p. 246), hot water freezes faster than cold possibly because its more rapid rate of evaporation causes it to lose mass and energy more quickly. The author says that the faster freezing of hot water has long been known to folk wisdom, and that science only recently proved it to be true.

CHAPTER 3

Some of the information about ancestors comes from short genealogies compiled by Alice and Grace Hursh, Martha Graf Bachman, and Ruth Frazier. (Thanks to my second cousins Doug and Gregory Frazier for helping me with the Frazier forebears, and for sending me copies of what Aunt Ruth wrote.)

A much more detailed document, and one of great use to me, is *Whence We Came: A Study of the Ancestry of Ralph Wickham Jones, Marian Alvord Jones, and Charlotte Adams Jones*, compiled by Ralph Wickham Jones (1960). This is a carbon copy of a typescript; I do not know how my parents got it. It traces ancestors back to the eleventh generation, to the mid-sixteenth century. Much of what I know about distant Wickham and Preston ancestors comes from it. I never met Mr. Jones, and I never will; the last time I strolled in the Norwalk cemetery, I came across his marker. He died in 1977. I thank him anyway for his scholarship and his humor.

Other useful sources were *Out of the Everywhere*, by Marian Warner Wildman Fenner (no date), a manuscript genealogy of the Wildman and Patch families; and typescript genealogies of the Benedict and DeForest families with no authors and no dates.

41 The story of Thomas Benedict, the first of the line in America, comes from *Genealogy of the Benedicts in America*, Vol. I, a book I found in the library of the Scott-Fanton Museum and Historical Society in Danbury, Connecticut.

42 The historian Francis Parkman mentions John Lovewell and his battles with Indians in *A Half-Century of Conflict: France and England in North America*, part 6, Vol. I (1899), pp. 250–71. A band of Pequawkets attacked the town of Dunstable in 1724, took two men captive, and ambushed and killed most of a ten-man party sent after them. In retaliation, John Lovewell organized several expeditions to hunt and kill Indians; in the middle of the winter he and his men surprised two wigwams, killed all ten Indians inside, and brought back scalps. In the spring of 1725 Lovewell and others were ambushed by a party of Pequawkets and pinned against the shore of what is now called Lovewell's Pond. Parkman describes the fight in which Lovewell lost his life as "one of the most obstinate and deadly bush-fights in the history of New England." John Lovewell's brother Zaccheus (1701–72) was the great-great-grandfather of Lucy Preston Wickham (see p. 65).

42 The statistic about the leading causes of death in women in colonial days I learned from a guide/historian at the Scott-Fanton Museum.

43 None of the genealogies I consulted, including Mr. Jones's, say that ancestors participated in the slave trade. I happened to learn this fact by accident. A friend, Robert Blaisdell, gave me a copy of *Black Cargoes: A History of the Atlantic Slave Trade 1518–1865*, by Daniel P. Mannix in collaboration with Malcolm Cowley (1962). I was reading it with interest when I found, in the chapter "The Yankee Slavers," this sentence: "Most of the Rhode Island shipowning families were concerned in the [slave] trade." A footnote elaborated: "For records of Rhode Island families engaged in the trade, consult the index to Donnan III [Elizabeth Donnan's *Documents Illustrative of the History of the Slave Trade to America*, Vol. III (1930–35)]. Do not consult the *Dictionary of American Biography*, which regards slaving as an unmentionable subject." I did consult Donnan, which turned out to be a remarkable four-volume compilation of documents of every sort, and there found evidence of Joseph Wanton's and Thomas Wickham's participation in the trade. The genealogical records on which I had previously depended evidently came from nineteenth-century sources in which my (Republican) forebears had edited that uncomfortable detail from their past.

44 Among my sources on American religious history in the first half of the nineteenth century are:

The Philosophy of Sectarianism; or, A Classified View of the Christian Sects in the United States, by Rev. Alexander Blaikie (1855). Blaikie was a Boston Presbyterian and wrote from a stern Presbyterian point of view.

Sectarian Shackles, by Libbie Miller Travers (1926). Travers, though not a minister, came from a Midwestern family who belonged to the Disciples of Christ.

The Old Northwest Pioneer Period 1815–1840, by Roscoe Carlyle Buley (1950). This two-volume survey of frontier life in Ohio, Indiana, Illinois, Michigan, and Wisconsin—the Old Northwest—is a very good book, and one I used a lot in research about that period. Its section about religion discusses sects and the spread of revivalism.

Righteous Empire: The Protestant Experience in America, by Martin E. Marty (1970).

A Religious History of the American People, by Sydney E. Ahlstrom (1972).

44 The divisions among the Presbyterians are enumerated by Blaikie. The Constitutional
Presbyterians were ones that had agreed to merge with the Congregationals, so I assume
they could also be called New School Presbyterians. The New School faction included
some of the most progressive Presbyterian ministers; a leading New School minister
was Rev. Lyman Beecher, kicked out of the church by the Presbyterian General
Assembly in 1838. Beecher was a strong antislavery advocate and the father of Harriet
Beecher Stowe, author of *Uncle Tom's Cabin*. Rev. Beecher deeply regretted the split
in his church and said, " 'Twas slavery that did it" (*Patriotic Gore*, by Edmund Wilson
[1986 ed.], p. 15).

The question of whether a group of worshippers represented a sect could of course
become murky, especially among denominations like the Congregationals, where every
congregation prized its independence. For every sect there were thousands of smaller
schisms which eventually healed. The Baptists generally believed in congregational
independence also, and my list of their sects is partial. Among the Baptists, Blaikie
wrote, "the sects are beyond comparison numerous." Groups like the Fourierists, whose
aim was more social than religious, I have omitted from my list of sects, as well as
smaller religious sects like the Rosicrucians, Edsonites, Bethelites, and Schwenkfelders.
Voltaire's remark about the English—that they had a hundred religions but only one
sauce—could also have applied to the Americans of these years.

46 Information about the history of the Disciples of Christ Church comes from sources
listed, and from *Hoosier Disciples: A Comprehensive History of the Christian Churches
(Disciples of Christ) in Indiana*, by Henry K. Shaw (1966). Details about the Disciples
Church building in New Washington, Indiana, may be found in an article by Marguerite
Fisher and Mary A. Walters in *New Washington Community History*, edited by Bertha
Giltner, Charlotte Adams, and Helen Wiggam (1990), in the Jefferson County Library
in Madison, Indiana.

48 Englishman John Newton, a slave-ship captain out of Liverpool in the years 1750–54,
later became an Anglican minister. He wrote many hymns, some in collaboration with
the poet William Cowper. See *An Ancient Mariner: A Biography of John Newton*, by
Bernard Martin (1960).

49 Further details about New Washington and environs are found in *Baird's History of
Clark County, Indiana*, by Captain Lewis C. Baird (1909), also in the Jefferson County
Library. (My thanks to librarian Cheryl Marriage.)

49 Details about nineteenth-century religious contention in the U.S. come from books
cited above, and from such works as *A Dialogue, Between a Predestinarian, and his
Friend*, by John Wesley (1796); and *Sectarianism Is Heresy*, by Rev. Andrew Wylie
(1840). Also helpful was *The Life of Our Blessed Lord and Saviour Jesus Christ*, by
Rev. John Fleetwood, D.D. (1822). That book's full title takes up most of a title page,
and proclaims it *A Full Defence of the Christian Religion, In which the Evidences of
Christianity Are Clearly Stated, the New Testament Proved to Be Genuine, and the
Religion of the Great Redeemer of Mankind Truly Divine*.

51 Information about my ancestors' whereabouts in the year 1800 comes from family
sources and the second U.S. Census (1800).

52 Family stories about the British raid on Danbury, Connecticut, are preserved in the
manuscript *Autobiography of Frederick Augustus Wildman* (1894) and *Out of the
Everywhere*, by Fenner (cited above). Many thanks to Cousin Winthrop Wickham's
daughter Joan Jones for sending a copy of the Wildman autobiography to me. Among
published sources, I referred to *Records of the State of Connecticut, 1776–1778*, Vol. I;

and *History of Danbury*, by James M. Bailey (1896); and *Connecticut Attacked: A British Viewpoint, Tryon's Raid on Danbury*, by Robert F. McDevitt (1974).

54 The establishment of the Connecticut Western Reserve is described in a number of books, notably *The Western Reserve: The Story of New Connecticut in Ohio*, by Harlan Hatcher (1966).

56 The story of Platt Benedict and Elisha Whittlesey and the founding of Norwalk comes from family sources, and articles in a historical journal called *The Firelands Pioneer* (March 1859; May 1859) on file in the Firelands Historical Society Library in Norwalk. Historian Henry Timman, in his interesting column in the Norwalk *Reflector-Herald* (April 21, 1972), goes into more detail about the partners' lobbying efforts to get Norwalk made county seat. (They hired a lobbyist and evidently feted legislators with brandy.) Details about the hanging of the Ottawas are found in *Historical Collections of Ohio*, by Henry Howe, LL.D., Vol. I (1904), p. 942.

59 An article in the *Reflector* of November 6, 1866, describes Platt's funeral. Thousands viewed him in his glass-topped coffin of silver-ornamented mahogany as he lay with wreaths of myrtle on his breast and around his head. Five hundred Masons marched in his funeral procession. Mourners filled the church he had founded, and three thousand more gathered around it.

CHAPTER 4

60 Many first-person narratives survive from people who traveled on the Ohio and Indiana frontiers. Some of the books from which details in this chapter are taken:

Notes on a Journey in America, from the Coast of Virginia to the Territory of Illinois, by Morris Birkbeck (1818).

Sketch of a Journey through the Western States of North America, by William Bullock (1827).

Personal Narrative of Travels in Virginia, Maryland, Pennsylvania, Ohio, Indiana, Kentucky, and of a Residence in the Illinois Territory: 1817–1818, by Elias Pym Fordham (1906).

The New Purchase, or Seven and a Half Years in the Far West, by Bayard Rush Hall (1843).

Narrative of Richard Lee Mason in the Pioneer West, 1819.

Letters from the West, Comprising a Tour through the Western Country, and a Residence of Two Summers in the States of Ohio and Kentucky, by George W. Ogden (1823).

Indiana Miscellany: Consisting of Sketches of Indian Life, the Early Settlement, Customs, and Hardships of the People, and the Introduction of the Gospel and of Schools . . . , by Rev. William C. Smith (1867).

Also of interest was *The Western Gazetteer; or Emigrants' Directory*, by Samuel R. Brown (1817), a guidebook with much specific information about the Western Reserve for settlers. Details about travel may be found in *The Old Pike: A History of the National Road*, by Thomas B. Searight (1896) and *Historic Highways of America*, Vol. 5: *The Old Glade (Forbes's) Road (Pennsylvania State Road)*, by Archer Butler Hulbert (1903).

Other details come from sources named in Chapter 3 notes above, especially Buley and Hatcher.

64 Absalom Frazier's removal to Indiana and career there emerge from family sources, census data, and Indiana county histories named above.

65 The story of the Preston family's move West is told in a memoir Lucy Preston Wickham wrote in 1895 with the aid of her daughter Catherine Wickham Christian. (It appeared in *The Firelands Pioneer* of January 1920.)

66 The Wickhams' story comes from Jones (see above). The poem about their Newport house is "The Old Homestead," by Angelica G. Gardiner (1845), on file at the Firelands Historical Society Library.

67 The Wildman and Patch families' emigrations are described in Frederick Wildman's autobiography (see above).

69 Further frontier details come from sources named. The quote about the claustrophobic qualities of Connecticut federalism is found in *The Old Northwest*, by B. A. Hinsdale (1888), pp. 389–90.

72 Charles Dickens does not seem to have had a very good time on his American journey in 1842. He arrived justifiably angry about the widespread reprinting in America of his books, for which he received no money, due to the absence of international copyright laws. He had hoped to persuade people that such laws were necessary, but found little sympathy for his position. Much of America appalled him, especially the frontier; many travelers from more civilized regions shared his reaction. In general, European visitors did not begin to write with enthusiasm about America until it got rich after the Civil War. Dickens hated slavery, and a list of advertisements for escaped slaves he compiled on his travels is a remarkable nonfiction document (see Chapter XVII, "Slavery," in *American Notes*). Of Tiffin, Ohio—a town which would be of some importance to my family—he says only that he arrived at noon, dropped off his hired carriage, and left two hours later on the train.

74 The Englishman who commented on how the people on the frontier looked, and about their affection for whiskey and religion, was Elias Pym Fordham (see above).

76 Information about geological analysis of Lake Erie sediments comes from *Erie: The Lake That Survived*, by Noel M. Burns (1985), p. 81.

CHAPTER 5

Most of the details in this chapter are found in family sources cited above. I learned about David Benedict's college years from the Kenyon College *Reveille* and other publications on file at the Kenyon library (my thanks to librarian Allan Bosch).

84 Phillip Hursh is buried in Oak Grove Cemetery near Fort Jefferson, Ohio. His obituary notice appeared in the Greenville (Ohio) *Democrat* of January 8, 1873. His wife's appeared in the *Democrat* of September 2, 1896.

85 The strength of antislavery sentiment in the Western Reserve is discussed in Hatcher (see above), Hinsdale (also above), and in *Ohio and Her Western Reserve*, by Alfred Mathews (1902). *Western Reserve and Early Ohio*, by P. P. Cherry (1921), describes the incident in Iberia, Ohio. Rev. George Gordon, sentenced to six months in jail for inciting the Iberia mob, later received a pardon from President Lincoln, but died of consumption he caught in jail (Cherry, p. 315).

87 The story of David Benedict's Civil War soldiering comes largely from the diaries he sent home to his wife. My thanks to my second cousin Frank I. Harding III for showing the diaries to me, and for his typed transcription of them. Solon Hyde's account of

how he and David Benedict were captured is in his *A Captive of War* (1900). General Benjamin Cheatham may have had his own reasons for not joining his fellow Confederate General Forrest in boycotting the Yankee doctors' offer of coffee. Cheatham's reputation for drunkenness was well known; according to General Braxton Bragg, Cheatham was so drunk at the Battle of Murfreesboro that a staff officer had to hold him on his horse. Another account said that attempting to exhort his troops at the Battle of Stones River, he "rolled off his horse and fell to the ground as limp and helpless as a bag of meal." Perhaps General Cheatham welcomed the coffee for his hangover. (See *No Better Place to Die: The Battle of Stones River*, by Peter Cozzens [1990], p. 213.)

88 The installments of *Our Mutual Friend* which David Benedict read in *Harper's Magazine* (its full name then: *Harper's New Monthly Magazine*) were Chapters 8 through 13, mostly about Mr. Boffin, Mr. Podsnap, and Podsnappery.

CHAPTER 6

91 *Trials and Triumphs: The Record of the Fifty-Fifth Ohio Volunteer Infantry*, by Hartwell Osborn (1904), gives the basic history of the regiment. A fuller picture emerges from the letters which Charlie Wickham, Will Wickham, and other soldiers wrote home, and which appeared in the Norwalk *Reflector*. That newspaper came out on Tuesdays, and almost every issue between late 1861 and mid-1865 carried news or letters from the regiment.

92 Frederick Boalt's battlefield bravery was a favorite subject of Charles Wickham's. The story of his murder near Voltaire, Kansas, may be found in the April 26, 1887, *Reflector*.

95 The importance of the B & O Railroad in keeping Maryland in the Union is mentioned in *The History of the Baltimore & Ohio, America's First Railroad*, edited by Timothy Jacobs (1989).

96 The *Reflector* of February 25, 1862, has Charles Wickham's long and detailed account of the skirmish at Moorefield.

97 Stonewall Jackson's angry letter to Congressman Boteler is reprinted in *I Rode with Stonewall*, by Henry Kyd Douglas (1940). That is my favorite of all the books on Jackson. Douglas recounts an exchange which took place when he and Jackson were picking blackberries: "After a little he paused and turning to me, with a large shining berry poised between his thumb and finger, enquired maladroitly in what part of the body I would prefer being shot. I replied that primarily I'd prefer being hit in the clothes . . ." Douglas's book is good reading and a believable picture of the general.

97 Some other sources on the life of Stonewall Jackson:

Stonewall Jackson, by Lenoir Chambers (2 vols., 1959).

Life and Letters of General Thomas J. Jackson, by Mary Anna Jackson (1892). This book by Jackson's second wife tells personal details found nowhere else.

Stonewall Jackson and the American Civil War, by G.F.R. Henderson (1898).

Mighty Stonewall, by Frank E. Vandiver (1957).

Stonewall Jackson: The Good Soldier, by Allen Tate (1928). Tate sometimes gets carried away—for example: "[Jackson's] visual memory was so retentive and accurate that, finishing a book, he knew every word of it by heart" (p. 52).

I also learned much information from "Stonewall Jackson: Molding the Man and Making a General," by James I. Robertson, Jr., in *Blue & Gray* magazine, Vol. IX, issue 5 (June 1992); and from a visit to Jackson's restored house in Lexington, Virginia.

The Virginia Military Institute (also in Lexington) is said to have the India-rubber overcoat Jackson was wearing when he was shot, and the bones of Jackson's horse, Little Sorrel.

100 The story of the Norwalk Soldiers' Aid Society is told in "Women's Work During the War," by Charlotte Wooster Boalt, in *Trials and Triumphs*; as well as in the pages of the *Reflector*.

CHAPTER 7

117 The battle of August 29 and 30, 1862, has come to be called the Battle of Second Manassas. I choose to call battles by the same names used by the men of the 55th; they called this one Second Bull Run.

118 Telegrapher George Kennan was a teenager during the war. After it he led an expedition attempting to build a west-to-east telegraph line to Europe via Siberia. His Siberian travels, which he wrote about in *Tent Life in Siberia* (1870), made him famous. A later book, *Siberia and the Exile System* (1891), gave the West its first close look at the prisons there. Anton Chekhov, preparing to research his book about the prison colony on Sakhalin Island, said he did not expect to be as careful a chronicler as George Kennan was.

127 Jackson's doings in the months before the battle are described in sources named above. That Jackson considered sending his men into battle naked after the victory at Fredericksburg is mentioned in *Attack and Die*, by Grady McWhiney and Perry D. Jamison (1982).

130 Many books describe the Battle of Chancellorsville and the events that led to it. My first overview of the battle and the war came from reading Shelby Foote's excellent three-volume *The Civil War: A Narrative* (1963). Anyone who wants to learn about the war should begin with this book. For specifics of the battle I relied heavily on *The Campaign of Chancellorsville*, by John Bigelow, Jr. (1910), which I found thorough and reliable.

Other sources were:

The Battle of Chancellorsville, by Samuel P. Bates (1882).

The Campaign of Chancellorsville, by Theodore A. Dodge (1881).

The Battle of Chancellorsville, by Augustus Choate Hamlin (1896).

Autobiography of Oliver Otis Howard (1907).

The 25th Ohio Veteran Volunteer Infantry in the War for the Union, by Edward C. Culp (1885).

"The First Division, Eleventh Corps, at Chancellorsville," by Captain E. R. Monfort, 75th Ohio Volunteer Infantry. This and other reminiscences of the battle may be found in *Grand Army of the Republic War Papers: Fred C. Jones Post*, Vol. 1 (1891).

"Afield with the Eleventh Corps at Chancellorsville," by Owen Rice, Captain, Company A, 153rd Pennsylvania, in *Military Order of the Loyal Legion of the United States: Ohio Commandery*, Vol. 1 (1888).

137 Looking back at Chancellorsville, the 55th could take some comfort from the fact that several histories mentioned the determined fight put up by its picket line as an important brake on Jackson's total assault, and also from the judgment of the 11th Corps historian, Augustus Choate Hamlin, who said of the 55th and the other veteran regi-

ments from Ohio, "It would be difficult to find six trustier regiments in all the armies of the United States" (Hamlin, op. cit., p. 40).

138 Charles Devens, heedless general of the 11th Corps's 1st Division, was held in such regard by his fellow citizens of Massachusetts that they erected two statues to him. One stands on the grounds of the State House in Boston, and one, an equestrian monument by Daniel Chester French and E. C. Potter, in front of the courthouse in Worcester.

139 According to Bigelow, after Princess Salm-Salm kissed Lincoln, "a bevy of female companions" followed her example, and Mrs. Lincoln, not present at the time, became angry when she found out. Prince Salm-Salm and his wife were among the interesting minor characters of the war. Princess Salm-Salm, of French Canadian background, accompanied her husband on campaigns and worked as a nurse and in soldiers' relief organizations. Prince Salm-Salm, a Prussian who had been decorated by Kaiser Wilhelm I for bravery, came to America, offered his services to Lincoln, won a colonelcy, and served throughout the war despite his lack of English. Afterward he went to Mexico and became aide-de-camp to Emperor Maximilian. Captured by Benito Juárez when Maximilian's government fell, Salm-Salm was condemned to death. After his wife flung herself at Juárez's feet and pleaded for her husband's life, Juárez freed him. Salm-Salm died a few years later in the Franco-Prussian War.

145 The exploits of the 55th Ohio from Chancellorsville to the end of the war could fill many more pages. A recent book, *Gettysburg: Culp's Hill and Cemetery Hill*, by Harry W. Pfanz (1993), gives a good picture of the regiment's difficult skirmishing near the foot of Cemetery Ridge, where they were under sniper fire from two directions. In front of their lines at Gettysburg, a soldier from another Ohio regiment won the Medal of Honor for crawling near the enemy to rescue a mortally wounded man, Private George Nixon, great-grandfather of Richard M., the President. (For this bit of information, and for Civil War expertise in matters large and small, I am indebted to John Howell, of Memphis and New York City.)

148 Most of the account of Jackson's death is taken from *Life and Letters*, by Mary Anna Jackson.

CHAPTER 8

For an overview of America in the half century after the Civil War, see *The Emergence of Modern America 1865–1878*, by Allan Nevins (1927), and *The Rise of the City*, by Arthur Meier Schlesinger (1933). Of the two, the second book has more scope. Both books are included in the twelve-volume *A History of American Life*, edited by Schlesinger and Dixon R. Fox.

151 The town of Saratoga's claim to the invention of the potato chip finds support in *Forty Years an Advertising Agent; 1865–1905*, by George Presbury Rowell (1906), p. 131.

152 Data about the burgeoning size of Americans appeared in a survey published in *Science* magazine in 1887: "The American Physique," by Edward Atkinson (Vol. X, p. 239).

152 A book which notes the fondness of Americans for spitting and chewing, as well as other details of the American scene, is *A Frenchman in America*, by Max O'Rell (Paul Blouët) (1891); O'Rell says at a theater he attended, "nineteen mouths out of twenty were chewing . . . All the jaws were going like those of so many ruminants grazing in a field."

152 *A Popular History of American Invention*, edited by Waldemar Kaempffert (1924), is mostly about America's technological advances of the nineteenth century. *The History of the Telephone*, by Herbert N. Casson (1910), discusses the persistence and ingenuity of Alexander Graham Bell. For a while Bell used a real ear—an eardrum and accompanying bones, cut from a dead man's head—in his experiments. He spoke for the first time over his invention in 1876, and it was the hit of the Centennial Exhibition in Philadelphia that year.

153 For a history of the screw-back earring, see *Accessories of Dress*, by Katherine Morris Lester and Bess Viola Oerke (1940), p. 115.

155 Many interesting details about the nineteenth-century career of the Ku Klux Klan appear in *A History of the United States since the Civil War*, by Ellis P. Oberholzer (1926–31), Vol. II, pp. 344ff.

155 The near-universal antipathy of white Americans for blacks in the latter half of the nineteenth century may be found in many sources. Robert Todd Lincoln's statements about Pullman porters were made when he was chairman of the board of Pullman; see *Robert Todd Lincoln: A Man in His Own Right*, by John S. Goff (1969).

157 Rudyard Kipling recorded his opinion of Americans in his *American Notes* (1891).

157 To fill in local details, I read many issues of the Norwalk *Reflector* from the years 1865 to 1900. I found information about David Benedict in the society column, and lists of goods for sale at his store in the ads. Facts of Louis Severance's biography come from the *Dictionary of American Biography* (1963) and *History of Cleveland and Its Environs*, by E. M. Avery (1918), among other sources. For facts about Louis Severance and Wooster College, I thank Denise D. Monbarren and Catherine Smith, of Wooster's Andrews Library.

160 Allan Nevins tells the story of John D. Rockefeller and the rise of the oil industry in *John D. Rockefeller: The Heroic Age of American Enterprise* (1940). The book is a more than sympathetic portrait of the magnate, and perhaps a reaction against the anti-Rockefeller and anti-Standard Oil books of earlier in the century, e.g., Ida Tarbell's *The History of the Standard Oil Company* (1904).

162 *The Stone That Burns: The Story of the American Sulphur Industry*, by William Haynes (1942), describes the career of Herman Frasch and the success of his sulphur-mining technique. An issue of *Architectural Record* (June 1917) ran a long article, illustrated with photos and floor plan, about John Severance's mansion in suburban Cleveland.

165 Some of the facts about Simeon Frazier and the Disciples of Christ Church come from Shaw's *Hoosier Disciples*, cited above. Others, including Simeon's obituary and the train timetable from the *Christian Standard*, I found by sending inquiries to the Disciples of Christ Historical Society in Nashville, Tennessee. (Many thanks to assistant librarian May F. Reed.)

170 A biography of Dio Lewis appears in the *Dictionary of American Temperance Biography*, by Mark Edward Lender (1984); a more complete account is *The Biography of Dio Lewis, A.M., M.D.*, by Mary F. Eastman (1891). That book also tells the story of the Ohio Women's Crusade in some detail. News items in the Norwalk *Reflector* followed the movement almost from its beginning. *On and Off the Wagon: A Sober Analysis of the Temperance Movement from the Pilgrims through Prohibition*, by Donald Barr Chidsey (1969), says that Lewis "is credited with the invention of the beanbag" (p. 27).

171 For more on the Women's Crusade and Prohibition in general, see also *The Evolution*

of Prohibition in the United States of America, by Ernest H. Cherrington (1920). (Cherrington was an officer of the Anti-Saloon League.) Northern Ohio has always been the capital of America's forces for temperance; soon after the repeal of Prohibition, Alcoholics Anonymous was founded in Akron.

C H A P T E R 9

174 Misfortune can have the effect of preserving a family's history. Teddy Frazier, an invalid, enjoyed reading stories about the family, so his grandfather Louis Wickham supplied him with a number of typescript reminiscences. They are my source for information about Louis's boyhood.

177 Charles P. Wickham wrote letters to the Norwalk *Reflector* while on the long Western trip he took with his wife and son in 1874. They add details not included in the story of the trip Louis Wickham wrote many years later. For a summary of the Modoc War, I relied on *The Reader's Encyclopedia of the American West*, edited by Howard R. Lamar (1977).

182 I had often heard the story about Louis Wickham blowing the windows out of a building on the Hudson campus. (According to the story, the building in question was a dormitory called the Atheneum.) My uncle Louis Frazier untangled the story for me in a way that made it more plausible and specific. Louis Wickham recalled his time at Princeton in notes submitted to alumni publications over the years; I thank Rick Ryan of the Alumni Office for sending me copies of those notes, and University Archivist Ben Primer for sending me and explaining the semester listings of Louis's grades.

183 For a discussion of painter Charles C. Curran's portrayal of women, see "Floral Femininity: A Pictorial Definition," by Annette Stott, in *American Art* (Spring 1992), pp. 61ff. (Thanks to May Castleberry for finding this article and sending it to me.) I heard of Mrs. Reagan's fondness for *Lotus Lilies* from a source close to museum founder Daniel Terra; a written inquiry to Mrs. Reagan on the subject went unanswered.

186 The baby Louis brought back from Colorado was Cousin Winthrop Wickham, who I interviewed in California—see the notes to Chapter 1.

188 The advent of Prohibition is explained in many books, including some cited above, and in *The Long Thirst: Prohibition in America, 1920–1933*, by Thomas M. Coffey (1975). For the story of Mail Pouch and Lucky Strike and the cellar burglaries I have depended entirely on the Norwalk *Reflector-Herald* to elaborate and substantiate a family story passed down from Lillie Wickham to her daughter Anne Belle.

191 For recollections of Louis Wickham by those who knew him, I thank my relatives Lane W. Barton, Ellen Harding Anderson, Frank I. Harding III, Evelyn Frazier, Jim Moses, and Frances Moses Thomson.

C H A P T E R 1 0

198 A good summary of the history of Hudson, Ohio, appears in *Hudson: A Survey of Historic Buildings in an Ohio Town*, edited by Lois Newkirk (1989). (Thanks to Priscilla Graham for sending this book to me.)

For additional Hudson information I am grateful to Cele Klein and Cynthia Longstreth.

201 Schlesinger's *The Rise of the City* (cited above) tells the story of the rural-to-urban population shift. See also *The Urbanization of America, 1860–1915*, by Blake McKelvey (1963). For the effect of this trend on northeastern Ohio, see "Expressions of Urbanism in the Sequent Occupance of Northeastern Ohio," by James S. Matthews (1949), a thesis written at the University of Chicago (on file at the New York Public Library).

The best book on America's move to the suburbs (in my opinion) is *Crabgrass Frontier: The Suburbanization of the United States*, by Kenneth T. Jackson (1985). Also helpful were *Borderland: Origins of the American Suburb, 1820–1939*, by John R. Stilgoe (1988), and *Bourgeois Utopias: The Rise and Fall of Suburbia*, by Robert Fishman (1987).

CHAPTERS 11 AND 12

Most of the sources for these chapters are documents—letters, scrapbooks, diaries, high-school and college yearbooks, newspaper clippings, programs from theatrical productions—found in my parents' apartment. For events surrounding my father's christening I referred to the Norwalk *Reflector-Herald* of June 1, 1920.

Also, I learned a lot from interviewing people who had known one or both of my parents. I am grateful to Louis Frazier, Evelyn Frazier, Donna Cosulich, Mrs. Paul Stewart, Phil Swartz, Ted Horvath, Dolores Hawthorne, Ellen Harding Anderson, Sarah Margaret Wallar, and Everett Hughes. Dr. Hughes also told me some of the history of Standard Oil of Ohio and of its early efforts in research and development. Other information I found in an anonymous typescript history of the company written in 1975.

CHAPTER 13

246 The story of the arrival of television in Tucson, Arizona, is taken from the Arizona *Daily Star* (February 1, and 2, 1953) and the Tucson *Daily Citizen* (January 27, February 2, 1953).

248 My father kept his home and work lives separate, and I met almost none of his colleagues until after his death. A pleasure of writing this book was meeting the great people he used to work with. Staffers from the old lab seemed to enjoy talking about it and about him. For giving me their time, and especially for their patience in explaining recondite problems of statistics or chemistry, I thank Ernie Milberger, Phil Fay, Marian F. Chew, Everett Hughes, Glen Brown, Bill and Martha Fitzgibbons, and Fran Gaylor. Ernie Milberger, Everett Hughes, and Glen Brown each talked to me about the invention of acrylonitrile; Jim Idol lucidly summarized the whole acrylonitrile process for me over the phone when I became confused. An in-house history of the invention, written by Jim Callahan, also helped a lot. The EPA's rating of the deep-well wastes from the Lima plant appears in "Hot Spots and Bright Spots," an article about toxic-waste sites in Ohio, in *Ohio* magazine (May 1991), p. 39. An Associated Press story in the New York *Daily News* of April 4, 1994 (p. 50), lists BP America as the tenth-worst toxic polluter in the country, with 54.4 million pounds of toxic chemicals released into the environment per year.

I especially thank longtime Sohioan and co-inventor of Boron gasoline, Lorry Szabo. She told me many stories about my dad, gave me addresses of other colleagues from the lab, and supplied company histories and other documents saved from when she used to edit the company's in-house magazine. I could not have sketched my father's career without her.

CHAPTER 14

271 Cousin Jim Moses still lives in a farmhouse near the lake, with his wife, Lois, in Huron, Ohio. They have three grown children. Jim operates a dredger, does construction work, and sells boat motors. In his spare time he coaches a girls' fast-pitch softball team. Though he is over sixty, he can still pick up a railroad tie.

275 Much of the information about the decline and partial revival of Lake Erie I learned from *Erie: The Lake That Survived*, by Noel M. Burns (1985), a thorough and clear description of the lake and its problems.

277 The arrival of detergents on the home-cleaning market after the Second World War got a lot of press—for example, "Soapless Cleaners," by Helen W. Kendall, in *Good Housekeeping* of March 1946; or "Cleaners: Soapless Soap," in *Newsweek* of April 28, 1947; or "Four Popular Synthetic Detergents" in *Consumers' Research Bulletin*, May 1954. *American City* magazine ran several articles (December 1947, October 1952, January 1953) about the problem of suds overflowing sewage treatment plants. See also *Synthetic Detergents*, by A. Davidson and B. Milwidsky (1967), and *The Pollution of Water by Detergents*, by J. Prat and A. Giraud.

279 The Cuyahoga River caught fire on June 22, 1969. Although the river had burned before—a fire in 1952 burned tugboats and did far more damage, and floating wastes used to catch fire regularly during the early days of Standard Oil—politicians used the 1969 blaze to draw attention to the lake's problems and to get support for pollution control. See "The Whole Truth," by Sue Gorisek, in *Ohio* magazine (August 1991, p. 29).

280 The Terminal Tower's descent in rank among the tall buildings of the world was chronicled in a newspaper article marking the completion of Society Center, Cleveland's new tallest building. See "Terminal Tower to Lose 'Tallest' Crown Next Week," by Bill Sammon, in the Cleveland *Plain Dealer* (November 20, 1990, p. 1).

281 Details about the more recent condition of the lake come from "Great Lakes, Bitter Legacy," a 1992 documentary produced by the National Audubon Society, and from a newspaper article ("Progress, Not Victory, on Great Lakes Pollution," *The New York Times* [May 7, 1994, p. 1]).

CHAPTER 15

I thank Louis Frazier, Lane Wickham Barton, Bill and Virginia Hursh, John and Lydia Hursh, Elizabeth McLean, and Alice Cooper for kindly allowing me to interview them. For additional information and insights, I thank Libby Frazier Root, George and Betty Barton, John C. Hursh, Mary Hursh Bartok, Katie Wickham Fremont, Mrs. N. Carter Hammond, Kay Gatrell Morton, and Dorothy Jane Frazier.

Dorothy Jane Frazier was the wife of my grandfather Ray's brother Dick. Uncle Dick died of a heart attack at the cottage on Lake Erie in 1959, leaving Dorothy Jane with three young children. She never remarried and put all the kids through college working as a secretary at General Tire in Akron. Growing up, I did not see much of her or her children. I learned what a remarkable person she was only recently, as we talked and corresponded about the family. She would have liked to have seen this book finished, but she died in 1992.

CHAPTER 17

I read a lot of books about religion in America. In fact, once I started, even books on other subjects—especially nineteenth-century books—seemed to be mainly about religion. The whale in *Moby Dick* seemed like the Transcendentalist oversoul turned almost comically evil, Hester Prynne and little Pearl seemed like personified rebukes to Calvinism, and Huck and Jim's conversation about King Solomon (". . . de man dat think he kin settle a 'spute 'bout a whole child wid half a chile, doan' know enough to come in out'n de rain") like an only slightly exaggerated version of the doctrinal disputes that were epidemic back then.

For historical survey, I relied on *A Religious History of the American People*, by Sydney E. Ahlstrom (1972), and *Righteous Empire: The Protestant Experience in America*, by Martin E. Marty (1970). The first places Protestantism in the context of other religions in America, and the second follows the decline of Protestantism with reference to the economic forces that contributed to it. Another good book was *The Protestant Temperament: Patterns of Child-Rearing, Religious Experience, and the Self in Early America*, by Philip Greven (1980).

Tracing the many Protestant sects, a job which so daunted Protestant historians, apparently was more fun for Catholics. A helpful basic study of the larger Protestant divisions is *The Protestant Churches of America*, by John A. Hardon, S.J. (1964).

Many sources say that Ralph Waldo Emerson was the most important American thinker on matters of religion and philosophy in the nineteenth century. I read his *Selected Essays*, edited by Larzer Ziff (1982), which included "An Address Delivered Before the Senior Class in Divinity College, Cambridge 1838," "Self-Reliance," and "The Over-Soul." I wish I could say I made a lot of sense of Emerson, but I didn't. I got more out of authors he supposedly influenced, like Whitman. Psychologist and philosopher William James was said to be as important to the twentieth century in America as Emerson was to the nineteenth. James's *The Varieties of Religious Experience* (1902) is indeed fascinating, a work to hold the interest of religious skeptics. Especially good are the quotations from religious documents of the past. James's personal, experiential, pragmatic approach to religion provided a basis for Alcoholics Anonymous, and similar inspirational disciplines of this century.

A more recent book, and perhaps the most helpful, is *The American Religion: The Emergence of the Post-Christian Nation*, by Harold Bloom (1992). Bloom believes that the true American religion is not Christianity or any other imported faith, but rather a home-grown version of Gnosticism—the mystic belief in the self as solitary with God, and as possessing a spark of holy fire which has been one with God since before the creation. Bloom sets forth the theory that in America, Christianity became the most personal form of the religion in the world, and that the loneliness of the frontier people who attended revival meetings produced a uniquely private American Jesus. He talks a lot about Mormons and Baptists—he thinks Mormonism is the one quintessentially American religion—and considers the bad social and political consequences of a widespread system of belief centering on the self.

Other sources on frontier religion, and on the advent of Prohibition, appear in notes to Chapters 3 and 10, above.

For a discussion of America's vision of itself as a nation destined to lead mankind to Christian utopia, see *Redeemer Nation: The Idea of America's Millennial Role*, by Ernest Lee Tuveson (1968).

An interesting study of apocalyptic beliefs in American history and especially in the twentieth century is *When Time Shall Be No More: Prophecy Belief in Modern American Culture*, by Paul Boyer (1992). Boyer draws comparisons between the growth in numbers of preachers of apocalypse in this century and the proliferation of sects in the last. He also notes the similarity between the old Calvinist belief in predestination and the modern apocalyptic belief that a chosen few will survive Armageddon.

The minister who compared Protestantism to a petered-out vein of gold was Burris A. Jenkins, in his *The Protestant: A Scrap-Book for Insurgents* (1918). Theologians Reinhold Niebuhr and his brother H. Richard Niebuhr wrote about the transcendence of God over worldly concerns, and led a religious movement of the 1920s and 1930s called Neo-Orthodoxy. Some people considered Reinhold Niebuhr a prophet. Of the Niebuhrs' many books, I read H. Richard Niebuhr's *The Kingdom of God in America* (1937).

It was President Dwight Eisenhower who said that he didn't care what religion America had, as long as it had one. Among the popular books on religious themes in the 1950s and '60s were *The Power of Positive Thinking*, by Norman Vincent Peale; *Peace with God*, by Billy Graham; and Bishop Fulton J. Sheen's *Guide to Contentment*.